George Norton

Commentaries on the history, constitution and chartered franchises of the city of London

George Norton

Commentaries on the history, constitution and chartered franchises of the city of London

ISBN/EAN: 9783741163067

Manufactured in Europe, USA, Canada, Australia, Japa

Cover: Foto ©ninafisch / pixelio.de

Manufactured and distributed by brebook publishing software (www.brebook.com)

George Norton

Commentaries on the history, constitution and chartered franchises of the city of London

COMMENTARIES

ON THE

HISTORY, CONSTITUTION, & CHARTERED FRANCHISES

OF

THE CITY OF LONDON.

BY

GEORGE NORTON,

FORMERLY ONE OF THE COMMON PLEADERS OF THE CITY OF LONDON.

THIRD EDITION, REVISED.

LONDON:
LONGMANS, GREEN, AND CO.
1869.

PREFACE

TO

THE THIRD EDITION.

THE scope and object of this treatise, and the circumstances under which it was first submitted to the public, have been fully explained in the Preface to the First Edition. The second was merely a reprint. Both have been long ago out of circulation.

The issue of this Third Edition is due to the Corporation of London (to whom the copyright of the work has been presented by the author), and who have passed a resolution for taking three hundred copies for the use of its members and officers. It has appeared to them that such information as the writer has attempted to contribute towards elucidating the early history of the City, the origin and nature of the civic constitution, and the quality of its franchises, might also deserve the attention of their fellow-citizens. The author allows himself to share in that hope, and ventures to think that such a work may not be without interest to some of the class of general readers.

It cannot be doubted that the system of municipal government in the cities and boroughs of England—and more particularly that of the City of London—is of national concern. On that system, and on the franchises through which it is maintained, the principles of self-government, as far as is conceded by the English Constitution, is in a very great degree founded. The personal interests and the social position of a large portion of the public are also intimately involved in these civic institutions, and in the authority which they exercise. The political power possessed by municipal corporations is a subject of still more important consideration. The student of general history and of antiquarian literature finds his enquiries continually directed to the effects of the corporate rights and privileges enjoyed by great cities, and their influence on the manners and customs of the inhabitants, as well as on the national weal. In no point of view are these topics unworthy of enlightened investigation, or of the notice of the public at large.

All these rights and privileges depend on charters, or are derived from ancient customs. But the unlearned enquirer, desiring to obtain some knowledge of the nature of these civic charters, and of the customary rights and liberties secured by them, would feel compelled to acknowledge that the meaning of the early, the most important, and the most really effective of these charters, and of these ancient customs, have become, through the lapse of ages, for the most part unintelligible without the help of legal and antiquarian study. As little would such a reader gather from the bare perusal of the City Charters, or of the documentary evidence through which these ancient customary franchises are established, their bearings on the interests of the people, and particularly of the citizens, at the present time. Consequently, every assertion of these privileges, essentially requisite to be maintained, every effort for the expedient modification of others, and every tendency to the judicious abandonment of such as are no longer beneficial, become (as in times past) a theme for controversy rather than for wise regulation. The mass of the citizens most concerned in the right conclusions, and in the most suitable measures, find themselves altogether at the mercy of the few who may choose (or perhaps only pretend) to make themselves acquainted with the subject proposed to be dealt with. At no period throughout the history of London, could the attention of the citizens to their ancient rights and customs be more appropriately called for than at the present time, when their municipal government and franchises have become the matter of much public criticism, and even of Parliamentary discussion.

The work now submitted to the public is confined to an attempt at explaining, in as popular a manner as the subject will admit of, these chartered and customary rights and liberties. The author has felt how impossible it is to accomplish such a task without reviewing, historically, the rise and progress of this great city of the world, in its relative connection with the history of the English nation itself. This historical account, however, was originally intended to be merely introductory to a larger treatise, and such only can it perhaps be properly considered. The elaborate professional work of Mr. Serjeant Pullen, on the Laws and Customs of the City of London, has supplied all that the author had further proposed; and the author is happy in thus reciprocating the compliment paid him by the learned Serjeant in saying that, had the author's full purpose been carried out, it would have superseded his own labours. An abstract and explanation of the Charters of London forms, however, no part of Mr. Serjeant Pullen's treatise. Neither would historical dissertations have consisted with his strictly legal and practical design. The author's work may therefore claim the character of a substantive treatise in itself. Superficial it may be, and for that reason, perhaps, the better adapted to the ordinary reader. At the same time, to those who may be disposed to turn their minds to more profound researches, and a more accurate knowledge of details, in this branch of historical literature, the great mass of references quoted may prove a repertory, and possibly a guide.

It is with much misgiving that the author—after a long life passed in a distant part of the empire, and in avocations which have no affinity with such researches—has undertaken a revisal of his work. A comprehensive exposition of the constitution and franchises of the City of London would better befit one who, with more learning than he could pretend to in his earlier years, or than he can now be at the pains to acquire, would apply his hard-gained knowledge to such a task. The author's own experience, however, has taught him the difficulty of compressing so complicated a subject within the limits of a single volume, while very few would, perhaps, be attracted to the perusal of a more minute and extended treatise. In a literary field, where hardly any reputation and no profit can be looked for, it is almost vain to expect a labourer.

The encouragement afforded by the Corporation of London, and more immediately by its Library Committee, demands the just acknowledgment of all cultivators of this department of constitutional literature, and of the public. Their liberal patronage of Mr. H. A. Riley's numerous translations from the City Archives, illustrating the manners and habits of the citizens in early times, and annotated with so much multifarious learning, is entitled to appropriate mention. No restriction prohibits consultation of these ancient records. If any reservation is made, it applies only to documents strictly affecting proprietary rights. The courtesy of the Librarian, Mr. W. H. Overall, in supplying ready assistance to the curious enquirer, as well as to the student, will be gratefully appreciated by all who have occasion to seek it. The author desires also to record his thanks for the assistance he has received from the City Solicitor, Mr. Nelson, and more particularly for that afforded by the City Town Clerk, Mr. Frederick Woodthorpe, similar to that rendered him, in times long past, both by his father and grandfather—all successively Town Clerks of London. And, lastly, the author gladly takes this opportunity of tendering his thanks to the Library Committee, and to their Chairman, Mr. Benjamin Orridge, himself a contributor to several publications on subjects of civic interest, for the honour done him by moving the Resolution unanimously adopted by the Court of Common Council, which has led to the undertaking of this new edition.

That he may do no discredit to this enlightened spirit displayed by the Corporation, or to this mark of respect for his own labours, the author has endeavoured, by a careful revision of his work, to render it better worthy of their acceptance. He has redistributed some of the chapters, and has made many corrections and several additions, though he has not essentially altered the original text. Some of the disquisitions incorporated may appear too digressive, but this was hardly to be avoided in an attempt to explain the subject-matter of ancient charters, and the various and changing interests affected by them. His object has been to supply easily accessible information, at least to such as are most concerned in attaining it; but neither to them, nor to the general reader, can he profess to offer other entertainment than what attends the rational pursuit of useful knowledge. His gratification will be sufficient if he may fairly indulge a consciousness of having contributed something to the service of the public.

Dedication of the First Edition.

TO THE
RIGHT HON. WILLIAM THOMPSON, M.P.
LORD MAYOR,

THE ALDERMEN AND COURT OF COMMON COUNCIL
OF THE CITY OF LONDON,

THIS ATTEMPT TO ELUCIDATE THE HISTORY AND CONSTITUTION,

TO EXPLAIN THE CHARTERED FRANCHISES, AND

TO ESTABLISH THE CORPORATE RIGHTS OF THEIR ANCIENT CITY,

IS,

IN RECOLLECTION OF OBLIGATIONS FORMERLY RECEIVED,

GRATEFULLY INSCRIBED

BY THEIR FELLOW-CITIZEN AND OBEDIENT SERVANT

THE AUTHOR.

PREFACE

TO

THE FIRST EDITION.

There are few subjects in English History more involved in obscurity than the original constitution and progressive condition of cities and boroughs. A theme of such national importance has by turns exercised the pens of legal, of statistical, of political, and of historical writers; but although their labours, and particularly those of Madox and Spelman, have scattered much light over its darker topics, yet the public have still to regret the want of a connected and systematic treatise comprehending the whole of the subject. Those authors who have pursued their enquiries with so much industry as to advance theories, may be said rather to have raised controversies than to have established principles : and no positions have been more confidently disputed of late years, than those regarding the origin and mercantile quality of town communities, propounded by Dr. Brady in his elaborate Treatise on Boroughs.

It may readily be imagined that the City of London, the most ancient constitutional borough in England—which has preserved its ancient Saxon independence and its political and judicial customs inviolate—which has constantly exercised such a decided influence in the State, and always maintained an internal self-jurisdiction—which has been the very cradle of civil liberty and civilisation in this country,—would have furnished the best materials for the work, if not the best writer upon a topic of such universal interest—that it would at least have presented to the public a compendious account of its own privileges and of the nature of its own constitution, by which that of other cities might have been greatly illustrated. Materials, indeed, of great antiquity and peculiar value the City possesses amongst its records, and sufficient for the substantiation of all its legal rights: but amongst all the eminent characters engaged in the higher and literary professions to whom the City has given birth, or the Corporation a livelihood, not one has, except in a very superficial degree, devoted himself to this task; and of all the writers on civic affairs in general, the most learned in London antiquities was a tailor.[1]

The author of the following work attained, at an early period of life, an office in the City of London, which imposed, as a professional duty, the obligation of some acquaintance with its laws and customs. In his anxious endeavour to acquire that information, from which alone all the value of his services to the Corporation could be derived, he very soon found reason to lament the absence of any work calculated even to direct his studies, much less to explain the object of them. The older chroniclers, to whom the ancient constitution and customs of London

---

[1] Stow, the author of the Survey of London. Subsequent editors, however, and more particularly Strype, have supplied the greatest part of the legal matter of the work.

were the most familiar, have expended all the energies of their labour and of their intellect in the description of churches, tombstones, and civic pageantry; and modern civic historians have done little more than extend their researches over the same surface. The professed expositors, both ancient and modern, of the polity, the chartered franchises, the privileges of the City, and the laws and practice of the civic courts, are very few in number; most of them anonymous, who quote one from another, without acknowledgment, a dry list of charters, customs, and decisions, which, so far from attempting to explain, their very phraseology proves them not to have understood. In the meantime a host of controversial pamphleteers have virulently disputed on some of the more constitutional and essential characteristics of the citizens and of the civic community; until, at times, the authority of the Legislature, or of a superior court of law—both more ignorant, perhaps, than these controversialists, of the true nature of the rights under contest—has by some enactment or absolute decision swept many of them altogether away. In short, such is the perplexity which the alterations of times and circumstances, and changes in practice, have introduced; so contradictory are the writers on isolated topics; so widely dispersed, or so difficult of access, the genuine authorities from which information is to be derived, and so utterly barren the treatises of those who have pretended to collect them—that to obtain a clear and accurate knowledge of the City law has been declared by one,[1] the most capable perhaps

[1] William Holland, Esq., afterwards a Baron of the Exchequer, who has been for more than twenty years one of the City Counsel, and who at an

of any man now living to form an opinion on the subject,
to be a task likely to baffle the most enterprising industry
and the most matured reflection.

The writer of these pages, however, had not proceeded
far in his investigation of the subject, when he felt that
it possessed an interest sufficient to reward amply the
curiosity both of the learned and the unlearned, and
meriting the consideration as well of the Englishman as of
the citizen. While the nature of that civic constitution,
under which London from its humble origin has emerged
the metropolis of England, could not fail to supply an
attractive source of reflection to the general reader, inquisitive in all that deeply concerns the history of his
country, or warm in his attachment to the free principles
of its government, the peculiar quality and purport of
the City charters and laws could not but excite some
attention amongst the more enlightened of that immense
population who live and thrive under their administration.
Avoiding the investigation of the more obsolete customs of
the City, now deservedly lapsed into desuetude, the first
topic appeared to the author capable of great elucidation;
the other, of a systematic exposition. Of the internal civic
polity he conceived, that it not only presented an epitome
of the original Saxon system of free government in this
country; but embodying with the most complete and
beneficial practical effect the principles of self-government,
it exemplified in the composition of its deliberative and
executive assemblies, in the free election of all its magis-

early period of his professional career, and before other increasing duties commanded his avocations, made laborious collections on the law administered in the City Courts; for the free perusal of which, the author has to testify to that gentleman the sincere acknowledgments of a friend.

trates, in the minute subdivisions of delegated authority, in the extent and quality of the elective franchise,—the best as well as the purest model of a free representing and representative community which can exist under a limited monarchy. Of the law, as administered in the City Courts, his experience in them induced him to think that it evinced a simple and effectual medium, through which, amidst a vast and concentrated population of traders, cheap, prompt, and pure justice was afforded to suitors, valuable in proportion to the accumulated intricacy and expense in other departments of the English law. Considerable intercourse with the citizens of all classes has served to confirm these sentiments. And now that all personal interest in the prosperity of the civic community, save that which may arise from a general regard for the welfare of his country at large, has long ceased, while his acquaintance with the rights of the London citizens has perhaps increased, his opinion remains unchanged.

Actuated by these impressions, he began to dedicate the leisure which professional engagements would allow, to the task of collecting and digesting the materials to which he has adverted, with a view to compile a treatise, confining its subject to the rise, progress, and present constitution of the Corporation of London, and to an exposition of the law and practice of the City Courts. In the prosecution of this design, it was his original intention, after giving some historical account of the City, and examining the tenor of its charters, to have pursued his undertaking systematically, by displaying the quality of the free citizens and of their elective franchises, the appointment and functions of the various civic magistrates and chief officers, and the composition and powers of the constitutional assemblies of the Court of Aldermen, the Court of Common Council, and the Hustings Court of Common Hall. In treating of the civic law, he would have examined into the nature and jurisdiction of the many City Law Courts; as the Hustings Court, the Lord Mayor's Court, the Sheriff's Courts, the Court of Conservancy, the Orphans' Court, the Chamberlain's Court for apprentices, and the Appeal Court of St. Martin's-le-Grand: and, in adverting to the exercise of the various legal functions of these Courts, it would have been incumbent on him to notice many City customs still in practical operation; more particularly the Law of Foreign Attachment, so peculiarly productive of beneficial results in a mercantile community. If he was encouraged in this attempt by a sincere ambition to render at least some service to his fellow-citizens, if not valuable information to the public at large, his zeal was not less sanctioned by the example of many great and learned characters, whose projected efforts in the same undertaking would no doubt have been crowned with success, had not more important duties intervened to direct their public labours in a different channel.[1]

Whatever objects in succeeding or hopes of success

---

[1] Lord Coke and Mr. Calthrop (both Recorders of London) edited superficial and short dissertations on City Law; and the former almost in terms recommends a more detailed work on the subject. Lord King, who was likewise Recorder, and afterwards Lord Chancellor, also collected materials for a work on the Law of Foreign Attachment. Mr. Kyd, who wrote on Corporations, projected a distinct work on that of London; and it is believed, that the learned Mr. Hargrave collected his valuable materials on City Law with a similar design. Lastly, Mr. Whitaker, whose History of Manchester proves his ability for the task, had designed A History of London, which he contemplated 'as quite new and original.' The last three were arrested in their progress by death.

the author may have conceived in the full accomplishment of his original design, they have been suddenly extinguished by a change in his circumstances, which has at once removed him from the chief sources of information, and imposed duties which fully engross the time requisite for the just fulfilment of his wishes. He may, perhaps, be thought deservedly to suffer imputation by not retiring, in deference to the example of more competent individuals, altogether from the further prosecution of them. If the only alternative had been to produce a scanty and incoherent dissertation on the subject, it would have manifested a contemptible ambition of authorship to have deluded the public by the publication of it. But as his researches upon some parts of his projected work had proceeded to almost their full extent, and were already digested into composition, the author indulged the idea, that merely to deduce the civil and political history of the City, to exhibit the fundamental principles of the municipal constitution, and to explain the tenor and effect of those highly valued charters, the purport of which are so little understood,—would be to convey some valuable information, and to perform no unwelcome service. Had he not hoped to accomplish so much of his task with some success, he would, though with reluctance, have resigned the project which had so long engaged his zealous pursuit. If, however, he has formed an erroneous estimate of his capacity to perform it in this limited degree, he must submit without murmur to the mortification incurred by his own mistaken pretensions. He might certainly have suspended his labours in expectation of more favourable opportunities hereafter; but he is aware, that if there is any value in the present treatise, the precarious tenure of his life in a noxious climate forbids any confident hope of its ever becoming enhanced by the contribution of his future exertions.

These particulars of the following work it has been thought expedient to premise, not out of any vain desire to deprecate that censure which the public interests require should pursue all literary failures, but for the purpose of precluding any ill-founded expectations, and of accounting for the desultory character of some discussions introduced into the body of it. Had the composition proceeded according to its original arrangement, many of the statistical particulars embodied in the history, and much of the subject-matter of the charters, would have been distributed under more specific and appropriate heads. As it is, without wandering beyond the legitimate bounds of digression, some topics which have appeared to be of more than ordinary interest, have been canvassed at somewhat greater length, perhaps, than the occasion would seem naturally to suggest.

To the learned reader the author feels that he has little occasion to appeal, either for a calm and deliberate consideration of those positions he may be disposed to dispute, or for a candid allowance for those errors which may be pronounced unavoidable, in a work embracing so many obscure and intricate points. His liberality will induce him to confess, that, upon subjects from which, shrouded as they are in the darkness of antiquity, many able men have shrunk with dismay, and over which learned disputants have struggled with all the honest warmth of mutual conviction, he might himself draw a mistaken conclusion.

Nor can the author better vindicate his sincere purpose of communicating information rather than party zeal, and of establishing truth rather than theory, than by scrupulously referring those who may correct him, to the sources and authorities of almost every fact he advances. It is true, that the authorities quoted may not always be exactly precise to the point submitted; sometimes the combination of many are relied upon, and sometimes the general discussion of one, as justifying the resulting position. Such a course is occasionally unavoidable in weaving a multifarious subject into a connected narrative; and the reader may be reminded that Gibbon remarks 'how much 'particular knowledge is requisite for general description, 'the author of which ought to be much more learned 'than his work.'[1] But if too little caution or discrimination is sometimes evinced in drawing these inferences, at least the means are honestly furnished by which the public may be undeceived.

A desire to render these pages attractive to the general reader, has induced the introduction of some matter which would hardly be sanctioned in a work strictly of a legal character, and perhaps a more discursive style in the historical part than the nature even of that part of the subject would warrant. The statement of some simple and notorious truths, in history or in law, the learned enquirer, should he deign to direct his eye through these pages, will pass over with indulgence; remembering that what is needless information to him, may form valuable knowledge to others. On the other hand, the more general reader, whose instruction is as much

[1] Introductory letter to 'The Antiquities of the House of Brunswick.'

sought as his amusement, may readily excuse the apparent parade of learning which disfigures each sheet; in the recollection that, wherever popular rights or historical facts are discussed, the only knowledge, which can be either useful or satisfactory, is that which can be traced to its source.

The author has but few acknowledgments to make for assistance afforded him; his most valuable acquisitions having been derived from the patient industry of one individual, by whom the public expression of his gratitude is not looked for as a recompense. But having already alluded to the kind assistance of Mr. Bolland, he is still less disposed to repress the testimonial of a sincere friend to the ready zeal and cheerful exertions of the City Solicitor, William Lewis Newman, Esq., in communicating from the wealthy stores both of his library and his own mind, and in collecting with critical judgment for his service many of the scarcer materials of this work. By his friends the late Town Clerk, Henry Woodthorpe, Esq., and the present Town Clerk, Henry Woodthorpe, Esq., LL.D., the author has been placed under similar obligations; and he has lately availed himself of some judicious hints with which he has been favoured by a distinguished prelate,[1] recently deceased, whose literary reputation cannot be advanced by a more particular mention of him on this occasion.

MADRAS: 1828.

[1] Bishop Heber.—EDIT.[*]

---

[*] The editor (in the absence of the author in India) of the first edition was Mr. Edward Tyrrell, Barrister, son of the then Remembrancer of the City, and himself Remembrancer subsequently.

CONTENTS.

BOOK I.
HISTORICAL ACCOUNT OF THE RISE AND PROGRESS OF THE CITY OF LONDON.

CHAPTER I.
Of the earliest Foundation of the City; and its Occupation by the Romans 1

CHAPTER II.
From the Invasion of the Saxons to the Norman Conquest—Internal Condition of London at the time of the Norman Invasion . . . 14

CHAPTER III.
Survey of the Changes introduced into the Laws and Government of England by the Conqueror—Of the Establishment of the Feudal System—Of the Privileges of the Citizens, which consisted in an exemption from the effects of these Changes 40

CHAPTER IV.
From the Norman Conquest to the Accession of Edward I. . 54

CHAPTER V.
From the Accession of Edward I. to the Death of Edward II. . 70

CHAPTER VI.
Account of the Original Qualifications of the Free Citizens, and of the First Establishment of the Mercantile Quality of the Civic Corporation in the Reign of Edward II. 91

CHAPTER VII.

From the Accession of Edward III. to that of Henry VII. . . . 108

CHAPTER VIII.

From the Accession of Henry VII. to the Death of Elizabeth—Of the Civic Processions and Pageants—Of the Interior Conditions, Population, Style of Building and Manner of Living within the City at this Period 131

CHAPTER IX.

Review of the Progress of Trade generally in England and in the City 157

CHAPTER X.

Inquiry into the Nature and Effect of the Exclusive Trading Privileges of the City of London 174

CHAPTER XI.

From the Accession of James I. to that of Charles II. . . . 189

CHAPTER XII.

From the Accession of Charles II. to the close of the Reign of George II.—Survey of the Measures of Charles II.—Seizure of the City Franchises by a Writ of Quo Warranto—Survey of the Measures of James II.—Confirmation of the City's corporate Rights, Franchises, &c.—Privileges by the Statute of 2 William III.—Nature and effect of the Statute of 11 George II. for regulating the elective Franchises—Summary of subsequent Legislation and of the Civic elective Franchises at the present time—Conclusion of the First Book 220

BOOK II.

OF THE CHARTERS OF LONDON.

CHAPTER I.

Charter of William the Conqueror	253
The Portreve	258
The Borough Barons	260
Citizens to be Law-worthy	262
Right of Heirship	265

CHAPTER II.

	PAGE
Charter of Henry I	267
Holding Middlesex to farm	268
Citizens to appoint their own Justiciar	270
Not to plead without the Walls	277
Exemption from Scot	281
Exemption from Danegeld	283
Exemption from Murder	283
Exemption from Waging Battle	284
Purgation in Criminal Pleas	285
Lodgings for the King's Household	287
Exemption from Toll, Passage, and Lestage	287
Of the City Soc	289
Amerciaments and Weres	292
Miskennings at the Hustings	294
Attachments for Illegal Toll-taking, and for Debts	298

CHAPTER III.

Charter of Henry II.	301
Pleas of Foreign Tenures	302
The King's Moneyers	302
Portsoken Ward	302
Bridtoll	303
Childwite	303
Jeresgive	303
Scotale	304
First Charter of Richard I.	305
Second Charter of Richard I.	305
Weirs to be removed from the Thames	305
First Charter of John	306
Second Charter of John	306
Sheriffwick of London and Middlesex	307
Blank Money	307
Removal of Sheriffs	307
Presentation of Sheriffs	312
Sheriffs' Accounts	312
Sheriffs' Amerciaments	312
Third Charter of John	313
Fourth Charter of John	313
Weavers' Gild expelled	313
Fifth Charter of John	315
Grant of the Mayoralty	315
Presentation of the Mayor	317
Chamberlainship reserved to the King	318

b

CHAPTER IV.

	PAGE
First Charter of Henry III.	319
Second Charter of Henry III.	319
Third Charter of Henry III.	319
Fourth Charter of Henry III.	320
Fifth Charter of Henry III.	320
Warren of Staines	320
Sixth Charter of Henry III.	321
Queenhithe granted	321
Seventh Charter of Henry III.	323
Allowance in the Sheriff's Court for the Liberty of St. Paul's	323
Eighth Charter of Henry III.	324
Ninth Charter of Henry III.	324
Pleading without the Walls	326
Swearing on Graves	327
Prisage of Wines	328
Making Attorneys for pleading in the Courts	328
Inrolment of Debts of Citizens	330
First Charter of Edward I.	332
Presentation of Mayor and Sheriffs	332
Second Charter of Edward I.	333
First Charter of Edward II.	333
Articles for the better Government of the City, and for regulating the City constitutional Franchises confirmed	333
Second Charter of Edward II.	344

CHAPTER V.

First Charter of Edward III.	345
Infangtheft and Outfangtheft	347
Bequeathing in Mortmain	349
Amerciaments of Sheriffs for Escapes	351
Custody of those escaping to Sanctuaries	354
King's Clerks of the Market to have no jurisdiction in the City	355
Mayor to be Escheator	356
Citizens to be exempt from Prises of Victuals taken by the Constable of the Tower	357
Recording of Charters in the King's Courts	359
Citizens to be taxed as a Commonalty and not individually	359
King's Officers not to trade in the City	360
Citizens' Lands without the City as well as within liable for City Officers' defaults	360
Criminal Inquisitions to be held only at St. Martin's Le Grand besides those at the Tower and at the Gaol-delivery at Newgate	361

	PAGE
Second Charter of Edward III.	303
Grant of Southwark	303
Third Charter of Edward III.	303
Exclusive Trade	303
Fourth Charter of Edward III.	304
Power of making Bye-Laws	305
Fifth Charter of Edward III.	305
City Maces	305

CHAPTER VI

First Charter of Richard II.	307
Protections of persons engaged in the King's service not to avail against suits for Victuals.	369
Second Charter of Richard II.	370
First Charter of Henry IV.	371
Custody of City Gates—Tolls of Markets	371
Second Charter of Henry IV.	371
First and Second Charters of Henry V.	372
Charter of Henry VI.	372
Grant of Common Land within the City	372
Purprestures and Improvements	372
First Charter of Edward IV.	375
Certifying City Customs	375
Second Charter of Edward IV.	376
Tronage	376
Third Charter of Edward IV.	379
Purchasing in Mortmain	379
Fourth Charter of Edward IV.	379
Scavage	380
Package, Pickage, and Portage	382

CHAPTER VII

Charter of Henry VII.	384
Wholesale Dealers—Office of Gauger	384
First Charter of Henry VIII.	385
Tronage	385
Second Charter of Henry VIII.	385
Inquisitions at St. Martin's Le Grand transferred to Guildhall	385
Third Charter of Henry VIII.	385
Confirmation of Tronage	385

CONTENTS.

	PAGE
Charter of Edward VI.	388
Land granted in the Borough of Southwark	388
First Charter of James I.	389
Conservancy of the Thames	390
Office of Measurer	392
Metage Duty on Goods on behalf of Funds of City Orphans	394
Second Charter of James I.	396
Search and Survey of Goods	396
Third Charter of James I.	397
Weighing and Metage of Goods	397
First Charter of Charles I.	398
General confirmation of all preceding Charters *nominatim*	398
Moorfields — Markets	400
Second Charter of Charles I.	404
Scavage and Waterbaillage	406
Charter of Charles II. — General confirmation of all previous Charters, and reciting at large their Contents	407
Charters of William and Mary, and of George II.	407
INDEX	409

COMMENTARIES ON LONDON.

BOOK I.
HISTORICAL ACCOUNT OF THE RISE AND PROGRESS OF THE CITY OF LONDON.

CHAPTER I.
OF THE EARLIEST FOUNDATION OF THE CITY, AND ITS OCCUPATION BY THE ROMANS.

THE natural interest which all feel in tracing the history of the place they inhabit, or with which they may be otherwise intimately connected—an interest which rather increases than diminishes in proportion as the sphere within which it operates becomes contracted—would in itself, perhaps, be a rational and sufficient inducement to preface a treatise upon a topic so local as the elucidation of the Constitution and Privileges of the City of London, with some account of its origin and progress. It will, however, upon reflection, presently suggest itself, that a due comprehension of its laws and customs, as well as of the civic government in general, must greatly depend on a competent acquaintance with the history of the times in which they originated, and of the manners of the age which gave rise to, and serve to illustrate, them. A dissertation of this nature, therefore, becomes not only apposite, in deference to common feelings of curiosity, but even necessary for the purposes of the present undertaking. Many of the ancient privileges and customs of London, being

CHAP. I.
B.C.

no longer applicable to the present state of society, are continually liable to be misunderstood: many commercial rights, though highly prized in former times, and still valuable, have, through the gradual changes in mercantile intercourse, sunk into disregard, and are in danger of being for ever lost; and much of that power and authority anciently exercised both in a judicial and ministerial capacity by the superior members of the Corporation, has, through the alteration of times and circumstances, naturally become subject to doubt or misconstruction. Difficulties of this kind can only be removed by directing our attention to those passing events, and that state of things, by which all laws and rights are influenced; and such attention becomes the more requisite, according as the laws and customs enquired into have a more peculiar and limited import.

The many ample and laborious works which have been already devoted to this subject, might seem, perhaps, to render an attempt of this nature superfluous: nor can there be any doubt, that whoever is curious to enquire into all the public events in detail connected with the history of the City of London, may gratify his wishes to the fullest indulgence by resorting to those volumes. It will nevertheless be seen upon examination, that, in all the accounts of London which have hitherto appeared, the writers have, for the most part, contented themselves with a minute, though very superficial, statement of historical facts and particulars; but have altogether withdrawn from the more difficult and uninviting task of enquiring into, and explaining, the progressive state of the civic government and constitution, and the relative condition of the City with respect to the rest of the kingdom. Consequently, for want of such illustration, much of their narration becomes barren and unsatisfactory; and in many of those particulars which concern the ancient and present rights and privileges of the citizens, impossible to be properly comprehended. In this undertaking, therefore, it will be attempted to supply such deficiency, by deducing a history of the legal constitution and government of the City of London, rather than to record those casual events, which, however interesting as connected with it, are foreign from

the purposes and object of the present work. Towards the
accomplishment of this design, much reference must necessarily be made to the political history of the nation at large;
but in so doing, every caution will be observed in introducing
no more of it than will serve to explain, or at least throw
light upon, the peculiar civic history of London.

In taking this brief retrospect into the history of London,
we shall purposely abstain from more than alluding to those
strange accounts of the remote origin and antiquity of that
City—fables which are now generally and justly deemed of
comparatively modern fabrication. The secret, and perhaps
unconscious, desire of flattering the propensity in human
nature to venerate antiquity, has prompted many, and particularly the more ancient authors of English history, in
treating upon a favourite topic, to strain arguments beyond
the limits of conjecture, and even to indulge in the most
absurd inventions, for the sake of assigning a very early
period to the establishment of the British polity and seat of
government. Thus Geoffrey of Monmouth, as he is called, a
monk who wrote in the twelfth century, ascribes, on the pretended authority of an ancient British manuscript, the foundation of the City of London to Brute, a descendant of Æneas,
who migrated to this country, according to his relation, about
half a century after the destruction of Troy: and he reckons
from him seventy kings, who reigned successively before the
arrival of Julius Cæsar. The reveries of this chronicler seem
to have been adopted by several of our early historians; and
they gained so much credit with our unlettered ancestors,
that they have been with difficulty exploded in later and
more civilised ages.[1] Even the accurate and learned Coke,
indulging the bias of his veneration for the antiquity of the

CHAP.
I.
B.C.

[1] Geoffrey's account of the foundation of London is inserted by way of preface to a book belonging to the City of London, denominated *Liber Horne*, from the name of the chamberlain who compiled it; which book is a compilation of all the laws and customs of the City of London, written in the reign of Edward II.; and the same account was even pleaded as good authority in point of law in the reign of Henry VI., as may be seen in the Tower Records.—Vide *Lib. Albus*, an old book of copied records in the Town Clerk's Office.

Bishop Gibson, the editor of Camden's Britannia, endeavours to support the credit of Geoffrey and his work.—Camden's *Brit.* 1772, vol. i. p. 5.

Common Law of England, quotes this account of the colonisation of England with respect; and labours strenuously to prove its laws and customs to be of Grecian origin.[1] We cannot but wonder, however, by what means it has escaped the recollection of those who have adopted or acquiesced in the notion of the settlement of Brute in this island, that the ancient Britons were ignorant of letters till long after Cæsar's invasion; so that any legend deducing the history of the country, which could have been composed, even at the very earliest period at which letters became known, must have been compiled out of an immense mass of traditions transmitted orally through a series of at least twelve hundred years. Allowing also the real existence of the British manuscript, from which Geoffrey, as he professes, translated his history, it may be safely averred that there has been no *other* work yet discovered of a prior date referring to the British dynasty before the Roman incursion. It appears, however, by its own internal evidence, that this manuscript must have been compiled many centuries after the introduction of letters into this country; indeed, there is much reason to believe, after the Norman Conquest.[2] When it is considered, therefore, that the materials for composing such a history could only have been collected from oral traditions, many of which must have survived the lapse of twenty barbarous ages, it becomes impossible to encourage the least faith on its testimony; and we may rest satisfied with the conviction, that all enquiries into the exploits and government of our uncivilised ancestors, before they were discovered by the Romans, would be as vain, as incapable of conveying any genuine instruction.

Having recourse then to those sources of information which alone deserve to be entitled authentic, we shall be

---

[1] Lord Coke's Preface to the Third Part of his Reports.

[2] The author of the British manuscript quoted by Geoffrey, calls himself Walter Archdeacon of Rhylyers (Oxford), so that he must have written some time after the establishment of Christianity in Britain, which can hardly be dated earlier than the close of the fourth century. He also alludes to the denomination of the City of London as *Londres* by foreigners who had subdued the country. By these terms must of necessity be understood the *Normans*. —Maitland's *History of London*, 1772, vol. i. p. 11.

readily disposed to think, that upon the arrival of Cæsar in this country, there existed no place of habitation on the present site of London, or indeed in any other part of this island, which could properly be denominated a city. Speaking of the most considerable station of which he gained any knowledge, that general says, 'The Britons deem 'a thick wood, fortified by a ditch and mound, a town; and 'retire thither for the purpose of securing themselves from an 'invading enemy.'[1] The circumstance of his not mentioning any town or fortress of a more regular construction, although he must have been very near the spot on which London now stands, if not actually upon it, tends most strongly to confirm the conclusion that no such place had at that time been established.

Indeed all the writers who lived at or near the age to which we are alluding, and who furnish any account of the inhabitants of Britain at that period, concur in representing their manners and customs to be of a nature quite inconsistent with the establishment of cities, or indeed of any stated and regular form of government. They were but half clothed, and that with the skins of beasts; they dwelt in huts built of hurdles and mud, which were the only kind of habitations they were capable of rearing. Agriculture was rarely and in very few places followed; but, subsisting chiefly by pasture, and the produce of forests and marshes with which the country was covered, their lives were passed in perpetual migration.[2]

Julius Cæsar, it appears from his own narrative, may be rather said to have shown the country to the Romans than to have reduced it under their dominion; and almost a hundred years elapsed after that event, before the Britons were again molested by any foreign enemy. In the second year, however, of the reign of the Emperor Claudius, a powerful armament was fitted out, under the command of Aulus Plautius, a very able general, for the purpose of making a complete conquest of the island. The Britons fought desperately in defence of their liberty; but being defeated

[1] Cæs. Com. de Bel. Gal. lib. 5.   Geog. lib. 4; Dion Cassius in Vit.
[2] Ibid.; Diod. Sic. lib. 60; Strabo.   Ner.

in several engagements, which appear to have taken place on the banks of the Thames, Claudius himself was invited over, in order to reap the honour of finishing the war. That Emperor, therefore, taking upon himself the personal command of the army, attacked the Britons, who were posted on the brink of the river Thames in the neighbourhood, as is supposed, of Chelsea, and entirely routed them. Thence penetrating into Essex, and overcoming all opposition, he left Plautius in possession of the country through which he had passed, and returned to Rome in triumph.

All these transactions took place in the immediate vicinity of London; and Claudius, in his progress into Essex, having to pass over the identical spot on which London stands, would hardly have failed, according to the Roman rules of war and policy, to have made himself master of the capital of the country; as, indeed, he did of Camalodunum, now supposed to be Maldon in Essex, which is described as the royal seat of Cynobelin. But Dion Cassius, who relates all the events of this war, makes no mention whatever of the City of London; and there is, therefore, every reason to conclude, that, even at this period, no such place was distinguished either as the seat of government or as a fortified position of any importance.

It is very probable, however, that even before the time of Julius Cæsar, the district which London now occupies might have been an occasional rendezvous of the description of those which he characterises; and it is not unreasonable to suppose that the advantages of its situation might render the stay of the natives within it less precarious and inconstant than usual. This circumstance might, in the progress of their intercourse with more civilised foreigners and neighbours, gradually lead to such an improvement, as well as increase, of the original assemblage of habitations, as would in the course of a century constitute a place of some local distinction and consideration, without the favourite solemnity of a formal foundation by men acquainted with the laws of civil society. The name 'Londinium,' by which the City was recognised within a very few years after the Romans became

[1] Dion Cass. lib. 60.

term expressive of a regular city, but even appears to avoid communicating such impression by the phrases he employs. When obliged to give it some appellation, he calls it '*oppidum*,' a word by no means so significative of a city of importance as '*urbs*;' nor does the commerce carried on at this time appear to have been of such a description as implies old mercantile establishments; but rather denotes that of an infant colony. The terms '*negociatores*' and '*commeatus*,' which Tacitus adopts in reference to the trade for which it had become famous, would, perhaps, be rendered better by the words *brokers* or *contractors*, and *provisions*, than by *merchants* and *merchandise*, according to the more usual translations.

Nevertheless, many persons, and especially the earlier writers of English history, who had not the opportunity of knowing what experience has proved with respect to the sudden and rapid growth of new colonies, have been much struck with the relation of the prodigious slaughter just described as taking place in London, as well as with the magnificent description Tacitus gives of its trade; and have thence drawn conclusions, in palpable contradiction to contemporary writers, that London must have long previously been a city of regular structure, subsisting under digested laws and a settled government. Of late, however, we have had reason to know that, under favourable circumstances, the growth of population is so rapid as in a few years to increase a very small community into a city as important as London is represented to have been at the time of its destruction by Boadicea.[1] It must be recollected, that the situation of London is one of great and peculiar advantage in a commercial point of view, and was occupied by inhabitants not altogether unacquainted with traffic. If therefore the Romans, on taking possession of the country, determined to fix on this spot as the central mart and emporium of the kingdom, it is easy to conceive how great an accession of inhabitants

[1] The population of the province of New York in America increased from 34,000 to 959,000 from the year 1790 to 1810 (Seybert's *Statistical Annals* of the *United States*); that of the city of Baltimore, from 13,000 to 46,000 in nineteen years; and many other towns in a like proportion (Fearon's *America*).

this would occasion in a place where constant supplies were required, and in which a regular intercourse with foreign nations was kept up. But, supposing one-half of those who fell victims to the slaughter inflicted by Boadicea's followers perished in London, it would be very erroneous to conclude that all these 35,000 were actually local residents. Upon the news of such an irruption, all who dwelt within the surrounding district would naturally fly to a place containing a large population, for refuge; and especially when it was known that an army of veterans was hastening to its protection. These observations may serve to illustrate the foundation and rise of the City of London: and perhaps any attempt to give more precise information, upon a subject so much involved in uncertainty as the origin and infancy of ancient cities, would be useless.

Julius Agricola, about the year 70, fifteen years after the defeat of Boadicea, was appointed governor of Britain, and continued in that authority for the space of sixteen years. We find that even, at this period, the Britons had barely emerged from a state of barbarism, and were unaccustomed to regular habitations—a circumstance strongly corroborating the presumption that the City of London, properly so denominated, and as it appeared in the time of Nero, was originally built by the Romans. For Tacitus informs us, that Agricola, having finally completed the conquest of the whole island, and having settled the country securely under the Roman dominion, began to exhort the natives to the structure of temples and houses, and to instruct them in the liberal arts of peace and civilisation.[1] These efforts, however, had but a very partial effect; for, in the time of the Emperor Lucius Septimus Severus (A.D. 210), the natives, according to Herodian, were still almost all in a state of barbarism. They went naked; they wore iron rings round their loins and necks, which they considered as a proof of wealth; they marked their bodies all over with grotesque stains. Even in the time of the Emperor Theodosius (A.D. 368), Ammianus Marcellinus writes, that the natives were perpe-

[1] Tacit. Vit. Agric.

ually wandering from place to place, and making irruptions on the Roman stations. The same writer also relates, that Theodosius made a progress throughout the country, beginning from London; and effected much towards the general civilisation of the inhabitants, whom he calls barbarians, by collecting them into cities and teaching them the arts of fortification.¹ These are still more conclusive proofs that all the cities and stations existing before his time were, strictly speaking, of Roman foundation.

Later writers, in recounting the visits of the Emperors Adrian and Severus to this country, and the transactions of subsequent Roman governors, make scarcely any allusion to London; so that it is from two or three historical facts only that we are acquainted even with its existence during the latter ages of the Roman sway. About the year 288 Carausius, who was in command of the Roman fleet stationed at Boulogne, having rebelled against the Emperor Diocletian, with the help of an army of Franks, usurped, and maintained for some years afterwards, the sovereignty of Britain. He was at length assassinated by his minister Allectus, who thereupon assumed the government. This last usurper was, however, totally defeated in the west of Britain by the Roman general Asclepiodotus, commanding the advance of an army under Constantius, who had undertaken the recovery of Britain. On this occasion (being about the year 298), we are informed the City was pillaged by a party of Franks, who were in rapid flight after the defeat of the army of Allectus, in which they had served, and hoped to have escaped with their booty across the sea. In this object, however, they were disappointed, being intercepted before they left the City, and cut to pieces by the Roman force under Constantius, which arrived suddenly.² In the reign of the Emperor Julian (A.D. 360) an expedition under Lupicinus was sent from Gaul against the Picts and Scots, who made London the place of muster.³ In the year 368, the Emperor Theo-

---

¹ Ammianus Marcellinus, lib. 18.
² Panegyr. Vet. delivered to the Emperor Maximian and to Constantius (nur. by Mamertinus and others; quoted in Camden's Brit. 1772, vol. i. p 331; Gibbon, Rom. Emp. vol. ii. chap. xiii.; and in Dr. Stukeley's Medalic Hist. of Carausius, 1757, p. 271.
³ Ammianus Marcellinus, lib. 20.

BOOK I.
A.D. 70 to 448.

dosius the elder arriving in Britain, drove the northern barbarians from the vicinity of London, after routing them in several engagements, and entered the City in formal triumph.[1] It is not probable, therefore, that at either of these periods the City was fortified by a wall; otherwise it must have been much more capable of defence than on these several occasions it appears to have been.

The Romans, compelled to rally in defence of their very seat of empire against the irruption of the northern barbarians, took their final leave of this island about the year 448, having been masters of the most considerable part of it nearly four centuries. During the latter period of their sway, the City of London made a very considerable advancement both in grandeur and civilisation. It was generally their chief station, and was very numerously inhabited. It was dignified with the name of Augusta—a name, however, which does not appear to have superseded its more ancient appellation, or indeed to have been long retained.[2] From the remains and antiquities which have been from time to time discovered, it is evident, not only that the City was adorned with temples and buildings constructed in no common style of architecture, but that many of those arts and conveniences of life were cultivated which betoken a considerable progress towards a state of refinement. Its wealth and prosperity could hardly have been of trivial consideration, when we find it, at different periods, an object of the first regard, as a scene of plunder or of victorious triumph. Nothing, indeed, can better prove the importance and comparative grandeur of the City, than the very extensive and substantial wall, which the Romans some time before their departure raised round it,[3] and of which very considerable vestiges even still remain. This wall was strengthened and adorned by them with many towers, of so firm a structure,

---

[1] Ammianus Marcellinus, lib. 17. He calls the City at this period 'Vetustum oppidum.'

[2] It was called London Ceaster, London Byrig, and London Wic, by the Saxons on their arrival (Camden. Brit. 1772, vol. i. p. 330); and was not called Augusta till after Theodosius's time (Ammianus Marcellinus, lib. 17).

[3] Woodward's Remarks upon the Ancient and Present State of London, 1723, p. 15.

that two existed two centuries ago;¹ and there is no reason to doubt that nearly the whole circuit of the City wall, as it stood in 1707, was erected upon the old Roman foundation, comprehending an area of more than three miles in circumference.²

¹ Maitland's London, 1772, vol. L. p. 31.
² Woodward's Remarks upon the Ancient and Present State of London, 1723, p. 70.

CHAPTER II.

FROM THE INVASION OF THE SAXONS TO THE NORMAN CONQUEST—INTERNAL CONDITION OF LONDON AT THE TIME OF THE NORMAN INVASION.

BOOK I.
A.D. 520 to 874.

WHATEVER may have been the state of magnificence at which London arrived under the government of the Romans, it rapidly declined upon being deserted by its powerful protectors. The Picts and Scots, at all times with difficulty restrained within their boundaries, no sooner felt themselves released from the terror of a disciplined force, than they poured in upon the southern provinces of Britain, spreading ruin and desolation throughout the whole country. In vain the Britons sought for protection from the Saxon barbarians, whom they called to their assistance. Their new and faithless allies soon either joined with or emulated their northern foes; and, arriving in large numbers at different times and in different parts of the kingdom, finally established that dominion over the whole of it, which has since passed by the name of the Saxon Heptarchy. Hengist, the first of the Saxon chiefs who landed, after many bloody engagements, established his government over Kent, Essex, and Middlesex, and fixed upon Canterbury as his capital in preference to London—a manifest proof of the decay of the latter city. Essex and Middlesex were, about the year 520, wrested from the successors of Hengist, and being incorporated with Hertfordshire, formed the kingdom of the East Saxons, of which London was made the capital. The kingdom of the East Saxons was reduced again to a sort of vassalage under Ethelbert, who began to reign over Kent in the year 564, but he was not induced to transfer the seat of his government to London, or to add that City to his own proper dominions.

INVASION OF THE SAXONS.

Towards the latter end of this king's reign, about the year 600, Christianity was first publicly preached to the Saxons in Britain, by Augustine, a monk sent for that express purpose from Rome by Pope Gregory the Great.[1] Having converted the Kentish and East Saxons, Augustine was consecrated Archbishop of Canterbury, which may therefore reasonably be supposed to have been at that time the city of the greatest consequence in those provinces. He ordained Mellitus Bishop of the East Saxons, who converted that kingdom to the true faith, and King Ethelbert built a church for him and his successors in London, dedicated to St. Paul. 'At this time,' says Bede, 'London was a mart town of many nations, which 'repaired hither by sea and land.'[2] Still, however, it must have been very far from that flourishing state in which it was left by the Romans; for no architecture in brick or stone was attempted by the Saxons till the year 680;[3] and the churches and monasteries were most of them built of wood down to Edgar's time in 974.[4]

In the confused and perpetual wars of the Heptarchy, nothing of any consequence can be traced as regarding London. We may believe, however, that throughout the universal scene of change and bloodshed which characterised a country divided into petty barbarous principalities, its relative importance did not decrease: for, on the various Saxon states being finally united under the sole dominion of the victorious Egbert in the year 827, he fixed upon this City as the seat of his residence and the metropolis of his empire; which rank it has ever since maintained. This may be assumed as a sort of second era of the foundation of London: it having from that period always held the first rank in national consideration, and gradually increased in wealth and influence till it arrived at its present flourishing condition.

Egbert was scarcely seated on his throne, when the Danes

CHAP. II.

A.D. 520 to 974.

---

[1] Christianity had made some progress among the Britons before Augustine's mission; but after the arrival of the Saxon Pagans, it was no longer acknowledged as the national religion.

[2] Bede, lib. 2, cap. 3.

[3] Ibid. lib. 2. Stow's Surrey, 1754, vol. i. p. 9.

[4] Edgar's Charter to the Abbey of Malmesbury. Stow's Surrey, 1754, vol. I. p. 9.

BOOK I.

A.D. 520 to 974.

first began those invasions, which, in the three subsequent reigns of his unwarlike successors, had wellnigh overwhelmed the whole kingdom with ruin. Their original design appears to have been plunder and devastation, rather than regular conquest: fire and sword marked their progress in every direction; and among many other cities London was sacked and burnt by them. At length, resolving to subjugate the island altogether, they took possession of the City and fortified it; and proceeding from one success to another, they had all but accomplished their enterprise, when the genius of the great Alfred enabled him to raise the nation from despair, and at last to save it by the expulsion of these merciless invaders. After gaining several great and signal victories, he besieged the Danes in London, who capitulated after some resistance. Alfred instantly began to repair and reinstate the walls and buildings of the City; which he accomplished in so effectual a manner, that it was able to withstand the most desperate sieges in after times successfully: and having finally either driven the Danes out of his kingdom, or so settled those who remained as to disable them from making any further attacks, he began to establish on a firm basis—though he cannot claim the honour of inventing—a more regular system of law and government than the nation had hitherto enjoyed—a system from which, it is not too much to say, the present liberties of England have been mainly, though gradually, derived.

In the benefits of this settlement of the national law and constitution, there is no doubt the City of London very largely partook. Indeed it may be satisfactorily shown, that the most prominent of those free customs and privileges, as well as that peculiar internal polity which, in a subsequent age of almost universal slavery, distinguished the City of London from the rest of the nation, were not only coeval with, but originally formed part of, that general law of the land which has, time out of mind, passed by the name of the Common Law of England; and which owes its first regular establishment to Alfred the Great.

That prince, it appears, collected together all the various customs and laws which prevailed in different parts of his

realm, and out of them he constructed one universal code, called the Dombok, which was to be the rule of law throughout the kingdom.¹ This body of laws was subsequently revised by Edgar, who incorporated with it many of the Danish customs, which had gradually gained ground; and was more completely established and confirmed in its full operation by Edward the Confessor. This free system of law was, however, almost totally overthrown at the Conquest, and gave way to the tyranny of the Norman laws and the feudal scheme of government, from which the nation after long struggles through many ages hardly at last emerged.² Nevertheless the Conqueror, desirous of acquiring the good-will of the most powerful body among his new subjects, reserved to the citizens of London, by his first charter, the high privilege of being governed by their ancient laws; declaring, that '*he grants them all to be law-worthy, as they were in King Edward's days*.'³ To know the purport of this charter, the nature of the privileges conferred by it, and the true date of the foundation of them, we must look back to the original establishment of the Common Law by Alfred; and if any further proof were wanting that he was the true founder of the municipal laws and privileges of London, we shall amply trace it in the identity of many of them with the provisions of that ancient Saxon code. It has been

CHAP. II.

A.D. 520 to 97 L.

¹ Blackstone's Commentaries, vol. iv. p. 411. The Dombok, though containing one general rule of law operating throughout the whole kingdom, comprised many distinct codes—such as the Wessex law, the Mercian law, the Danish law, &c.—which prevailed in different parts of the kingdom, and were added to the general code from time to time, as the various districts, into which the kingdom was divided, became again united under the same authority. Alfred's original Digest did not comprise the Danish law.—Heywood's *Dissertation upon the Ranks of the People*, 1818. Introduction, p. xxiii.

² Blackstone's Commentaries, vol. iv. p. 414, et seq. So attached were the people to these ancient laws, and so clamorous for their observance, that the first Norman kings often pretended to restore them, when either through fear or ambition they wished to cultivate the good opinion of their English subjects. Thus the Conqueror, in the fourth year of his reign, had a Digest composed of the laws observed in the Confessor's time; and Henry I., after a more systematic collection of them, swore to establish them (Heywood's *Dissertation upon the Ranks of the People*, 1818. Introduction, p. xxiii.). Every attempt to restore them proved abortive; and in the meanwhile the feudal system became thoroughly interwoven with the Constitution.

³ First Charter of William the Conqueror. Vide post, p. 257.

said that this original Dombok, or a copy of it, was carefully preserved among the City Records; and the Mirror of Justices, which was a book written in the reign of Edward II. by Horne, who was Chamberlain of London, seems to have been compiled from that very work.[1]

To specify a few instances: Among the institutions of the Common Law it was provided, that justice should be administered throughout the kingdom in local courts, over which the Earl (or Alderman, as he was originally termed) or the Reve,[2] together with the Bishop, were to preside;[3] and so accordingly we find in the time of Athelstan, who reigned within twenty-four years after Alfred, and afterwards in that of the Conqueror—these magistrates, or at least the two latter, were at the head of the judicial authorities in London.[4] The privilege of a special legal jurisdiction has always been considered by the citizens as one of their most valuable immunities. It was secured to them in express terms by one of the laws of Edward the Confessor, and by the earliest of their charters which refer to any of their privileges in detail.[5] Another of the ancient Saxon institutions established by Alfred was, that the members of the various districts, into which the kingdom was divided, should elect freely their own magistrates.[6] This also is a right which has always been deservedly prized by the City of London as one of the highest importance, and was in very early times granted, or rather confirmed, to it by charter;[7] for it was evidently enjoyed under the Saxon dynasty. The first civic temporal magistrates at that period were the Reves; and they appear to have exercised an authority, even in a legislative capacity, quite independent of the king. 'This,'

[1] Edinburgh Review, vol. xxxiv. p. 187. There is reason to believe that Magna Charta, which was framed in London, was founded on some such document.—Vide Ch. II.; and Lyttelton's *History of King Henry II.*, 4to. 1767, vol. i. note to p. 99.

[2] As to the quality and functions of these dignitaries, who seem originally to have performed the same magisterial duties under different appellations, vide Book II. Ch. I. p. 258. 'Portreve.'

[3] Ingulphus, p. 870.

[4] Wilkins, Leges Anglo-Saxonicæ, 1721, p. 65. First Charter of William the Conqueror. Book II. Ch. I. p. 257.

[5] Charter of Henry I. Wilkins, Leges Anglo-Saxonicæ, p. 197.

[6] Blackstone's Commentaries, vol. iv. p. 413.

[7] Charter of Henry I. Book II. Ch. I. 'Portreve.'

begins one of Athelstan's laws, 'is the agreement which the 'Bishops and Reves belonging to the City of London have 'resolved upon and sworn to observe:' and then are recited many resolutions for mutual defence against robbery and violence, entered into by the *free gilds*, or fraternities, over which they presided.¹ The Conqueror, on his arrival, appears readily to have acquiesced in the authority and title of the Portreve, who then, as chief magistrate, governed the City; and neither that king, nor any of his immediate successors, prior to the charter confirming the liberty of choosing a chief magistrate, seems, in any one instance, to have interfered in the appointment of the chief magistrate, except under some plea of forfeiture; when the king, for a time, seized the government of the City into his own hands.² Again, by the Common Law, though the Danish burthen of *heriot*, and some other taxes and services were due in respect of lands, yet the possessors of land were free from all the

---

¹ Wilkins, Leges Anglo-Saxonicæ, p. 65.—A Gild was an association of men who contributed for political purposes to a joint stock; from the Saxon 'Gildan' to pay (Spelman's *Glossary*, 1687: 'Geldum'). 'Frith' is an ancient Gothic word signifying peace.

² Although it seems clear that the citizens of London in the Saxon times appointed *most* of their own magistrates, yet it is not so certain that they had always appointed *all* of them. If the City was put on a par with counties in point of jurisdiction, it would follow that the Reve or Portreve or Sheriff (who was at that period the Mayor or chief magistrate) would, in conformity with the Saxon system of law, be *elected* by the citizens. Indeed, if they belonged to no superior lord, but were freemen, it could not be otherwise, because the *lordship* carried with it the magistracy and jurisdiction. Yet still, as the king sometimes appointed Earls, or, as they were anciently termed, *Aldermen*, to exercise the Shrieval authority over counties, and who, even after sheriffs superseded their ordinary functions, still possessed a concurrent jurisdiction with them, and, in some respects, a superior jurisdiction over several counties; so the king might, perhaps, do the same occasionally in London; and we find that Alfred appointed one Alderman to have jurisdiction over *all* London (*Saxon Chronicle*, A.D. 886). This, however, is the only instance on record of any other than the Reve and Bishop, and the Aldermen in their Gilds, having authority in London in the Saxon era. The Bishop, who acted as a magistrate, was appointed by the Archbishop of Canterbury. The Aldermen of the London wards or gilds (though it does not seem probable that the governors of those districts were known by that name in the time of the Saxons) were evidently appointed by the inhabitants; as we find that the king gave Knighten-gild, which was the ancient name of Portsoken ward, to the *knights* or *men* of that district; and it is certain that they, being so liberated from *demesne*, (i.e. the pure proprietorship), gave the gild to the Prior and Canons of the Holy Trinity at Aldgate; and the Prior *thereby* became an Alderman.—Vide post, p. 59. and Ch. VI. 91 et seq.

BOOK I.
A.D. 520 to 974.

more oppressive feudal services which characterised the Norman sway.¹ From these feudal grievances also the citizens of London were always privileged, and held their property according to the tenure of Saxon times.² So, by the ancient Common Law, every freeman possessed the right of disposing of his real property by will—a right which was overthrown by the Normans, as incompatible with that system of feudal tenure which they introduced;³ but this right was preserved to the citizens, as a peculiar custom. Another remarkable coincidence between the ancient City customs and the provisions of the Common Law appears in regard to the residence of foreign merchants; which, by a law of Athelstan and according to ancient usage in the City, was restricted to forty days.⁴ Lastly, the citizens always retained the ancient constitutional trial *by Jury* and *by Wager of Law*, as established by Alfred's code; and were expressly exempted from the necessity of submitting to the *trial by Battle*, as introduced by the Normans⁵—a privilege which existed, as a matter of right, in no other part of the kingdom.

One of the regulations adopted by Alfred in the administration of his government, was, that the assembly called the *Wittenagemote*, should meet twice a year in *London* for legislative purposes.⁶ The precise meaning of the term *Wittenagemote* is, a 'deliberation of wise men;' but much dispute has arisen upon the quality and functions of this assembly. We

---

¹ Blackstone's Commentaries, vol. iv. p. 413.
² Brady on English Boroughs, 1777, p. 29.
³ Coke on Littleton, lib. 2, sect. 167; Hargrave's Notes, p. 136; Selden's Notæ et Spicilegium ad Eadmerum; Leges Edwardi, xxxvi.
⁴ Vide Ch. VI. pp. 91, 92; Ch. VII. 120.
⁵ Charter of Henry I. Justice Blackstone, indeed, attributes this exemption of the citizens from trial by Battle to an idea of 'fighting being 'foreign to their education and employ-'ments' (Blackstone's Commentaries, vol. iv. p. 347). The reason assigned in the text appears more consistent with the history of the age. It is to be recollected, that in early times, the citizens of London, so far from evincing an unwarlike disposition, were the most efficient soldiers in the kingdom. Fitzstephen, who wrote in Henry the Second's time, says that the City mustered 80,000 troops—a number probably more than equal to the whole male population capable of bearing arms: and although little credit can be placed on such a calculation, yet we may collect from it that the military strength of the City was very considerable.
⁶ Hume's History of England, vol. i. ch. ii. Le Mirrour de Justice.

may gather that at all events it was of a parliamentary
nature. This Council had been summoned in much earlier
times, at the royal discretion, to London and elsewhere; and
usually attended at whatever place the king might happen to
hold his Court at the time he thought proper to summon it;
if, indeed, it is not rather to be considered as part of the
King's Court itself. The fixing of a stated period and place
of its future meeting may serve to show the advancement of
the national policy, and the relative importance of the City
of London, in the reign of Alfred.

We learn from a circumstance mentioned in the laws of
Athelstan that, in his reign, London still maintained the rank
of the first city in the kingdom. Upon the occasion of the
general coinage which took place throughout the realm,
eight moneyers were appointed for London, six for Canterbury, and a smaller number for several other cities.[1] A
remarkable statute also passed during the reign of the same
monarch, by which we may judge how great a national
object the encouragement of commerce had become, and can
estimate the consideration in which those engaged in it were
held. By this law, which chiefly, if not solely, affected the
citizens, as may be collected from the circumstance of its
being annexed to the 'Agreement' of Londoners before
alluded to, forming, as it were, a code of civic ordinances, it
was ordained, that a merchant who had made three long
sea voyages on his own account, should be entitled to the
quality of a thane, or nobleman.[2]

A more accurate judgment, however, may be drawn from
other sources, of the real condition of the metropolis and
of the quality of its inhabitants, as we advance towards the
close of the Saxon ascendency. We have observed that in
Edgar's time (A.D. 974) almost all the buildings throughout
England, both public and private, were built of wood.[3] And
we are not to suppose the extent of London was equal to the
present site of that part of it called the City. The walls,
indeed, remained the same as in the time of the Romans;
but we are informed that in Ethelred's reign (A.D. 1000), there

[1] Wilkins, Leges Anglo-Saxonicæ,
721, p. 59.
[2] Ibid. p. 71.
[3] Supra, p. 15.

were very few houses within the City walls; and that a large area in the middle was left vacant.¹ These walls, however, were preserved in such strength and condition, that when at the latter end of the reign of Ethelred London was invested by Sweyn at the head of a most powerful army of Danes— an army which had marched in victorious triumph from one end of the kingdom to the other—the citizens opposed so effectual a resistance as to oblige him to abandon the siege.² His son Cnut, in the succeeding reign of Edmund Ironside, twice furiously assaulted the City in vain; and so intent was he upon the reduction of it, to ensure the conquest of the whole kingdom, that, by the incredible labour of a very numerous armament, he cut a canal from below London bridge—then lately constructed, and which had been securely fortified by the citizens—round by the south side of the Thames, in order to invest the City on all sides.³

Notwithstanding his utmost efforts, the citizens so successfully maintained their ground, that Cnut was fain to compromise the struggle for dominion with Edmund, and, the kingdom being divided between them, London was ceded to the former.

Edmund, the favourite of the Londoners, whose cause they had espoused with so much zeal and courage, was murdered very soon after this arrangement; which removed the only obstacle to the sole dominion of Cnut. The former had been elected to the throne, and crowned in London with great pomp and splendour, chiefly through the influence of the citizens, in opposition to the original claims of Cnut in right of his father Sweyn, who had gained possession of the sovereign power in the lifetime of Ethelred.⁴

Almost the first act of Cnut on his accession was to levy a contribution from the whole nation of 83,000*l*.—an enormous sum in those days; out of which the City was taxed to supply no less than 11,000*l*.; being nearly a seventh of the whole. It is to be confessed, however, that this monarch was, throughout his reign, ever mindful of the true interests of

---

¹ Fabian's Chronicles, 4to. 1811. p. 202; Sim. Dun. Hist.
² Saxon Chronicle, 4to. 1823. p. 181.
³ Ibid. p. 197.
⁴ William of Malmesbury, A.D. 1016.

the country. He turned an anxious and patriotic attention to the revision and establishment of the laws upon the original Saxon system; and took care that justice was administered with strictness and impartiality towards all classes of his subjects.[1] The nation flourished under his wise and temperate administration; and London, in particular, opulent as it appears to have been at his accession, and notwithstanding its vigorous opposition to his original usurpation, advanced under his government very considerably both in prosperity and political importance.

At the close of his reign, we find the citizens represented at a Wittonagemote, summoned at Oxford, on no less a national occasion than the choice of a successor. Those who attended on behalf of the City are termed in the Saxon Chronicle 'the Lithsmen' of London—an expression not easily translated at the present day, though probably meaning merchants;[2] at all events, we may suppose them to have been the men who possessed the highest civic dignity at that period.

It has been conjectured, rather hastily, from the City having a voice in the national assembly, that it had already become one individual and chartered body politic.[3] In answer to this conjecture it may be alleged in the first place, with some confidence, that the elective franchise of sending representatives to the national council, or, as it afterwards became, the Parliament, was *not* originally and constitutionally a *corporate* privilege in any of the cities or boroughs in England, but that the assumption of such privilege by the *corporations* of towns was, in truth, an usurpation over the more ancient system of borough representation.[4] The hypothesis, there-

---

[1] Hume's History of England, vol. i, p. iii.

[2] Maitland and Northouck in their Histories of London have, apparently without consideration, adopted the most ready translation, and have rendered *Lithsmen* by *Mariners* (Maitland, 1772, vol. i. p. 36; Northouck, p. 17). The term is derived from *Lithan, naviagare*, which is often used in a mercantile sense by the Saxon writers.—Lye's *Gothic Dictionary*, vol. i. 'Lithan,' 1772; Saxon Chronicle, A.D. 1035.

[3] Northouck's Hist. Lon., pp. 17, 18.

[4] Vide Book II. Ch. III. p. 313. This position is satisfactorily established by Merewether's Sketch of the History of Boroughs, 1822, p. 26. The subject, however, is by no means thoroughly discussed in that work, though much learning and ability is displayed. It may be seen by the City Records, that

fore, of the early existence of the Corporation of London built on such a foundation must fall to the ground. It may be doubted whether the *citizens at large* had, properly speaking, a voice in the Wittenagemote, for no trace can be found in the history of the times, of the mode of electing and deputing political *representatives*, or that any were deputed at all by the citizens themselves, in the strict character of free constituents. There appears greater probability in supposing that these *Lithsmen,* or merchants, of London who found a place in the Wittenagemote, attended rather in the character of *Thanes* than of burgesses, since the terms employed to designate the members of that council always imply *nobility*;[1] and we have seen that the more successful and prosperous of the London merchants were entitled by the laws of Athelstan to the dignity of Thanes.[2]

The conjecture that the whole mass of the citizens formed at this period one corporation admits of still clearer refutation. It is true, indeed, that corporations, considered as associations of many individuals for a permanent common purpose, are older, even in England, than the reign of Cnut, and older, perhaps, than the Saxon era.[3] The division of the kingdom into tithings, hundreds, and counties, may be considered in some sense a creation of so many corporations. But, even in this sense, the term will not apply to the City of London. For, although we find that in the reign of Athelstan[4] several *gilds* or fraternities, partaking, it may be allowed, very much of the nature of the hundreds instituted by Alfred,[5] existed in London; yet it seems plain,

---

the Members of Parliament were in fact for upwards of the first hundred years elected by the same persons as composed the Common Council; that is, householders of the wards paying scot, and indeed usually in the Common Council. Vide post, pp. 85, 87, 88. Book I. Ch. VI. Book II. pp. 336, 337.

[1] They are termed in the ancient historians, 'principes, satrapæ, optimates, magnates, proceres.'

[2] Vide p. 21. Tyrrell, in his Bibliotheca Politica, Dialogus VI. and in his Life of Richard the Second, makes it very apparent that the Commons of England had no *representatives* in Parliament till the 49th Henry III.; and this opinion seems to be established by the authorities adduced in the Report of the Lords' Committee appointed July 1815 on the dignity of a peer.

[3] Miller on English Government. Stewart on the Antiquity of the English Constitution.

[4] Vide pp. 18, 19.

[5] Vide Ch. II. & IV.

at they were distinct and independent of each other. One
strict in particular, within the liberties of London, namely,
at of Portsoken ward, anciently called *Knighten-gild*, was a
ld altogether distinct from the rest of the civic body,
roughout the Saxon times; and remained so to the time of
enry I., possessing independent franchises, and at the same
me all the judicial privileges which belonged to any part of
ondon.[1] In the reign of Henry I. this *gild* was bestowed
y the men of the *gild*, with the king's charter of confirmaion, upon the prior and canons of the Holy Trinity in Aldate; by virtue of which title, the prior afterwards, when as
t may be presumed the whole City with its liberties became
strictly one corporation, held the rank of an Alderman.[2]
There is no mention made of London as *one gild* or fraternity
in the Saxon times; nor are the citizens spoken of in a corporate capacity by William the Conqueror's charter, or by
those of his immediate successors. *Gilds*, however, if they
are to be considered in the light of corporations, were, according to the well authorised opinion of Madox, very different
from, and far more ancient than, town corporations, strictly
so called: and that author adds, that the practice of gildating or embodying whole towns sprung up, in all probability,
in imitation of them.[3] Anciently, many towns and districts

---

[1] Stow's Survey, 1755, vol. i, p. 348; Madox's Firma Burgi, 1726, ch. i. sec. 9, p. 23, and note (1).

[2] Ibid. Vide p. 38, note 4.

[3] Madox's Firma Burgi, 1726, pp. 23, 27. It must not, however, be supposed that the practice of gildating or incorporating whole towns as *mercantile* corporations arose in imitation of these gilds. That the term *gilda* originally had no *peculiar mercantile* signification is clear; for there were many associations, both in the country and in cities, passing by that name, which were composed of the inhabitants of particular districts; indeed, the members of the *berkenfriborkes*, or *friborgys*, were also termed members of *frithgilds* (Spelman's *Glossary*: 'Geldum'). There is no trace of any mercantile incorporation of London, nor of its ever having been a general mercantile gild; though *gilds*, both mercantile and territorial, were common enough within it: and yet this City is universally considered as one of the oldest in England. It was common for a particular body of townsmen, and still more so for individuals, to have a gild in propriety, and with it *sac* and *soc*, or a civil and criminal jurisdiction (Madox's *Firma Burgi*, p. 23), which, it is presumed, is quite sufficient to show that these *gilds* were not considered merely as associations of trading individuals. When such an association was incorporated in a town, it was so termed expressly; viz. that the town should have a '*Gilda* or *Hansa mercatoria*;' but when the whole town itself was incorporated, it was said to

BOOK I.
A.D. 947 to 1066.

which were not incorporated, nevertheless possessed exclusive immunities,[1] and even rendered in an aggregate capacity ser-

have a community, 'communio, communes, communitas;' that is, according to Dr. Brady, a representative faculty (Brady on Boroughs, 1777, p. 30; Madox's Firma Burgi, p. 35). So that, although these incorporations may truly have sprung from gilds, they were not raised in imitation of, nor had they much resemblance to, *mercantile gilds*. In process of time these *merchant gilds* grew to be the only gilds established under that name; and then the term, in all probability, began to be applied to such corporations *solely*; and thus the notion might arise, that to confer a gild on a town was in effect to make it a corporation of free citizens, which however, in strictness, depended on the nature of the gild. There can be no doubt that the engrafting a *commercial* constitution on the aggregate corporations of cities and boroughs, originated in usurpation; and, in all probability, took its rise in the following way. It was the ancient practice, in the Saxon times, to enroll all the dwellers in towns, as well as throughout the rest of the kingdom, in *frankpledge*, either as free householders, or as inmates, at the leets. This would make them citizens, as it were, of that leet. When a whole town became one associated body, apprentices, who, as inmates, were before in pledge within the City, would of course become entitled to enrolment in the civic community; accordingly, we find from the very earliest records now to be seen in the Town Clerk's Office, of enrolments of citizens in London (Lib. Ordinationum, temp. Edw. I. fol. 143 et seq. et Stat. Civit. Lond. 13 Edw. I.), that *apprentices* to tradesmen were enrolled upon having served their time. Being thus admitted as members, they naturally came to be considered as representing true citizens (which they certainly did not, in the original and *full* sense of the word, nor do they to this day in the City of London). At length, as scarcely

any resided in such towns but tradesmen and their inmates, the established mode of making free citizens began to be grounded on the absolute requisition of passing, actually or nominally, through a *trade*. In like manner those towns which could only trace title to a *mercantile gild*, and not to a *community* in any other sense, adopted the same mode of supplying *their* associations; and, since their trading privileges extended to nearly the whole of the inhabitants, the *gilds* would be co-extensive with the towns: and thus, that which was originally but a merchant gild, would be converted into a town corporation. There are two instances as early as the time of Henry III. of charters granted to cities, by which the qualification of the citizens are made to depend as well upon their freedom of the *merchant gild* as upon residency (Madox's *Firma Burgi*. pp. 270, 272). It is impossible to suppose that the erection of a *community*, or, strictly speaking, a *town corporation*, could, any more than that of a *gild* in a town, deprive the original inhabitants and their heirs or assigns of their free rights, as citizens, derived from actual tenancy; and those who would endeavour to prove by authentic evidence that genuine corporate privileges were originally granted to citizens in any other capacity than as mere tenants, or residents, will make the attempt in vain.—Vide Ch. VI. p. 101 and Book II. p. 313.

[1] That a grant made to the inhabitants, good men, or *citizens*, of any particular place did not thereby constitute them a *corporation*, is clear from the case of Norwich and other corporations (21st Edw. IV. 55, cited in Moore, 581), by which it is decided that any such grants should be enjoyed by the corporation of such place *in case it should afterwards be incorporated* by the name of the Mayor and Commonalty, or by any other name.

vices and dues, or fee farm rents in lieu of such dues, to the king or lord of whom the burgesses or citizens held.¹ A town corporate is one which has succession as a community modified or put into a particular form, and under a special denomination; as of Mayor, Bailiffs, and Community, or Mayor, Jurats, and Community; and the like.² What constituted a Town Corporation, says a learned French writer³ in treating of their origin, was a college or council, a mayoralty, a common seal, a bell to convoke the members of it, and a jurisdiction.⁴ These are terms (with the exception perhaps of the last) no way applicable to the condition of London in the age which we are considering. The practice of gildating or incorporating whole towns began first, according to Dr. Brady, in France, and not before the middle of the eleventh century. It was very soon followed in England and Scotland; though, with respect to London, the first express intimation to be discovered on record of its becoming one corporation, is the account of a general assembly of the nobility and citizens of London in the second year of Richard I., held by his brother John, then Earl of Moreton and regent of the kingdom, at which it was granted and solemnly confirmed by oaths, that the whole City should have or be represented by a *community*⁵ or corporation.

It seems reasonable therefore to conclude, that at the period when the citizens of London began to assume so important an influence in the affairs of the nation, the City was not repre-

---

¹ Madox's Firma Burgi, p. 85.
² Ibid. pp. 49, 50.
³ Du Fresne Glossary, 'Communia.'
⁴ In orig. Scabinatus, Collegium, Majoratus, Sigillum, Campana, Berfredus, et Jurisdictio.
⁵ Brady's treatise on Boroughs, p. 12. This author considers the term 'Community' to be synonymous with 'Corporation,' and produces many records in corroboration of that position. That the term 'Community' did not *always* imply a Corporation, is amply shown in Madox's Firma Burgi, p. 37, and the community of counties and hundreds is frequently mentioned in ancient records. In such cases the term appears usually to have been applied on occasions of a general assessment of a district to any fiscal payment. The citizens of London began to be recognised as a commonalty in records and deeds first in the reign of Henry III. (Madox's *Hist. Exch.* vol. ii. pp. 94, 247, 260). Their charters were granted to them, either in the name of the citizens or barons, till the reign of Henry III., when they began to be addressed by the name of Mayor and Citizens, and in the reign of Edward III. by the name of Mayor, Aldermen, and Commonalty, and of Mayor, Commonalty, and Citizens.

sented at the Wittenagemote in a *corporate* capacity. The national consideration and influence of the citizens may naturally be attributed to their collective opulence, derived from an increasing commerce, and to the individual wealth of many among them. They were possessed also of a strong and, in those days, an almost impregnable fortress, the command of which alone was almost sufficient to confer a sovereignty then subject to perpetual dispute. This will sufficiently account for their usual interference at the commencement of a new reign, as well as for their success in obtaining and preserving inviolate many privileges and immunities not possessed by the kingdom at large.

The two sons of Cnut, Harold Harefoot and Hardicnut, successively mounted the throne with the sanction of the citizens.[1] Their reigns were short and inglorious, and on their deaths without issue, Edward the Confessor obtained the crown under the same auspices.[2] This monarch, the last of the Saxon dynasty (if we except the second Harold, who may be said rather to have contended for, than to have attained, the crown), instructed in the good effects of a regular administration of justice by the example and prosperous reigns of the wisest among his predecessors, devoted himself to the adjusting and compiling the body of laws which had been accumulated by preceding legislators, and which, though now lost, was long an object of affection to the English nation. London seems to have held a conspicuous rank in the government throughout this reign; and it may be as well at this crisis—when a most important revolution is about to begin in the laws, the manners, and the policy of the country, in consequence of the Norman invasion—to take a survey of the internal constitution of the City, and the condition of its inhabitants, as far as can be ascertained from the scanty sources of information which are authentic. It must be confessed, however, that it is very difficult to form a competent judgment on the subject.

Although the great body of the people under the Saxon dynasty enjoyed the advantages of a free form of government

[1] Saxon Chronicle, A.D. 1035; Flor. Wigorn. Chron. 1592, lib. 3, p. 398. Sim. Dun. Hist. A.D. 1039.
[2] Saxon Chronicle, A.D. 1042.

—holding their possessions freely in their own right, appointing their own magistrates, interpreting and administering the national laws and customs themselves in their own local courts, and being exempt from the arbitrary control of any superior—a very considerable portion of the community, under the character of *serfs* or *villeins*, were doomed to a condition little, if at all, short of absolute slavery; which has been manifestly proved by the testimony and authorities produced by the most learned writers on the subject.¹ These were individuals who having, independently, no land of their own, were employed either in the personal service of the more powerful landed proprietors, or in the cultivation of their *demesne* land as it was termed; being that part of their possessions which they retained under their own immediate superintendence, for the support of their rank and household establishment. This class of persons were in a state of absolute dependency on their lord's will; they possessed no property which might not instantly be seized and appropriated by him; law and justice was administered in courts of his own, over which he exercised all but despotic power.²

Whatever may have been the *original* condition of the inhabitants of many towns in England, and whatever credit we may give the assertion of Dr. Brady, that most of them were *serfs* or *villeins*—it appears from Domesday Book, that at the period of the Norman Conquest, almost all the cities and towns of England were possessed either by the king or his nobles or chief clergy, as their *private property* or *in demesne*.³ They were all indiscriminately known by the name of *boroughs*;⁴ by far the greater portion of them, including

---

¹ Wright's Tenures. Turner's History of the Anglo-Saxons, 1823, vol. iii. p. 182. Robertson's History of Charles V., ch. i. note xi.

² 2nd Black. Comm. p. 91.

³ Madox's Firma Burgi, p. 4; and Millar, p. 279; also Coke Litt. p. 109. London and a few other cities are left out of the account of lands in Domesday Book altogether. The rest of the boroughs are enumerated among the demesne lands.

⁴ Ibid. There is some variance among the learned authorities in regard to the etymology of the word 'borough.' Some derive it from the Saxon Borh or Borhoe, a *pledge*, from which we certainly derive our 'headborough' or 'borhsolder,' and infer thence that all boroughs were originally nothing but those associations of a few families which have been commonly since known as decennaries or tythings, in which the ten were pledges for each other's con-

nearly all those which merited the appellation of flourishing cities, belonged to the king himself; and there is reason to believe, that even those few cities which, like London, were not held then *in demesne*, were nevertheless held of the king under some kind of tenure, and that most of, if not all, such cities had, at one time or other, been held *in demesne*.[1] The tenure by which the houses of the inhabitants of these *demesne* boroughs were held, was that of rendering certain fixed rents in kind and services. Their superior, whether the king or any inferior lord, also imposed various tolls, duties, and customs, to be paid by those attending the fairs and markets which he established in such districts; and which demands were, for a long time subsequent to the Conquest, regulated solely by his own discretion.[2] The situation of these borough tenants holding strictly *in demesne*, who neither enjoyed the positive right of being governed by their own customs, nor had obtained from their superiors any peculiar immunities, was, if the certainty and quality of their rents and services be excepted, such as differed little, if at all, from that of the common *villeins* or *serfs*;[3] and Dr.

---

duct, and one of them the *capital pledge* or *headborough*. This opinion, however, is quite inconsistent with history; for there existed many considerable towns and cities before the system of tything, or frankpledges, or the Saxon dynasty, all of which were subsequently called '*boroughs*,' though consisting of as many boroughs, in the sense of tythings or pledges, as there were tens of *families*. It seems more reasonable to suppose that the derivation is from the Saxon or rather Gothic, *Byrig, Burig,* or *Burh*, signifying, specifically *a town or castle:* thus London was called '*London byrig,*' and the Conqueror called the citizens in his charter '*Burh-waran;*' '*war*' signifying *a man*, and '*an*' the Gothic plural termination. So we derive St. Edmund's Bury, and many other places; as *Lothbury*, according to Stow, the dwelling of the tinworkers: and *Bucklersbury*, the buildings erected by one Buckler (Spelman's *Glossary:* '*Burgus*'). It is to be remarked also that the term Boph was used quite in a different signification from that of a town in records, where we may see this word Burig or Byrig expressly so applied.—Wilkins, *Leges Anglo-Saxonicæ*, 1721, pp. 78, 80, where in Boph and Bup b are distinguished.

[1] Vide p. 45, note.

[2] Vide p. 44, and notes.

[3] We find in Domesday Book an enumeration of the *burgesses held by the lords* in the account of almost every one of the boroughs. Such burgesses seem to have lived in the *demesne boroughs* on the same terms and conditions as the *villeins* lived on the *demesne farms* or *manors* of the lords, and were amenable precisely in the same way to the Lord's own Courts of Justice. There were many burgesses, Turner says, even in the most privileged cities, who were attached to manors (Turner's *Hist. of the Anglo-Saxons*, vol.

Brady's account of the English boroughs, as far as regards them, may be entitled to some deference.

There were, however, very few of these boroughs in which the inhabitants did not possess the privilege of having their respective rights regulated by their own customs—customs which time out of mind had gradually grown up among them, and many of which had originated among their British ancestors, and subsisted at the time when they fell a prey to their Saxon conquerors. Among the most valuable of these customs must be considered the right of heirship to their ancestor's estates, and the alienation of them under particular restrictions; rights which, though at variance with the condition of those who were tenants in the lord's demesne,[1] prevailed in one shape or other in several of the boroughs of England, and particularly the royal ones.[1] The burgesses who held their possessions under such a tenure and with such privileges, enjoyed some little share of liberty and independence; and might be regarded in the light of freemen, though still perhaps, strictly speaking, *in demesne*. Notwithstanding these privileges, unless some special and distinguishing immunities had been granted to them, they were all subject to the judicial control of their respective lords, who administered justice in their own courts, and claimed those

---

iv. p. 141.) A specimen of a town held *in demesne*, as proved by the liberation granted from all the slavish oppressions of a demesne tenure, is enumerated in the charter of Dunwich.—Madox's *Hist. Exch.* 1769, vol. i. p. 402, note *g*.

[1] That alienations by sale, will, or otherwise, and the claim of heirship, was not a common right in towns held strictly *in demesne*, appears clear from two records quoted in Mad. Hist. Exch. pp. 402, 412. That such rights were generally by common law in the Saxon times among *freemen*, vide Selden's Notæ et Spicilegium ad Eadmerum; Leges Edwardi XXXVI. Vide also Wright's Tenures, p. 171, and authorities; and Spelm. on Feuds, p. 12; and vide many records quoted in Turner's Hist. Angl. Sax. vol. ii. p. 172.

[1] The descent of land in the way of borough English, that is, to the youngest instead of the eldest son, is by virtue of an ancient Saxon custom, 2 Black. Comm. pp. 82, 83; and therefore it would appear to be of a much earlier date than the period when the inhabitants of boroughs grew rich and powerful enough to liberate themselves from a demesne tenure, and to acquire land in their own free right. However, Dr. Brady asserts, with good ground, that tenants *in strict demesne* had no right of heirship at the Conquest; and if so, this custom of borough English could only be referable to such inhabitants of boroughs as held their lands freely.

mulcts, fines, and forfeitures by which almost all crimes in those days might be expiated.[1]

A seigniory and jurisdiction of this nature, it may be easily supposed, would be rendered a source of oppression, both in regard to the dispensation of justice, and also with respect to the collection of the multifarious rents and tolls arising out of an increasing and prosperous city. Accordingly, we find in proportion as the wealth and influence of the burgesses increased, they manifested the utmost anxiety to rid themselves of so obnoxious a dependency. In many boroughs the most wealthy of the inhabitants, on one consideration or other, contrived to emancipate themselves, individually, from the demesne of their lords altogether, and held their possessions as of their own right;[2] others, forming themselves into *gilds* and fraternities, obtained from their lords, not only the free possession of their tenements, but also all judicial rights over the districts in which their property lay:[3] some few cities, which originally belonging to the king, had, either through royal indulgence or through their own influence, succeeded in liberating, in a similar manner, the whole body of citizens from the vassalage incident to the tenure *in demesne*; and some of them were also allowed to compromise, by paying one certain annual contribution by way of rent or tax, in lieu of all other payments and of all those customary dues, tolls, and other levies, which the king, as lord of the *demesne*, had been used to collect and receive; but which were afterwards levied by the citizens themselves, for the purpose of satisfying out of them the lord's rent.[4] These annual contributions were called the *farm* (ꝼeoꞃme Sax. Victum, alimentum). As early in the Norman government as the reign of Henry I., this farm was in favour of some particular cities, estimated at a specific sum, and made *perpetual*; upon which it was denominated a *fee farm*, and such cities were then said to be held of the

[1] Vide Brady on Boroughs. Spelman's Glossary: 'Sora,' 'Infangthefe.' Vide also p. 46, note.
[2] Vide Ellis's Introduction to Domesday Book: title 'Cities.'
[3] Ellis's Introd. to Domesday. Vide p. 26.
[4] Ibid. et Vid. Millar, pp. 379, 380. Madox's Firma Burgi. p. 232.

king *in capite*, or in chief, at *fee farm*.¹ The king was then considered to have relinquished the property of the soil, retaining nothing more than the mere seigniory.² The citizens who in the Saxon times held their possessions thus in their own right, and possessed judicial authority among themselves, but more particularly those citizens who likewise held *at farm*, were called *freemen* or free burgesses;³ not being subject to the arbitrary will of a superior, and entitled to be governed by their own customs or the general law of the land. This was the case with London at the Norman Conquest. It is possible indeed that it had never been in vassalage, or under the strict *demesne* of the king, but had always asserted its own independence, and claimed to be governed by its own laws in common with the free part of the national community. There are, however, certainly indications of its having been held in some sort of proprietorship even in the Saxon times; and it is not easy to account for such proprietorship at that period, on any other score than that of a *demesne* origin.⁴ From the grant of the office of Sheriff of the City to its inhabitants *in fee*, or at *fee farm*, by the early Norman charters, it must be considered that a proprietary title of some kind was vested in the king, which had descended to him from his Saxon predecessors. For, as we have already noticed,⁵ the citizens were allowed by a special charter of William the Conqueror to be as free in all respects as they were in the

---

¹ That this farm was paid in the Saxon times is not only evident from the Saxon derivation of the term, but from the circumstance of its being the common source of revenue to the Saxon kings, and paid by many other towns and whole districts in the kingdom to a stated amount.—Spelman's *Glossary*: 'Firma.'

² Madox's Firma Burgi, p. 15.

³ Brady on Boroughs; Mad. Hist. Exch. 407, note e; 421, note n.

⁴ Malmsbury says, Alfred gave London to Ethelred as the marriage portion of his daughter; or, according to the Saxon manuscript, 'he set London to Alderman Ethelred to *bdd*.' This grant may either mean to hold *in demesne*, or to preside over it in a magisterial capacity. The latter has been the acceptation among the learned (vide Malms. *de Gest. Reg.* lib. 2, caps. 4 & 5; Selden *Tit. Hon.* 650). So Richard I. said he would sell it, could he meet a purchaser (vide p. 65; though it is clear he had it not after the charters of William I. and Henry I.). But, in fact, during the sway of the earlier Norman princes, it was a frequent subject of dispute whether London was *in demesne* or not, and as such, subject to *talliaged*. Vide Mad. *Hist. Exch.* p. 712, note n.

⁵ Vide p. 17.

BOOK I.
A.D. 1066.

days of Edward the Confessor: but the charters by which the office of Sheriff was disposed of at *fee farm* to the citizens, did not imply an *assumption* of any *new title*, but rather the grant of *new* immunities, in order to promote the independence and welfare of the City. Madox states, that whenever a town was granted in *fee farm*, the king had been previously seised of that town in his *demesne*.[1] Contrary to his almost uniform practice, he does not in this instance adduce any direct authority for this assertion; and perhaps it may require some qualification: but the well-known caution and accuracy of this author will probably gain him credit at least so far as to induce a belief that such grants had a *demesne foundation*. It is however beyond a doubt that the City of London was not *in demesne*, either at the Norman Conquest or for some time previous.

As a necessary consequence of the City's free tenure of the ground on which it stood, the citizens possessed an independent jurisdiction both civil and criminal, to be exercised by magistrates of their own appointment.[2] Whether the latter was exercised by a general court of criminal judicature extending over the whole City, or whether all kind of criminal justice was administered in the separate and distinct *free gilds*, into which it appears the City was in the Saxon times divided,[3] is not easy to ascertain; but it is probable that criminal justice was dispensed in the separate free gilds. According to Spelman,[4] the term *Gild* (which originally signified an association of men paying to a common stock) was applied to the jurisdiction afterwards known by the term *Friborg*, from the Saxon Fpibophoe, *free pledge*. The assembly and review of the *Friborgs, free pledges* or *gilds*,

---

[1] Madox's Firma Burgi, p. 16.
[2] It appears from Domesday Book, that almost invariably where the burgesses possess the property of the borough, either in whole or in part, they held likewise what was called the *soc* and *sac* (terms which signify a civil and criminal court and jurisdiction over the district), just in the same manner as the barons anciently in their manor courts. In the enumeration of the dues and issues in lieu of which the *fee farm* rents of cities and boroughs were paid, *pleas and perquisites* are almost invariably mentioned.—Madox's *Firma Burgi*, p. 23; vide Ellis's *Introduction to Domesday Book*; vide also *Hist. Exch.* ch. x. and ch. xi.
[3] Wilkins, Leges Anglo-Saxonicæ, pp. 61, 65.
[4] Spelman's Glossary: 'Geldum.'

CRIMINAL JURISDICTION. GILDS. LEETS. WARDS.

was called the Court Leet, or Lað, from the word Laðian, *to assemble*,¹ the primitive of which seems to be Leoð, *people*: this meeting was held in each hundred of a county in turn by the reve or sheriff; by whom, according to the Saxon policy, the criminal law was formerly administered.² This leet jurisdiction was in ancient times usually possessed by the lords over their *demesnes*, and accounts for the leets held in manors which were carved out of the Sheriff *Turns*.³ It was no uncommon thing to grant precisely the same judicial powers to the civic authorities, or to a number of burgesses composing a gild, or possessing part only of the borough.⁴ The circumstance of these *free gilds* assembling in the reign of Athelstan for the purpose of passing penal resolutions against all offenders by robbery or violence,⁵ strongly corroborates this conjecture. The division of the City into *gilds*, was most probably the origin of the division into wards.⁶ There are many records in which *aldermen* are noticed as presiding over *gilds*;⁷ and the criminal jurisdiction of aldermen over their wards or *gilds*, was similar to that of the original lords of demesne over their demesne lands,⁸ or rather of the sheriff over his hundred.⁹

Throughout the Saxon era, the administration of criminal justice was very irregular and unsettled. The judicial pro-

CHAP. II.
———
A.D. 1066.

---

¹ Vide 2nd Co. Inst. Mag. Chart. c. 35. 4th Co. Inst. c. 54; but this derivation is by no means certain (vide Spelman's Glossary: 'Leta;' Lye's Sax. Dict.). The ancient Frisons had their *Lind-thing*, a sort of legislative assembly (Vide *Edin. Rev.* vol. xxxii. p. 14).

² Ibid. 4 Black. Comp. 273.

³ Ibid.

⁴ Vide p. 25, note. Thus the men of Knighten-gild held their property in the liberties of the City, with the right of sac and soc, infangthef, theam, toll, and all customs (terms implying a court and jurisdiction over all crimes, with the fines, mulcts, and forfeitures accruing to it), and subsequently granted the same, as appears from a charter of Henry I., confirming such grant to the Prior and Canons of the Holy Trinity, with all those rights expressly enumerated. Madox's *Firma Burgi*, chap. 1. And again. The men of Dover had a gild, and also with it the sac and soc, for which they paid the king a fee farm rent.—*Domesday Book*. And so many other burgesses, as may be seen in Mad. *Hist. Exch.*

⁵ Vide p. 19.

⁶ Thus Knighten-gild was as early as the reign of Henry I. identified with Portsoken Ward; and Fitzstephen, who writes in Henry II.'s reign, speaks of the division of the City into distinct districts as of no very recent date.

⁷ Madox's *Firma Burgi*, p. 30; Hist. Exch. pp. 562, 708, 709, 738, 739.

⁸ Maitland's Lond. vol. ii. p. 1199; Brady on Boroughs; LL. Edw. Lamb. Archaion. fol. 132.

⁹ 3rd Co. Inst. pp. 69, 70.

ceedings of their leets seem to have been neither systematic nor uniform. These courts had their jurymen, composed of neighbours *de viceneto*; but the verdict they pronounced was, in fact, the charge which they presented; and in many cases such *presentment* was in itself tantamount to a conviction. This may appear strange, and contrary to all principle and common sense, but can be explained with some shade of reason. It is to be assumed that some sort of trial, that is by testimony to the fact, really took place before these jurymen of leets or hundreds previous to their presentment of the crime as having been committed; a second investigation before the same jurymen might have been considered superfluous. There may have been, moreover, insuperable difficulties in assembling a second jury and all the witnesses before the tribunal which was finally to decide on the guilt and punishment, out of a sparse population with scanty means of locomotion, and for the most part sunk in ignorance and degradation. Further trials, however, if they can be so called, were often had; but such trials appear to have been nothing more than solemn appeals to the Deity by the accused, through the medium of ceremonials varying probably with the circumstances of the case, and with the district in which the trial took place. Sometimes the party denied the charge on his own oath and on that of his friends, who swore to their belief in his innocence, and were termed his Compurgators.[1] Sometimes the culprit took the *corsned*, or *sacred morsel*: sometimes he underwent the *ordeal*; that is, plunged his hands in boiling water, or walked over burning ploughshares, or pretended to do so with the assistance of the priests, in testimony of his innocence.[2] In the case of a culprit *taken in the manner*, that is, with the stolen goods upon him, no investigation seems to have taken place; but the seizure of him under such circumstances was a conviction,

---

[1] Vide Book II. Ch. I. p. 264. There is reason to conjecture that this trial (if the term can be allowed) by oath of compurgators, or wager of law, was the origin of the real trial by petit jury— who gave their verdict upon *evidence* of witnesses taken in court before them, instead of the oath of denial by the accused, and of that of his compurgators of *their* belief.—Vide p. 285.

[2] Vide ibid.

CIVIL JURISDICTION.

and summary justice was instantly executed by the lord of the soc or district, or the magistrate.¹ The blackest crimes might generally be expiated by a pecuniary mulct; in some cases fixed by positive law, but in others, *affeered*, or assessed, by persons delegated by the leet jury.² In short, there appears to have been no other rule of law or of judicial trial in the Saxon criminal courts, than what resulted from the resolutions of the proprietors of land associating together in their various gilds for mutual protection, or from the arbitrary will of such proprietors exercised over their own immediate vassal tenants.³

Of the administration of *civil* justice throughout the kingdom more specific information may be gained. In all the counties of England courts were established, in which every claim, whether of a personal nature or in respect of land, was tried: those between tenants *in demeene* were adjusted by the Lord in a court of his own¹—the Court Baron; those between free members of the same hundred, in the hundred courts;⁵ those between free members of different hundreds in the county court.⁶ This county court, called the *Sciregemote*, was held twice every year; and over it presided the Alderman or the Sheriff together with the Bishop.⁷ But in London a peculiar and separate legal establishment subsisted, in which all litigation between the citizens was decided. How rights of a *personal* nature were tried is not very clear. In all probability a court for these causes, when of importance, was occasionally held by the Reve or Portreve, to which court the present Lord Mayor's and Sheriff's courts may have succeeded. Possibly, however, for minor causes the Reve or Alderman of the *gild* might exercise a similar civil jurisdiction as the Sheriff in his hundred, or the Lord over his demesne; but these courts, not being of *record*, there are no traces of their trials. The Lord Mayor's and Sheriff's courts, in which alone all personal causes are at present sued, did not

---

¹ Vide Book II. Ch. V. p. 317.
² Vide Book II. Ch. IV.
³ Hume's Hist. Appendix 2nd; Brady on Boroughs; Wilkins, Leges Anglo-Saxonicæ, p. 65.
⁴ Brady on Boroughs; Madox's Hist. Exch. p. 107; and ch. xi.
⁵ Leg. Edwardi, c. 2.
⁶ Hume's Hist. App. 2nl: and authorities there quoted.
⁷ Ingulph. p. 870.

exist at this period, at least under those names, or according to their present establishment. It may be noticed, that personal property was very trivial and but little regarded in the laws of those early times. The only civil court particularised is that, the jurisdiction of which was always time out of mind confined to suits which either directly or indirectly affected land. This court, called the Court of Hustings, is described by old writers and in old records as one of the greatest antiquity and dignity. It was one common jurisdiction extending throughout the whole City, over which the first magistrature presided in conjunction with the Bishop, in a similar way as in the county courts.[1] The privilege of suing and being sued in this court only, and of being tried in their own criminal courts by their own appointed judges was, in these times, of great value to the citizens, and was anxiously secured to them in their earliest charters. They were thereby not only protected from the arbitrary jurisdiction of a demesne lord, who would have had an absolute dominion over the property of those who were strictly tenants in demesne, but they had the advantage of obtaining justice at their own doors on that spot where their laws and customs were likely to be best understood.

Such then was the state of freedom and independence enjoyed by the citizens of London when the Saxon Government, after subsisting upwards of six hundred years, was finally overthrown by the Normans. Holding their possessions in their own inherent right, they were entitled either to dispose of them at their discretion, or to transmit them to their posterity. Governed by their own magistrates,[1] and amenable only to their own courts, they were privileged in having justice dispensed to them, not according to the will of any superior, but according to the general law of the land, modified by their own peculiar customs. In short, they possessed all the legal rights and privileges which in that age distinguished men of the first rank among the Anglo-Saxons, being those who held their land independently in their own right, and which entitled them to the appellation of *Freemen*, in a country where a large class of the community was in a complete state of servitude. To this state of liberty undoubtedly must be attributed the flourishing commerce for which the City of London had, even at this period, become famous, and the opulence it seems in consequence to have acquired.[2]

[1] Vide pp. 19, 20.
[2] William of Malmesbury, who wrote in King Stephen's reign, speaking of London in Edward the Confessor's time, says, 'London was a noble city, frequented by merchants from all parts of the world.'

CHAPTER III.

SURVEY OF THE CHANGES INTRODUCED INTO THE LAWS AND GOVERNMENT OF ENGLAND BY THE CONQUEROR—OF THE ESTABLISHMENT OF THE FEUDAL SYSTEM—OF THE PRIVILEGES OF THE CITIZENS, WHICH CONSISTED IN AN EXEMPTION FROM THE EFFECTS OF THESE CHANGES.

BOOK I.
A.D. 1066.

IN consequence of the Norman Conquest, a vast revolution was gradually effected in the constitution and condition of the country. The first and immediate result was a change of proprietors of the greater part of the landed property in the kingdom. The battle of Hastings was attended not only by the death of Harold, who had assumed the crown, but also with a prodigious slaughter of the chief nobility and landholders in the kingdom. This enabled William the Conqueror to reward his followers with the possession of the estates of all those who had borne arms against him, as being confiscated by reason of such resistance. London, as a royal burgh, fell into the hands of the Conqueror himself, who, in order to ensure the allegiance of that place which had now become the very key to the empire, raised a fortress of great strength within the walls of the City, since called the Tower of London.[1] The citizens, perhaps not without reason, began to entertain apprehensions that the king, upon the assumption of his royal rights, might deprive them of all their immunities, and reduce them to the condition of strict tenants *in demesne*: and probably this measure had been enforced against some of the boroughs which fell to the lot of the new Norman lords. William, however, either induced by the civic magistrates—one of whom, namely the Bishop, was a Norman—or willing to attach the citizens to his government,

[1] Gul. Pict.

who had indeed readily submitted to him on his arrival, relieved them from this anxiety, and granted to them their first charter, by which he declares they shall be all *law-worthy*, and that *each man should be his father's heir*; the meaning and importance of which grants may be understood from what has already been premised.

Another important alteration, introduced by the Normans, was the extending the original jurisdiction of the king's own appointed judges, or justices, to all parts of the kingdom. We have seen that, by the Saxon policy, remedial courts of law were established in each county and hundred for the dispensation of justice, over which the local authorities presided:[1] and by the Saxon laws every man was forbidden to appeal to the king sitting in council, or wittenagemote, unless justice had been denied him in that court which was appointed for him in the first resort.[2] But by the Normans a specific and supreme judicial court, called the *aula regis* or *curia regis*, was established, over which an officer called the Capital Justiciar presided, who gradually assumed the authority by his process in the first instance to draw within his jurisdiction all causes arising within the kingdom beyond the value of forty shillings, and also to review all the proceedings of inferior local courts in an appellate capacity. This court was, indeed, no other than the king's supreme council of the realm; in which the chief justiciar, while he acted, supplied the place of the king himself; and it exercised the functions of the wittenagemote or parliament, as well as those of a court for the dispensation of justice both criminal and civil, as may be clearly seen by the tenor of a vast number of records.[3] For a long period after its first erection, it was

---

[1] Although, generally speaking, the earl or bishop together with the reve or sheriff presiding over the district administered justice in these courts, yet in the Saxon times the king's chief alderman, or judge occasionally, as it appears, travelled about to the local courts; perhaps as a kind of visitor, or for the purpose of settling some important dispute (vide authorities and records collected in Hunt's *Hist.* lib. 6; *Jani. Anglic.* p. 128).

[2] LL. Canuti; Lamb. Archaion. fol. 108.

[3] Madox's Hist. Exch. *passim*; and particularly in pp. 12, 14, 16, 20, 31, 36, 84, 87, 88, 93, 95, 103, 113, 119, 209, 210. So it is provided by Magna Charta, that barons and earls should only be *amerced* by their *peers*; which, in a record temp. Henry III., is explained, that they were to be amerced, *before the king's council only.*—Ibid. 529.

ambulatory, and followed the person of the monarch, who often presided in it personally—a circumstance calculated to occasion a great grievance to distant suitors. A much more serious evil, however, resulted from the establishment of this new judicial authority, in the change thereby introduced, both in the rules and practice of the law. The first judges who presided in this court, and who continued so to preside for many years, were Normans; who, understanding neither the English law nor language, clung, for the most part, to that of their own country. Consequently, all law proceedings were carried on in the Norman-French—a language never generally understood in England, and which very much contributed to hasten the surrender of the ancient maxims of the common law to Norman notions of jurisprudence. What still further contributed to the downfall of the Saxon judicial system, was the art and labour expended by the foreign practitioners in engrafting upon the law all those niceties and metaphysical distinctions and subtilties which were engendered by the study of the Aristotelian philosophy, to which the learned in those days were passionately addicted—subtilties and distinctions which, in spite of every legislative effort for many generations to eradicate, have ever since continued to deform and encumber the simple principles of the ancient law of the land. It is not surprising, therefore, that, under an arbitrary government, which administered justice from one court to all parts of the kingdom, through the medium of judges and lawyers who were foreigners, and whose minds were imbued with foreign prejudices and learning, the old national law, which depended much upon local customs, and which was a law of liberty, proceeding upon the principle that the whole people ought, as far as possible, to be judges of each other, should, not only in forms, but in substance also, be in a great degree superseded, though it never was altogether forgotten.

In this wreck of the valuable rights of the people, the citizens of London, as a peculiar privileged body, still preserved their independence, together with their ancient forms of law and municipal government. By a very early Norman charter, they were not to be impleaded out of the walls of the

INTRODUCTION OF FEUDAL LAWS AND TENURES.

City; and they were to have no foreign justiciar placed over them, but only such as they themselves elected, for the dispensation of penal or criminal justice.[1] We need not wonder at the earnest anxiety always manifested by the citizens in ancient times in regard to the privileges of their local jurisdictions, for to this circumstance alone can we attribute the preservation of their most valuable customs; otherwise these customs, together with the rest of the general law of the land, would either at once have been surrendered to new legal institutions, or have been gradually frittered away by the logical casuistry of the Norman jurists.

The introduction of the trial by *Wager of Battle* has been already noticed as another Norman innovation.[2] But the most important change in the constitution and legal polity of the country which followed the Norman Conquest, was effected by the institution of *feudal tenures*, by which, either purely or under modification, all the land in the kingdom began to be held. It is not consistent with the plan of this work to enter into a minute examination of the peculiarities and details of the feudal law, which, through the artificial refinements of the commentators upon it, has been rendered very abstruse; though it is not to be doubted that an intimate acquaintance with this branch of jurisprudence would serve to explain and illustrate, not only the present general system of English law, but also those peculiar laws and customs now prevalent in the City of London, either as contrasted or corresponding with the feudal doctrines.[3] It will be necessary, however, in order to convey anything like a competent idea of the nature and origin of many of the civic

---

[1] Charter of Henry I. There can be no doubt that these franchises were considered as peculiarly valuable at the times when they were granted. They were sought for with avidity by several cities. The City of York paid a large fine to obtain them only for a short time.—Madox's *Hist. Exch.* p. 387. It was the common practice to extort large sums in the shape of fines to the king for obtaining justice in the king's court, which were of course avoided by suing elsewhere.—Ibid. *passim*, ch. xii.

[2] Vide p. 20, and also Selden, Duello, cap. 6; and authorities there quoted.

[3] For an elaborate, and at the same time a clear, explanation of the law of Feudal Tenures, see a very learned and able note of Mr. Butler, Co. Litt. lib. 3, 191 *a*, note 77; from which, as well as from Wright's Tenures, Madox's Hist. Exch. and Firma Burgi, and the 2nd vol. of Blackstone's Commentaries, this brief account of the feudal system is abstracted.

privileges, and of the relative condition of the citizens during the earlier ages of the English government, to draw an outline of the distinguishing principles which characterised that scheme of law, which, in its consequences, gave a tone to the manners, and controlled the interests of the whole community of the nation.

Much dispute has arisen, both respecting the first origin of the feudal system, and the time of its first introduction into this country. It appears certain that, if it did prevail at all under the Saxon dynasty, it was not to such an extent as to supersede the plan, either of government or of law, which took its rise from the institutions of Alfred. Suffice it to say, that the Conqueror, in the twentieth year of his reign,[1] summoned together a great council of the nation; at which, with the consent of all present, a statute passed by which, in effect, the law of feudal tenure was engrafted on all the land held by freemen[2] throughout the kingdom. The fundamental doctrine of pure feudal tenure was, that all the land of a country was held immediately of the king. He was to be considered the original possessor of the whole; and, after his first acquisition, to have granted the greater part to those about him of the chief consideration and influence (as indeed was actually the case with respect to William and his followers), to be held by them, upon condition of rendering certain services, according to the nature of their respective tenures; reserving the rest for the support of his kingly dignity, under the appellation of his *royal demesne*. Those who thus received their lands from the king himself, were termed his *tenants in capite*, and were in fact the aristocracy of the nation. These tenants, however, of the king, assumed a power, inconsistent indeed with the pure principles of feudalism, of parcelling out their territories to other tenants, upon similar conditions

---

[1] There is every reason to think that William was tardy in introducing this great change in the laws and constitution of the country. That he originally professed at least a great anxiety for the full and universal establishment of the laws of Edward the Confessor, and to govern the kingdom by them, may be satisfactorily ascertained by consulting the Spicilegium of the learned Selden.

[2] The tenure *in demesne* or in villenage can hardly be termed a *feudal* tenure; and if it was, the tenure certainly existed in the Saxon times, as has been explained before.

EXPLANATION OF THE FEUDAL SYSTEM.

CHAP. III.
A.D. 1066.

to those under which they themselves held of the supreme lord; reserving, in a similar manner, and for the same purposes, *their* private *demesnes*; these sub-tenants, again, to still inferior dependants: till, thus, a regular gradation of subordinate feudatories was established; all, indeed, subjected to the same general allegiance to the king, but most of them owing also a more contracted and immediate duty to that lord from whose hands they received their estates or feuds. These intermediate lords were denominated *mesne lords*, and their inferior tenants, *tenants paravail*. To this practice of subinfeudation a stop was at last put by several statutes passed in the reigns of Henry III., Edward I., Edward II., and Edward III.; but not before it had proceeded to a very considerable extent.

Every free man[1] who received lands from his lord, by whatever services he held them, was, in the first place bound to take an oath of *fealty*, that he would be faithful to his lord, would do him suit and services in his court, and would defend him against all enemies: he was also compelled, upon his investiture, to *do his lord homage*, as it was termed, by kneeling before him and holding his hands together between those of the lord, and then declaring that he became *his man*. There were also other important *services* which all tenants were bound in some shape or other to render to their respective lords in virtue of their tenancies, into the nature of which it remains now to enquire.

The first species of tenure, and that which alone characterised a pure and proper feud, was that by *Knight's service*; by virtue of which tenure every tenant, possessed of such considerable quantity of land as would amount to what was termed a *Knight's fee*, was bound to attend his respective lord in his wars for forty days in a year, whenever he might be called upon, or to provide a knight who should so attend for each knight's fee. This power of suddenly and arbitrarily raising a body of bold soldiers, so attached by oath and a

---

[1] Villeins, when they came to hold land, were admitted to *fealty* and *homage*; but that *enfranchised* them in a degree, and they then became *tenants*. Originally they were not admitted to *fealty* and *homage*, and were considered merely as slaves.—Vide Wright, p. 216.

spirit of clanship to their lords, contributed to raise the political influence of the great barons and landholders who possessed a great number of knight's fees, to a very great height: for they soon began to exercise a kind of royal authority over their domains; and eventually, under the sway of the weaker Norman princes, as we afterwards find in the early history of the country, the combination of a few of them became a match even for the king himself. At the time of the Conqueror, the whole body of tenants holding by knight's service either of the king or of mesne lords amounted to upwards of 60,000, ready to be called together on any emergency, and attend in the field, under the penalty of forfeiting their estates.[1] This warlike service, according to the original principles of the feudal system, was all that could be required of the tenant, and all that was contemplated by our ancestors, perhaps, upon their first submission to the yoke of such a tenure. But the Norman lawyers, incited in all probability by the encouragement and rapacity of the first Norman princes, soon contrived to engraft upon this branch of feudal tenure a variety of burthens and taxes, which reduced the nation to almost an absolute slavery, and became at last so intolerably oppressive, as to occasion that famous rebellion in the reign of King John, the fruit of which was the granting Magna Charta, whereby some of the most prominent of them were removed. Still, however, many of the grievances incident to this species of tenure continued to harass the people for many generations; and although various efforts were from time to time made to get rid of them, they were not finally and entirely abolished till the reign of Charles II., when this tenure by knight's service was changed into *socage tenure*—a tenure which we shall presently have occasion to notice, and by which, in fact, all the freehold property in the kingdom is holden to this day.

The burthens, which were incident to the tenure by knight's service, were, first, *Aids*; which were a pecuniary contribution by the tenant, demandable on four different occasions: namely, to ransom the Lord's person when taken prisoner;

---

[1] Spelman's Glossary: 'Feodum.' Selden, Tit. Hon. part 2nd, chap. v. sect. 17.

to make his eldest son a knight; to portion his eldest
daughter; and, lastly, to pay the lord's debts. Secondly, the
Relief; which was at first an arbitrary, but after many struggles an ascertained sum, payable by the heir of the last tenant
upon coming to his estate. Thirdly, the *Primer Seisin*, incident only to tenancies *in capite*; which was the right to a
year's profits of the land held, whenever the tenant died; on
the ground that it behoved the supreme lord to hold possession of the land for one year, in order to protect it from false
claimants and intruders. Fourthly, *Wardship*; which was,
the privilege of holding possession of all the estates of heirs
until they became of age, who were then still further obliged
to pay the value of half a year's profits for the ceremony of
delivering the lands up; and, if he was a tenant *in capite*, he
was at this period compelled to take up his knighthood (an
order conferred with much pomp and solemnity) or else to
pay a fine to the king. Fifthly, *Marriage*; which was the
right of selling a ward to the best bidder, in marriage, provided it was no disparagement; and if the wards refused such
tender of marriage, they forfeited the value of it—that is, as
much as any jury would say a person of equal rank would
give for it to the lord; if they married without his consent,
they then forfeited the double value: this was, undoubtedly
the most oppressive hardship which arose out of the system
of feudal tenures. The principle on which *wardship* and
marriage were claimed, was, that the lord had an interest
in providing a sufficient tenant to render the service due to
him, and might run some risk of losing it if the tenant had
a discretionary power in marrying; and he actually did lose
it while the tenant was a minor. Sixthly, *Fines* upon alienation: these fines were in England exacted only from the
tenants *in capite*, who, not being allowed to sell their estates
without the king's license, were obliged to pay a heavy consideration for such liberty. Seventhly and lastly, *Escheat*;
which was the determination of the tenant's estate and the
resumption of it by the lord, either for want of heirs or in
consequence of the tenant's having committed treason or
felony; by which means his blood became corrupted and lost
all heritable qualities. In this enumeration of feudal bur-

thens, that of *Escuage* must not be overlooked; though it was not, strictly speaking, an incident of knight service, but rather the service itself. For these military tenants, galled by the dependency and uncertainty of their warlike duties, in process of time acquired permission, first, to serve by deputy, and afterwards, to make a pecuniary satisfaction in lieu of such service. This satisfaction was called the tenant's *escuage*, and the king by his prerogative levied it in an arbitrary manner, till that power, being grossly abused, the levying of escuage was first regulated by Parliament, and afterwards altogether prohibited without the previous consent of the legislature.

Another kind of tenure, namely that by *Socage-service*, prevailed also to a considerable extent in the kingdom, and which, under the Norman jurisdiction, bore many of the genuine marks of a feudal quality, though the services rendered by virtue of it were of an essentially different character. Those who held their estates under this species of tenure, instead of performing knight's service, which, though of a free and honourable nature, was nevertheless, from its uncertainty, very burthensome, rendered some certain rent or some stipulated acknowledgment, not of a military nature, by the discharge of which their land was preserved to them. This acknowledgment was sometimes the bare oath of fealty; sometimes it was of a personal kind; but usually, both that and the rent was of a trivial amount.

Tenure by *socage-service* had the advantage of that by *knight's-service*, not only in respect of certainty, but also inasmuch as it was exempted from many of those slavish consequences which have been mentioned as characterising the latter. For, in the first place, neither *wardship* nor *marriage* could be claimed by the lord, by reason that no personal military service being due, it was of no importance to him to secure an able and suitable tenant. Both *wardship* and *marriage*, therefore, were entrusted to that nearest relation of the socage tenant who could not by possibility succeed to the inheritance. Such guardian was bound to account to his ward, both for the profits of the estate and the suitableness of the marriage, in case he married his ward under the age of fourteen. In the second place, the other burthens of knight's service (with the exception of *aids*) namely, *primer seisins*, *fines* on alienation, and *escheats*, which were levied (legally or not) on cities and boroughs as being in *demesne*, as well as on those held on knight's service, came to be compromised for by a collective rent or farm.¹

A tenure so liberal in its terms as this, and so mild, when compared with the oppressive quality of that by knight's service, seems to have been a modified remnant of ancient Saxon liberty,² and to have been retained by those who had strength or influence enough to resist the Norman encroachments; as may be exemplified in the case of Gavelkind in Kent, which is a species of socage tenure, and was preserved to the men of Kent by their terms of capitulation to the Conqueror. It soon naturally became an object of general interest, especially among tenants who were not of the nobility, to emancipate themselves from the thraldom which a military tenure imposed, and to enjoy their estates under the easy and plain terms of socage tenancy. Gradually, as the slavish burthens of knight's service wore off, the two tenures approached nearer in quality; socage tenures grew more and more in vogue, and were the more easily granted; till at last, in the reign of James I., the total abolition of chivalry tenures, and the conversion of them into socage tenures, began to be seriously thought of, though the measure was not altogether completed till the reign of Charles II.

There was another tenure, not strictly feudal nor perhaps of feudal origin, but which may nevertheless be classed under the same system; under which tenure a very large class of the people served, and which was the lowest species of all; namely, that of *villenage* or *in demesne*. The villeins, indeed, were at the Norman Conquest little better than mere slaves, which they no doubt had originally been; and they could be sued for in courts of justice in the same manner as any chattel interest. As before stated, they were cultivators of the lord's *demesne* lands, and were *astricti glebæ*, being

¹ Vide p. 51.
² For an enquiry into the nature and derivation of this tenure, and into the etymology of the word, vide Book II. Ch. II.

unable to leave the land without the lord's permission. They were allowed a small portion of land for their own support, upon condition of doing the menial offices prescribed to them; to which land, however, they had no independent title of their own, but were liable to be dispossessed at a moment's warning, being tenants merely at the will of the lord. In process of time, these villeins became universally emancipated personally from the proprietorship of their superiors; and imperceptibly so gained ground on their lords, that at last they came to have a fixed interest in the soil they held, descendable to their heirs; an interest which, growing up in a gradual usage, has, by virtue of such usage, now become sanctioned in law as a right, under the modern title of *copyhold-tenure*.

Under one or other of these tenures all the land in the kingdom, with a few special exceptions, and excepting that of the superior cities, was held soon after the Norman Conquest.[1] The tenants occupying possessions in the inferior towns and boroughs were said indeed to hold by *tenure in burgage*; but this was a tenure in all respects similar to that in socage, and, in fact, as is said by Littleton, nothing other than a kind of *town socage*. It has been suggested, that these boroughs, so held by the inhabitants individually in burgage tenure, in all probability escaped the burthensome effects of a tenure by knight's service, from the insignificancy of the tenements; a hundred of them together amounting scarcely to a knight's fee.[2] They might, however, rather be considered as districts originally *in demesne*, and afterwards specially liberated and converted into socage: indeed, by the earlier Norman authorities, they were for all purposes of taxation still considered in principle as lands held *in demesne*;[3] and it is very probable, that on the arrival of the Normans, many of the boroughs and tenants in them, who had in the

[1] Tenures in Frankalmoign, in grand and petit serjeantry, and homage ancestral, are passed over, as being comparatively rare, and unimportant in a national point of view.
[2] Black. Comm. vol. ii.
[3] The records are very numerous in Madox's Hist. Exch. and Firma Burgi. in which the boroughs of England are *talliaged*, as being *in demesne*; and exemptions are claimed by some cities from this tax, on the ground that they are not *in demesne*.—Vide, p. 83.

Saxon times become emancipated, were reduced again under actual *demesne*, and subsequently liberated on terms. However, there can be no doubt that the independence and certainty which eventually characterised these burgage or socage tenures, most mainly contributed to improve the commerce and wealth, and thereby the importance, of these boroughs; till at last by their parliamentary and general influence they had a very considerable share in emancipating the whole nation from a state of comparative slavery, and in restoring the ancient constitutional liberty enjoyed by our early ancestors.[1]

But in great cities, as we have seen, a privilege prevailed, even in the Saxon times, of paying annually one aggregate contribution, called a farm rent, in lieu of all those services, duties, tolls, &c. which the king or other lord of the *demesne* had been used to exact from the inhabitants individually.[2] It is to be remarked, that in many boroughs where the inhabitants held by burgage tenure, their borough was after the Conquest let at farm; but whatever rank such cities might hold in the Saxon times and before the creation of perpetual *fee* farms, yet after the Norman Conquest, when these boroughs were not assigned to the inhabitants themselves at farm, or, if so assigned, were not held at a *perpetual* or *fee* farm, they could not be considered, although holding by burgage tenure and rendering either a free certain service or none at all, as altogether liberated from *demesne*, and to hold freely; at all events, they were not on a par with the tenants of those cities who held at *fee* farm. Their farm was liable to be changed or done away with, and the *demesne* perquisites resumed, by the lord in the cases where they held their borough at farm themselves in their own right: and, of course, when such borough was let to an individual, such demise only produced a change of master. Upon the introduction of the feudal system throughout the kingdom, this farm rent, being made perpetual or in fee, seems to have been converted into, or rather came to be accepted as, the condition or service by which these cities were to be held in

---

[1] Anderson's Hist. Com. vol. i. p. 169.   [2] Vide page 33.

the aggregate. Such a tenure would appear the most easy of any; for the inhabitants thereby not only enjoyed the advantages of the tenure in burgage, but, paying their dues to their lord in one collective capacity, they became thereby exempted even from those remaining feudal burthens which still attached to individual socage tenures; namely, reliefs, primer seisins,[1] fines upon alienation, and feudal escheat.[2] For as the citizens in a collective capacity could never die, or commit felony, or alienate the soil, it followed that none of these feudal dues, according to the Norman legal construction, could arise. It was a tenure, therefore, sought at the king's hands by the greater towns with the utmost avidity, and often largely paid for.[3] This fee farm rent was not, however, collected from the inhabitants by contribution, but arose, as we have observed, from certain issues and profits arising out of inland customs, fairs, markets, and other like franchises, which being originally enjoyed by the lord of the demesne, had been granted to, or at least were possessed by, the citizens; and, being received by the proper civic authorities, were accounted for at the rent fixed.[4] So that, in fact, the inhabitants of these privileged cities might be said to hold their estates as freely and independently as could be, in any way, consistent with allegiance to a superior.

In this manner was the City of London held from the earliest establishment of the feudal system in England, and that is what is meant when it is said in ancient records, that London is *held of the king in capite, in free burgage*. Thus we find that this City survived all the mighty innovations

[1] Lord Coke says, 'Neither shall the king have primer seisin of lands holden in burgage, as some have said; *for that it is no tenure in capite.*' This reason is completely disproved by the authorities quoted in the above pages, and still further by many records quoted in Madox's Firma Burgi, ch. i. It seems much more probable that the reason assigned in the text, therefore, is correct; and that although what 'some have said' as to the king not having primer seisin of lands held in burgage may be just, yet that the reason they assign can only apply to burgage lands in towns not held at fee farm.

[2] Escheats are to be here understood as distinguished from *forfeitures*, which were not of feudal origin. Aids, it seems, were paid in *all* cases by towns and cities held in capite (vide Madox's *Hist. Exch.* ch. xv.). Though, as socage tenures were exempt in most particulars, (vide ibid.) it is not easy to perceive the legal ground of such charge.—Vide p. 366.

[3] Vide Madox's Hist. Exch. pp. 397, 398, 399, 500, 503.

[4] Vide infra, p. 96.

introduced by the Norman Conquest. Retaining its ancient
laws and customs, governed by its own magistrates, who
dispensed justice according to the old established forms of
trial, preserving the exclusive jurisdiction of its courts, and
privileged from all those feudal oppressions which gave a
tyrannical and almost despotic authority to the king and his
barons, over nearly the whole population of the realm, it
presented the only genuine model of the free and independent
rights which prevailed in the Saxon times; and became in
fact the very ark of the constitution. It is true, indeed,
that this model of the civic constitution was seldom in a
perfect state during the early ages of the English government,
and that the rights and liberties of the City were continually
subject to invasion and interruption: still, however, they
were never lost sight of; nor did the citizens cease to assert
them whenever the first favourable juncture in political
affairs gave an earnest of success. In after times, when such
noble struggles were made for emancipation from the many
abuses of the Norman law, and for a more regular administration of justice, we find, not only that the citizens were ever
conspicuously active, but that Magna Charta itself was
framed in the very midst of them, confessedly on the basis of
the laws of Edward the Confessor. It would look, therefore,
as if the citizens were in a manner appealed to, as preserving
among themselves the sample of that legal polity, if not the
very laws themselves, so much venerated by the people, and
which they considered to embody the just constitutional
rights and liberties enjoyed by their ancestors.[1]

[1] Vide Blackstone's Introduction to Magna Charta. It seems pretty clear from that learned judge's account of the original of Magna Charta, that the story of its being formed upon the accidental discovery of Henry I.'s national charter is unfounded. That charter, as embodying some of the Confessor's laws and alluding generally to them, was no doubt, in one sense, the foundation of the great Charter; but the *details* of the latter must have been collected from other and more extensive sources (vide Litt. *Hist. of Henry II.*, vol. i. note to p. 142). If it is true, as has been said (vide *Edin. Review*, vol. xxxiv. p. 187, and Supp. p. 24), that a copy of the ancient Book of Common Law, called the *Domhok*, was preserved among the archives of the City, from which very work in the reign of Edward II. the compilation called the Mirror of Justices was made by Horne, then Chamberlain of London, this fact would almost substantiate the remark suggested in the text.

CHAPTER IV.

FROM THE NORMAN CONQUEST TO THE ACCESSION OF EDWARD I.

BOOK I.
A.D. 1066 to 1189.

To REVERT to a more direct and historical account of the progressive state of the City, it appears that, throughout the reign of William the Conqueror and that of his successor, the City of London sustained little or no molestation in its privileges; although the rest of the nation groaned, during the whole of that period, under a tyrannical and rapacious government. Henry I. upon his accession to an usurped throne, the more readily to secure the attachment of the body of the people, promised to observe the laws of the Confessor, and even granted a charter to that effect, enumerating many particular grievances which he professed to abolish.[1] But so little mindful was he of any such engagements after his present purpose was served, that the whole of his long reign was passed in the continual violation of all the articles of his charter;[2] and so rapidly did it fall into neglect and oblivion, that in one century afterwards it was with difficulty that any traces of it were discovered, to found the stipulations contained in Magna Charta.[3]

The reign of this monarch, however, is rendered remarkable by the grant of the first of the City charters which specify any of its liberties and privileges in detail—a charter conferred at his accession, and which, as is justly observed by Hume, seems to have been the *first step towards* rendering the City a corporation—for there does not appear anything in that charter indicating the previous existence of a body politic, or of a community having a modified and artificial succession according to the definition of Madox.[4] Neither does the charter, by its inherent force, create a cor-

---

[1] Matthew Paris, p. 71; Selden's Epinomis, ch. vi.
[2] Hume's Hist.   [3] Vide p. 53, note.   [4] Firma Burgi, ch. ii.

·oration. The privileges granted by it are, in fact, such as might be granted to any class of people, however unconnected with and independent of each other. It is directed, not to any magistrates or aldermen of the City, nor to the citizens generally, but to the dignitaries of the national council *nominatim*, and to *all* the king's subjects. It grants that the citizens shall have the right of appointing the sheriff of Middlesex, and also that of appointing their own Justiciar; and in these terms, there is reason to believe, were included the right of appointing the Sheriff of London, as well as of Middlesex, and the governor over the whole City, under whatever title he may have exercised his authority, whether that of Reve, or Portreve, or Sheriff.[1] It also grants that the Church, the barons (by which appellation it may be assumed was meant the aldermen), and the citizens should have their *socs*—in other words, the subsidiary government of their respective districts or *gilds*—afterwards called *wards*—in peace. These are all subjects which will be treated of more at large in future pages better appropriate to the consideration of them. It may be observed, however, here that these rights of self-government appeared to have been commonly exercised in the Saxon times by the citizens.[2]

The reign of King Stephen affords many unequivocal proofs of the great influence possessed by the City in the government; and we have also the testimony of a cotemporary writer[3] as to its internal grandeur and prosperity. Stephen, it seems, was so convinced of the powerful effect of its patronage, that during the latter years of the reign of Henry he studied by every art and address to acquire the affection of the Londoners.[4] No sooner had Henry breathed his last, than Stephen hastened at once to London, where he was immediately saluted king; and to bribe the favour of the people and give them an earnest of something like a restoration of their ancient liberties, his first act was to publish a charter, confirming, in general terms, that granted by Henry, and commanding the good laws of Edward the Con-

[1] Vide p. 60, and note, post: Charter of Henry I.
[2] Vide ibid.
[3] Fitz-Stephen, secretary to Thomas à Becket.
[4] William of Malmesbury, p. 179.

fessor to be observed. The vague terms of this charter seem to indicate, either that the king was cautious in binding himself by any fixed and specific rules, or that most of the laws of Edward the Confessor, if not the charter itself of Henry, had become obsolete and unknown. Whatever his intentions might have been in respect of the administration of his government (and from his personal character we are justified in forming a favourable opinion of them), his whole reign was so completely occupied by the intestine wars arising from a powerfully disputed succession, that he had no opportunity of evincing the sincerity of his patriotism. Obliged by the weakness of his regal title to cultivate the good-will of the greater barons, and depending much upon them for military assistance, he was compelled, in his turn, to connive at their usurpations of power, and the tyrannical authority exercised by them over their immediate tenants. Aristocratical power and the oppressions of feudal government arrived, therefore, in Stephen's reign to their greatest height; and consequently the people in general were sunk to the lowest state of degradation and misery.

From the striking contrast between the condition of the citizens of London and that of the rest of the people, we may gather the most incontestible proof of the value and importance of the rights secured to them, and that this superiority was owing to nothing but the preservation of their ancient institutions, and their exemption from the slavery of feudalism. A remarkable occurrence in Stephen's eventful reign will serve as a manifest illustration of this remark. In one of the many battles fought by that prince for his crown against the partisans of Matilda, who, as the only child of Henry, was the rightful heir to the throne, he had the misfortune to be made prisoner. Matilda, well aware of the all-powerful influence of the clergy in those days, instantly summoned an ecclesiastical synod, from which, rather than from the assembled states of the realm, she preferred to accept the crown; and by that assembly her title to the throne was instantly acknowledged. The only laymen called to this meeting were the citizens of London, who were bold enough to remonstrate against the imprisonment of

Stephen, and demanded his liberation. It was answered, that 'it ill became them, who were considered as noblemen 'in the kingdom, to take part with those barons who had 'deserted their king.'

In the meanwhile Matilda, swayed rather by her passions than by any true policy, delivered up both the office of justiciary of London and the sheriffwick to her partisan Geoffrey, Earl of Essex, who seems to have aimed at reducing the City to the same condition as the rest of the nation. The citizens soon besought a restoration of their laws and privileges, as enjoyed under the Confessor; but received a contemptuous answer. Exasperated by their situation and the little respect paid to their remonstrances, they no longer hesitated to revolt against the new government; and so immediate was the success of their influence, that Matilda was compelled within a few months to abandon the kingdom and to liberate her royal prisoner, who at the head of a powerful army, composed chiefly of Londoners, overcoming all opposition, again mounted the throne, which he continued to occupy during the remainder of his life.

This account of the political transactions of this era, extracted from the annals of cotemporary writers,[1] will suggest a magnificent conception of the influence commanded by the City in the affairs of the State. If we could attach any credit to the estimate made by Fitz-Stephen, who lived at this time, of the population and military establishment of London, we should have little cause to wonder at the haughty posture it assumed. This writer asserts, that the City mustered, according to estimation, no less than sixty thousand foot and twenty thousand horse, in the field; a number so incredible, that it requires little argument to show that it must have been most loosely and preposterously calculated.[2] We may collect, however, from this statement,

---

[1] William of Malmesbury; Gervas. Tilb.; Flor. Wig.; War. Annals.

[2] A numerical error may easily have crept into this account, when we consider that it existed only in manuscript for upwards of 300 years. It appears from Strype, the editor of Stowe, that this calculation was according to a very ancient and authentic copy of the manuscript kept in the Town Clerk's Office. In the translation of Fitz-Stephen's work by an 'antiquary' (Dr. Pegge), dated 1772, a note, p. 28, mentions that many MSS. copies had been consulted in vain

BOOK I.
A.D. 1066
to 1189.

that the City was possessed of very considerable military strength, the only efficient source of power in those days; and it is probable that such strength, from the free quality of the civic government, must have been composed of an independent soldiery. More reliance may be placed, perhaps, on the description drawn by this author, a citizen born and bred, of the domestic condition of the City and the manners of the inhabitants in the time of Henry II., under whose able sway the civil government was administered with comparative regularity, and the nation enjoyed the rare blessing of internal peace.

According to this author, the City was divided into distinct districts[1] at this time, in all probability in the same manner as at present into wards; though it is not easy to determine at what period this latter division specifically and in terms took place. The derivation of the term 'ward' is from the Saxon pæpan, pnpian, *custodire*, *tueri*, whence 'warda' (*tutela*, *custodia*), and is called 'garde' in law French; and we find this term came to be commonly applied in the old records to the districts of London, at least as early as the reign of Henry III.,[2] and there is one instance of it even as early as the thirty-first year of Henry II.[3] In each of these wards was held a court-leet,[4] having originally jurisdiction over all crimes and nuisances—an institution which is generally considered as old as the time of Alfred. Indeed the court-leet of the hundred, and the wardmote court, were anciently known by the same name—that of the Folkmote.[5] From the etymology of the word therefore, and the corresponding purposes of its judicial authority, there can be no doubt that the London ward came to represent the

to find a correction of the numbers stated in the text. Lord Lyttelton in his Life of Henry II., quotes a cotemporary letter from the Archdeacon of London to the Pope, in which it is reported that the whole population of London amounted to but 40,000.

[1] Literally, 'Hæc similiter illis (Trojanis sc.) regionibus est distincta.' Vide Book II. ch. II. pp. 270 et seq. 289; also supra, pp. 18, 24, 35, for further explanation as to different jurisdictions subsisting anciently in London.

[2] Records of proclamations in Lib. Horne and Lib. Alb.

[3] Mad. Hist. Exch. p. 583.

[4] Co. Inst. part iv. p. 469. *Soc* and *Sac* was also an appendage of these wards, which signifies a jurisdiction corresponding with that of a court-leet. —Heywood's *Dissertation*, p. 145.

[5] Vide Lib. Alb. fols. 9, 10; Co. 3rd Inst. C. pp. 69, 70.

ancient hundred, and the wardmote court the assembly of
the frithbourg, who were identified, according to Spelman,[1]
with the members of what were called the frithgilds; into a
number of which, as we have seen, the City was in early
Saxon times divided; and which were associations for the
purpose of preserving the common peace and property, with
liberty of *Sac* and *Soc*; or, in other words, a leet jurisdiction.
What tends strongly to corroborate this conclusion, is the
fact that, in the 26th year of the reign of Henry II.,
districts called *gilds* were still existing in London; for at
that period many *gilds*, some being of a commercial nature,
but most of them territorial, were amerced as being 'adulterine,'
or 'constituted without the king's authority,' over all
of which *aldermen* presided;[2] though it cannot be found
that *aldermen* ever presided over mercantile gilds in London,
except in these few instances[3] here recorded as of adulterine
origin. And we have observed already that Portsoken ward
was called *Cnighten gild* at least to the end of the reign of
Henry I., as appears by the charter of that king confirming
it to the church and canons of the Holy Trinity—indeed, the
prior of that church became an alderman of London merely
by virtue of his possessing this gild.[4] When the term *wards*
was first used they were not called by their present names,
but as the ward of such and such an alderman, in the same
way as the gilds were denominated.[5] In the time of Edward
I. they began to be called by their present *district*
names.[6] It would appear, therefore, that the term *ward* had
barely arisen at this period; though we may safely fix the

CHAP.
IV.

A.D. 1066
to 1189.

[1] Spelman's Glossary: 'Gilda.'
[2] Mad. Hist. Exch. p. 562. Bridge-gild is mentioned by name.
[3] Vide supra, pp. 25, 35; Ch. VI. p. 101; Book II. Ch. II.
[4] Strype's Edit. of Stow, lib. 2, p. 5. Another proof that gilds were not all originally mercantile, may be inferred from the circumstance, that in ancient records the gilds which are so, are termed 'Merchant gilds' (Gilda et Hansa Mercatorum): thus, a fine is recorded of Thomas of l'Ivet, paid for his being made an alderman of the Merchant gild of York (Madox's *Hist. Exch.* p. 397).

None of the gilds of London amerced for want of the king's warrant of authority are termed 'Merchant gilds.' And further, although all the corporate towns in England almost have had a specific and Merchant gilds granted them, yet the citizens of London never have, although *gilds* have been common enough, as well as a Gild hall, for the assembling of the *gilds*.—Vide supra, p. 25, and notes.
[5] Records in Madox's Hist. Exch. pp. 582, 708, 709, 738–9.
[6] Madox's Hist. Exch. p. 711.

BOOK I.
A.D. 1066 to 1189.

date of that appellation, as commonly applied to the civic divisions, between the latter end of the reign of Henry II and the beginning of that of Edward I.¹

Fitz-Stephen proceeds to state that the City had its annual sheriffs; that it had its lesser magistrates, and enjoyed a senatorial dignity. The magistracy and senatorial dignity was most probably attached to the alderman or barons of socs or gilds; by Henry I.'s charter the sheriffwick of *Middlesex* was freely granted to them, and there are good grounds for believing that the sheriffwick of London (the functions of which were exercised by the chief magistrate under the title of Reve or Portreve, before the creation of the mayoralty), was included in the same grant as an ancient prescriptive right of the citizens;² yet the privilege of choosing the sheriffs for London, if it was previously enjoyed, seems to have been very soon lost again, inasmuch as we find the citizens offering to purchase such privilege of

---

¹ The name of 'wards' was used in the time of Henry III. (vide *Hist. Eccl.* pp. 708, 709; but they were also occasionally called Aldermanries.—Madox's *Firma Burgi*, p. 92; and vide p. 58.

² It seems improbable that the citizens should have the privilege of electing a sheriff for Middlesex, which they had not for the City itself. Besides, by a record of the reign of Henry I. of an uncertain year, it seems they actually paid for that liberty (Madox's *Firma Burgi*, p. 165). And as the charter of Henry I. is also of an uncertain year, it is likely that such purchase took place previous to the charter. It is quite certain they enjoyed this privilege throughout the reign of Richard I. (ibid.), and there is no record of the grant of it. Indeed the terms of the specific grant of it by John's second charter acknowledges it as an ancient right; for it runs, 'Confirmavimus;' and the same identical farm rent, viz. 300*l.*, as established by Henry's charter, is reserved for the sheriffwick of *both* London and Middlesex, it being, as is therein stated, the *ancient* form. The grant of the appointment of their own justiciar in this charter of Henry I. may be construed into a grant of the sheriffwick of London; for the reve, or magistrate of the county court, and all other reves and magistrates, however inferior, were at first termed justiciars by the Normans; and till the appointment of a mayor in Richard I.'s or John's time, the only magistrates known in London were sheriffs or bailiffs, and barons or aldermen of socs; and no magistrate was ever known in London by the specific name of a justiciar, except as applied to the reve or portreve. Lib. Custom. de Justit. Strype's Stow, Book v. p. 340, quotes Lib. K. in Archiv. in which it is stated that the Shrievalty of London was expressly given by William I. with consent of *Parliament*. That, however, is at least an inaccurate expression. But that such a grant was in fact made, and that the record did actually exist in the possession of the City of London in the time of Henry VI., seems abundantly evident on consulting the Appendix to Strype's Stow. p. 18; Harg. MSS. No. 133, p. 149. Brit. Mus.

that monarch;¹ and it appears by Madox's extracts² from ancient records, that both Stephen and Henry II. appointed the sheriffs quite at their own will and pleasure, sometimes three, four, and five at a time. It is remarkable also, that in the charters granted to the City of London by Henry II., Richard I., and in the first charter of King John, no mention whatever is made of the sheriffwick of London or of Middlesex either.³

According to the same author, the City had its courts, both judicial and deliberative, and also its general meetings of citizens on stated days.⁴ These judicial courts, there can be no doubt, were the hustings, the portreve's or sheriff's courts, and the gild or ward courts leet of the aldermen;⁵ the deliberative, those of the portreve, or sheriff, and aldermen. There is no reason to think that the Court of Common Council, or any other representative body, could be intended either by the *deliberative courts* or the *meetings* of the citizens here alluded to. The latter, and perhaps the former also, must have been those general assemblies of the citizens at large, denominated in the ancient City records '*immensa communitas*,' or '*immensa multitudo civium*,' or '*Folkmote*,' in which elections, and most, if not all, other transactions of a public nature were carried on, till the reign of Edward I.⁶ At that period, and not before, it seems, these elections began to be carried on by citizens *specially summoned* for that purpose by the lord mayor,⁷ and occasionally, though, as far

¹ Firma Burgi, p. 165; Hist. Exch. p. 397.
² Ibid. vide Hist. Exch. vol. i. pp. 363-4, 397, 686.
³ There was no mayor at this time, nor till the time of Richard I. Lib. Custum. Town Clerk's Office, p. 89; Fitz-Stephen, Lib. Alb. fol. 29, a; Strype's edit. of Stow, vol. ii. pp. 73, 100, 153, 370; Bohun. 40. Harg. MSS. Brit. Mus. No. 153, fol. 113, quoting a variety of records. The mayoralty was first given in terms to the citizens by a charter of King John.—Vide infra, p. 68, note.
⁴ Literally 'habet suis diebus statutis Comitia.'

⁵ As there was no mayor, there was of course no Mayor's court, the functions of that court were performed by that of the sheriff, reve, or portreve. There is reason to think that the Hustings court was as well the common assembly of all the citizens for deliberative and political purposes, as a judicial court.—Vide Bohun, Priv. Lond. p. 239; and Strype's Stow, vol. ii. p. 370.
⁶ Vide post, pp. 74, 85, 115.
⁷ No traces are to be found of elections by a select or representative body earlier than the 26th of Edward I., at which time Walleys was chosen mayor by the aldermen and twelve commoners

BOOK I.
A.D. 1066 to 1189.

as appears, very seldom, a select number of the *discreeter sort*, as they are termed in the ancient City books, were summoned under the same authority to enact ordinances also.[1] In general, however, the great mass of citizens still continued to meet for the purpose of *ordinances* or *general resolutions*, till the reign of Edward III.,[2] when an attempt was first made towards the regular constitution of the Court of Common Council as a legislative and representative body;[3] though it was not, in fact, fully established upon the present representative system till the 7th year of Richard II.[4] They also persisted in attending *at elections* in great numbers, without any regard to a specific individual summons for that purpose, till the latter end of the reign of Edward II.[5]

Notwithstanding Henry II. exercised something like a despotic authority, so wise and paternal on the whole was the administration of his government, that, though internal disorders were not unfrequent, the City during the progress of his reign made great advancements in splendour and prosperity.[6] Its fame, says Fitz-Stephen, was spread wider

---

[1] from each ward (Strype's Stow, Book v. p. 74, quoting Lib. B. fol. 38 & p. 80). According to many records to be seen in Madox's Hist. Exch. vol. ii. p. 92, 93, 94, the mayor was elected by the *cives generally*; and there is one record of the date of 6th Edward I., in which it is said that he was elected by the *communitas* (vide ibid. p. 94). In the 29th, 31st, and 32nd years of Edward I. the mayor was chosen by a select body, sometimes called the *Common Council of the Mayor*, sometimes *good and lawful men summoned from each ward* (ibid. p. 75, Lib. C. fols. 62, 111, 112, 113). By a proclamation of Edward II.'s reign it is recited, that elections had been accustomed to be in former times by the mayor, aldermen, *and such discreet persons who were specially summoned for that purpose*: and then an order is made that none others interfere. — Lib. Horne, fol. 332 b.

[2] The earliest ordinance discovered in which any *select number* of the citizens only had a voice, is that of 5th Edward I. Lib. Alb. fol. 130. There are, however, but very few of this kind before the 20th Edward III., and these, as well as many subsequent ordinances, are to be considered rather as acts of the Court and Mayor and Aldermen than of the Common Council summoned; for the lord mayor and aldermen summoned just whom they pleased, and the members attending were up to the time of Richard II. called *his* (the Mayor's) Common Council, as appears by the City entries. — Vide Stow, Book v. p. 74, and note 6, p. 61.

[3] Vide note 6, p. 61 and the preamble to ordinance of 7th Richard II. Lib. H. fol. 173.

[4] Vide Lib. Legum, Town Clerk's Office, Lib. F. altimo, fol. 5 b; Hodge's List of Bye-Laws, and note 6, p. 61.

[5] Ibid. Lib. H. fol. 173; Hodge's List of Bye-Laws, and note 6, p. 61.

[6] Vide proclamation of 8th Edward II.; Lib. Horne. fol. 332 b, and *post*. p. 88.

[7] 'Urbs sane bona cum bonum habeat dominum,' writes Fitz-Stephen.

than that of any city on the earth, its trade extended to the very borders of the known world, and in it was to be found the produce of China and of Norway.¹ Its wall was strong and lofty, adorned with seven gates, and having all along the north side turrets at equal distances. Within it and its immediate suburbs were thirteen conventual churches, and one hundred and twenty-six parish churches. The king's palace is described as an incomparable edifice, and connected with the City by suburbs reaching two miles in length. From the specimens of an earlier period still remaining, namely Westminster Hall and Abbey,² which were in a manner appendages to this palace, we may judge that the architectural style of the age was far from contemptible. London bridge was also begun at this period, and took thirty-three years in building.³

To proceed with Fitz-Stephen's account:—Almost all the bishops, abbots, and noblemen of the kingdom resorted thither; living in beautiful houses, and maintaining very magnificent establishments. The citizens seem to have been very early initiated in the luxuries of good fare; for at this time there was an immense public cookery on the Thames side, at which dainties of all kinds, of a very expensive quality, could be had at any time of day or night. There were also, besides private seminaries, three great public schools of philosophy (if the logic and rhetoric taught in those ages can be justly so called), at which learned disputations were carried on in a manner which testified no moderate acquaintance with the *belles lettres*. Smithfield was at this time a great horse and cattle market; but part of it was devoted to horse-racing and the very prevalent exercise of warlike manœuvres and martial sports. Hunting and hawking

---

¹ In raising a tax for a Crusade, which was done after a very arbitrary fashion, London was assessed at twice the sum to that of York, which are the only two cities named by the historian.—Hoveden, P. II. p. 642, n. 20, 30, 40.

² Silk was imported at this period.—Madox's *Hist. Exch.*

³ The foundations only of the Abbey can be probably ascribed to an earlier period than the reign of Henry III., who built the most ancient part of the structure as it stands at present (vide Anderson's *Hist. Com.* vol. I. p. 215): and the same may indeed be said of Westminster Hall, which was rebuilt by Richard II. Ibid. 368.

⁴ Strype's edit. of Stow, vol. I. p. 53.

BOOK I.
A.D. 1189 to 1199.

were also very fashionable amusements among the citizens; which accounts for the insertion of that valued privilege of a free chase in most of the earlier charters.¹ The drama too was cultivated according to the taste of the age; for Fitz-Stephen, who was a monk, applauds the holy exhibition of the miracles and martyrdom of the saints. Such is the description given of London by a cotemporary writer, who, although a professed panegyrist, may perhaps be relied on as authenticating the more particular and leading facts of his account.²

In the reign of Richard I. some incidents occur which make it manifest that the indications of the external magnificence and political influence of the City related by Fitz-Stephen are not much exaggerated. For in the first year of that prince's reign, in consequence of the frequent fires, it was ordained by the Court of Aldermen that no houses should in future be allowed to be built of wood or to be thatched; but that all of them should have an outside wall of stone raised sixteen feet from the ground—an ordinance which seems to have been at that time carefully carried into effect.³

Richard, enthusiastically engaged in the war of the Crusades, passed a very small part of his short reign in his own dominions; and in his absence John, his successor, then Earl of Moreton, made every effort by flattering attentions to gain the hearts of the citizens, in hopes, through their assistance, eventually to acquire the crown in prejudice of the rights of Arthur the son of Geoffrey his elder brother. Accordingly the citizens assumed a prominent influence in

---

¹ An officer called the Common Hunt exists to this day, whose department has latterly been to attend upon the Lady Mayoress, on State days, as Master of the Ceremonies.

² Strype gives a translation of Fitz-Stephen's description; but it is too free, to say the least of it, to be relied upon as authority.

³ Lib. Constitut.; Lib. Horne; Lib. Clerkenwell. Twelve aldermen were consequently chosen at a full husting to superintend all City works, and settle disputes about enclosures, party walls, &c. This stability in the structure of houses did not last long; for according to cotemporary accounts, all houses in London were built of wood down to the reign of James I., at which time they began to be built of brick.—Vide Strype's edit. of Stow, book i. p. 7; Hume's Hist. App. to James I.; and Anderson's Hist. of Commerce, vol. i. p. 213.

RICHARD I. CITY FIRST INCORPORATED.

the affairs of the nation; and at a meeting held in St. Paul's Churchyard, in conjunction with many of the chief nobility, they deposed Longchamp, one of the two guardians of the realm appointed by Richard, and compelled him to fly the kingdom.[1] Upon this occasion, the assembled aristocracy, with John at their head, confirmed all the civic rights and privileges by oaths, and conceded to the citizens the immunity of becoming a body politic or Corporation.[2] But though the City enjoyed what little advantage could be derived from the patronage of a profligate court, the internal state of its police seems to have deeply experienced the effects of an incompetent administration. Murders, robberies, and the most licentious disorders prevailed to such a degree as to be openly perpetrated in the daytime, and the most avowed defiance was held out to the constituted authorities. One sedition, in particular, was so generally engaged in by the inferior orders of the citizens, that their ringleader, one Fitzosbert, appeared before the Archbishop of Canterbury with so large a retinue of his partisans as to intimidate that prelate from making any order upon him; and when he was on a subsequent occasion arrested, he with a few followers made a long and desperate resistance, and was secured at last with the utmost difficulty, after being burnt out of Bow Church steeple, in which he had taken refuge.[3]

Richard, though a magnanimous and kind-hearted monarch, was so entirely impressed with the chivalrous superstition of the age, that he considered no exactions from his subjects oppressive, when imposed for the purpose of furthering the sacred cause of the Crusades. Heavy taxes were levied from all ranks of people,[4] and offices of the greatest trust, which could easily be made the means of extortion, were openly exposed to sale.[5]

Exorbitant grants of royal lands, revenues, and perquisites were made,[6] and the king went so far as to declare 'he would sell London itself if he could find a purchaser.'[7] The royal

CHAP. IV.
A.D. 1189 to 1199.

[1] Rog. Hoveden.
[2] Ibid. Brady on Boroughs.
[3] Matth. Paris. Hist. Ang.
[4] Hume's Hist. Richard I.
[5] Ibid.
[6] Ibid.
[7] Matth. Paris. Hist. Angl. Hen. Hig. Polyc. After the charters of William I. and Henry I. the king could have but very little title in London.

BOOK I.
A.D. 1189 to 1199.

demesnes appear to have been the most immediate objects of his rapacity. The king assumed, by his prerogative, to have the sole despotic power over the whole internal and external trade of the kingdom.¹ Accordingly, tolls were levied in all the *demesne* cities and territories, for attending markets, for passing bridges, and for landing merchandise in any of the ports.² Fines, forfeitures, and amerciaments, were other sources of an abundant and arbitrary revenue;³ for at this period most crimes were expiated by pecuniary fines; and the offences against the rigorous clauses of the forest laws were, naturally, very numerous among a people passionately addicted to the sports of the field.⁴ But, as if all these ordinary modes of exaction were insufficient to satisfy the craving rapacity of a ruler who made his will the only measure of his power, the Norman invention of *talliages* was resorted to, by which all *demesne* lands were bound to provide an arbitrary sum towards the royal necessities, and which became a very fruitful source of extortion.⁵

Although the City of London was by no means exempted from her share in these manifold grievances, and particularly in the article of talliages, it had nevertheless influence enough to gain, at the king's hands, a remission of the more slavish

However, Richard and several of his successors were in the habit of usurping many profits to which they had no right. Vide p. 33, note 4.
¹ Hume's Hist. Appendix 2nd; and vide Madox's Hist. Exch. *passim*.
² Ibid.
³ Ibid.
⁴ Ibid.
⁵ *Talliages*, in the original signification, mean nothing more than *taxes*, from French 'tailler,' *to cut off*: they came afterwards to have a restricted meaning. They were not identically the same as *aids*: the latter were due as from tenants by *knight's service* upon stated occasions; the former were confined to *demesne* lands and lands in the king's own hands, and were arbitrary, being levied on whatever emergency the king happened to experience, or rather invite; such as an expedition abroad, and the like. It must be confessed, however, that the distinction is very subtle (vide *Hist. Exch.* p. 712, where the citizens claim to pay as for an *aid* and not a *talliage*; vide also Hume's *Hist.* 2nd Appendix; Cotgrave's *French and English Dictionary*; and Spelm. voce 'Tallinge'). Neither were these talliages gifts, or, as the common term was, *benevolences*, but were assumed to be due as *of right* demandable by the superior lord (vide Cotgrave's *Dictionary*; and vide also a record in Madox's *Firma Burgi*, p. 93, of a judgment that certain money was payable by the townsmen of Ormsby *not as a talliage, but as a gift to the lord*. Co. 2nd Inst. fo. 512). Sometimes, however, these payments were called *dona*, which was a common term occasionally applied to *aids* and *scutages* as well as talliages.—Madox's *Hist. Exch.* ch. xvii.

and oppressive part of them.¹ The circumstances of the times will, therefore, sufficiently explain why the citizens were so clamorous and urgent for the repeated confirmation of their charters, as each monarch successively mounted the throne, and will serve to illustrate the franchises and immunities granted by them; which, though at the present triumphant period of a free constitution, unmeaning and forgotten, were, in the age of which we are writing, the only and genuine fruits of comparative freedom and independence. Though the rest of the nation were evidently in a state of abject poverty, insomuch that 100,000 marks (equal to about 200,000*l.* in sterling silver of our present money) was with difficulty raised towards the payment of two-thirds of Richard's ransom from his Austrian captivity,² we find the City receiving that favourite prince with such a display of wealth and magnificence as to have occasioned a German nobleman to remark, that had the emperor (Henry VI.) known of the immense wealth of England, he would have insisted on a much larger ransom.³

The occurrences of John's reign, so glorious to the nation and so disgraceful to himself, are too well known to require particular notice here. Suffice it to say, that proceeding in the arbitrary steps of his predecessors, but possessing neither their capacity to govern, nor their disposition to promote the welfare of his subjects, he pushed his extortions and oppressions beyond the verge of endurance, and at the same time both roused the indignation and invited the resistance of an insulted people by his cowardly baseness. As before observed, he was ever assiduous in courting the attachment of the Londoners, seeking to separate their interests from that of the nation at large, and hoping to find in them a firm bulwark against the encroachments of his patriotic barons. The City

¹ Vide Charter of Rich. I. It is remarkable that Richard, in enumerating the many liberties and franchises granted by his predecessors, which he confirms, makes no mention of the Sheriffwick. It seems that both Stephen and his father Henry II. had usurped the appointment to that office (vide p. 61), and Richard was not disposed to restore it. John in his first charter makes no mention of it; but his second was granted for the sole and express purpose of restoring it after long and many usurpations, as may be collected from the tenor of it.
² Hume's Hist. Richard I.
³ Matth. Paris. Hist. Angl.

received at his hands no less than five charters confirmatory of their former privileges, and memorable for the restoration of the Sheriffwick, as well as for the first specific grant of the Mayoralty;[1] rights which had been wrested from the citizens at various periods since the Conquest, and the deprivation of which was the proximate cause of all the wrongs and degradations which they suffered from the Government since that revolution. It would seem, however, that the citizens had too much experience of the fickleness of John's character to entrust themselves to his despotism, or to waive the opportunity of fixing their own rights and those of the whole nation upon a solid constitutional basis. The articles composing the Great Charter were proposed, resolved upon, and sworn to, at St. Paul's Church; and upon the first intimation of the noble enterprise for the deliverance of the people from their feudal slavery having been actually undertaken by the barons, the City readily joined in their determination, and received with exulting welcome the army destined to so glorious a conquest. The king in vain endeavoured by delays and dissimulation to thwart the steady resolution of the national band of patriots; but after many fruitless efforts at accommodation, he was obliged at last, though reluctantly, to fix his signature to that instrument[2] which has ever been justly considered, with reference to the times in which it was procured, the standard and palladium of the liberties of England.

By this famous charter much was accomplished for the aristocracy of the nation, and much for the body of the people. It would be irrelevant to go into the details of the enactments of it; the celebrated 29th chapter has become

[1] The first civic magistrate had begun to be called by the name of 'Mayor' towards the latter end of Richard's reign. This term may have been originally though remotely derived from the *Mayor of the Palace*, who was nominally the Chief Governor of Paris, but who in fact held the sovereign power in France; and subsequently indeed usurped the sovereignty itself. It was from a Mayor of the Palace that the imperial family of Charlemagne descended. Before this period the functions of the mayor were executed by the portreve, portgrave, meaning sheriff of the port; also called provost and bailiff (vide Stow, book v. and the early charters; vide also authorities quoted p. 61, note 3; and Book II. Ch. III. p. 315).

[2] Vide Blackstone's Introd. to Magna Charta.

the very alphabet of the language of freedom, and proverbialised in the mouths of Englishmen.[1] What more essentially concerns and serves to illustrate the rights and privileges of the City of London is the circumstance that now, for the first time since the Conquest, the nation at large began to enjoy a participation in the more important part of them. It is provided by the Charter, that merchants should be allowed to transact their business without being exposed to arbitrary tolls; that the king's court for common pleas should no longer follow his person, but be stationary in one place; that circuits should be established and held every year, and that the inferior local courts should be held only at their regular and appointed times, those jurisdictions having been much abused in harassing and extorting from the people; that the sheriffs should not be allowed in their districts to hold the pleas of the crown; that no aids should be demanded of the people, except by consent of Parliament, and in the three cases of the king's captivity, the making his son a knight, and the marriage of his daughter, which latter aids were to be in proportion to such reasonable contribution as was levied upon London. And lastly, as an object of national concern, it was expressly provided, that London and all the cities and boroughs of the kingdom should preserve their ancient liberties, immunities, and free customs.[2]

The Charter was scarcely granted, when John prepared to violate it; and by a sudden and unexpected muster of a large number of his military tenants *in capite*, made such progress towards the subjugation of the country, that the barons and citizens were compelled to resort to the desperate remedy of inviting over Louis, the son of the French king, to take possession of the throne. Though the death of John, almost as soon as Louis had set his foot on English ground, released the nation from this melancholy resource, yet Louis

[1] 'Nullus liber homo capiatur, vel imprisonetur, aut disseisietur de libero tenemento suo, vel libertatibus, vel consuetudinibus suis, aut utlagetur, aut exuletur, aut aliquo modo destruatur; nec super eum ibimus, nec super eum mittemus, nisi per legale judicium parium suorum, vel per legem terræ. Nulli vendemus, nulli negabimus, aut differemus rectum vel justitiam.'

[2] The liberties of London are protected by one special clause; those of the other cities by another general one, beginning 'Prætera volumus,' &c.

was enabled, through the support of the citizens, to maintain his position in the country for about half a year, against a very general combination of the barons in favour of the young king Henry III.

Through the wise and liberal negotiations of the Earl of Pembroke,[1] Henry soon found himself seated on an undisputed throne; and the people may have augured well of his reign, when they learned the very first royal act was to confirm the Great Charter.[2] Pembroke, unfortunately, did not long survive this auspicious settlement, and, from the time of his death, began one continued course of exactions, oppressions, and misgovernment, which lasted half a century. When Henry's character began to develop itself, it proved very evident, from the incapacity of his mind and the meanness of his disposition, that he was ill calculated to sway the sceptre over a turbulent nobility and a haughty people, who had already tasted the sweets of liberty. He soon gave himself up entirely into the hands of his ministers and favourites;[3] and, unhappily for him and for the nation, his partiality was lavished upon foreigners distinguished by no quality so much as their rapacity. Hubert de Burgh, after the death of Pembroke, had become the chief minister and justiciary, and though an able, and in many respects a virtuous statesman, yet he set the fatal example of some arbitrary measures, contrary to the letter and spirit of Magna Charta; and particularly in the execution of the ringleader of a popular tumult in London without trial.[4] He even went so far, under pretence of this riot, as to seize the City liberties into his own hands and appoint a custos over it,[5] and afterwards, upon a remonstrance against these infringements of the Great Charter, demanded a fifteenth of all movables for granting a restoration of it.[6] These, however, were but the signals for future grievances. As if to remove at once all obstacles or hesitation in the violation of the Great Charter, it was in the 11th year of the king's reign formally cancelled by the advice

[1] Hume's Hist.
[2] Blackstone's Introd. to Magna Charta.
[3] Hume's Hist.
[4] Matth. Paris. Hist. Angl.
[5] Brad. Appendix Hist. Engl.
[6] Matth. West.

of Hubert de Burgh: and afterwards, when the king ruled for himself, he strictly forbad any schools of law to be longer kept in the City, where lectures had begun to be read, taking as their theses the clauses of the Great Charter and that of the Forests.¹

Upon the king's coming of age, Hubert was displaced, and a shoal of Poictevins, with their countryman the bishop of Winchester at their head, took possession of the reins of government.² It would be a tedious and useless task to detail all the many exactions and oppressions endured by the nation under the government of this weak and infatuated monarch. They are most amply dwelt upon by Matthew Paris and many other writers of that age, and seem to have comprehended every class and almost every individual capable of contributing to the royal necessities.³ The fact, however, seems to be, that Henry, either fearing to offend his barons, or conscious that his lavish partiality to favourites gave him but little title to their good-will, seldom dared to propose any general national supply, nor was his authority strong enough to enable him to levy any general tax without the concurrence of the king's Council of State.⁴ Indeed, on one or two occasions, when such an appeal to the national council was made, it was met with that sort of remonstrance on his measures which rendered him very averse to repeating the attempt.⁵ The consequence was, that being continually preyed upon by the exorbitant avarice of those around him, and cajoled into expensive wars and projects, he perpetually found himself loaded with debts and difficulties, from which he had no means of extricating himself but by extortions and every species of abuse of his prerogative. We may judge of the distress to which this miserable ruler was at times reduced, and at the same time of the opulence of the citizens, in spite of the continued extortions they were compelled to undergo, from the circumstance that he actually sold his plate and jewels to them. On enquiring where he

¹ Co. 2nd Inst. proœm. Rot. Claus. anno 19th Hen. III. memb. 22.
² Hume.
³ Edinb. Review, No. 69, p. 22. in which the various exactions and abuses of power are enumerated.
⁴ Hume's Hist.
⁵ Ibid.

could meet a purchaser, it was suggested to him the citizens of London. 'On my word,' indignantly said the king, with characteristic ignorance of a monarch's true interests, '*if the treasury of Augustus were brought to sale, the citizens are able to be the purchasers: these clowns, who assume to themselves the name of barons, abound in everything, while we are reduced to necessities.*'[1]

Certainly, however, among those few of Henry's subjects who possessed the means of acquiring wealth, the citizens of London did not suffer the least. False charges were repeatedly made against them, for the purpose of exacting money:[2] exorbitant sums were demanded for purchasing the king's 'good-will,'[3] and for the granting of charters, no less than nine of which were, at various times, signed by the king; though except in a few trivial particulars they are merely confirmatory of ancient rights and privileges which had been conferred and enjoyed before. Indeed, the very fact of these numerous confirmations clearly shows the want of all principles of justice and regular government. It was a government under which, as is justly observed by Hume, 'laws seemed to lose their validity unless often renewed.' On frivolous pretences, the liberties of the City were seized upon by the king's ministers, and a custos appointed; the citizens all the while protesting against any arbitrary inquisitions upon the charges affected to be made against them, and demanding to be tried by jury and the laws and customs of the City.[4] Talliages were levied at discretion, and with or without a pretence;[5] though this tax was only legally demandable from *demesne* tenants, which the citizens clearly were not. No occasion was suffered to pass by, however ridiculous, for soliciting *presents*; and if any refused, they did not fail to be reminded of the omission. In short, schemes of begging, borrowing, and pillaging, under the cloak

---

[1]. Matth. Paris. p. 501. For an explanation of the title of the citizens to the denomination of *barons*, vide Book II. Ch. I.

[2] Fabian's Chronicle, p. 7. Matth. Paris, *passim*.

[3] 'Pro bona voluntate habenda.'— Vide *Record*; Madox's *Hist. Exch.* p. 475.

[4] Fabian's Chron. Lib. de Antiquis Legibus, fol. 72. Hist. Exch. p. 711.

[5] Matth. Paris. For an explanation of talliages, vide p. 66, note 5; and post. p. 88, note 2.

of purveyance,¹ were carried on with such unremitting zeal and assiduity, that the citizens, never cordially affected to Henry's government, at last contracted such a thorough hatred of that monarch and indignation at his measures, that they never ceased, throughout the troubles of his reign, to render the most active assistance to those barons who were leagued against him.²

From the various fortunes of the barons' wars, the citizens derived very little advantage; and when they were finally composed, through the conduct and gallantry of Prince Edward, the citizens lost their liberties, as might be naturally expected. During the time they were in the king's hands ample revenge was taken on the principal men concerned in the barons' insurrections. Their houses were pillaged, and heavy fines set upon them:³ and the king finally demanded sixty thousand marks as an atonement of past offences; although afterwards he consented to take twenty thousand.⁴ The City, however, at length recovered its privileges, though four years elapsed before all its rights were completely restored.⁵ Prince Edward, who had in the mean time been governor of the City, and indeed chiefly managed the affairs of the kingdom, soon after departed for Palestine; and the consequence was, that the kingdom, and particularly the City, began to fall into its old distracted state.⁶ Riots and disorders multiplied, and robberies were openly avowed; when at last the nation was released from the heavy burthen of its monarch by his death.

Amidst the distractions of this unfortunate reign, the administration of the law seems to have been arbitrary and uncertain wherever the Crown was concerned; though, with respect to suits between private individuals, the proceedings in the administration of the general common law began to be methodised into some regularity.⁷ The barons' wars will ever be memorable as the epoch of the first establishment

---

¹ For an explanation of Purveyance, vide p. 108; Book II. Ch. II. p. 287; and Ch. V. p. 160.
² Matth. West. Flor. Wigorn. Hist. Wike's Chron.
³ Fabian's Chron.
⁴ Ibid. Madox's Hist. Exch. p. 476.
⁵ Madox's Hist. Exch. Fabian's Chron.
⁶ Hume's Hist.
⁷ Bracton's Treatise gives competent proof of this.

74   HISTORICAL ACCOUNT OF LONDON.

BOOK I.
A.D. 1199 to 1272.

of the commons house in Parliament; for it was in consequence of the victory at Lewes that Leicester sent writs to all the counties and chief boroughs in England, summoning knights and burgesses to meet and legislate on the affairs of the nation.¹ It was in the beginning also of Henry's reign that the Saxon trial by ordeal was abolished.²

The citizens, we have seen, held a high tone in respect of their laws and privileges, and seem to have been fully aware of the importance of them in respect of their trials for offences.³ The public affairs of the City were, without question, at this period conducted at what was called the Folkmote; being a meeting of the whole body of citizens,⁴ at St. Paul's Cross, convened by the sound of a bell. This mode of assembling continued to the latter end of Edward the Second's reign,⁵ if not to that of Edward the Third; though, as we have seen, the mayor sometimes summoned specially certain individual citizens to elections, and occasionally others, of the discreeter sort, to pass ordinances as a deliberative assembly. To this folkmote we find the king continually appealing in his correspondences with the City, and treating with them, as representing the citizens at large.⁶ The civic trade, we may gather from a list of customs for foreign merchandise, and of dues for the

---

¹ Hume's Hist. Doddridge's tract on Parliaments.
² Blacks. Comm. vol. iv. p. 425.
³ Vide p. 72.
⁴ As called in the ancient City Books, lib. Leg. &c., 'immensa multitudo,' and 'immensa communitas civium' (vide p. 61, and pmt, 85, 115). But that which was subsequently, and is now, called the Wardmote, was also at this time called a Folkmote.—Vide *Lib. Alb. de Wardmotis.*
⁵ Pleadings on a quo warranto case 14th Edw. II. lib. N. fol. 51, and vide pp. 77, 78.
⁶ Fabian's Chron. In the 9th year of this king's reign, a common seal was granted to the City, according to Stow, lib. 5, p. 102; though it does not appear on what authority the assertion is made. However, as the seal in Richard II.'s reign was destroyed on account of its antiquity (Lib. II. fol. 132 b.), there is reason to believe the statement correct. That the citizens, as a community, used a common seal in the 31st year of the reign of Henry III., is proved by the charter concerning Queenhithe; and also in the 44th and 50th years of Henry III. (vide *Lib. de Ant. Leg.* fol. 122 a. 142. Harg. MSS. Brit. Mus. 277). The possession of a common seal may be said to fix the period of its becoming, strictly speaking, incorporated in fact, if not in name: for whatever acts, by-laws, and regulations, the citizens might make *as a community* for the government of the members of it; and so, in one sense, as a legislative body possessing a local jurisdiction, be entitled to be denominated a Corporation—it is certain they could do no act

privileges of foreign merchant settlers, quoted by Madox,[1] must have been very considerable: nor can we doubt of the increasing and comparatively prosperous state of its commerce, when we reflect on the exactions to which, in consequence of their wealth, the citizens were continually exposed. Great jealousies were manifested at this time against foreigners to the freedom of the City, who by ancient custom and regulations were not allowed to reside more than forty days;[2] and it was a law well recognised, that if they sold any of their goods to others foreigners in the City, those goods were forfeited.[3]

in the management or disposition of property, or institute legal proceedings for the recovery of any rights in the manner of a private person, without a common seal. Indeed it is quite clear that in the 30th year of Henry III. the citizens had no notion of any possessions or property from which a revenue was derived in a *corporate capacity*; for at that period the sheriffs themselves were personally answerable for the fee farm, and distrained on any individuals for the payment of it, until such distress was replevied by particular citizens delegated for that purpose.— Madox's *Firma Burgi*, p. 183. If the sheriffs could not obtain payment or security for it, they went to prison, or else the liberties were seized. It would seem from a charter of Edward IV. allowing purchasers by and grants to the City in mortmain, that the corporation did not begin to possess, in a corporate capacity, any *productive private* property in land till that period; though the civic government might, and certainly did, exercise a sort of jurisdiction over common and waste land in and about the City, and other land too for *public purposes*. The earliest traces we find on record of a civic proprietorship of land, is 50th Edw. III.; when it was recited by way of complaint in an act of the commonalty, That the mayor and aldermen had been used to make grants under

the City seal of the City lands, without the authority of the commonalty. This was probably common public land, over which the City authorities held a political jurisdiction, and not land held in a corporate capacity. The tenor of the record, and the nature of the complaint, would seem to testify that even this assumption of proprietorship in land by transfer of it under the City seal was but of recent origin. The oldest *private* landed property, if indeed it ever was possessed as such by the corporation, is *the Forge* in St. Clement's, for which a rent of horse shoes and nails is paid to this day in great form at the Exchequer. But this property did not come into the possession of the corporation, at all events, till after the reign of Edward II., and it is quite uncertain *when* it was first granted.—Vide records in Madox's *Hist. Exch.* vol. ii. p. 100. In truth, this forge has long been altogether lost and unknown—a pretty clear proof that it was neither private nor productive.

[1] Hist. Exch. vol. i. pp. 708-9.
[2] Fabian's Chron.
[3] Vide record of goods of foreigners forfeited to a very considerable amount, as sold contrary to the laws and customs of the City.—Madox's *Hist. Exch.* vol. i. pp. 708-9. These forfeitures are very numerous throughout the early City records.—Vide post, p. 170, and Book II. Ch. VI. p. 371.

CHAPTER V.

FROM THE ACCESSION OF EDWARD I. TO THE DEATH OF EDWARD II.

BOOK I.
A.D. 1272 to 1327.

THE first care of Edward upon his accession, was to adjust upon a firm basis the shattered constitution, and thoroughly to revise the civil administration of the realm. The dominion of the law is of slow growth: its establishment springs not from the effort of one mind, nor even from the concentrated wisdom of an entire nation; it derives its real origin from arbitrary wrongs and violence, and is first suggested for purposes of redress. But though repeated oppressions may rouse the spirit of freedom and resistance, the intellect of ages must combine and labour with it, to produce the grand result of a constitutional plan of power, which sets up the law, as the supreme sovereign of a free nation. Gradual, however, as must be the perfect growth of a dominion emanating from such sources, so numerous were the grievances under which the nation suffered during the last reign, and at the same time so prevalent among the people were those yearnings for liberty and justice which Henry had in all his measures defied, that the reign of Edward, whose mind was constantly devoted to the redress of oppressions and the establishment of those great public rights which had now gradually become as well known as valued, became at once, as it were, the epoch of the national law and of the principles of the constitution. Indeed, it is observed by Sir Matthew Hale, that more was done in the first thirteen years of his reign to settle and establish the distributive justice of the kingdom, than in all the ages since that time put together.[1]

[1] Hale's Hist. C. L. p. 158.

EDWARD I. REFORMS IN CIVIL GOVERNMENT.

CHAP. V.

A.D. 1272 to 1327.

Edward was sensible that most of the disorders and outrages which prevailed in the kingdom, were as much owing to the great barons and chief officers of the late king, as to Henry himself. In order therefore to curb these powerful despots, to ascertain the real complaints of the people, and to dispense an equal measure of justice to all ranks of his subjects, he summoned a parliament, composed of representatives elected by the people from all the counties, as well as of the barons, and subsequently of deputies from all the boroughs.[1] To give a history of the statutes passed in these parliaments would be to give a history of the English law itself. It will be necessary, however, to advert to a few of the most important particulars, in order to convey a just notion of the true meaning and value of many of those peculiar rights and privileges which are the subject matter of the ancient civic charters, and to illustrate the history of the times when those rights and privileges were practically enjoyed.

From the Conquest to Magna Charta the government of England had been gradually undergoing great and successive alterations. The establishment of the feudal system, cautiously introduced, drew on one by one, and almost imperceptibly, those various and overwhelming oppressions by which its final ascendency was characterised. The power of the king, aided by his barons when they could be kept under his control, became more and more absolute and settled over the people at large, in proportion to the high authority exercised by the barons themselves over their immediate inferiors; and, much as the cause of English freedom is indebted to the liberal views and patriotic principles of those who obtained Magna Charta from King John, there can be little doubt but that the charter itself originated more from the rigour and exactions practised against these petty potentates, and their spirited resistance against them, than out of their regard for the general liberties of the country at

[1] It appears from some records quoted by Brady on Boroughs, p. 65 et seq. that for some years before the burgesses were summoned to Parliament, the taxes had been imposed on cities, burghs, and towns, by the king's commissioners, as if all were held in demesne. London was first applied to, and their grant set an example to all other cities, burghs, and towns.

large, or from the independent exertions of the people for their own emancipation. While the prevalence of absolute principles of government increased, those resources which were derived from the continental territories and from the extensive private demesnes of the crown, were wrested from it by conquest, or lost by improvident alienations to powerful favourites. The revenues, too, which had previously been derived in great abundance from customs and tolls at ports and markets—revenues always in themselves of an arbitrary and, consequently, of an odious nature—experienced a very considerable reduction from the charters of emancipation and peculiar exemptions granted to most of the considerable towns of England, either without any, or for a very inadequate, consideration. To supply those royal necessities, which rather increased than diminished by the advancement in civilisation and the temper of the times, recourse was necessarily had to other sources; and the system of judicial administration then established, unhappily furnished the readiest medium through which the monarch could enforce upon the property of his subjects the assumed and arbitrary powers of his feudal prerogative.

The Conqueror, we have shown, instituted one judicial court, which very soon engrossed almost the whole legal proceedings of a *civil* nature in the kingdom; and the local courts of the county, the hundred, and the manor, over which the king possessed but little influence, gradually fell into decay. The sheriffs, coroners, and barons, however, in their courts leet maintained for some time a sort of exclusive jurisdiction over *criminal* matters; an authority which, it seems—either to satisfy the king for the demands made upon them in respect of the fines, forfeitures, and levies, made in their respective districts, and for which they were personally responsible,[1] or to gratify their own private interests—they very much abused.[2] But this power was likewise in

[1] Madox's Firma Burgi. p. 86, recites many records to that effect.

[2] The abuses may be collected from Coke's reading on the stat. Westm. I, 2nd Inst., and are generally enumerated in the Edinburgh Review, vol. xxxiv. p. 22; also from Matth. Paris; and Madox's Hist. Exch. vol. i., in which all the judicial exactions of this period, composing the chief part of the revenue, are detailed and explained.

process of time superseded by the king's justices; for by a law of Henry I., all jurisdiction was taken from the sheriffs of punishing capitally;[1] and in the time of Henry II. justices in *Eyre*, or itinerant, were appointed to traverse the whole kingdom at stated periods, invested with supreme jurisdiction over all pleas criminal or civil, by whose arrival the authority of all other inferior courts was determined.[2] And, finally, we we have seen that, by a provision of the Great Charter, sheriffs were forbidden to hold any pleas of the Crown whatever. In the result, therefore, the sole and universal charge of dispensing justice, both criminal and civil, was committed to the hands of judges dependent altogether on the king, and who were, in fact, his more immediate ministers and agents. In the exercise of the vast power delegated to these judges, it is very certain that no object was so zealously prosecuted as that of filling the royal treasury out of those funds from which the revenues were almost solely to be derived; and the *iters* of the justices are known to us at the present day, only by the fines and exactions recorded in the king's exchequer.[3] Many of the oppressions exercised by them under the sanction of the Crown, and particularly with regard to the feudal claims of lords over their tenants, were professed, indeed, to be redressed by Magna Charta: the provisions, however, of that code were continually violated; and where that was not palpably the case, other indirect modes of extortion were resorted to, which were not contemplated or provided against. The check given by the Great Charter to the universal abuse of the royal prerogatives, had perhaps the effect of more especially directing the rapacity of the Crown to the *demesne* lands, and to the cities and boroughs whose tenure was originally *demesne*, over which its control was less limited and ascertained.

The justices in Eyre were armed with commissions contain-

CHAP.
V.
A.D. 1272
to 1327.

---

[1] L. L. H. 1. c. 2. Wilkins, p. 146.
[2] Hale's Hist. C. L. 4th Inst. p. 185. Co. Litt. p. 293. Hoveden, part. ii, p. 313.
[3] Madox's Hist. Exch. *passim*. The

Justices in Eyre had the same power as Barons of Exchequer; and accordingly had the collection of, and jurisdiction over, all matters of revenue.—Ibid. p. 200.

ing articles of enquiry of a multifarious kind, according to the circumstances of the times, but which usually amounted to about one hundred and thirty-eight in number.[1] In pursuance of the authority delegated to them, they imposed tallages on the cities, boroughs, and demesne lands, to an arbitrary amount;[2] they obliged all those who owned franchises and liberties from the Crown to come before them to substantiate their claims;[3] which gave rise to many exactions and much bribery in securing the allowance of them. They amerced arbitrarily individuals, and even whole districts, in common, for offences easily alleged; and particularly those in misgovernment, or in the abuse of power:[4] and, when all these taxes and penalties were adjudged, the sheriffs and constituted authorities of the district assumed and exercised the power of assessing the apportionments among the people at their discretion, and of adopting such mode of exacting them as might best suit their own views[5]—a power most obviously liable to every species of mismanagement and abuse. Personal crimes and transgressions of almost every description were also visited by the same system of punishment—that of pecuniary mulct; the unrelenting severity of which seems to have been measured only by the necessities of the king and

---

[1] Co. 2nd Inst. p. 211.

[2] Fœdera, vol. i. p. 815. Brady on Boroughs, pp. 58, 66, quoting records to that effect beginning as early as Henry II.; and Madox's Hist. Exch. passim.

[3] Co. 4th Inst. p. 184. Case del Abbot de Strata Marcella Co. Rep. 9, 24. Co. 2nd Inst. p. 493. Madox's Hist. Exch. vol. i. ch. xi. and passim. And it was common enough to amerce these unsuccessful claimants like other suitors at law as 'pro falso clamore.'—Ibid. p. 558.

[4] Madox's Firma Burgi, p. 86, Stat. West. 1, C. 1. Co. 2nd Inst. p. 196; and Madox's Hist. Exch. ch. xiii. and xiv. passim. Amerciaments ought regularly by law to have been assessed as to amount for offences of which parties might be convicted by a jury; but the amerciament was often, and indeed usually, admeasured by the justices, and sometimes by the king himself (Madox's Hist. Exch. ch. xiv.). The earls and barons had by a clause in Magna Charta the privilege of being amerced only by their peers. It was the legal doctrine, that for those crimes which were to be punished by pecuniary amerrement, no trial was allowed; the inquisition or presentment of a leet jury or the jury of the Eyre was sufficient, and such presentments were not traversable. Only pleas of the Crown were traversable, i.e. subjects of trial; and the distinction between pleas of the Crown and presentments seems to have been, that the former were subject to some fixed or stated punishment, as death, pillory, or fine; the latter, only to the offered amercement (vide Book II. Ch. II. p. 292; V. p. 361).

[5] Vide note 3, p. 83; Ch. II. p. 292.

the opulence of the culprit.¹ Even the administration of civil justice between man and man was made the subject of open traffic; the very liberty of suing at law in the king's courts was to be paid for, and that arbitrarily: and nothing was more common than for a suitor to purchase the interference of the king in the progress of his suit, by his mandates to the justices.²

In the meanwhile the sheriffs and inferior magistrates were by no means wanting either to the royal interests or their own, as far as regarded the means of extortion which they possessed. Although the judicial authority of the sheriff was greatly eclipsed by the institution of the Eyres, he still retained a formidable power of a fiscal nature, in the district entrusted to his jurisdiction. He was at the head of the finances; and, in fact, the issues of his office composed almost the whole of the regular national revenue.³ But besides the duty of collecting, according to his own discretion, the levies of his district, he was the conservator of the peace,⁴ fulfilling the office of the present committing country justice: and by virtue of that authority, not only decided on the commitment of all malefactors, but levied fines for their escapes, and exercised an arbitrary discretion in bailing those only whom he held in favour.⁵ He collected also, on behalf of the king, all tolls in the public markets not let to farm, and on bridges, and ferries; and, in like manner, the lords of particular franchises and boroughs, and the citizens holding of the king at fee farm, exacted them as of their own right in their demesnes and other territories.⁶ This latter right, as well as the ministerial duty of the sheriff, was often made a pretence for exorbitant charges at the arbitrary pleasure of the proprietors,⁷ and loudly called for a remedy. And in short, to omit many

---

¹ Madox's Hist. Exch. ch. xiv. sect. 6, and passim, enumerated in one view in Hume's Hist. Appendix II. Foster's Crown Law, p. 287.
² Ibid. Madox's Hist. Exch. ch. xii. passim, chap. xiii.
³ Ibid. p. 354, and vol. II. p. 128. Madox's Firma Burgi, p. 86.
⁴ He is said to have been so created by West. 1, cap. 15. Hale's P. C. 2nd p. 44. Hawkinson's P. C. vol. II. p. 32.
⁵ Westm. 1, caps. 11, 15. Numberless were the appeals and payments to the king for liberty to be out on bail; and many of the cases were of a civil nature, or misdemeanours only.—Vide Madox's Hist. Exch. vol. i. p. 403.
⁶ Ibid. cap. 31. Co. 2nd Inst. p. 219.
⁷ Ibid.

other particulars, so universal was the system of appropriating whatever could with any semblance of pretence be wrested from the owner, that all vessels and merchandise which happened to be wrecked, were instantly seized as lawful plunder to the use of the king.[1]

Much as had been accomplished by Magna Charta for the relief of all orders of the people against national grievances, most, if not all, the oppressions just enumerated, continued to harass the people with more or less severity up to the accession of Edward I. Indeed, there were very few of the provisions of the charter itself which were not subjected to open violation or warm contest, when opposed to the craving pecuniary necessities of the monarch; and it was far from being considered as comprising the essential and constitutional basis of the law of the land. It is not surprising that such a state of things should occasion disorders of all sorts in the state, and that at last a crisis should arrive when so harsh and tyrannical a course of government could be endured no longer. Edward, whose excellent abilities, swayed by honourable and liberal feelings, taught him this lesson, soon found how expedient it was to adopt some more constitutional plan of ruling the kingdom, and of supplying those revenues which, however necessary, were no longer to be obtained by unequal and arbitrary extortion. He formed, therefore, at once, the resolution (as already mentioned) of summoning a parliament which should be composed of the freely elected representatives of the people; and determined to throw himself on their voluntary support, for those contributions which the dignity of the crown and the wants of the state required. Having taken this important step, and thereby rendered himself independent of those arbitrary extortions by which his treasury had before been precariously supplied, and which alone were the sources of all the grievances which the nation suffered, the path of reformation became smooth. The very first parliament convoked, voted him a fifteenth of all movables;[2] and then engaged, under the king's direction, in the great task of correcting the numerous abuses which existed, and of

---

[1] Ibid. cap. 4. Blacks.Comm. vol. i. p. 291.   [2] Hume's Hist. Statutes at large.

putting the administration of the government and of the
laws into a regular and equitable course. The greater part
of these reformations were effected in this parliament;
though some of the evils which prevailed were remedied
more tardily, and by the king's sole authority. However,
it will be more convenient and plain to sum up under one
view all those measures which we shall have occasion to
mention.

With regard to the justices, it was ordained that tallages
should no more be levied upon cities, boroughs, towns, or
other of the king's demesnes, without consent of Parliament;[1]
that the justices in Eyre should no more amerce counties
and districts in common, for the offences of particular
individuals: but that such amerciaments should be imposed
only upon the parties actually guilty; and that, wherever a
general or common amerciament might be imposed, the
sheriffs should not have authority to assess the proportions
of any amerciament at their discretion; but that the assessments,
as respected the apportionment, should be made by a
jury, and estreated by the justices into the exchequer by
parcels;[2] that cities, boroughs, and towns, should no longer
be amerced without reasonable cause, nor to a ruinous
extent;[3] that the king should never interfere by his mandates
in private causes.[4] With regard to sheriffs and other
magistrates holding inferior courts, boundaries were set to

---

[1] Stat. de Tall. 34. Edw. I. Co. 2nd Inst. p. 532. According to Calthorp, who in his Book of Customs, Usages, &c. quotes Lib. Alb. fol. 40, it was ordained *by charter* in the *first year* of Edward I., that the City should no more be *tallaged*, but pay their *aids* according as the *counties* did, and not as the cities and boroughs. This is however a mistake, and Calthorp means the 1st of Edward III., when a charter was granted to this effect. That is the charter in Liber Albus.

[2] Stat. West. 1, cap. 18. Co. 2nd Inst. p. 196. For the nature of amerciaments, vide Book II. Ch. II. p. 292.

[3] Stat. West. 1, cap. 6. Co. 2nd Inst. p. 169. That is for any *general* delinquency, such as riot, misgovernment, not paying their farm, &c. By a previous clause they were not to be amerced in *common* for the offences of any *individuals*.

[4] Blacks. Comm. vol. I. p. 425. Hale's Hist. C. L. Stat. Artic. Sap. Chart. It must be confessed, however, that neither Edward nor any of his immediate successors were very strict in observing this law (vide Ryley, p. 525). There were instances of such interferences even down to the time of Elizabeth. A remarkable letter of Recorder Fleetwood in that reign, complains of the bribes and interference of the courtiers in regard to convicts. — Vide Maitland's Hist. vol. i. p. 263.

their jurisdiction,[1] so that they should set no more penalties upon the mere presentment of juries in their leets, for the escapes of felons,[2] or for offences of any kind which were properly the subjects of trial before the judges;[3] nor should they exercise a discretionary power in respect to the bailing or detaining in prison persons accused of crimes.[4] It was ordained, that magisterial proprietors, and those holding at fee farm of the king, should no longer take outrageous tolls in mercantile districts; and that if they did, the franchise, on the ground of which such extortionate toll was taken, should be forfeited to the king, whether the district was held of the king at fee farm, or belonged to any private lord;[5] and with respect to wrecks, it was emphatically provided, that if any thing alive escaped from the vessel, it should not be adjudged a wreck.[6] Lastly, to remove all confusion in the various functions of the king's court, the office of chief justiciary was abolished, and the court itself divided into several branches, with distinct duties prescribed to each:[7] although these distinctions, adapted to an earlier stage of our constitution, were, through the invention of some modern fictions very beneficially practised in the enlarged state of private property, in most cases abolished, and have been directly so by recent legislation. Improvements so great as these in the constitution and administration of the laws, have justly gained Edward the title of the English Justinian;

[1] Hale's Hist. C. L.
[2] Stat. West. 1, cap. 3rd.
[3] Ibid. Co. 2nd. Inst. p. 183. Vide further on this subject Book II. Ch. V. pp. 292, 352.
[4] Stat. West. 1, cap. 12, 15. Co. 2nd Inst. p. 185.
[5] Stat. West. 1, cap. 31. This law, however, did not prevent the king from regulating the amount of tolls and customs arbitrarily—a practice which continued for many centuries afterwards.
[6] Ibid. cap. 4. Blacks. Comm. vol. i. p. 291. Co. 2nd Inst. p. 166. There is no doubt that such was the old Common Law; though it is plain it was little observed. A Saxon law of the age of Ethelred, enacted that all vessels and their crews, even public enemies, which were wrecked and took refuge on the English shores, should be at peace and enjoy their own.—Vide Selden, *Analecta Anglo-Britannica*.
[7] Sellon's Practices. Introd. to Hale's Hist. C. L. Blacks. Comm. vol. iv. p. 425. Spelman's Gloss. 'Justiciarius.' Gilbert's Hist. of the Exchequer, p. 9; and Madox's Hist. Exch. The Common Pleas had been in a manner separated before by Magna Charta; but suits at law were nevertheless still brought before the Court of Exchequer, and indeed indiscriminately before any of the king's judges.—Vide Madox's *Hist. Exch.* ch. xxii.

and it has been correctly observed by a philosophic and judicious historian,¹ that Magna Charta could never till now be said to be fully established; and that afterwards, although practices contrary to its true spirit often prevailed, and were even able to establish themselves into settled customs, its validity was never formally disputed.

To revert to what more immediately relates to the City of London—it appears that, in consequence of a general riot which took place immediately after the king's return from Palestine, which was produced by a contested election of a mayor, Edward thought it requisite, by way of showing his determination to repress the disgraceful disorders which had been so common in the preceding reign, instantly to appoint, by a stretch of his authority, a custos over the City. Having manifested by this rigorous measure what his resolution was, upon the election being finally decided, he returned to the citizens their franchise.²

At this period, as it has been already observed, the division of the City into Wards began to be known solely under such denomination;³ the wards chose, in their respective wardmote courts, or leets of the wards, certain inhabitants to be of council to the aldermen; not, however, as of right representing the whole community of the corporation, for that '*immensa communitas*' still continued to assemble for public purposes.⁴ Whatever elections or ordinances were made by select bodies, as to representing the corporate community, were made by those summoned by the lord mayor according to his discretion, and called by distinction *his* common council. It seems reasonable to suppose that they were appointed originally as mere assistants to the aldermen in the government of their respective wards; though it appears that the lord mayor summoned *his* council out of the same individuals.⁵ The juries of the several wards, taking advantage of the disposition of the king to redress abuses,

---

¹ Hume.
² Fabian's Chron. 7.
³ Lib. Alb. fol. 116. Names of the wards as at present denominated, and those of the common councilmen there mentioned, and vide supra, p. 59 and notes. There is an instance, however, of an 'Aldermanry' mentioned in a record as late as the 6th Edward I.—Vide *Firma Burgi*, p. 15.
⁴ Vide pp. 61, 74, 115.
⁵ Vide p. 115.

BOOK 1.
A.D. 1272 to 1327.

upon the arrival of the justices in Eyre at the Tower in the third year of his reign (being the same year in which he held his first parliament), presented to them that the mayors and guardians of the City had been used to load them with arbitrary and unauthorised tallages, and unequal assessments of such tallages.[1] It does not appear, however, that any particular notice was at that time taken of such delinquencies, but these complaints may have served to promote that general system of reform which Edward was anxious to put in force. In the 12th year of this reign, the mayor, aldermen, and sheriffs, having been summoned before the justices in Eyre at the Tower, to give an account of the peace of the City, the former, conceiving he was not bound to go out of the City upon such inquest, formally deposed himself before he entered the Tower gates; and went in as a private citizen, under no magisterial reponsibility. It is probable that this conception arose out of an overstrained construction of ancient usages and of the earlier charters, which grant that the citizens shall appoint whomsoever they please to be justiciar over them, and shall not be compelled to plead in any pleas without the walls of the City—immunities which may be thought rather to refer to the internal dispensation of justice among the citizens at large, than to any exemption of the magistrates from reponsibility to the Crown. The king was so incensed at this conduct of the magistrates, that he immediately seized the franchise into his own hands, and appointed a custos, who held the authority of the mayor for no less a period than twelve years.[2] This seizure of the government seems by no means to have ameliorated the police of the City; for the frequency and boldness of crimes of all kinds, which were openly perpetrated in the streets, occasioned the passing a statute,[3] by which it was directed, that the aldermen should make strict

[1] Bag. de quaranto London, 3rd Edward I. No. 4 in Scaccario.
[2] Lib. Horne, Lib. F. ad fin. It is to be remarked, however, that the citizens had formerly, though in very few instances, attended the inquests of the justices held at the Tower. In the list of all the items for the time between Henry II. and Edward I., London is only twice or three times mentioned.—Vide Madox's *Hist. Exch.* ch. iii., and ibid. p. 568.
[3] Stat. Civ. Lond. 13th Edward I.

search for offenders, and allow none but freemen to reside in the City—a regulation which appears by the ancient City Books to have been very early enforced, as one of the civic privileges in regard to foreign merchants, who were provided with lodgings by the aldermen, and not allowed to remain even there longer than forty days.[1]

In the 26th year of Edward's reign the City liberties were restored; not, however, without the payment of a large fine for the concession.[2] Upon this the aldermen, with twelve men selected and summoned by them from each ward, chose the new mayor;[3] and we may collect, both from the special mode of summoning by the aldermen on this occasion and the number summoned, evident proof that the persons summoned for the election of the mayor were not the regularly elected body constituting the ward councilmen of the aldermen, since we find that the names of all the common-councilmen elected for the wards in the year 1285 (ten years only previous) are recorded;[4] and they will not allow the proportion of *two* (nor have they ever amounted to the average of *twelve*) for each ward.[5] This mode of election of the mayor by selected members of the ward was a novelty, and it certainly did not last long. For in the next reign important changes were introduced in the qualifications for the civic freedom, and subsequently in the elective franchises and constitutional government of the City, which will be among the subjects discussed in future chapters. The City was never afterwards in this reign molested in its rights; and so firmly does the supreme authority of the law appear to have been established, that upon a mandate coming from the king, directed to the mayor and sheriffs, which appeared to infringe on the privileges of the City, they did not hesitate to return for answer — that they could not be charged to obey it; and they actually refused so to do with impunity.[6]

---

[1] Vide Calthorp's Customs, Usages, &c., p. 11. Lib. Alb. fol. 89, b. c. Fabian's Chron. 7. Lib. Horne, p. 272. Vide supra, p. 75 and post, p. 120; and Book II. Ch. II. p. 289.

[2] Lib. Nigr. fol. 34.

[3] Lib. B. fol. 88.

[4] Lib. Alb. fol. 116.

[5] Vide p. 114.

[6] The mandate was to obey the Stat. of Winchester in regard to the apprehending felons, and returning inquisi-

BOOK I.
A.D. 1272 to 1327.

The sceptre was now transmitted from the powerful hand of Edward to that of his feeble-minded son Edward II. A prey to favourites during almost the whole of his reign, and incapable of checking the turbulence of his barons, who resolved by force of arms to deliver themselves and the nation from such pernicious influence, the country naturally fell again into disorder and confusion. The authority of Parliament seems hardly yet to have been established, and still less the inviolability of its statutes. The king, though continually referring with submission to the principles of Magna Charta, thought himself at liberty to transgress against many of the other laws enacted in his father's time; and his measures do not appear to have been remonstrated against as illegal or unconstitutional on *that* account. Thus the old grievance of talliages, the imposition of which was especially and solemnly prohibited in the late reign, without consent of Parliament, was revived on the ancient arbitrary principles by Edward II.[1] It is remarkable that, although the citizens strongly opposed the tax, yet they grounded such opposition rather upon peculiar privileges of exemption, than upon its inconsistency with the law of the land.[2] At this period, elections of mayor and sheriffs were commonly made by persons specially summoned for that purpose, as we have seen was the case in the last reign; and though the great body of citizens would upon such occasions press in, yet their interference was strictly forbidden.[3] The consequence of this was, that the same persons were elected, or rather held over, for many years successively; and they gradually assumed an

---

tions respecting them out of the City, Lib. Horne, fol. 314 b. Lib. Major Nig.

[1] Madox's Firma Burgi, p. 185. Vide supra, p. 88, note 1.

[2] Lib. Horne, fol. 324. The citizens said that they were not *in demesne*; that they paid a fee farm in lieu of all talliages; and that therefore, though the king might by right talliage his demesnes, they were not liable—a plea rather ignorantly framed, for the king had no right to talliage even his demesnes after the statutes 'de talliagio non concedendo' (24th Edward I.) with-

out consent of Parliament; and the farm was not paid instead of talliages, for the talliages had always been used to be paid, as well on behalf of towns held at farm as others, the farm being merely the substitution for the ancient issues and profits from customs, fairs, pleas, &c. (Vide Madox's *Firma Burgi*, ch. xi., and vide Madox's *Hist. Exch.* ch. x. p. 357, where the men of Ipswich are threatened with the loss of their *fee farm*, if they did not pay their *talliages*.)

[3] Vide Proclamations of 8th Edward II. to that effect, Lib. Horne, fol. 332 b.

illegal power in the City which they very soon abused, particularly in the main article of talliages. Sometimes they would raise talliages of their own authority; sometimes they would leave themselves, the aldermen, and a few others, out of the rate, upon some frivolous pretence of exemption; sometimes, after the talliages had been assessed by the competent men in the ward-motes upon the individuals, to be levied by the aldermen, as the practice was,¹ they would heighten the respective sums; and it is not without reason to be suspected that they embezzled a great part of them.² Upon the remonstrances of the citizens it was ordained, with the sanction of the king's letters patent of approbation,³ that the mayor should be elected according to the old charters;⁴ and that neither he, nor any alderman, should remain in office more than one year, and that the latter should not be re-elected for the ensuing year. The abuse respecting talliages was, for the time, corrected; and many regulations were passed respecting the commercial privileges of the citizens, and the admission of strangers to the freedom, which testify something like a constitutional regularity in the civic government.

But the government of the king was too weak and unstable to enforce his commands over the civic magistrates; who continued the same unjust and illegal practices, in spite of presentments made against them at the Eyres of the judges, the consequences of which presentments in these turbulent times they had power enough to evade.⁵ Often as talliages were imposed in this reign, even by royal sanction, they were always met by murmurs and discontent, and an appeal to Parliament for further consideration of the subject was as often contended for, the effect of which usually was a compromise with the king at a smaller sum than what was

---

¹ Madox's Firma Burgi, p. 185.
² Vide Ordinances sanctioned by letters patent of Edward II. Rec. Tower, pat. 12th Edward II. p. 2, m. 2. Strype's Stow, vol. ii. p. 361; and vide articles in the first charter of Edward II.
³ Ibid.
⁴ This ordinance, however, had not the effect of gaining for the citizens the full right of electing their mayor: for until the 49th Edward III. that magistrate continued to summon at his discretion those who should attend for elective purposes.—Vide *Ordinance of Edward III.* Lib. Leg. fol. 25 b.
⁵ Tho. Wals. Hist. Angl.

originally demanded.[1] Throughout the troubled fortunes of this unhappy monarch the City seems to have experienced the most sudden changes of favour and persecution, according as his moments of fear or exultation predominated; and if a charter of confirmation or protection was granted at one time, it was sure to be violated at another, if an emergency occurred, when such violation appeared safe or profitable. On the whole, however, we may judge from the circumstance of the City having been, on an occasion of a general conscription, required to provide five times more men than any other City, that its relative wealth and influence had risen to a very high ascendency.[2]

[1] Lib. Horne, p. 324 et seq.   [2] Tho. Wals. Hist. Angl.

CHAPTER VI.

ACCOUNT OF THE ORIGINAL QUALIFICATIONS OF THE FREE CITIZENS, AND OF THE FIRST ESTABLISHMENT OF THE MERCANTILE QUALITY OF THE CIVIC CORPORATION IN THE REIGN OF EDWARD II.

IT is in the reign of Edward II. that we discern the first authentic mention of the *mercantile* constitution of the civic corporation, and of the *mercantile* qualifications requisite in the candidates for admission to the freedom of the City. By one of a number of articles of regulation ordained by the citizens for their internal government—which articles were confirmed by the king, and afterwards incorporated into a charter[1]—it was provided, that no person, whether an inhabitant of the City or otherwise, should be admitted into the civic freedom, unless he was a *member of one* of the *trades* or *mysteries*, or unless by the full assent of the whole commonalty convened; only, that *apprentices* might still be admitted according to the accustomed forms.

CHAP. VI.
A.D. 1272 to 1327.

Some remarks have, as occasion suggested, already been made with reference to the original nature of the civic community, and the quality of its members;[2] but the article just noticed induces in this place some further observations, tracing from their origin the present and actual qualifications of a free citizen of London.

In the Saxon times immediately preceding the Conquest, and certainly for a long time subsequent to that event, which so materially changed the constitution and laws of England, we have seen that the City maintained the same legal polity and constitution which distinguished a county

---

[1] Vide Book II. Ch. IV. p. 334.
[2] Vide pp. 24 et seq. 61, 74, 243; and Book II. Ch. III. p. 309 et seq.

92   HISTORICAL ACCOUNT OF LONDON.

BOOK I.
A.D. 1272 to 1327.

under the Saxon government. It was a concentration of leet jurisdictions, each comprising a ward, or, as the division was then termed, a *gild*; and the whole superintended by one magistrate, or by him and the bishop. It was, in fact, a county in itself—with this important distinction, that it contained no *villeins* or slaves, so numerous in the counties; but all its inhabitants were free men and law-worthy.[1]

As in the counties the districts over which the lords or great landed proprietors possessed a leet jurisdiction were called their *sokes* or *socs*,[2] so in the City, the *gilds* or districts over which the civic magistrates held their leet jurisdictions, were likewise called their *sokes*.[3] It was a provision of the very earliest City charter granting any privileges in detail, 'that the barons' and citizens should have their *sokes* in peace, and that guests tarrying within any of these *sokes* should pay custom to those only to whom the *soke* belonged.'[5] The city and county *sokes* had, in truth, the same origin, and were governed and regulated on the same principles: they were both districts originally held *in demesne*, or considered so to have been, and in which all or many of the tenants had become emancipated.[4] The tenants in *free socage* of the counties, and the burghers or tenants in *free burgage*, were of the same quality; for the tenure of *free burgage*, as has been before remarked, was no other than a species of *free socage*. The *proprietary* title of the alderman to his *soke* in London

---

[1] Vide pp. 17, 29 et seq. 51; and express authorities to this effect in Year Book, Pasch. 7 Hen. 6ti. pl. 36, 42. Do. Pasch. 4 Edw. 4ti. pl. 32. Vide also Co. Rep. 9, p. 36 b.

[2] Sac and Soc were the rights which comprised the baronial jurisdiction (vide Domesday Book). Ellis's Introd. p. 87. Lambard's Archaion. Legem Ed. 21. Spelman's Gloss. Lye's Dict. Hist. Exch. vol. i. pp. 107, 724, 725, notes. Also Selden's Tit. Hon. pp. 476 et seq. 719, 732. And Heywood's Dissertation on Saxon Ranks, pp. 145, 216.

[3] Thus *Knightengild* was called *Portsoke*, and Aldgate ward was called the *inner soc*. (Vide supra, pp. 35, 49;

and vide Strype's Stow, vol. 1. Aldgate ward; and vide *Records Hist. Exch.* p. 693. 'The burgesses and tenants of the soc,' &c. 724, 725, where many other town *socs* are mentioned. Vide also *Lib. Horne*, fol. 130, quoted by Stow, book v. p. 319.)

[4] For the meaning of this term as applied in the earlier times to the citizens and civic magistrates, vide infra, charter of William the Conqueror, Book II. Ch. I.

[5] Charter of Henry I.; and vide *infra*, Book II. Ch. II.

[6] Vide authorities quoted pp. 94, 96, notes.

was certainly of short duration, and perhaps never universal throughout the City. It probably arose with the introduction of the feudal system, and expired with the grant of those exemptions from it secured to the citizens by their early charters, the establishment of a community, and the election of their own magistrates. But that these *sokes* did at one time actually belong to the aldermen or barons, at least in their magisterial capacity, as heritable property, is too clear to admit of a doubt.

If we proceed to examine still further, and compare in detail the qualities and internal government of these respective *sokes*, we shall not only perceive plainly their original identity in principle, but shall also gather clear indications of what were the original qualifications of the free constituent members of both.

When the proprietor or lord first assumed possession of the soil composing his demesne or *soke* (such a possession as was taken by the Saxon invaders of Britain), it is probable that all the individuals within it were reduced to a state of absolute dependence, if not slavery. Long, however, before the Norman Conquest, in the gradual approach towards a regular and settled form of government and more reformed social habits, the tenants within those districts had become divided into three distinct classes. The lowest were those whose oppressed condition we have often had occasion to mention, who never emerged from their original bondage, but continued the personal and proprietary slaves or *serfs* of the lord, employed in whatever occupations he considered most advantageous, and subservient entirely to his will. The next were those who, although they had contrived to loose themselves from the more galling links of their chain, had by no means acquired the blessings of a free condition. These were the villeins,[2] who, being for the most part husbandmen, cultivated the soil of their demesne lords, and were for such service requited with some small allotment of land. The tenure of

---

[1] Firma Burgi. p. 14.

[2] The term 'villeins,' it seems, was at a later period applied generally as well to serfs or personal slaves, as to the rustic labourers; but still the distinction was kept up, the former being denominated *villeins in gross*, and the latter *villeins regardant*.—Vide Lytt. Sect. 181. Co. 120 b.

this land was, however, entirely at will; the occupiers had no power of leaving the soc; they were themselves, their children, and their possessions, the absolute property of their demesne master; and they had claim to no personal rights whatever, either legal or political. It has been elsewhere observed,[1] that by gradual usage a fixed interest was attained in the land by such villein tenants, through the benevolent facility of their masters, who considered it hard to strip a deserving tenant of all his possessions without any adequate or reasonable cause; which interest finally grew up into a right, descendable to their heirs. Many of these villein or demesne tenants did however, in the Saxon times, acquire, from especial favour of their lord, or through purchase, accomplished out of the accumulated savings of successful industry an entire emancipation from servitude, and a free right to their tenements;[2] and this emancipation gave rise to a third class, of whom we are now to speak.

This third class was composed of freemen, or free tenants, who, passing under various names, were still tenants, owing certain duties and services within the soc.[3] They were sometimes called *Coleberti*,[4] and likewise *Radmen*, from *pat* or *pebe* (Sax.) an *agreement, compact*[5] (because their services were fixed, and by compact), but were all known by the common appellation of *sockmen*, sokemen, or socmen.[6] They are described as *free tenants* who *ploughed*, or *fenced*, or *reaped*, or *mowed, within the lord's manor*.[7] Living within the soc, and subject to the soc jurisdiction, both slaves and villeins might be said indeed, in that sense, to be *sockmen*: the term, however, was never applied to the former, which may be easily accounted for. They were, in truth, held in very little

---

[1] Vide p. 49.

[2] Co. Lytt. 'Villenage' passim. Turner's Hist. Ang. Sax. 4th ed. vol. iii. pp. 181, 182.

[3] Thus we hear in records of 'my men, both servile and free.'—Turner's *Hist. Ang. Sax.* vol. iii. p. 85.

[4] The precise etymon of this word is difficult to ascertain—that of Spelman's Gloss. appearing very unsatisfactory. Coke (Lytt. 56) says it is expounded of record, and in Domesday Book, to signify *tenants in free socage at free rents*. Brissonius explains it as 'con liberti,' De Verborum Dig.

[5] Ibid.; but Coke says 'rad' or 'rede' signifies *firm* or *stable*; a construction not borne out by Lye's Dict. It is here taken in a more authorised, and perhaps more correct sense.

[6] Ibid.

[7] Ibid.

higher estimation than the cattle they tended; and as on the one hand they possessed no legal rights, so on the other they were not allowed in the smallest degree to participate in the administration of justice. They were not even members of the tythings, borhoes or decenniaries; for although they were, together with every other individual, in Frankpledge, yet they were not themselves free pledgers, but were *answered for* by their lords or others.¹ Much also as these base tenants subsequently gained ground in legal, in judicial, and in constitutional rights; yet it is very certain that, in the Saxon times, the *free tenants* were the only persons who owed *suit* and *service* to the lord's court;² they only gave their judgment as the *peers* of those who resorted thither for justice; they only had the privilege of access to such jurisdiction, as *law-worthy* men; and they only, together with the presiding lord, composed the court,³ which was itself sometimes called the soc, and which seems, indeed, to have been its primitive signification; though afterwards, by a metonymy, applied to the district.

It would seem, therefore, that the original tenants in *free socage* (although the term came to be applied generally to the common free tenants of a hundred or county who were under the general jurisdiction of the sheriff), were no other than these socmen; and that they were so called from their belonging to the lord's district, originally demesne, and from their attendance on his court. It is conceived that, at all events, enquirers into this much disputed topic may by this suggested derivation relieve themselves from the very discrepant and unsatisfactory explanation of this tenure proffered by Somner and Lyttleton, with which, for want of any other, the learned have been hitherto obliged to rest contented.⁴

---

¹ Mirroir de Justice, 'De viewe de frankpledge.' ch. i. sect. 17; and 3rd art. of the View.

² Ibid.; and the common mention in Domesday Book of the sockmen and free tenants, who *owed suit and service* to the lord's court.

³ The *Secta* (suit, i.e. the attendant oty of freehold peers of the court) is given by Lye as the original meaning of the soc: so also by an ancient writing drawn up, according to Strype (vide Stow, book iii. p. 107), by some ancient lawyer for the use of St. Martin's liberty.

⁴ Wright's Ten. p. 141. Lyttleton derives the tenure in socage from *soca*, 'a plough;' and says it was so called from the tenure being originally by *plough service*. Somner derives it from

BOOK I.
A.D. 1272 to 1327.

It is curious to observe how, conformably with the imperceptible gradations towards civil freedom in this country, the socage tenant advances into the independent freeholder, on a par and blended almost with the freeholder of a county or hundred; the villein grows up, under the name of copyholder, into the true original socage tenant; while the wretched bondman, or slave, disappears altogether from the face of the land; so that in the reign of Elizabeth not one was to be found throughout the whole realm. But serfs, boors, and slaves, either in name or quality, still subsist in those countries where constitutional rights have not yet overcome the despotism entailed by feudal principles; and in those countries most where political freedom is least understood.

As proprietors of the soc, the lords claimed a great number of fees and perquisites, payable by all classes of people, whether free or servile, who negotiated any affairs within the soc, and which no doubt formed in themselves a considerable source of revenue. It is probable that the judicial fines imposed in their courts, and the tolls, composed the chief part of this fiscal revenue. They likewise had the *view of frank-pledge*, which was the right of assembling the whole male population of the district above the age of twelve years (with the exception of the clergy, earls, barons, knights, and those disabled by infirmity), at the leet or soke court, to take the oath of fealty to the king, and for the capital frankpledgers to give account of the peace kept by the individuals within their respective tythings.[1] In other words, he had the general superintendence of the conduct and affairs of every individual within the range of his territory.

When a stranger first came into a soke, the person under

soc, which he translates a *liberty*, and says it was called *socage* because it was a *free* tenure. With regard to the first etymon, it is not only far from clear that plough service ever was the service of a socage tenant, but the word soon never appears to have been used in the sense of plough, when the plough service is alluded to, but the word *syll*, as vide record quoted Turner's *Angl. Sax.* vol. ii. p. 179. With regard to the latter,

soc never was used for the word *liberty*, in the abstract sense of freedom; although it stood for a *franchise* of holding a court, &c. According to Somner's derivation, too, tenure in free socage would labour with the tautological meaning of a tenure in *free freedom*.

[1] Mirroir de Justice, 'Viewes de Franckpledge,' articles of Wardmote Inquest. Stow, book iii. p. 313 et seq.

whose roof he took his permanent abode was responsible for his good behaviour.[1] If, however, he lodged but one night, he was considered altogether as *a person unknown:*[2] the second night he was denominated his *guest*:[3] but by the third night it was conceived that his entertainer had, or ought to have, some certain knowledge of his inmate; and consequently, the stranger was then set down as the host's own *man*.[4] If he stayed forty days, it was incumbent on him to be enrolled in some tything, either as a *socman*, or capital free-pledger, himself,[5] or else as an inmate in the pledge of some other. He then became a regular resident member of the society into which he had migrated. Thus the owner of the *soke* became apprised of the number and character of all the inhabitants within his district; and a system of police surveillance was established upon a principle of mutual protection, which extended to the very threshold of each man's habitation.[6]

As in the county *sokes* great precautions were observed with regard to the reception of strangers, so in the early ages of the civic constitution, great vigilance was exercised with regard to the access and resiance of new-comers into the city for any purpose. This vigilance, although it was prompted in later times by a virulent jealousy of their participating in the many monopolies and commercial privileges accorded from time to time to the true citizens, yet did not derive its source originally from any such interested feeling. That legal system for the repression, the detection, and the punishment of violence, for mutual protection and mutual responsibility, established under the ancient Saxon polity, prevailed in the fullest force within the City of London. We may trace in those civic regulations of the reign of Athelstan, which we have noticed as passed by the citizens in their *gilds* or leet jurisdictions, the same principles of administration of the criminal law, as those which characterised the *frith gilds* and

---

[1] Lamb. Archaion. Ll. Ed. 'De hospitibus.' Spelman's Gloss. verbo: 'Third nights, awn hynd.'
[2] 'Uncuth.' Ibid.
[3] 'Twa nights, geste.' Ibid.
[4] 'Third nights, awn hynd.' Ibid.
[5] Vide pp. 20, 129, note 4.
[6] Upon this subject Granville Sharp has commented fully in his desultory work 'On Congregational Courts.'

leets of the counties.¹ So in Edward the Confessor's laws, and in subsequent laws of the Conqueror, it was ordained, that *all freemen* of the kingdom (without any distinction), whether in *cities, boroughs, castles,* or *hundreds,* should provide themselves with arms, according to their means, and according to their *fees and tenements,* and should produce them at their leets.² So by ancient civic ordinances it was required, that strangers should remain no longer within the walls than forty days, without being enrolled in frank-pledge.³ So again, notice was required from those who received strangers, upon their remaining two days.⁴ So also, every adult, after a year's residence, was bound to present himself to be sworn to his allegiance in the leet.⁵ But these requisitions, prescribed by ancient civic ordinances, were the same as those which we have observed were applicable to the whole people at large—they were precisely such as qualified the inhabitants of counties, and the members of the *sokes* or *friburghs* or *frithgilds.*⁶

Within the City of London the court leet was held with precisely the same jurisdiction as that of the county soke;⁷ and the most prominent part of its duties was to hold the view of frank-pledge.⁸ As in the county soke, so in the City ward, *all* inhabitants were not equally constituent members, exercising the full functions of freemen, and enjoying the political or municipal rights of the association. Neither in the City, any more than in the country *soke,* did *inmates, lodgers, persons under age,* or *villeins,* possess these rights.⁹ The *mere inhabitancy* within the walls was, at least after a year and a day, a badge of *freedom* in one sense; that is, it conferred an exemption from villeinage or slavery. In the

¹ Vide pp. 19, 34, 59.
² Lib. Rub. in Custod. Rememb. Regis; and vide LL. Wilkins. 'De Greve.'
³ Vide post, 120.
⁴ Articles of Wardmote Inquest. Stow, book v. pp. 313-365.
⁵ Vide ibid.
⁶ Vide Leges Athelst. Wilkins. Mirroir de Justice. ch. i. sec. 3, ch. v. sec. 1.
⁷ Vide Book II. Ch. II. pp. 274. 290,

notes 3 and 4.
⁸ Vide ibid.
⁹ The authorities are very numerous to show that only free tenants or dignitaries composed the judicial members of the leet. Vide Mirroir de Justice. ch. i. sec. 3-17, ch. iv. sec. 27; 29th law of William the Conqueror; and Kelham's Notes: also Lib. Rub. in Custod. Rememb. Regis. Leges Edwardi. Wilkins. 'De Greve.' Co. 4th Inst. p. 259. Bracton, lib. iii. c. 10.

free boroughs and cities, neither villein tenants or serfs had, properly, any place as regular residents. So high were the privileges of such towns estimated, that by an ancient Saxon custom, secured to most of them by charter, the law was, that if a serf or villein fled from his master's soke, and continued unreclaimed for a year and a day within the walls of a free borough, he thereby effected his effranchisement.[1] The kind of resiancy, therefore, by which an inhabitant acquired the *full* franchises of a citizen, was that which distinguished the *freeholder, free-pledger*, or *socman* in counties; he who with his peers formed a component and judicial part of the leet: it was the resiance of a person *holding a tenement*,[2] or, according to the now long-received appellation, a *householder*. All persons above the age of twelve years were obliged annually to appear at the leet and take the oaths of allegiance, and be enrolled in frank-pledge, as living or resiant with it; but they were not *all* members of the leet for the purposes of enquiring and adjudicating upon matters occurring within the jurisdiction; they were not all *frank-pledgers*: but far the greater number were merely *in* frank-pledge, that is, pledged *for* by others. The only true and full freemen of the leet were those who had a local stake and free tenure; either magistrates, free owners of land (*terrarum domini*), or those holding something which should suffice for their frank-pledge; as dignity, station, or *in cities, immovable property*:[3] and as all tenures within London were free in their nature, it followed, that any occupation of a tenement came up to the requisition of holding it freely, which was not necessarily the case in counties.

In counties, it seems, a freeholder, though *conversant* and resiant in another county, might still exercise his rights and functions at the leet;[4] but in London, as it was from the

---

[1] This was a common privilege in most boroughs.—Vide Madox's *Firma Burgi*, p. 271; also a very ancient book of Records in the Town Clerk of London's office, entitled 'De antiquis legibus,' in which this custom is stated as existing long before the Conquest. Now, book v. p. 316.

[2] For an explanation of the quality of this *holding* or tenement, or of resiancy, vide p. 243, and Book II. Ch. IV. p. 341.

[3] 'Sicat dignitatem, vel ordinem, vel in *civitate rem immobilem*' (vide p. 98, note 9).

[4] Co. 2nd Inst. 121, on stat. of Marlebridge.

BOOK I.
A.D. 1275 to 1327.

earliest times required that the full citizen should be in *lot and scot*;[1] that is, to be ready to *sustain leet offices* in his turn, and *pay his share* towards the common civic burthens,—it may be inferred that resiancy or occupation, or being *conversant* in the leet, was another criterion of his rights.

It would seem plain, therefore, that during the early period of the civic constitution, resiancy, as a householder, formed the only requisite qualification of a free citizen. But this will appear more distinctly, if we consider the total silence of all charters, legal documents, and records, as to any other civic qualification, down to that period of the reign of Edward II. now under consideration. Inhabitancy as a *householder* is in fact still termed the *common law* qualification of burghers.[2] The invasion of the Normans, followed by the change of territorial property, the introduction of the feudal system and Norman customs, overthrew, in great measure, the political rights, and the local laws and government of counties; but the pride and distinction of the Londoners in early times consisted in the preservation of their ancient common law constitution and franchises, which were prevalent throughout all England in the days of Edward the Confessor. The Conqueror granted, in few words, that the citizens should continue, *as before*, to be law-worthy, and should retain the right of heirship; and the subsequent royal charters, until the reign of John, confer very few new and peculiar privileges, certainly none that might not, in the same language, have been conferred on the inhabitants of any county, or even upon the nation at large.

From the reign of King John to that of Edward II. we can trace no other qualification than the resiancy of a householder, noticed as characterising the free citizen; no allusion to mercantile distinctions—no *corporate* freeman's oath (the earliest of which bears internal evidence by its phraseology of a date at least as modern as Edward III.); nor any reference to a *corporate* admission to freedom: because, in fact, no

[1] Year Book. 38 Lib. Ass. p. 13. 45th Edward III. pl. 39. (Vide post, pp. 243, 384, 341) and authorities. Freeman's oath. Also a record of 38th Edward III Harg. MSS. No. 139, p. 9.

Brit. Mus. Also a record of a City law of 39th Edward III. Lib. G. p. 173; and Lib. Alb. pp. 200, 224.)

[2] Serj. Glanville's Report.

uch political body as a general town corporation, in the modern sense of the word, existed until the latter end of the reign of Richard I.¹ In short, the vigilance exercised in the City with regard to the reception of strangers, was founded on the same principles as that prevailing in the county leet; and as the *same* grounds operated in excluding persons from these political associations, so it may be presumed the *same* qualifications entitled to admission.

From the earliest times to the present period, whatever innovations have been made in regard to the characteristics of a citizen, and whatever additional qualifications have been required, it has ever been acknowledged that the only *complete* and full citizen, enjoying *all* the privileges as such, is the *householder paying scot and bearing lot*.² Usage, since the incorporation of the City, has established the requisition of enrolment as a citizen: ancient ordinances of the City have added the *mercantile* qualification: other ordinances and a statute have conferred some elective franchises on enrolled freemen who are not householders, as in the instances when liverymen vote.³ Still, however, the *scot and lot householder*, when admitted a freeman, according to civic ordinances and statutes, remains the only true and efficient citizen for *all* civic purposes.⁴ It is to him only that the many chartered rights and immunities were originally applicable, and it is to a portion only (however important) that others not resiant have, under certain civic or mercantile qualifications, been admitted: it is he only that can become, or vote for, a representative in the great corporate assembly of the common council: it is he only that can vote for the aldermen and councilmen of wards and ward officers. Such citizens alone, through their representatives in common council, with the aldermen as conjoint members of it superior in rank, and the Lord Mayor as the President, conduct the municipal

---

¹ Vide pp. 23, 64, 65, 74, note 6; and Book II. Ch. IV.
² Vide p. 100 and authorities, note 1.
³ Vide pp. 126, 243, *et seq.* Vide a series of acts of Com. Co. and stat. 11th Geo. I. c. 18.
⁴ Mayor of London v. Lynne Regis; and the numerous authorities there referred to. 1 Bos. and Pul. p. 498. Hale concerning Customs, 3rd part, ch. 3. Priv. London, p. 148; and the cases there quoted. Calthrop's Reports, p. 31; and *post*, 243, 276, 281, 331, 341.

government of the City in its legislative capacity, and constitutionally form the Corporation of the City of London.

During the absence of Richard I. in the Holy Land, and under the usurpation of his brother John, the *community*, or representative and corporate faculty of the citizens of London in general, as one body politic, took its origin. This was an association of a totally different quality from that of the leets. It was an assemblage of all the leets for general municipal purposes. It was endued with a voice, and with a political locality and rank: it became a member of the national council; it possessed common political rights; and regulated, through the medium of municipal representatives, common property and common privileges. It was natural therefore, and indeed almost necessary, that a new form of admission and enrolment into the fellowship of this grand civic body should now be adopted, and that the civic freedom should take a new and different character from that of the ancient Saxon freedom of the leet. This enrolment into the civic and corporate freedom, it seems evident, was solemnised at the great hustings court, being the highest and most dignified court of record in the City: and as such admissions are occasionally referred to as in common course so early as the reigns of Edward I. and Edward II.,[1] it may be safely inferred that such course was adopted very soon after, if not immediately upon, the foundation of the Corporation itself.

Still, however, no mention occurs of any *mercantile*, or indeed of any other qualification being required to entitle the householder to his admission into the Corporation, until the period of the regulation noticed at the beginning of this chapter: and from the language of some records of a date so recent as the reign of Edward I. and the beginning of that of Edward II., it may be concluded that no such qualification was insisted upon.[2] How this revolution in

[1] As may be seen in the charter of Edward II., an article of which has been quoted at the head of this chapter. Lib. Ordinationum, fol. 143 *et seq.* refers to this course of admission as the established mode in the time of Edward I.

[2] Lib. Ordin. fols. 113, 191, 192, where qualifications are spoken of, as by swearing, by apprenticeship, or by admission by full commonalty: and, again, the *commons* of London are termed 'aussi bien *terres tenants* quo *moebles*' (owners of personal property).

the quality of civic freedoms—a revolution which gradually overspread most of the town corporations in England—arose, is a subject well deserving of some further consideration and enquiry. This revolution appears, in a political point of view, the greatest inroad upon the genuine principles of the English Constitution which has ever been made. Its effects operate to a most important degree at the present hour; and it has been said that the corporate borough system, as it is called—of which the exercise of the elective franchise for members of Parliament by *corporation* freemen forms a prominent feature, and which this change in the nature of civic freedoms was a main cause of introducing—must, if not skilfully attempered, in the gradual progress of corruption, one day overwhelm the British Constitution.[1]

It is obvious that the very essence of any civic association (except where individuals unite for the mere purpose of defence) is trade. The support of citizens must altogether depend on commerce and proficiency in the mechanical arts. It would seem, therefore, but a natural result of the first formation of town corporate communities, that the members should approve themselves as sustaining some commercial character. With regard to the City of London and other English town corporations, as the civic qualifications by resiancy were already fixed by law, and notorious, we must look for some more direct and immediate source for that which became the essential characteristic of the citizen; and enough may be gathered from the early history of civic communities, to enable us to trace with some plausibility the origin of this additional requisition.

The existence of mercantile gilds in England cannot be traced to so early a period as that of the territorial, which were common during the Saxon era. It seems reasonable to believe that the former took their rise from the latter, and that they were introduced from the continent by the Normans. These mercantile gilds were very common long before

---

[1] By the great Reform Act of 2nd & 3rd William IV. the voters for all new boroughs then created, are required to be occupiers paying rates. By the recent Act of 1867, the voters for *all* boroughs must be householders paying rates. The author has not thought it to alter the original text advocating these constitutional principles. Vide *post*, 243 *et seq*.

the reign of Edward II.¹ They were, in truth, combinations for the purpose of regulating and monopolising the respective trades in which each society was conversant. It is generally admitted that these associations originated on the continent;² of which the term *mysteries*, by which appellation they were as commonly denominated, gives some assurance. They derived their constitution and monopolous privileges, both in England and abroad, either from the express or implied sanction of those needy princes who, endued with very political foresight, were open to the temptation of large bribes for such concessions.³ By degrees, most of the larger towns in Europe, and more especially on the continent, became altogether occupied by these commercial subdivisions:⁴ and during the reign of Henry II. these gilds had increased to such an extent in London, that their evil tendency became obvious to that wary prince, and many of them were abolished;⁵ though more, it may be presumed, remained. In the end, when entire town corporations were founded, in professed imitation, as it is said,⁶ of the old gildated associations, or territorial gilds, it may be easily concluded that the influence of the *mercantile* gilds, or, as they are now termed, *companies* (absorbing as they did almost the whole bulk of the civic population), would be powerfully exercised in regulating the constitution of the new civic body.

The immediate and prominent object of these gildated communities was, the establishment and preservation of their exclusive privileges of trade. Their natural interests directed them to restrain the number of competitors, and enhance the value of their merchandise. Many were the by-laws and regulations by which these interests were secured; but none were so decisively effectual as those by which long *apprenticeships* were ordained.⁷ The scion thus grafted upon the stock of monopoly was, like the parent plant itself, originally of foreign growth; but very soon became in most mercantile

---

¹ Madox's Firma Burgi, ch. i.
² Ibid.; and Smith's Wealth of Nations, book i, ch. x. part 2.
³ Ibid.; and Robertson's Charles V. vol. i. p. 36.
⁴ Ibid.
⁵ Vide p. 59.
⁶ Madox's Firma Burgi, ch. i.; and *supra*, p. 25, note 2.
⁷ Smith's Wealth of Nations, book i. ch. x. part 2.

corporations in England the only branch which produced the fruit of civic freedom. It is remarkable, however, that although service by apprenticeship became by degrees the regular and more usual path to enfranchisement in London, this burthensome progress was never universally established amongst the trading companies, or as of absolute necessity in the civic corporation itself. Any inhabitant, or even stranger, might, and may still, be admitted a member of many, if not most, of the companies; and also to the freedom of the City by virtue of his title by birth or patrimony; or he might become a candidate for admission either by donation or upon a pecuniary payment usually exacted on such occasions.[1] In the latter case he became free by what was termed *redemption*; an expression implying the purchased acquisition of the more authentic title.[2]

What materially contributed to impose a trading character on the Corporation of London, was the granting so many peculiarly commercial privileges to the citizens by the charters. As these privileges could only be enjoyed by persons engaged in trade, or in other words the members of the companies, the grant of them would naturally lead to the conclusion, that the civic body was to be considered as one concentrated *mercantile* gild, composed of many gildated subdivisions; instead of a concentration of *territorial* gilds or leets, which, in a political and more constitutional sense, it really was.[3] The City being engrossed by the members of the various trading companies, it was obviously their joint interest to exclude from the participation of their chartered monopolies those who had not earned or paid for their fellowship in one or other of their associations. By these means not only was the number limited and competition restrained, but the more immediate advantages of the services or purchase-money of the candidates were gained. It is not to be doubted that in these early and unsettled times, the good government and

[1] Mayor of London v. Lyme. 1 Ros. and Pul. p. 496; and the numerous cases on that subject. Calth. Rep. Prisage case, p. 31. 3 Rubtrale 4 and 9. Harg. Law Tracts. Hale on Customs, part 3, ch. ii.; and Lib. Ordin. fol. 143.
[2] Vide last note.
[3] Vide p. 25, note 2.

well ordering of the whole community formed a more honest inducement on the minds of many; and it is therefore not surprising that what good policy and self-interest combined to suggest, the authority and power of those influenced should carry into execution.

This revolution in the original character of the civic community was neither affected suddenly, nor does it seem to have sprung immediately from the establishment of its corporate quality. In the reign of King John, apprenticeship service does not appear to have been common, if indeed it had been introduced at all in England. It is probable it came into general use during the succeeding reign of Henry III., for apprentices both to trades and to the law are noticed in records of the reign of Edward I. It was then the custom to enroll apprentices into the freedom upon the expiration of their service; though it is plain from the same records which testify this as an approved course, that such service was not the *only* course of obtaining admission, nor indeed that it conveyed an absolute title to the franchise.[1] Enrolment was a positive requisite;[2] but it seems clear both from the language of the records last noticed, and from that of the article quoted at the beginning of this chapter, that a title to enrolment might, previous to this charter of Edward II., have been gained, not only independently of any apprenticeship, but independently of any trade; and it is fair to conclude, as resiancy was the original title to enfranchisement, and as no earlier trace can be found of that additional mercantile qualification required by the express enactment of the article just noticed, that such qualification was neither constitutionally essential, nor of long previous introduction.

It has been already observed, that those invested with the bare corporate or mercantile freedom are still not *complete* and *full* citizens. The only full citizens, capable of exercising *every* civic function and of enjoying *every* chartered privilege

---

[1] Lib. Ordin. fol. 143; where titles to admission are spoken of as by birth, or by apprenticeship, or by donation of the full commonalty; and fols. 191, 192, where '*terres tenants*' are spoken of as citizens.

[2] Stat. Civit. Lond. Edw. I. cap. 13.

and right, is he that is clothed with the ancient and original common law qualification as a resiant householder,[1] as well as the corporate or mercantile franchise. A word, therefore, may be added as to the nature of the bare *corporate* freeman's franchise. Apart from the privilege of engaging in trade, within the civic limits (a privilege which he could hardly exercise without becoming a householder), it is in fact a mere inchoate right. Some few other unimportant privileges, not of a political character, but purely of an internal and municipal nature, he might legally enjoy; but in other respects, until the freeman became a householder, and paid *scot* and bore *lot*, mere freemanship was but a nominal distinction, and conferred no positive advantage. There was, accordingly, always an acknowledged difference between those citizens who were *dotati* (endowed), or even *inquilini* (mere inhabitants), though not admitted to the corporate franchise, and those who were citizens *re et nomine*[2] (both in fact and in name); and although from the uncertainty which prevailed in early times as to the constitutional quality of a free citizen, it is probable that the bare corporation admission may have been considered, for a season, as co-extensive with the civic franchise of the actual residents, when admitted to the corporation freedom, it is certain that such impression must have been very soon corrected; and that neither elective nor chartered franchises have ever been successfully claimed, under that corporate title alone, since the reign of Edward III. The statute of 11th Geo. I. cap. 18, bestowed on the corporate freeman, though not a resiant householder upon taking up his company's *livery*, all those important elective franchises exercised in Common Hall: but, originating as that Act did, in times of dispute and turbulence, and hastily and inconsiderately carried by a party, it evinced a most manifest violation, in that respect, of the original and genuine political constitution of the City.[3] There will be occasion to revert to this topic in a subsequent page.[4]

CHAP. VI.

A.D. 1272 to 1327.

[1] Vide pp. 99, 100; and authorities quoted in notes.
[2] Vide ibid.
[3] For the discussions and progress of this bill, vide 1 Maitland, p. 534 *et seq.*; also the City Journals of disputed elections from 1710 to 1734.
[4] Vide Ch. XII. p. 243 *et seq.*

CHAPTER VII.

FROM THE ACCESSION OF EDWARD III. TO THAT OF HENRY VII.

BOOK I.
A.D. 1327 to 1377.

THE reign of Edward III. began with the most auspicious indications of royal regard and protection; for in the very first year an important charter was granted, not only confirming in the most ample manner those of his predecessors, but adding many immunities of peculiar value to the citizens. Of these we shall have occasion to speak hereafter. It will be pertinent, however, to notice, that tallages were again by this charter prohibited, and the numerous abuses of *purveyance* strictly denounced. This grievance of *purveyance* had arisen out of the circumstances of the times; and as it was a subject of perpetual complaint in the City, it may be as well perhaps to give some account of the practice. Originally, the royal household was supplied with all articles of consumption from those extensive demesnes which long before and subsequent to the time of the Conqueror belonged to the Crown.[1] Afterwards, when, in consequence of the large alienations of the Crown property, provisions from the demesnes began to fall short, while in the meantime money became more common, a market was held at the palace gate, under the regulation of an officer of the king, for the purchase of whatever articles might be requisite.[2] In the many royal progresses, however, which were made with a very numerous retinue,[3] this mode of supply by an attendant market gradu-

---

[1] Co. 2nd Inst. pp. 542, 543.
[2] Ibid.
[3] This retinue, it would seem, claimed to be entertained at their discretion in the houses adjacent to the place wherever the king might be—for in an ancient book of the Liberties of London called Lib. Horne, which was written in the time of Edward II. after noticing (fol. 230) the privilege (which is amply confirmed by charter) that none of the king's court should take lodgings by

ally became defective, and officers called *purveyors* started up who ranged about, levying contributions from all parts adjacent to the king's domicile, wherever it might happen to be [1]—a practice soon imitated by the powerful barons.[2] Still, by law, the king's prerogative in this particular was so far restrained, that he had no right to take anything without first agreeing with the proprietor for the price, or, otherwise, paying the current price of the market.[3] As may naturally be surmised, in violent and tyrannical times this privilege was exercised in a most grievous and oppressive manner.[4] Sometimes purveyors paid nothing for the property seized;[5] sometimes they paid too little;[6] they constantly made a profit of their authority, by embezzlement,[7] or by the sale of their protection; and it was by no means uncommon for persons to act as purveyors without any warrant.[8] The regulation and restriction of this vexatious prerogative became a constant object of anxiety with the people, and it formed an important feature in the Great Charter itself. In subsequent reigns many statutes passed with the same views, amounting to no less than forty-eight in number; the chief of which was that of 30th Edward III. cap. 2: but the practice was not finally and completely abolished till the restoration of Charles II., when this tyrannical right was purchased from the Crown by Parliament.

England enjoyed under the government of Edward a longer period of domestic tranquillity than it had been blest with at any former period. Throughout his reign parliaments were frequently summoned, and he affected to consult them upon all important occasions: at the latter end of his life, this assembly took upon itself to remonstrate with him

---

force, or without the host's permission; it is added, that if any person were killed in the attempt, the host might clear himself, by the oath of any six, that he slew him for such cause. A curious illustration both of the state of the law, and the manners of the times.— Vide infra, Book II. Ch. II. p. 267.

[1] Co. 2nd Inst. pp. 512, 543.
[2] Ibid. pp. 33, 170.
[3] Ibid. p. 543, Artic. Sup.Chart. cap. 2.

[4] Vide the list of statutes passed in consequence of complaints and remonstrances on this topic under the heads 'Protections,' 'Purveyance,' Cotton's Abr. Index.
[5] Artic. Sup. Chart. cap. 2. Co. 2nd Inst. pp. 542, 543.
[6] Ibid.
[7] Ibid.
[8] Ibid.

about a mistress he kept, and he was obliged to remove her from Court.¹ The authority of Parliament, however, was by no means settled on a firm and certain basis; for on one occasion when it passed an act,² even sanctioned by the king's dissembled consent, by which he was to be put in a great measure under the tutelage of a council, Edward, as soon as he had procured a vote of money, at once annulled it of his own authority, as contrary to the law of the land and his prerogative. But afterwards, when freed from his necessities, he obtained from another parliament a legal repeal of this obnoxious statute.³ It must be confessed that, in respect of pecuniary supplies also, many arbitrary impositions were resorted to, contrary to the known law of the land,⁴ from which, under the pressure of urgent necessity, the king still thought himself authorised to deviate.⁵

Nevertheless, taxes were for the most part furnished by regular parliamentary grants; and in a war so successful and glorious to the national arms as that by which France was overrun, they were cheerfully supplied to a very enormous amount.⁶ Amongst other modes of raising supplies for this war, the king issued a writ to the sheriffs of London, commanding them to require every citizen possessed of tenements of the value of 40l. per annum to take upon himself the order of knighthood—a ceremony which the king well knew would be compromised for by a fine. The citizens resisted the order, on the ground of their tenure being by free burgage, and not by knight's-service; a plea which seems to have been too well founded and clear not to be ac-

¹ Hume's Hist. Thos. Wals. p. 180.
² 15th Edward III.
³ Cotton's Abridgment, pp. 38, 39.
⁴ Ibid. pp. 38, 39, where many instances are collected together with remonstrances of the Parliament upon the subject.
⁵ Ibid. p. 138.
⁶ Statutes at Large: Edward III. A singular testimony exists on record, both of the popularity of the French wars, in which so much of the nation's blood and treasure was expended, and of the estimation in which the citizens,

who, it may be presumed, contributed a great share of both, were held. Edward the Black Prince wrote a letter to the Mayor, Aldermen, and Commonalty, informing them of his heroic victory and describing the battle of Poictiers. It is inserted among the City Records, Lib. G. fol. 53 b. [This interesting document is printed amongst the Illustrations to 'A Chronicle of London from 1089 to 1483,' 4to. 1827, p. 204, published by the Editor, Mr. Tyrrell, who, in the absence of the author, edited the first edition.]

quiesced in.¹ It would therefore be a great mistake to suppose that in this reign, productive as it was of many enactments calculated to protect the rights and liberties of the subject, the constitution and the administration of the government had arrived at any such stage of perfection as has been often alleged: and, if any further proof were wanting to justify a contrary conclusion, it may be obviously inferred from the circumstance of the Great Charter having been confirmed no less than twenty times;² which could hardly have happened but in consequence of occasional and palpable infringements.

The dispensation of criminal justice was conducted throughout this reign comparatively upon a regular system; and upon the same principles as at the present day. Inquisitions were taken by jury in most cases which affected the life or liberty of the subject, before trial;³ and though, with respect to the punishment of offences and the jurisdictions under which they were enquired into, great changes have since been made, yet every man could at least be sure of having all accusations against him duly heard and decided upon by his peers; and the iniquitous system of punishing by amercement upon the mere inquisition or presentment of a leet or Eyre jury without trial, was seldom resorted to except in respect of the most trivial offences of a public character, or in cases of abuse of power in magistrates.⁴ Even the attainder of Mortimer, which had been sanctioned by Parliament, and whose violent usurpations of the royal prerogatives were notorious, was nevertheless in the twentieth year of Edward's reign solemnly repealed, as having taken place

---

¹ The writ and the return are quoted at length in Maitland, vol. i. p. 127, but he does not mention his authority.

² Hume's Hist. Edward III.

³ This appears evident from a variety of commissions directed to the judges and the civic authorities, to enquire into offences by oath of jury, and to detain or try those accused by them according to the king's further direction. Rec. Turr. Pat. 2nd Edward III. p. 2, m. 11. Ibid. in dorso, where the inquisitions taken are directed to be tried and determined. The jurisdiction of the Star Chamber, and the power of instituting ex officio informations, seem hardly to have been known, much less acted upon, in these times; though said to be as old as the common law itself.—Vide Shower's Rep. vol. i. p. 108; Blacks. Comm. vol. iv. p. 309.

⁴ Vide p. 80 and notes; and post. 292, 351.

without his being regularly arraigned. The citizens seem to have been engaged in continual disputes with the king's justices respecting their authority to take inquisitions within the walls of the City, and to summon the citizens without the walls to any inquisition; and for the most part the citizens prevailed in obtaining the royal sanction of their exclusive privileges in that respect. Their rights were now better ascertained, in regard to their own criminal jurisdiction, than at the time when the institution of justices in Eyre was a matter of novelty; for, whether from the continual disorders which prevailed in London, or from a desire on the part of the king to show respect to the civic authorities, or from a deference to the chartered rights of the citizens to a specific criminal jurisdiction, the lord mayor was by charter constituted one of the judges of Oyer and Terminer and gaol-delivery for the gaol of Newgate.³ During the king's absence in France, the lord mayor together with the aldermen were commissioned specially to enquire into and speedily punish those who had been guilty of some flagrant riots:⁴ an authority which the mayor exercised with such promptitude and rigour, as to try in a very summary manner and immediately behead two of the principal offenders. But, however well justified this magistrate might have conceived himself in such a measure from the urgent necessity of the case, it is evident that it was considered an unwarrantable stretch of power; for the king thought it incumbent on him, in approving the act, to grant an indemnity to the mayor from the consequences which might arise from it.⁵ Many statutes

---

³ Cotton's Abridgment, pp. 85, 86.
⁴ Hollinshed's Chron. A.D. 1341, and Lib. Horne, fol. 302; in which is recorded a petition to the king, upon the subject of the steward of his household drawing citizens *out of* the City to be impleaded before him; which was accordingly forbidden, and inquisitions directed to be always taken within the City for facts arising there. It is also stated in Lib. Horne, fol. 230 (written in the time of Edward II.), that it was an ancient privilege of the citizens, that they should not be bound to answer the king or any other by him appointed, *without* the walls of the City. This privilege seems to be confirmed, rather than granted, by charter of Henry I.; but it must be considered as a private and *personal* privilege of individuals.
⁵ Edward III.'s charter, *anno primo*. This may be rather looked upon as a compromise than a grant; for, strictly speaking, the right of the citizens to a criminal jurisdiction is by charter of Hen. 1, *exclusive*.—Vide Book II. Ch. II.
⁴ Rymer's Fœdera.
⁵ Maitland's Hist. vol. i. p. 126, Rec. Turr.

afterwards passed, in which the systematic mode for taking inquisitions for offences was regulated; and in particular that of 18th Edw. III. cap. 1, enacted that no commissions of new enquiries should issue.¹

It has been generally supposed that during the reign of Edward III. foreign commerce made rapid advances in England; but there is little foundation for that belief. It is true that Edward passed many laws for the encouragement of manufactures and trade, and particularly that of woollen cloths,² which in all probability had a very considerable effect in extending the *internal* commerce of the kingdom. Many of these laws, however, were of a very injudicious tendency as far as regarded foreign commerce; and among the most prominent of them are to be reckoned those fixing the staples or established markets to which all goods of a particular class were to be brought. One law was made to prohibit all woollen goods, leather, and felts, being brought to any other staple than that of Calais;³ a measure which, however well adapted to the prosperity of that single city, was a manifest hindrance to the advancement of the general export commerce of the kingdom. At the commencement of the reign of Richard II. a complaint was made in Parliament, that the shipping had so grievously decayed during this reign, that, in consequence of the continual seizure of vessels, the whole kingdom did not contain the number formerly to be seen in one sea-port.⁴ It was the policy of Edward to excite a manufacturing spirit amongst his own subjects, and to direct their attention to learn the arts and manufactures carried on in neighbouring countries; a policy which, although highly beneficial to the progress of the national trade eventually,

---

¹ Statutes at Large.
² 11th Edward III. cap. 5.; Rymer's Fœdera, vol. iv. p. 723; 11th Edward III. cap. 2; Acts passed to encourage the settlement of foreign weavers, and to prevent the wearing of any cloth but of English fabric; and many others in the *Statutes at Large*.
³ By 27th Edward III. cap. 7. Another grant of a monopolising staple was expressly bestowed in consideration of the declining state of that town.—Rymer's Fœdera, vol. vii. p. 116.
⁴ Cotton's Abridgment of the Records, pp. 155, 164. Edward III. had such success in establishing woollen manufactures in England, that it became no longer necessary either to export the raw wool or to import it when manufactured, which till his time was the constant course. To a certain extent, therefore, foreign commerce would decrease in proportion to the increase of the internal trade.

would in its *immediate* effects, by reducing the exports of the raw material and the imports of the same when converted into manufactures, have a tendency to diminish rather than increase foreign trade. The people would thus be rendered more independent of foreign supplies, but it would require some time to rival established manufactories in a general course of trade. With a view to this policy, Edward gave the greatest possible encouragement to the settlement of foreign artificers; and this measure was carried to such an extent, and so suddenly, as to occasion the most melancholy decay of some of the cities in which they were previously established. Many complaints were made by the City of London,[1] whose ancient privileges were violated by the introduction of these merchant strangers.[2] But, though the privileges were acknowledged, and in one charter expressly reserved from the operation of the statutes allowing the free trade and residence of foreigners in all parts of the kingdom,[3] complete restrictions against the invasion of them were not obtained till the subsequent reign, when all dealings carried on between foreigner and foreigner within the City of London were emphatically prohibited.[4]

The reign of Richard II. is a remarkable era in the annals of the Corporation, as we must refer to this period the constitution of the City government as at present established in the Commonalty in Common Council assembled. Many abortive efforts had been made from time to time in and since the reign of Edward I. for the election, or selection, of particular citizens to act for the whole body, and for convening them for the purpose of conducting the legislative and municipal government of the City. In the 20th year of Edward III. a representative plan of government was more formally attempted through an ordinance passed in the assembly of the citizens at large, by which it was enacted, that each ward, at the annual wardmote, should choose a certain number, *eight*, *six*, or *four*, according to its size, who were to be summoned, as occasion required, *to deliberate* con-

---

[1] Charter of 50th Edward III. Cotton's Abridgment of the Records, p. 111. Cottonian MSS. App. 11. Brit. Mus. And 1st Charter of Richard II.

[2] City of London Case, Coke's Rep. vol. viii. p. 251.

[3] Charter of 11th Edward III.

[4] Charters of 1st and 7th Richard II. Cottonian MSS. Records, Appendix 11. fols. 294, 406. Brit. Mus.

cerning the common interest of the City.¹ By the same ordinance it was provided, that a certain number only, *twelve, eight*, or *six*, from each ward, according to its size, should come to the respective assemblies for *electing* the Lord Mayor, the sheriffs, various other corporate officers, and members to serve in Parliament; and that none but those especially summoned for that purpose should attend. From which it may be collected, that the *elections* to such corporate offices and of representatives in Parliament were to be made by a different body from that which was summoned to meet as a Common Council on behalf of the Citizens at large for deliberative purposes.² This arrangement seems to have occasioned some abuses; for, in the 49th year of Edward's reign, a special meeting of a great number of the chief citizens was called together, who passed an ordinance, by which, after noticing the many complaints made of the discretionary power assumed by the lord mayor and aldermen, in *selecting* out of those chosen and delegated at the wardmote to be Common Councilmen, those who were to be in fact *summoned* to Common Councils,³ it was ordained, that the members of Common Council should be nominated in future by the *trading companies* instead of the wards; and that the *same* persons, so nominated as Common Councilmen, and none others, should be summoned to attend *both* at Common Councils and at elections.⁴ Great confusion, however, and irregularity seems still to have prevailed, both at the meeting of Common Council and at elections, at which the citizens at large still persisted in interfering. At length, after many consultations on the subject, the *deliberative* assembly was again detached from that convened for *elections* to the above mentioned corporate offices and of parliamentary representatives; and it was finally arranged in the 7th year of the reign of Richard II., by an

CHAP. VII.

A.D. 1377 to 1422.

---

¹ Lib. Leg. F. ultimo fol. 5 b. Town Clerk's Office.
² Vide p. 88, where it may be seen that this was in all probability the case before.
³ This had been the usual course for a great number of years; and there is nothing in the ordinance of 20th Edward III. from which it may be collected that the exercise of this discretion in regard to the summoning particular Common Councilmen, as representatives of the rest of the community, however illegal in its commencement, was considered irregular, or was meant to be circumscribed.
⁴ Vide Ordinance in Lib. Leg. fol. 25 b.

ordinance of the whole community, or '*immensa communitas,*' specially called together for that purpose, that, in regard to the *former,* the election of Common Councilmen should be again restored to the wards; and that four persons should be annually elected at the wardmote for each ward (since increased to larger numbers, according to the growing population of the respective wards), who should be the regular standing representatives of the whole body of citizens upon all common and corporate occasions of a deliberative nature.[1] Since this ordinance, the citizens at large have entirely ceased to meet in a *legislative,* and also in a corporate capacity, except with respect to their several assemblies in Common Hall for *elections* to corporate offices and to serve in Parliament; which latter assemblies, not being affected by the ordinance of the 7th Richard II., continued to be convened under that of 49th Edward III. for eighty-four years longer, according to the special summons of the lord mayor, out of those *nominated* for such purpose by the *trading companies.*[2] This course of specially summoning out of those nominated as electors by the trading companies, conflicts with this ordinance of 49th Edward III., which provides that the *same* persons as thus nominated for attendance at Common Councils, should attend at elections in the Common Hall. But such course more or less prevailed from the time of Edward I. till the Act of Common Council of 15th Edward IV. appointed specifically the *liverymen* only of the companies to attend.

Although the whole kingdom, during the greater part of the reign of Richard II. was a scene of turbulence and misgovernment—the latter occasioned chiefly by the disputes between him and his barons, who appear on each side to have been guilty of unconstitutional oppressions—yet the citizens of London had no cause to complain that their rights and privileges were not duly respected. The charters granted by this monarch were peculiarly liberal; and we may judge of the consideration in which the citizens were held, from the circumstance, that in the assessment of the famous poll tax which gave rise to Wat Tyler's rebellion, the

[1] Lib. Leg. II. fol. 173.
[2] Acts of Common Council. 7th and 15th Edward IV. Lib. Leg. L. 53, fol. 98; also that of 15th Edward IV. Lib. Leg. I. fol. 113. And vide *infra,* p. 120.

lord mayor ranked as an earl and the aldermen as barons.¹ It is related of one of the latter, by name Philpot, that he, at his own private expense, fitted out a fleet of vessels containing a thousand men, and sailed with them, for the purpose of attacking a pirate who had long infested the coast and had made very numerous captures. The gallant citizen was completely successful in his expedition, and returned to the City in triumph after taking or destroying the whole of the enemy's ships.² He was afterwards questioned by the King's Council on the subject: but it nevertheless affords a striking proof both of the wealth and personal importance of an individual in undertaking and executing an enterprise of so national a character.

The part which the citizens acted on the occasion of Wat Tyler's insurrection, and the exploit of the lord mayor Walworth in killing, or at least assisting in the destruction of the rebel chief, in the very presence of his army, are too well known to need repetition here.³ But it may be remarked, that the walls and military strength of the City were at this time of such a description as to be capable of resisting even the overwhelming force which Tyler commanded, and which is estimated at 100,000 men. His first efforts failed to give him an entrance; and he succeeded at last in gaining a peaceable admission only by threatening to ravage with fire and sword the adjacent suburbs.⁴ It may also be noticed, that one of the main articles which the rebels insisted upon was, that all people, whether strangers or not, should be at liberty to sell and buy freely in all cities and boroughs;⁵ which shows that the exclusive privileges of the citizens in this particular were at this time notorious and ascertained.

The reign of Richard II. is particularly distinguished by his having refrained from any attempt to levy direct taxes on the people without the consent of Parliament.⁶ But the

CHAP. VII.
A.D. 1377 to 1422.

¹ Cotton's Abridgment of the Records.
² Thos. Wals. Hist. Angl.
³ Vide note p. 366 as to the mode of Walworth's exploit in killing Wat Tyler.
⁴ Thos. Wals. Hist. Angl. Froissart's Chronicle.
⁵ Ibid. It will be seen hereafter how these principles of free internal trade, as advocated by Tyler and his followers, have been recognised by the citizens themselves, and their exclusive trading privileges almost altogether abandoned voluntarily by the Corporation. Vide post, p. 194.
⁶ Hume.

Parliament being then much under the influence of a nobility bent on circumscribing the king's authority, were little disposed to encourage the king's lavish expenditure, and he was accordingly reduced to employ such indirect means of obtaining supplies, as tended ultimately to deprive him of his crown. The citizens of London had been often applied to by the king for loans of money; and such was the independent tone which the state of the government enabled them to assume, that in one or two instances they refused compliance.[1] The king, in great indignation, took measures for seizing the liberties of the City, as forfeited in consequence, as was pretended, of some riot, and, according to the usual practice, proceeded to exact large sums of money by way of ransom.[2] In many instances afterwards, on one pretence or other, gross expedients of extortion were resorted to; and particularly on one occasion, he compelled many of the principal citizens to sign and seal blank grants of money, which he filled up at his discretion.[3] This arbitrary conduct so completely lost Richard the affection of the Londoners, that upon the landing of the Duke of Hereford (afterwards Henry IV.) in Yorkshire, he was instantly invited to the City; and was consequently enabled to present so formidable an aspect to Richard, that the latter had no other resource than to resign his crown[4]—a resignation which was soon followed by his death.

Richard was the last monarch who assumed, for the *individual* offences of the magistrates or others, to seize into his own hands the liberties of the City;[5] for the well known forfeiture in Charles II.'s time was grounded on corporate acts of the *whole body* of citizens. It had been expressly provided by the 1st charter of Edward III., that no forfeiture should be incurred by any *individual* misconduct, and that the parties offending, only, should be responsible for their respective acts; but it had been so long the practice of preceding kings to seize on the City liberties at their

[1] Walsing. Hist. Angl.
[2] Ibid. Fabian's Chron. p. 7. Rymer's Fœdera. Madox's Firma Burgi.
[3] Ibid.
[4] Tyrrell's Gen. Hist. Eng. MSS. in bib. Lamb. Froissart's Chron.
[5] Pollexfen's Argument in the Quo Warranto case.

own discretion, that Richard had the less hesitation in following their example. They were, however, on this occasion immediately restored;[1] though not without the usual compromise of a sum of money, which was indeed the real, though not the ostensible cause of such frequent invasions of the corporate privileges. There can be no doubt that most, if not all, of these seizures of the civic liberties were contrary to the principles of law even as then established. At first, upon these occasions of forfeiture, the kings of England seem to have appointed governors over the City, and to have levied contributions in the way of fine arbitrarily; and though, afterwards, there was usually the form of a judicial trial observed, and a judgment recorded of the cause of forfeiture (more particularly by the justices in Eyre), yet it seems to have been assumed as a right vested in the king's prerogative, to decide what should amount to such forfeiture of the franchise[2]—a prerogative which the king certainly never had a right to exercise.[3] Indeed, it is powerfully urged in the argument of Pollexfen in the Quo Warranto case, that these seizures took place in times of trouble and confusion, and can never be drawn into precedent as legal authorities.

In the many troubles which attended the usurpation of Henry IV., the citizens continued faithfully to adhere to his interests; and we may form no incompetent judgment of the important influence their attachment had in securing his throne, when we learn that in the beginning of his reign, a most powerful insurrection, headed by the first noblemen of the kingdom, was suppressed almost solely by the citizens, who, at a moment's warning, furnished Henry with the major part of 20,000 men. From the suddenness with which 6,000 men were supplied at the very first intimation of the king's impending danger, it would appear that such was the constant force kept up at this time by the civic authorities.[4] In return for such timely and valuable support, the king granted the City, both in and out of Parliament, some very indulgent

---

[1] Rymer's Fœdera.
[2] Vide the records of the various appointments of custodes of the City, and the various forfeitures of the liberties.—Madox's *Firma Burgi*, Index 'London,' Henry II.
[3] Rex v. Amory. Term Reports, vol. ii. p. 515.
[4] De Word. ad Polyc. Wals. Hist. Hall. Chron.

BOOK I.
A.D. 1377 to 1422.

charters; and testified an anxious desire to preserve their privileges inviolate.[1] In particular, with regard to merchant strangers, their liberty of free trade by *wholesale* with other strangers which had been conferred on them first by Edward III., and which, as contrary to the civic rights and customs, had occasioned continual jealousies and disputes, was in the 9th year of his reign finally taken away, and such wholesale trading restricted to that between them and citizens.[2] Nevertheless, Henry seems to have been disposed to encourage the settlement of foreign traders, as far as he could consistently with the welfare, or claims, of the Londoners; for an act was passed in the 7th year of his reign, by virtue of which Italian merchants were allowed to provide lodgings for themselves at their own discretion, instead of being billeted out by the citizens themselves.[3] This custom of providing all merchant strangers with lodgings, as well as that of limiting their residence to forty days, appears by the old corporation books to have been of long standing, and till the reign of Edward III. constantly exercised.[4] After that period, in consequence of the free trade opened by him throughout the City, the merchants gradually acquired a firmer footing within the walls; especially as some foreign companies, who by royal charters and the concession of the citizens themselves, had been long previously settled, began at that time to exercise a very considerable traffic.[5] But the custom of billeting out the merchant strangers did not

[1] Charter 1st Henry IV. Act of 9th Henry IV. cap. 1. Rot. Turr. Cotton's Abridgment.
[2] Ibid.
[3] This Act is quoted in Anderson's Hist. of Commerce; vol. i. p. 383, and in Maitland, vol. i. p. 184. And vide *infra*, Book II. Ch. II.
[4] Liber Albus. Lib. Horne. Petitions in parliaments Edward III., Richard II., and Henry IV. Statuta de Civitate Lond. 13th Edward I. Calthorpe's Usages, &c. &c. The true origin of this restriction in regard to the residence of strangers is to be traced perhaps to the laws of Alfred, who ordained that no man should be suffered to reside in England above forty days without being enrolled in some tithing or decennary (Blackst. Comm. vol. i. p. 114; Mirroir de Justice, cap. 1. sec. 3, cap. 5, sec. 1). And that no foreign merchant should stay in the land beyond forty days (ibid. LL. Athelst. cap. ii.; and vide *supra*, 20, and notes).
[5] The Hanse, French, Italian, and other foreign merchants, who had, some of them, settled and been incorporated as early as Henry III.'s reign.—Anderson's *History of Commerce*. passim; Northouck's *History of London*; Rymer's *Foedera*, vol. v. p. 105; and vide *infra*, Ch. IX. p. 150 et seq.

entirely cease for some time after this period; as we find several acts passed from the reign of Henry IV. to that of Henry VII., by which this practice was directed to be observed throughout all the towns in England.¹ It is to be understood that, at this period and for many subsequent reigns, all wholesale dealing was carried on in the public open markets, and was not allowed to be conducted elsewhere.²

In the time of Henry IV. and of his son Henry V., we trace many indications of the prosperous and improving condition of the metropolis. So valuable, indeed, were the privileges enjoyed by citizens, and so much had the interests of trade advanced, that Henry IV. passed a law to repress the avidity of the inferior classes to become apprentices. The statute, after complaining of the want of husbandry labourers, by reason of the peasants becoming bound to learn trades in the cities and boroughs, and the consequent impoverishment of the nobility, enacts, that none shall so put their children out as apprentices who are not possessed of land to the amount of 20s. per annum.³ At this period Guildhall was built;⁴ which building, though it has in subsequent times been frequently beautified by external and internal decorations, and more particularly after the great fire of London, still rests on the same ancient foundation. The walls of the City were kept in a regular and complete state of repair; and care was taken to preserve a wide and clear ditch round the whole area, so as to render the fortifications the more complete⁵—an object which we may believe at this period was of some consequence, as we find that a new gate

¹ Stat. 5th Henry IV., cap. 9. And Stow, book v. p. 205.
² This is sufficiently apparent from the many acts of Common Council against forestalling goods coming to market; those establishing public warehouses, which expressly state that all goods of merchant strangers had been used to be sold openly in markets; the many statutes passed beginning in the time of Edward III., fixing the staples; a proclamation of Elizabeth (Rymer's Fœdera, vol. xvi. p. 213,), regulating in which markets the various goods should be sold in London. Player and Hutchins, Harg. MSS. Brit. Mus. No. 56, p. 23, in which Sir O. Bridgman says that the public open markets were the only places for strangers to sell in; also Stat. 1st and 2nd Phil. and Mary, cap. 7; and Anderson's *History of Commerce*, passim.
³ Stat. 7th Hen. IV. cap. 17. This statute was repealed as regards the citizens of London by 8th Henry VI. cap. 11.
⁴ Fabian's Chronicle. Mait. vol. i. p. 185.
⁵ Ibid. p. 186. Stow's Survey.

was built in the reign of Henry V.¹ The streets were now, for the first time, under the direction of the lord mayor, lighted at night by public lanterns;² from whence we may justly infer that the internal police of the City was under tolerably good regulation.

It is remarked by Hume, that during the reigns of the Lancastrian princes, the authority of Parliament seems to have been more confirmed, and the privileges of the people more regarded, than during any former period: an observation which appears justified by the history of the times. Nothing, indeed, could more contribute to such influence than a doubtful title to the throne, while occupied by men of spirit and abilities, or the minority and personal weakness of a subsequent monarch who claimed by a more regular succession. Accordingly, we find that, from the accession of Henry VI., the Parliament assumed almost the whole prerogatives of government; and throughout the contests between the Lancastrian dynasty and that of the House of York, its concurrence was courted and appealed to by both parties. Upon the death of Henry V., totally disregarding that monarch's own destination, it gave a new arrangement to the whole administration.³ The policy pursued by Parliament during the progress of the ensuing reign was directed, still more decidedly, to weaken the king's authority, and to detract from his dignity and predominance. Although vast sums were necessarily required in the French wars, and in keeping possession of those conquered countries which the nation were as little disposed as the Court to resign; yet the Parliament were neither willing to aid, in the first instance, the very inadequate resources of the royal treasury in maintaining those wars, nor, subsequently, to relieve the king from the load of debt unavoidably contracted during the continuance of them.⁴ The consequence was, that the king's ministers were forced to recur to many old abuses, and particularly to the arbitrary practice of purveyance;⁵ till by

---

¹ Moorgate. Fabian's Chron. Mait. vol. l. p. 186. Stow's Survey.
² Ibid.
³ Rymer's Fœdera, vol. x. p. 261 Cotton's Abridgment, p. 564. Hall,
fol. 83. Monstrelet, vol. ii. p. 27.
⁴ Hume's Hist.
⁵ Ibid.; and Petition of Commons presented to the king, Parl. Hist. vol. ii. p. 263.

degrees, not only the allegiance of Parliament was withdrawn, but the affections of the people greatly estranged, both from the king and his government.

This was very seriously and plainly manifested by Cade's rebellion; who, although a man of low condition and bad character, had influence enough, by the bare assumption of the name of Mortimer, and by holding out the prospect of a redress of grievances, to collect about him a body so numerous and strong as nearly to overturn the government. Advancing from Kent, he and his followers were, after some hesitation, admitted within the City gates, where, at first, they conducted themselves with comparative moderation. Their first measure, however atrocious in itself, nevertheless affords some illustration of the settled notions entertained of the sovereign dominion of the law, and the universal reverence paid to the regular forms observed in the administration of justice; especially as regarded the legal institutions in the City of London. Cade, having apprehended Lord Say the high treasurer, had him arraigned for his political conduct before the lord mayor. That nobleman refused to plead before a jurisdiction so constituted and so convened; and by these means avoided that judicial trial which the rebels had conceived themselves, under any circumstances, bound to concede to him. Accordingly, Cade had him taken from the bar and instantly beheaded.[1] This violence was very soon followed by other indications of bloodshed and plunder; and the citizens, at last roused to a due sense of their danger, during a temporary absence shut their gates against the insurgents. The next day a severe battle was fought: the citizens successfully defended the bridge against their intrusion;[2] and so much were the rebels dispirited by the loss they sustained on this occasion, that, upon a promise of pardon, they all dispersed. Cade made the best of his way alone towards the coast, but was soon detected and killed by a private gentleman in the county of Sussex.[3]

The general discontent, however, at the measures of the king's ministers, by no means diminished. Parliamentary

---

[1] Stow. Hall Chron. Fabian's Chron. [2] Hall Chron.
[3] Hist. Croyland. Contin. p. 526.

remonstrances grew bold, and demands were made which seemed to arrogate little short of supreme authority.¹ In this state of things a competitor for the throne appeared in the person of the Duke of York, whose interests were very warmly espoused by a large class of the people, and particularly by the citizens. Independent of the general grievances which the City, in common with the rest of the nation, may be well supposed to have undergone, a personal and common hatred was conceived against the leaders of the Lancastrian, or royal party, who with the queen were strongly suspected of the assassination of the Duke of Gloucester, the king's uncle; a prince who had rendered himself, by his many amiable qualities, a great favourite with the people.² That the oppressions of which the nation and the Parliament complained were real, and their complaints not the result of a factious support of a popular nobleman, we may justly infer from the circumstance, that after the first battle fought between the two parties, when the Duke of York had the manifest advantage, and had, indeed, reduced the king entirely under his power,³ the Parliament contented themselves with passing some few regulations of government, and renewed their oaths of fealty to Henry.⁴ The Duke of York saw how expedient it was to have his claim recognised by the Parliament, which, in consequence of some desperate battles terminating in favour of the Yorkists, was soon afterwards formally done;⁵ subject to the possession of the crown by Henry during his life. An arrangement so incompatible with the feelings and views of the two contending parties could hardly long continue. The civil war soon raged again with its wonted fury. The duke was killed in battle, and his son immediately hastened to London, where he was cordially received, and had confidence enough openly to assume the sceptre under the title of Edward IV.

Amidst these violent transactions the progressive influence gained by the Parliament and the people in the Constitution is obvious. During the struggle for dominion, the Yorkists having to contend against the established order of govern-

¹ Parliam. Hist. vol. ii. p. 263.   ² Hume's Hist.
³ Hume's Hist.   ⁴ Cotton's Abridgment, p. 686.
⁵ Now, pp. 388, 389. Hollingshed, Grafton, p. 617.
p. 633.

EDWARD IV.   CONTESTS FOR THE CROWN.   125

ment, would naturally find their interest, not only in fomenting discontent, but in promoting all popular interference for reformation and redress. Accordingly, we find that scarce a step was taken, either by the Duke of York or his son Edward IV., without first warily sounding the disposition of the people. They uniformly professed, as their prominent object, emancipation from arbitrary and tyrannical measures, and endeavoured to identify their cause with that of an oppressed and suffering nation.[1] Even the assumption of the crown by Edward was speciously grounded on national consent;[2] and, while every art was employed by the Yorkists to cultivate the good opinion of the inferior orders, on the part of the Lancastrians the usual licentiousness which prevails among mercenary troops, suddenly raised to be as suddenly dispersed, was from necessity indulged.[3] It is no wonder, therefore, that in a contest which so long and so doubtfully divided the whole kingdom, the City of London should exemplify as conspicuous an attachment to the House of York as an aversion to that of Lancaster.[4] In truth, the goodwill of the citizens was thought by Edward to be so main a bulwark of his throne, that he never failed, during the course of his reign, to use every means of preserving it. Besides securing to them in the most ample manner their ancient privileges, he increased them by the grant of several very beneficial charters; and even condescended to live among them on terms of convivial familiarity.[5]

It may be doubted whether the City of London ever stood so high in national influence and consideration, as during the reign of Edward IV. The decided expression of its support may be said more than once to have conferred the crown. For, not only did the first reception of Edward after the death of his father, under very untoward circumstances, enable him successfully to assert his claim to the throne;[6]

CHAP. VII.

A.D. 1422 to 1485.

---

[1] Stow, p. 394. De Worl. ad. Polychron. Fab. Chron. pp. 7, 14, 50.

[2] Account of Edward's election in London, in Stow, p. 415. Hollingshed, p. 661. Grafton, p. 653.

[3] Hume's Hist.

[4] Maitland and Northouck in their Histories of London detail very particularly many proofs of the citizens' attachment to the House of York.

[5] Hume quoting Polyd. Virg. p. 613, and Biondi.

[6] Stow, p. 415. Hollingshed, p. 661. Grafton, p. 653. Fabian's Chron. and Hall's Chron. ann. 1460.

but afterwards, when, in the strange vicissitudes of the times, he was compelled rather to seek refuge in the City as an exile, than to resort thither as the leader of a formidable party, the unabated zeal and support of the citizens at once elevated him again to the situation of a conqueror and a monarch.[1] Nor was the City unqualified from its local strength to take a prominent part in settling the government. Its fortifications were in so complete a state, and so well guarded, as to defy the attacks of a potent army; and nothing tended more directly to the ruin of the Lancastrians than the steady refusal of the Londoners to admit them within the walls.[2] They were consequently twice subjected to furious assaults; once by Lord Scales, who, having possession of the Tower, incessantly for several days, though in vain, plied the City with ordnance;[3] and again by the Bastard Falconbridge, who, at the head of 17,000 men, attempted to storm the City in two places at the same time, but was repulsed with great slaughter by the citizens with very little extraneous assistance.[4]

It was in the reign of Edward IV. that the liverymen *at large* of the trading companies were first associated with the electors at the Common Hall. We have noticed,[5] that, in the 49th year of Edward III., these electors, who were originally summoned by the lord mayor out of the men chosen by *the wards*, were ordained by a regulation of that date to be nominated as delegates by the whole number of the *trading companies* for the exercise of the elective franchises, out of whom the lord mayor summoned the actual electors; and so they continued to be till this period. But, as neither a *fixed number* nor a *fixed class* was settled by this ordinance, it seems that much irregularity ensued, both with respect to the mode and authority of summoning them to elections, and in the number of persons summoned. It was accordingly enacted in the 7th year of Edward IV., that the election of the mayor and sheriffs should be in the Common Council, together with the

---

[1] Comines, lib. 3, ch. vii. Grafton, p. 702.
[2] Fabian and Hall's Chron. ann. 1460.
[3] Ibid.
[4] Vide p. 115.
[5] Ibid.
[6] Acts of Com. Co. 7th and 15th Edward IV.

masters and *wardens* of each mystery. The number, however, of voters appearing by this regulation to be too much narrowed, it was at last established by act of Common Council of the 15th of Edward IV., that the masters and wardens should *associate with themselves the honest men of their mysteries*, and come *in their last liveries* (or clothings) to the *elections* by the several assemblies of the citizens in Common Hall of corporate officers and members to serve in Parliament; and that none other, but themselves and the members of the Common Council, should be present.[1] This is the first origin of the elective franchise of the *liverymen*, as a distinct class of those admitted to the freedom of the trading companies. By the operation of the previous ordinances of the City, the nomination to the right of electing these functionaries in Common Hall was, in a manner, *shared* between the companies and the mayor—the companies selecting the particular electors, and the mayor selecting (if he pleased) the actual electors out of them. Under this act of Edward IV., the *undivided* nomination was transferred finally to the companies, who might, and do, grant liveries according to such rules and terms as they prescribe to such of their members who may be considered to deserve the denomination of '*honest men*,' or '*of the discreeter sort*,' or of '*probi homines*.'

On the death of Edward, the reins of government were committed into the hands of his brother, Richard Duke of Gloucester, as protector during the minority of his infant son, Edward V. In tracing with hasty steps, and for an ulterior object, the thread of English History, the adult reader must be *again* informed, though succinctly, that Richard, who from his childhood had been bred in the midst of carnage and violence, and who had given many proofs of a ferocious disposition, as well as of great talents for government, instantly determined to usurp the throne. The many obstacles which stood in the way of his elevation, and which would at once have disheartened a man of moderate courage, or one imbued with any natural feelings of humanity, had no

[1] The City elections were further and finally regulated by Stat. 11th Geo. I. cap. 18, by an act of Common Council passed in 1834, and by the Great Reform Acts of 1832 and 1867. The subject will be again reverted to. Vide Ch. XII. p. 243, *et seq.*

influence on a heart hardened by long experience in bloodshed and disorder. His first step was to murder those noblemen, who, from their personal influence as well as impregnable attachment to the issue of Edward IV., he knew would make a powerful and warlike opposition to his claims.¹ Among these, Lord Hastings, whom Richard by well dissembled familiarity had inveigled within his grasp, was suddenly seized at the Council table in the presence of the Protector, and at his command, upon a most extraordinary and absurd charge of witchcraft; and was as suddenly beheaded on Tower Hill.² An apology for this summary outrage was instantly read throughout the City of London in the form of a proclamation; but in such haste was it got up, that, as was sarcastically observed by a citizen, *it certainly seemed penned in the spirit of prophecy.*³

Richard appears to have founded his chief hopes of success in his ambitious project, on the concurrence of the citizens. Aware of the important effects of their allegiance during the reign of his brother, and of the influence acquired by their united strength in a nation divided throughout by many contending interests, he judged that, if his authority was once established in London, he had little to fear or expect from opposition in any other quarter. Accordingly, he bent his most artful attention to gain over the City to his interest; and, mindful of that election which first seated his brother on the throne, he resolved, if possible, to have his own title recognised in a similar manner. For this purpose Shaw, the lord mayor, who had become a creature of Richard, and privy to all his designs, was employed to entrap the citizens into a kind of popular expression in favour of the Protector's title.⁴ His first attempt, however, which was to raise the semblance of a public acclamation through the medium of a popular appeal introduced into a sermon preached by his brother at St. Paul's, most awkwardly and entirely failed of the concerted object.⁵ The lord mayor then summoned a general assembly of the citizens, at which the Duke of Buckingham, who is said to have possessed

¹ Hume's Hist. Edward V.
² Sir Thos. More's Life of Edward V.
³ Fabian's Chron.
⁴ Ibid.

great oratorical powers, attended.¹ At this meeting the duke harangued the citizens, at great length, on the pretensions of Richard; but the assembly, either through astonishment at the impudence of such claims, or through a steady resolution to oppose them, maintained a perfect silence. The Recorder was then instructed to address them to the same effect; but, speaking cautiously and with some equivocation, he had no better success. At last the duke peremptorily required an opinion one way or the other; and, on some few voices being feebly raised, he, with formal solemnity, announced that he had heard the sentiments of the nation sufficiently declared.² Richard accordingly, with ill-disguised alacrity, accepted the crown; and the first act of his supreme authority was the murder of the two young princes, the sons of Edward IV.³

The citizens attended the usurper's coronation, with the lord mayor as cupbearer, in great pomp; and their claim in this particular was formally allowed, and still remains on record.⁴ Richard showed a continual anxiety to conciliate all ranks of the people to his government, and as soon as he deemed himself securely settled on his throne, passed in Parliament several popular laws. He likewise intended to strengthen his title to the crown by marrying Elizabeth, the daughter of Edward IV.; and although he had murdered her two brothers, he met with no opposition to his addresses either from herself or her mother. Everything, therefore, seemed to promise a triumphant issue to all his crimes, and an eventual stability to his throne.⁵

The nation, however, was incapable of enduring so baleful

---

¹ This appears to have been a meeting quite out of the common course, and neither a meeting of the Common Hall under the regulation of the 15th Edward IV. or of the established Common Council, but a general assembly of the citizens at large. No entry is made in the City Books of this meeting; although in the few instances in which Common Halls have been held for other than elective purposes (as to have a proclamation or a royal letter read, or under a special order of Parliament), such meetings have always been regularly recorded. All the other acts of Richard III.'s time are duly entered.

² Sir T. More's Life of Edward V. Fabian's Chronicle.

³ Ibid.; and vide note Q. 2 to Hume's Hist.

⁴ Lib. L. fol. 191 a & b. Town Clerk's Office.

⁵ Hume's Hist.

a prospect. Henry, Earl of Richmond, who stood nearly related to the throne, and an exile in Brittany, was strenuously urged from all quarters to appear in England; and, by placing himself at the head of an indignant people, at once to save them from impending tyranny, and prevent a marriage which would prove as fatal to his own hopes as to those of the whole nation. He accordingly hastened over; but, such was the activity of his able adversary, that, before he could call together more than a handful of partisans, he found himself compelled to contend in a bloody battle for a crown and for his life. In the memorable field of Bosworth, however, Henry proved victorious. Richard found in the field a death too honourable for so execrable a man: and his competitor, by marrying Elizabeth, the true heir to the throne, succeeded to the undisputed possession of the royal authority.[1]

[1] The author gives all due credit to the ingenious reasoning of Walpole in his Historic Doubts; but he has not been induced to alter his opinion, formed from the usual sources of historical information, on the character of Richard III.

CHAPTER VIII.

FROM THE ACCESSION OF HENRY VII. TO THE DEATH OF ELIZABETH; OF THE CIVIC PROCESSIONS AND PAGEANTS; OF THE INTERIOR CONDITION, POPULATION, STYLE OF BUILDING, AND MANNER OF LIVING WITHIN THE CITY AT THIS PERIOD.

WE have now traced the progress of the City of London through a series of barbarous ages to a period when the better features of modern civilisation may be said to have become general throughout the nation, and many, though certainly not all, of the great principles of its government had attained a settled foundation. The issue by Henry's marriage with Elizabeth put a final close to those contests which had so long attended a disputed succession. The laws of the land began to be reduced to a system, and to become a favourite study among the better orders, who consequently felt a peculiar and personal interest in the maintenance of them.[1] The constitution and prerogatives of Parliament began to be better known and appreciated, and it became universally considered as the organ and arbiter of the national legislation. It is true that, in the reign of Henry VII., as well as in those of several of his successors, many arbitrary practices prevailed, evincing rather the despotic power than the controlling influence of the monarch; the laws, too, were occasionally strained to effect illegal and tyrannical objects; and many royal prerogatives, totally incompatible with the supremacy of the law, were exercised, the assumption of which by Charles I. brought that ill-fated monarch in bolder times to the scaffold. It is difficult to specify precisely *any* period

CHAP. VIII.

A.D. 1485 to 1509.

---

[1] Fortescue writes, that in the reign of Henry VI. the Inns of Court contained 2,000 students, most of them men of honourable birth.

in the English history in which our own genuine constitution can be said to have existed, free from the tinge of autocracy on the one hand or that of corruption on the other; and nothing is more certain, than that he who attempts, by looking back to former ages, to affix any point of time for a truly constitutional plan of power, will be scared by the irregularities or enormities of each age as he recedes, till at last he takes refuge in that entangled wilderness of our early history, where he may just descry the primitive efforts at government which barbarians adopt in associating together by bands for mutual protection. Still, however, from the accession of Henry VII., most of the fundamental maxims of the English constitution were at least *acknowledged*, and the common rights and liberties of the people ascertained. The administration of government and of the laws proceeded for the most part in one and the same course, in spite of temporary checks and convulsions, and extended an uniform influence over all classes of the people; there will therefore be the less reason for any detailed reference to it for the purpose of illustrating any *distinguishing* privileges of the citizens. The history of London becomes more local; and ceases in great measure to be involved in that of the times, and of the nation at large.

The frequent rebellions which mark the progress of this king's reign, gave many occasions for the irregular exercise of his authority. But, in most instances, Henry, whose ruling passion was the accumulation of wealth, was satisfied with the exaction of ruinous fines and forfeitures, which, while they strengthened his own power, at the same time depressed that of his enemies. The whole policy of Henry's government seems to have been the amassing treasure; a policy which we may conceive to have been as much suggested by the difficulties into which former kings had been placed, through the loss of their private demesnes and their consequent dependence on the will of Parliament, as by a natural disposition to avarice. But, although this was, directly or indirectly, the chief object of all Henry's cares, he knew too well the temper of his people to resort to those barefaced extortions which marked the reigns of his earlier

predecessors. On one occasion, only, he ventured to levy
a *benevolence* of his own authority,[1] to which the citizens of
London were, as usual, obliged very largely to contribute;[2]
but he had the prudence to obtain from the first Parliament
which met afterwards a sanction to this measure.[3] Sensible
of the dangers and disorders attending a direct and general
taxation of his subjects, Henry devised a safer mode of
attaining his ends, by craftily framing new laws, which tended
to multiply and facilitate the forfeiture of estates, and by
rigidly enforcing, and even perverting, those laws by which
fines and forfeitures were incurred. For this purpose he
employed, as his ministers, the notorious Empson and Dudley,
lawyers of great learning and experience, who devoted,
throughout the whole of Henry's reign, the most industrious
sagacity in contriving specious methods of oppressing the
people under the forms of law. Under his sole authority
they new modelled the Court of Star Chamber, and supplied
it with jurisdiction to try offences without jury, and with
power almost unlimited over the persons and properties of
subjects.[4] They directed crown informations instead of
indictments to be at once received, without the intervention
of grand juries, not only at assizes, but even at sessions of
the peace, for the purpose of levying heavy penalties.[5] They
issued new and strange commissions for the trial of offenders.[5] They raked up old and long forgotten penal statutes,
on which prosecutions were directed against persons totally
unconscious of offence.[6] And whatever remained of the oppressive system of the feudal law was wrested to the harassing and
plundering of all those who could in any shape be brought
under the king's authority as his tenants.[6]

Henry commenced his exactions from the citizens of London

CHAP.
VIII.

A.D. 1485
to 1509.

[1] Rymer's Fœdera, vol. xii. p. 486.
[2] According to Fabian, to the amount of 15,000*l*. a sum equal to at least 100,000*l*. in the present times. Chron. part vii. This species of tax, for such it was in reality, is first mentioned in the time of Richard II. (vide Hume's *Hist.* ch. xvii. ad fin.), and was occasionally levied till the 1st year of Richard III., when it was abolished by Act of Parliament. It was resorted upon, however, both by Henry VII. and his successor, and was altogether arbitrary in amount and mode of collection.
[3] Parliament held 1495. The bene-volence was levied in 1491.
[4] Bacon's Life of Henry VII. Black-stone's Comm. vol. iv. p. 429,
[5] Hollingshed, p. 501. Polydore Virg pp. 613, 615. [6] Ibid.

in the mild form of *borrowing*;[1] but, though supplies to a moderate extent, and more than sufficient to meet his very limited necessities, were cheerfully advanced, the king's rapacity was not of such a quality as to be satisfied with such slender acquisitions. Under the pretext of having transgressed against an old penal statute, Alderman Capel was fined 2,700*l*.;[2] and this case formed the precedent for the numerous extortions which followed. Five thousand pounds were paid by the Corporation for a confirmation of their charter; principally with regard to their right to the forfeiture of all goods bought within the City by strangers from strangers (i.e. others than citizens) or sold there by strangers to such strangers;[3] the charter, however, contained no grant of any new privileges or franchises. Every effort seems to have been exerted by the citizens to conciliate the king's favour, both by the lavish magnificence displayed by them in their attendance on his person, and in the reception of his family in the City, and also by their zealous alacrity in defending his interests against the continual attacks of rebels.[4] But these attentions and services had no effect on his cold and calculating temper; and his reign finished, as it had begun, by cruel impositions on the wealthier citizens, many of whom, and among the rest Capel, were liberated from prison at his death, where they were confined for non-payment of heavy fines.[5]

Almost the first act of Henry VIII. after his accession, was to gratify his subjects by beheading Empson and Dudley who had so justly drawn upon themselves the unqualified hatred of the whole nation. The wealth accumulated by his father furnished the young monarch with ample means to indulge that fondness for magnificent revelry which characterised his natural disposition; and the unbounded display of his liberality as well as of his accomplishments in the numerous tournaments and carousals which succeeded each other, it may be believed, contributed in no small degree to

[1] Fabian, part vii.
[2] Bacon's Life of Henry VII.
[3] Fabian, part vii. Charter of 20th Henry VII. Inspeximus charter of

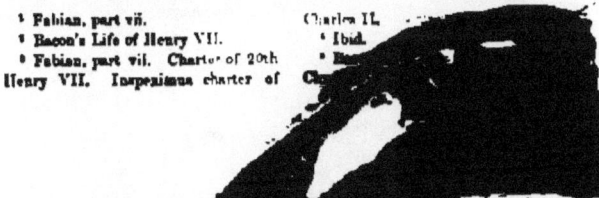

attract the affections of Henry's new subjects, who had been so long both oppressed and disgusted by the sullen qualities of the late king. Most of this dissipation was carried on in the City;[1] and it is impossible to read without surprise the splendid accounts, given with so much solemnity of detail by contemporary chroniclers, of the magnificent feasts, processions, and public spectacles, which mark a period when domestic arts and luxuries were so little known or appreciated.

The citizens appear from very early times to have evinced a strong propensity for expensive and pompous shows. Not to mention the entry of Richard I. after his captivity, which may be considered as a great national occasion of display, we are told that on the reception of Edward I. from the Holy Land, the walls of the houses were hung with silks and tapestries; the conduits ran with rich wines; and the wealthier citizens threw gold and silver among the people.[2] After the battle of Poictiers, John, king of France, with his illustrious captor Edward the Black Prince, were ushered through the City in a procession so numerous as to last from three in the morning till noon. On this occasion there was a most profuse display of pageants, rich tapestries, plate, silks, and every species of warlike accoutrements. Richard II. was twice publicly received in the City, with still greater splendour; when the citizens who lined the streets vied with each other in the richness of their apparel and the display of their individual wealth. The conduits ran with wine; pageants, in the form of castles fancifully adorned, were erected; a boy, habited like an angel, presented the king with a gorgeous crown set with jewels, and another to the queen; while four young ladies scattered leaves of gold over the king's head.[3] In the reign of Henry V. a similar procession took place attended with equal magnificence; on which occasion tapestries embroidered with a representation of that monarch's exploits in France were suspended from the houses.[4]

---

[1] Stow, An. Engl. A.D. 1510. Stow's Survey.
[2] Hollingshed, A.D. 1271. Nic. Triv. Annals.
[3] Tho. Wals. Hist. Aug. Hen. Knight's Chron. Fabian, part vii.
[4] De Worde ad Polychron. Tho. Wals. Hist. Ang.

In the several successive reigns there was no diminution either in the number or in the splendour of these public displays: but in that of Henry VIII. the magnificence of them rose to such a height as to be almost incredible, did we not know from incontestible authorities the pompous habits of that age. Upon the ceremony of mustering the nightly watch, the king with his royal consort attended as spectators. No less than 2,000 men, on foot and on stately horses, all dressed or armed in a very costly manner, and marching in several divisions, with bands of musicians, pages, dancers, and pageants interspersed, made up the procession. The lord mayor himself, mounted on a charger richly trapped, and attended by a large retinue of servants, together with the sheriffs, also composed part of this spectacle. This ceremony of mustering the nightly watch was afterwards prohibited by Henry, on account of its great expense. The citizens, however, seemed resolved to seize every opportunity throughout this reign which could enable them to exhibit the exuberance of their wealth. Whenever a crowned head, or even an ambassador, approached the walls, he was sure to be welcomed by a public reception. But the manner in which Anne Boleyn made her public entry into the City preparatory to her coronation may well serve as an example which it would be difficult to surpass, in point of splendour, even in the present age; and which proves the enormous riches at that time individually possessed by the chief citizens. The full account of this ceremony is to be found minutely detailed in Stow's English Annals, to which the curious reader is referred—suffice it to say, that with respect to the profusion of gold and silver, silks and embroidered tapestries, gorgeous dresses, and stately pageantry, this appears to have thrown all other public exhibitions completely into the shade.

These magnificent shows continued to be exhibited with their accustomed splendour, and to characterise the taste of the age for several reigns subsequent. The entry of Queen Elizabeth into London before her coronation, was particularly remarkable for this mode of expressing the national exultation at her accession.[1] The reign of James afforded few

[1] Hollingshed. Maitland's Hist. vol. i. p. 266.

occasions for similar parade; but nothing can more clearly evince the early and general attachment of the people towards his ill-fated successor, than the manner in which he was conducted into the City upon his return from a long absence in the North, and the extravagant magnificence displayed at a civic entertainment given him upon that occasion.[1] The austere habits which prevailed during the Puritan times of the Commonwealth, indisposed the people to maintain, or partake in, festal solemnities of this nature; and though, upon the restoration, the ancient style of receiving and welcoming the monarch was once more revived,[2] the frequency as well as splendour of these shows and processions rapidly declined from that period.[3]

---

[1] Maitland's Hist. vol. i. p. 340. Stow's Survey.

[2] Echard's Hist. Eng. Cook's Life of Charles II.

[3] The estimation of shows and pageantry did not begin to decline until the latter end of the sixteenth century; for the great Midsummer night watch which was put down by Henry VIII. was revived again, and not finally abolished till the year 1569; and it was long after referred to in the City with every mark of admiration. In a burlesque play of the year 1613, a young citizen is made to exclaim:

' — My valiant love will batter down Millions of constables, and put to flight E'en that great watch of Midsummer day at night.'
  Beaumont and Fletcher: The Knight of the Burning Pestle.

Towards the beginning of the seventeenth century, the dramatic poets regarded the civic mummery as a very fruitful source of ridicule; and the solemn descriptions of them by the chroniclers Hollingshed, Baker, Stow, and others, were equally derided. The following scenes will at once exemplify the strange nature of these shows, the estimation in which they were held by the citizens, and the growing contempt of them arising among the higher orders. In the play last quoted, a citizen grocer is made to say, addressing a kind of stage messenger—

' Citizen. Let Ralph come out on a May day in the morning, and speak upon a conduit, with all his scarfs about him, and his feathers and his rings and his knacks.——I'll have him come out, or I'll fetch him out myself. I'll have something done in honour of the City.——Bring him out quickly; or, if I come in amongst you——

' Boy. Well, sir, he shall come out.

' Citizen. Bring him away then!

' Citizen's Wife. This will be brave, 'faith. George, shall he not dance the morris too, for the credit of the Strand?

' Citizen. No, sweetheart, it will be too much for the boy. Oh! there he is, Nell!—he's reasonable well in apparel; but he has not rings enough.'

[Ralph is here exhibited in a fancy costume at the top of one of the City conduits; and he spouts some wretched doggrel in honour of the City, and of May day.]

In another play of the same date, Spendall, a young citizen, thus expresses himself:—

' By this light, I do not think but to be lord mayor of London before I die, and have three pageants carried before me, besides a ship and an unicorn.'—Green's Tu quoque, 1614.

In a play of the year 1633, the next-

We should be much deceived, however, if from these instances of public parade we should draw an inference favourable to the general state of refinement, either in the arts and luxuries of life or in the domestic comforts enjoyed by the people in the age of which we are now writing. It is true that great wealth was accumulated in the metropolis; but we may gather that it was engrossed by comparatively a very few individuals, when we consider the enormous possessions acquired by some of the citizens of this period. The whole of the foreign and wholesale trade was confined to the hands of a few great capitalists; and a London merchant has been the origin of some of the most illustrious families in the kingdom, not to mention that which gave to England one of its greatest monarchs.[1] The trading companies, both foreign and English, under which all the citizens of London are classed, were not only opulent in a corporate capacity; but interfering with and regulating, as they did in these times, the dealing of all those of the same trade, they commanded in no small degree the resources of their respective members. The City companies divided the citizens into so many clans, professing one common interest and feeling. In imitation of the Court and more powerful of the nobility, the Corporation of London, who had the superintendence of these associations, assigned to several of them a peculiar costume, denominated a *Livery*, and required of such *Livery companies*, that they should attend in that garb at all civic solemnities.[2]

[jected] means which a young spendthrift acquires of paying his debts is thus referred to.

'*Tapwell.* He has found out such a new way
To pay old debts as 'tis very like,
He shall be chronicled for it.
'*Froth.* He deserves it.
More than *ten pageants.*'
Massinger: *New Way to Pay Old Debts.* 1633.

[1] Queen Elizabeth's great-great-grandfather by her mother's side was Geoffrey Boleyn, a mercer living in the Old Jewry, and lord-mayor an. 1457. Stow, book iii. p. 44; book v. p. 175.

[2] The court of aldermen has always exercised the right of authorising companies to wear liveries and admit liverymen, and in most cases it has expressly granted the liveries in the first instance (vide further on this subject, Book II. Ch. III. p. 313). Assigning *liveries* to dependants and followers was very common in England from the time of the Conquest. The providing them for the king's family, servants, judges, military officers, and retainers of all classes, was a common subject of the rent of farmers of demesnes and cities, and of the farm of sheriffs (vide *Hist. Exch.* vol. i. pp. 204, 220). The nobility and the most powerful subjects used to clothe so many of their followers, about the time

CIVIC PAGEANTRY AND SPECTACLES. 139

At a time, therefore, when the middle classes of society, who now form the great mass of the independent portion of the community, could hardly be said to exist; when the whole people were divided into the rich and powerful, and those who were their dependants and retainers; when most of those numerous luxuries which are now considered as necessaries in private life, were but little, if at all, known—we may easily account for that large expenditure which was devoted to public spectacles and festivities. In fact, it was an expenditure which formed almost the only channel through which the exorbitant wealth of the higher orders could flow, and to direct which the public spirit of associated bodies combined with the prevalent taste of the age. Less independent than in the present times, both in their persons and their circumstances, the inferior orders regarded public spectacles and revelry as their only solace and sources of amusement. They considered such indulgences as no more than what they had a right to expect from their superiors, and as the only possible return for their services and dependence. But when, through the gradual improvement of the constitution, the lower orders became more and more emancipated from the control of those above them; when, in consequence of such independence, the aggregate wealth and resources of the nation became more equally diffused among all classes of the people—a corresponding change was produced in their tastes and habits: every man, as he acquired substance, wished to appropriate to his private interests and enjoyments the fruits of his own industry; the elegancies and refinements of art grew up with the ability and disposition of the people to relish them; and as, on the one hand, the taste for pomp and grandeur decreased, so, on the other, the private means of individuals to administer to it diminished. So that we may consider it as a criterion of the general prosperity and state of civilisation in a country, when the people,

CHAP. VIII.
A.D. 1509 to 1558.

of Richard II., for the purpose of maintaining their state and their quarrels, that they began then to be denounced by statutes under the name of *Maintenances*. Other statutes to the same effect passed in several subsequent reigns (vide Anderson's *Hist. Com.* vol. i. p. 365, vol. ii. p. 17). Numerous also were the City ordinances limiting the number of liveries to be granted by the mayor, sheriffs, and others.

instead of regarding with universal and fond delight splendid but extravagant public pageantries, place their ideas of comfort and felicity in the more refined luxuries of private life.

It is certain that in the time of Henry VIII. the manner of living in London among the generality of the people was, according to modern notions, wretched in the highest degree. Erasmus, in a letter to Dr. Francis, says, 'The floors are commonly of clay strewed with rushes; 'under which lies unmolested an ancient collection of beer, 'grease, fragments, bones, spittle, excrements of dogs and 'cats, and everything that is nasty.' He attributes the frequent plagues which ravaged the City to the crowded manner of building and the almost total exclusion of light and air from the houses. The suburbs of London were at this period almost totally void of buildings. From an ancient map, dated about the year 1560,[1] and which is perhaps the oldest map of London extant in print, it appears, that almost the whole of the metropolis was confined at that time within the City wall. There were a few straggling houses leading up the Strand, and a few more round about Smithfield. The open fields came close up to the City wall throughout almost the whole northern and eastern circumference; and those houses which stood without them were for the most part detached, and accommodated with gardens. Charing Cross appears in some degree to have been connected with the City by an irregular train of houses. The village of St. Giles lay entirely isolated, across the open country. A single street led up Holborn about as far as the Bars; between that point and Somerset House the space was entirely occupied by fields and gardens. There were also many gardens and open spaces within the City, and more particularly in the immediate vicinity of the wall, within which a considerable space was kept clear round the whole circuit. The largest area occupied by gardens was immediately behind Lothbury, where several acres seem to have been so laid out. In the eastern and south-eastern parts of the

---

[1] By Ralph Aggas. 'Circiter A.D. 1560' is printed on the map.

City there were likewise a great many spots similarly appropriated.¹

Within this very limited compass of inhabited ground was crowded a population of constant residents amounting to not less than 130,000. The estimate, however, of the population at this period must be made on very different principles from one formed of the present. Owing to the enormous increase of the trade of the metropolis, one half of the City at least may now be calculated to be occupied by warehouses and counting-houses. Public offices and buildings of that nature also take up a very considerable space. Much even of the retail trade and handicraft occupation is carried on in houses in no part devoted to regular family residence. Add to this, that the great change in domestic habits and manners has engendered a love of privacy and retirement, which prompts many persons, even at some sacrifice of pecuniary interest, to withdraw themselves as much as possible from the bustle of business, to a neighbourhood where they may enjoy better air and more cheerful society. The consequence of this is, that, out of the vast numbers who resort daily to the City to pursue their regular avocations, not one twentieth proportion of them are to be reckoned among the constant inhabitants ; and that proportion is for the most part, though certainly not entirely, composed of the inferior orders. The tide of population flows in large streams into the City every morning, and is again disgorged at the close of the day. The City properly so called may now be considered rather as a vast mercantile emporium or factory, than as a place of general habitation. When we speak, therefore, of the present population of London, we must be careful to distinguish between those who pursue their daily employments and occupy tenements within the City for the purpose of trade merely, and those who are strictly to be accounted inhabitants.

---

¹ Gardens seem to have been common throughout the City, to the beginning of the seventeenth century. In 'The Puritan,' a play written about 1607, the first scene is laid in a garden behind the widow's house in Watling Street. The widow in another part says:

'Will you wa'k a while in the garden, and gather a pink or a gilliflower?'

One part of the plot in the same play is to hide a citizen's chain of three thousand links among the shrubs in this garden.

the population of the City
in the reign of Henry VIII. it must necessarily that the general style of living amongst
have been, according to our present notions,

An old and humorous play in Elizabeth's
reign is entitled "The Roaring Girl."

very wretched, but that the general aspect of the City must
have been mean and unsightly. The private houses for the
most part were built of wood, were much lower in altitude,
and capable of containing fewer inhabitants than the present
buildings. Taking these circumstances into our consideration, and likewise that much of the area within the walls was
left open, we must naturally conclude, to account for the
existence of so large a population, that several families must
have resided in the same house and ' in a sort smothered;' *
that the houses were comparatively small; that they were
crowded very much one upon another; and that the streets
were much narrower than at present. This conclusion is
completely corroborated by the ancient maps, and more particularly by that already referred to; by which it appears
that, formerly, the streets were much more numerous than
since the fire of London; and that alleys, courts, and by-
paths abounded in every direction. The almost total absence
of wheel-carriages no doubt conduced very much to this incommodious and confined arrangement of the streets. The
only vehicles of this nature known in London were carts;
and those which plied for hire were restricted to the number
of four hundred and twenty.² There appears to have been
but one commodious and regular street, which led through
the heart of the City, from Aldersgate to Ludgate; and the
breadth of way throughout the course of Cheapside was
much greater than at the present day. This street, which
was the scene of all processions and civic grandeur, was justly
esteemed the most beautiful part of the City; and much
attention on the part of the civic authorities, as well as of the

---

¹ Brick houses were not built until the reign of Henry VIII. in any part of the kingdom (Hume's *Hist.* ch. xxxvii. note L); and such houses were not begun in London till James I.'s reign, before which time they were invariably built of wood.—Hume's *Hist.* Appendix to James I. note 41; Strype's *Stow.* book i. p. 7.

² Words of a proclamation of James I. against increase of buildings and dividing of tenements in London.—Vide *Dissertation*, Appendix.

³ Vide Act of Common Council, 1601, Brown mayor. Queen Elizabeth was the first who made general use of a coach; the fashion was introduced in the year 1580 by the Earl of Arundel (Anderson's *Hist. Com.* vol. i. p. 425). No doubt the common use of coaches very much impaired the splendour of, as well as the taste for, processions, shows.

BOOK I.
A.D. 1509 to 1558.

If we calculate the population on the latter basis, the City must be considered, even with reference to the present liberal style of house-keeping, as half deserted: if on the former, we shall readily conclude that but a small proportion, probably not more than a twentieth part, could by possibility become inhabitants, if any regard be had, not merely to that luxurious ease which the circumstances of many of them can command, but to what, at the present day, are considered the common comforts and necessaries of life.

But at the time of which we are writing, not only did all those who employed themselves in their daily occupations within the City reside there with their families as constant inhabitants, but it may even be doubted whether the City did not contain within its walls a larger population by night than by day. From the earliest period of the civic history, down to that under present notice, the City gates and the bank of the river were strictly guarded at night by armed men;[1] and we have seen with what ceremony the watch of citizens was set to parade the streets and to take their stations at the gates. None were allowed to wander about the City between dark and light. Night-walkers and riotous persons[2] were instantly arrested, and promptly tried and punished. There were scarcely any suburbs; and it is not to be supposed that many of the common people would come from any distance to their employments within the City, and return to their families by night: and at this time country-houses and villas were altogether unknown and unsought for by the trading citizens. The daily influx of non-residents would be, therefore, for the most part confined to those who attended the markets for the sale of provisions; and it is reasonable to think that they would be far exceeded in number by those who passed out of the City to their labours in the neighbourhood immediately adjoining.

If, however, we are to compute the population of the City only at 130,000 in the reign of Henry VIII., it must necessarily follow, not only that the general style of living amongst the citizens must have been, according to our present notions,

[1] Lib. Albus, passim.
[2] Termed 'roarers' in the City books. An old and licentious play in Elizabeth's reign is entitled 'The Roaring Girl.'

very wretched, but that the general aspect of the City must have been mean and unsightly. The private houses for the most part were built of wood,¹ were much lower in altitude, and capable of containing fewer inhabitants than the present buildings. Taking these circumstances into our consideration, and likewise that much of the area within the walls was left open, we must naturally conclude, to account for the existence of so large a population, that several families must have resided in the same house and 'in a sort smothered;'² that the houses were comparatively small; that they were crowded very much one upon another; and that the streets were much narrower than at present. This conclusion is completely corroborated by the ancient maps, and more particularly by that already referred to; by which it appears that, formerly, the streets were much more numerous than since the fire of London; and that alleys, courts, and by-paths abounded in every direction. The almost total absence of wheel-carriages no doubt conduced very much to this incommodious and confined arrangement of the streets. The only vehicles of this nature known in London were carts: and those which plied for hire were restricted to the number of four hundred and twenty.³ There appears to have been but one commodious and regular street, which led through the heart of the City, from Aldersgate to Ludgate; and the breadth of way throughout the course of Cheapside was much greater than at the present day. This street, which was the scene of all processions and civic grandeur, was justly esteemed the most beautiful part of the City; and much attention on the part of the civic authorities, as well as of the

---

¹ Brick houses were not built until the reign of Henry VIII. in any part of the kingdom (Hume's *Hist.* ch. xxxvii. note L.); and such houses were not begun in London till James I.'s reign, before which time they were invariably built of wood.—Hume's *Hist.* Appendix to James I. note 41; Strype's Stow, book i. p. 7.

² Words of a proclamation of James I. against increase of buildings and dividing of tenements in London.—Vide *Dissertation*, Appendix.

³ Vide Act of Common Council, 1661, Brown mayor. Queen Elizabeth was the first who made general use of a coach; the fashion was introduced in the year 1580 by the Earl of Arundel (Anderson's *Hist. Com.* vol. i. p. 421). No doubt the common use of coaches very much impaired the splendour of, as well as the taste for, processional shows.

government, was bestowed to preserve its uniformity. It was
chiefly occupied by goldsmiths' shops, and care was taken to
exclude all trades of a less splendid appearance.¹

No inference, therefore, can be drawn of the relative advancement in the arts and elegancies of life, or of society, from the splendour displayed in civic processions, or from the cumbrous though magnificent style of hospitality displayed by the comparatively few individuals who engrossed the wealth and resources of the kingdom. It may even be doubted whether the manner of living in these times among the very lowest artisans does not evince more comfort and cleanliness, though not more plenty, than was to be witnessed in the houses of the most opulent tradesmen in the time of Henry VIII.

The progress of Henry's reign was marked by bold and continual efforts for the establishment of absolute power, and the gradual extinction of those constitutional rights and privileges which had begun to gain ground during the reign of his predecessor. Able in capacity, and imperious in disposition, he was but too successful in triumphing over the remonstrances and murmurs of his people at each encroachment on their liberties; which served only to indicate that the spirit and principles of freedom existed in the nation, though held in subjection; and that the legal rights of the subject were not altogether unknown or abandoned. Nothing can more strongly testify the almost uncontrollable authority of the king's will, than the arbitrary and fanciful innovations which he introduced into the system of national faith—innovations so frequent and inconsistent with each other, that it is not too much to say, the established doctrines of the English Church were made to depend, as far as regarded the outward conformity of the people, upon the royal interests and passions, and even caprices. Indeed Hume does not scruple to declare, that no prince in Europe was possessed of such absolute authority as Henry.²

The practice of imposing taxes without the consent of

¹ Vide Orders, Proclamations, &c. upon this subject, collected passim in Maitland's Hist. of London, Index, title 'Cheapside.'
² Hume's Hist. ch. xxxi, and note YY.

Parliament, that most dangerous stretch of the royal prerogative, was again revived during this reign. These impositions were disguised under the names of loans and benevolences; but such were the demonstrations of discontent and impatience on the part of the people, that the king ventured on these invasions of their rights with the utmost caution. The Parliament, however, of this period was too subservient to complain of these infringements on the constitution; and even the judges are said to have gone so far as to pronounce the legality of the king's commissions to levy these taxes;[1] although by an Act of 1st Richard III. they were expressly abolished. The only check, therefore, to the entire overthrow of the liberties of the nation, was the opposition to these measures which was manifested by the people themselves. The City of London was the first to evince a determination to resist these illegal demands. In 1525 a commission was issued to levy a benevolence to enable the king to carry on the war in France. The mayor and aldermen were called before Wolsey, and directed by him to make the necessary assessments. The recorder, upon this, intimated it was contrary to the statute of Richard III.; but this objection was treated with the highest contempt by the cardinal. The citizens then craved to consult the Common Council upon the subject; and that court, upon hearing all the particulars, rejected the payment of this imposition with indignation. This opposition of the City was so implicitly followed by the country at large, that on this occasion the king derived scarcely any other consequence from his attempt, than that of raising the indignation of his subjects.[2]

At the latter end of Henry's reign, when his authority was more firmly established, an alderman of London absolutely refused to comply with a similar demand: but such was the power of prerogative assumed at this time, that for this disobedience to the king's will the citizen was immediately enrolled as a foot-soldier and sent off to the Scottish wars.[3] Another, who showed himself equally refractory, was cast

[1] Hume: but he refers to no authority.
[2] Herbert's Life of Henry VIII. a.d. 1525. Hall's Chron.
[3] Hall's Chron. a.d. 1545.

BOOK I.

A.D. 1509 to 1558.

into prison, and compelled to ransom himself by a heavy composition.[1]

At this period the greatest possible animosity prevailed against the foreign merchants and artisans; who were very numerous in London throughout this reign.[2] The citizens conceived the pursuing their occupations within the walls to be not only prejudicial to their individual interests, but in direct violation of their customs and charters which gave them the privilege of exclusive trade. This privilege had, indeed, been asserted time out of mind, and secured by the authority of Parliament as well as by charter; but, by the introduction of various chartered companies of foreigners, the various practices resorted to by others, and the frequent grants of monopolies by the king, this privilege had from time to time been very much encroached upon.[3] At last, so great was the indignation of the citizens against foreigners, that in the beginning of this reign a furious insurrection broke out against them. Many of them were murdered, and their houses plundered. It was with some difficulty that this riot was eventually quelled. Upwards of 400 rioters were taken prisoners, thirteen of whom were condemned for high treason and executed: the rest, with ropes about their necks, fell down on their knees before the king, who, as Hume says, knew at that time how to pardon, and were dismissed without punishment.[4]

[1] Goodwin's Annals. Hume's Hist. ch. xxxiii.

[2] Fifteen thousand Flemings were obliged to leave London at one time by order of Council. Le Grand, vol. iii. p. 232.

[3] An exposition of the privileges of the City of London in regard to exclusive trade was published in 1821 by the author, in which the subject of the encroachments of foreigners is fully discussed.—Vide also p. 188 et seq. and Book II. Ch. IV. pp. 334, 341.

[4] Fab. Chron. Hall's Chron. A.D. 1517. The day of this riot was long known in the City by the name of Evil May-day, and is constantly alluded to by the older poets and others, who treat of City affairs and manners. It was almost a proverbial allusion down to the reign of Charles II. May-day was for ages a kind of Saturnalian jubilee among the citizens, who used to collect in bands, according to their companies and wards, and sally out, headed by a mock nobility and mock officers, into the adjacent fields to bring home garlands for the City May-poles and to practise sports—chiefly archery. This was called going a Maying. It was on one of these occasions that the citizens more than usually incited by the 'amor dapis atque pugnæ,' gave loose to their vengeance against the hapless foreigners. Maitland and Stow give a long account of this catastrophe. A ludicrous scene

MAY-DAY REVELLINGS.

It was in this reign that the Court of Conscience, or, as it is now called, of Requests, was first established in London; in an old play of the year 1613, the main drift of which is to ridicule the manners of the citizens and their propensity to mummery and shows, will perhaps amuse the reader in its illustration of this custom of Maying.

'*Citizen* (*addressing his apprentice*, RALPH). Come hither, Ralph; come to thy mistress, boy.

'*Wife.* Ralph, I would have thee call all the youths together in battle-ray, with drums, and guns, and flags, and march to Mile-end in pompous fashion, and there exhort your soldiers to be merry and wise, and to keep their beards from burning. Ralph; and then skirmish and let your flags fly, and cry "Kill, kill, kill!" My husband shall lend you his jerkin, Ralph, and there's a scarf; for the rest, the house shall furnish you, and we'll pay for't. Do it bravely, Ralph; and think before whom you perform, and what person you represent.

'*Ralph.* I warrant you, mistress; if I do it not for the honour of the City, and the credit of my master, let me never hope for freedom!

'*Wife.* 'Tis well spoken, i' faith! Go thy ways; thou art a spark indeed.

'*Cit.* Ralph, Ralph, double your files bravely, Ralph!

'*Ralph.* I warrant you, sir. [*Exit.*

'*Cit.* Let him look narrowly to his service; I shall take him else. I was there myself a pikeman once, in the hottest of the day, wench; had my feather shot sheer away, the fringe of my pike burnt off with powder, my pate broken with a scouring stick, and yet, I thank God, I am here. [*Drums within.*

'*Wife.* Hark, George, the drums!

'*Cit.* Ran, tan, tan, tan, ran, tan! Oh, wench, an thou hadst but seen little Ned of Aldgate, drum Ned, how he made it roar again, and laid on like a tyrant, and then struck softly till the ward came up, and then thundered again, and together we go! ta, ta, ta, "bounce,"

CHAP. VIII
A.D. 1509 to 1558.

quoth the guns! "courage, my hearts!" quoth the captains! "Saint George," quoth the pikemen! and withal, here they lay and there they lay! and yet for all this I am here, wench.

'*Wife.* Be thankful for it, George; for indeed 'tis wonderful.

(*Enter* RALPH *and his company, with drums and colours.*)

'*Ralph.* March fair, my hearts! lieutenant, beat the rear up. Ancient, let your colours fly; but have a great care of the butchers' hooks at Whitechapel; they have been the death of many a fair ancient. Open your files that I may take a view both of your persons and munition. Serjeant, call a muster.

'*Serj.* A stand! William Hamerton, pewterer!

'*Ham.* Here, captain.

'*Ralph.* A corselet and a Spanish pike! 'tis well. Can you shake it with a terror?

'*Ham.* I hope so, captain.

'*Ralph.* Charge upon me. 'Tis with the weakest. Put more strength, William Hamerton, more strength. As you were again. Proceed, serjeant.

'*Serj.* George Greengoose, poulterer!

'*Green.* Here!

'*Ralph.* Let me see your piece, neighbour Greengoose; when was she shot in?

'*Green.* An't like you, master captain, I made a shot even now, partly to scour her, and partly for audacity.

'*Ralph.* It should seem so, certainly; for her breath is yet inflamed. Besides, there is a main fault in the touch-hole, it runs and stinketh: and I tell you, moreover, and believe it, ten such touchholes would breed the pox i' th' army. Get you a feather, neighbour, get you a feather, sweet oil, and paper, and your piece may do well enough yet. Where's your powder?

'*Green.* Here.

'*Ralph.* What, in a paper? As I'm a soldier and a gentleman it craves a

L 2

which originally had jurisdiction to the amount only of 40s.[1] In the 10th year of the same reign, the taking of inquisitions

martial court! You ought to die for 't. Where's your horn? Answer me to that.

'*Green.* An't like you, sir, I was oblivious.

'*Ralph.* It likes me not you should be so; 'tis a shame for you, and a scandal to all our neighbours, being a man of worth and estimation, to leave your horn behind you: I'm afraid 'twill breed example. But let me tell you no more on't. Stand till I view you all. What's become o' th' nose of your flask?

'*1st Sold.* Indeed la, captain, 'twas blown away with powder.

'*Ralph.* I'm on a new one at the City's charge. Where's the stone of this piece?

'*2nd Sold.* The drummer took it out to light tobacco.

'*Ralph.* 'Tis a fault, my friend; put it in again. You want a nose, and you a stone; Serjeant, take a note on't, for I mean to stop it in the pay. Remove and march! [*They march.*] Soft and fair, gentlemen, soft and fair! Double your files; as you were! faces about! Now, you with the sodden face, keep in there! Look to your match, sirrah, it will be in your fellow's flask anon. So; make a crescent now; advance your pikes; stand and give ear! Gentlemen, countrymen, friends, and my fellow-soldiers, I have brought you this day from the shops of security, and the counters of content, to measure out in these furious fields, honour by the ell, and prowess by the pound. Let it not, oh! let it not, I say, be told hereafter, the noble issue of this City fainted; but bear yourselves in this fair action like men, valiant men, and free men! Fear not the face of the enemy, nor the noise of the guns; for believe me, brethren, the rude rumbling of a brewer's cart is far more terrible, of which you have a daily experience: neither let the stink of the powder offend you, since a more valiant stink is nightly with you.

'To a resolved mind, his home is every where:

I speak not this to take away
The hope of your return; for you shall see
(I do not doubt it), and that very shortly,
Your loving wives again, and your sweet children,
Whose care doth bear you company in baskets.
Remember then whose cause you have in hand,
And, like a sort of true-born scavengers,
Scour me this famous realm of enemies.

'I have no more to say but this: stand to your tacklings, lads, and show to th' world you can as well brandish a sword as shake an apron. Saint George, and on, my hearts!

'*All.* St. George! St. George!
[*Exeunt.*

'*Wife.* 'Twas well done, Ralph! I'll send thee a cold capon a-field, and a bottle of March beer; and, it may be, come myself to see thee.

'*Cit.* Nell, the boy hath deceived me much! I did not think it had been in him. He has performed such a matter, wench, that if I live, next year I'll have him captain of the gallifoist, or I'll want my will.'

Beaumont and Fletcher: *Knight of the Burning Pestle.*

Afterwards Ralph, in a kind of burlesque dying speech, says, giving an account of his exploits:—

'I then returned home, and thrust myself
In action, and by all men chosen was
The Lord of May; where I did flourish it
With scarfs and rings and posy in my hand.
After this action I preferred was
And chosen *City Captain at Mile-end*,
With hat and feather and with leading staff,
And trained my men and brought them all off clear,
Save one man, that berayed him with the noise, &c.'—*Ibid.*

'It was first established by Act of

by the king's justices, which by a charter of Edward III. was directed to be taken at St. Martin's-le-Grand, was granted to be taken at Guildhall instead, St. Martin's-le-Grand being out of the civic jurisdiction. Another charter was also granted in the 22nd year of this reign, but which was only confirmatory of former grants in respect to the right of weighing all merchandise imported.¹

The reign of Edward VI. and of his sister Mary may be passed over with slight notice; it being no part of the design of this work to characterise either the qualities or measures of the English princes, except so far as they may bear upon the history of the civic constitution. It is plain that the City still maintained the highest influence amidst the political divisions of the government. The Duke of Somerset, as Protector, had acquired at the beginning of Edward's reign almost the whole regal authority in his own person. The lords associated with him in the administration were resolved to overthrow his ascendency, which had become generally unpopular. Their first precaution was to coalesce with the City magistrates; who, at their instance, called together a Court of Common Council, in which it was proposed to levy a force to be at the disposal of the lords, through whose assistance, it was hoped, the Protector would be brought to account. This bold measure, though introduced by the recorder, was, nevertheless, with some hesitation, rejected; but the lord mayor and aldermen, with the cordial sanction of the court of Common Council, deputed one of their members to represent their complaints to the king. The alderman executed his trust so emphatically in the presence of the Protector himself, that he was fain to yield to the powerful combination against him, and was soon after committed by his opponents to the Tower; to which place he was conducted by the citizens in a manner savouring very much of a triumph.²

Common council, 9th Hen. VIII., and afterwards by Act of 3rd James I. cap. 15. By later acts the jurisdiction has been increased to 5*l*. The jurisdiction of the Civic Courts over causes of limited amount has been, in recent years, largely extended on the model of the general County Court Acts.

¹ Vide post, 'Charters.'
² Grafton's Chron. Engl. A.D. 1549. Hayward's Life of Edward VI. Mait-land, p. 240. Hollingshed. p. 1057.

BOOK I.
A.D. 1548 to 1603.

In the progress of Wyatt's rebellion, the particulars of which can only be here made a matter of reference, Queen Mary had great reason to apprehend the entire defection of the City. This occasioned her such alarm, that, on the news of Wyatt's approach, she suddenly repaired to the Guildhall; where she was met by the lord mayor, aldermen, sheriffs, and the chief of the City companies. She then addressed the citizens in a very conciliatory harangue which had the good effect of preserving their allegiance; on which at this crisis it appeared very evident that the stability of her throne altogether depended.[1]

It was for a long time the fashion, in defiance of the most palpable historical evidence, to extol the reign of Elizabeth as a period in which the genuine principles of the English Constitution prevailed in the highest purity, and characterised all the measures of government. But we have only to refer to the pages of Hume for an ample exposure of such unfounded paneygric: and, although that historian may be charged with an intention to propagate his own political opinions, the records and authorities he refers to speak a plain tale. The administration of justice had become, through the various though partial enactments of Edward I. and Edward III., comparatively regular and uniform: legislative forms, when laws were professed to be enacted, were duly observed; but an obvious opinion must be inferred of the spirit of that government, in which the powers of the royal prerogative were neither ascertained or controlled; and in which Parliament had scarcely acquired the freedom of debate. The unlimited authority which Henry VIII. had on so many important occasions exercised was fresh in the recollection of Elizabeth and of her submissive people; and she possessed too haughty a nature to resign more of it than

[1] Stow, Ann. Eng. Spread's Hist. Brit. It may be argued from this passage, that the Livery, or meeting in Common Hall, was considered the general representative assembly of the genuine citizens. But this meeting must be considered as called very suddenly together on a peculiar emergency; and it will be seen, in examining into the origin and functions of the assembly in Common Hall, that it cannot be considered as entitled to such regard. This meeting is not recorded even among those of the Common Hall, as in such case it would have been.

the circumstances of the times were calculated to wrest gradually from her hands. Throughout her reign she laboured to rule rather by prerogative than by law; and was notoriously disinclined to parliaments. She endeavoured to restrict the functions of that assembly within limits which would have implied that its members were merely her discretionary advisers. All state affairs, she informed them, were *not there to be meddled with*.¹ She even proceeded so far as expressly to forbid certain discussions; though involving the most important considerations which could possibly occupy the attention of a legislature; namely, those concerning the national religion, and the succession to the Crown.² From this formidable assumption of prerogative, however, she had the prudence decently to retire; and it must be confessed, that in spite of the prevalent subserviency of Parliament, many indications of independence in that house may be discovered in the speeches of some of the members.

The prerogatives which, as exercised throughout this reign, were most hostile to the just liberty of the subject may be shortly summed up. Elizabeth had continual recourse to the jurisdiction of the Star Chamber—a jurisdiction altogether unlimited and undefined in its extent, its process, its mode of trial, and its judgments. The Court of High Commission, established on her sole authority for the trial of all offences in matters of religion, that is, all aberrations in faith from one arbitrary standard, as well as many moral transgressions deemed of ecclesiastical cognisance, was an Inquisition in its worst sense. It was discretionary in all its powers, both of investigation and of punishment. Martial law was frequently ordered to be put in force upon all offenders whom the queen determined to consider as promoting disorders or mutiny in the government. But of all the privileges assumed by the Crown in this age, none were more prejudicial to the national interests or more offensive to the body of the people, than the power of dispensing with, and even of indirectly enacting, laws by royal proclamations, and that of granting exclusive monopolies to favourites and purchasers by royal

¹ Hume, ch. xl.   ² Hume, chaps. xxxix. xli. xlii.

patents. By the latter, the Crown arrogated no less a right than that of circumscribing at discretion the private wealth of all the industrious individuals of the kingdom, by absolute interference with the profits of their labour: by the former, it is plain that the engrossment of the whole authority of the legislature was despotically aimed at.

Under such a dynasty it is apparent that the condition of the people must have depended altogether on the accidental qualities of the ruler; and these, it must be acknowledged, were, in regard to Elizabeth, of a description eminently successful in promoting her own prosperity and that of her subjects. Frugal in the highest degree in all her expenditure, both public and private, and cautiously abstaining from all unnecessary wars, she avoided that common stumbling-block to the authority of monarchs occasioned by burthensome taxation. Sagacious in the choice of wise ministers, she maintained, through their agency, that just equilibrium between popular concession and coercive severity, as to ensure the greatest deference to all her measures. By a sedulous attention to the ports and shipping, she may be said to have restored the naval glory of England; and by the promotion of commercial speculations (however ignorantly and imperfectly regulated) she diffused a vast increase of wealth and industry amongst her people. Her success in effectually humbling her powerful enemies, while it flattered the high spirit of the nation, at the same time preserved it from the degradation and disasters of foreign conquest. But above all, generous and intrepid in her disposition, she ever manifested that personal confidence in the attachment of her people, with which it is a quality in human nature itself under any circumstances to be fascinated. It is to these peculiarities in the character of Elizabeth, and in that of the times, rather than to the forms of government which prevailed, or the enjoyment of anything like pure constitutional liberty by the people, that we must attribute the universal popularity which attended this glorious reign—

[1] It was a saying of Queen Elizabeth's that 'her purse was the pockets of her people.' On one occasion she sold many of her private demesnes and even her crown jewels, to support a necessary war.

ELIZABETH. ASSUMPTIONS OF PREROGATIVES.

a popularity which, being faithfully handed down to posterity, has served to blind those who are not careful to distinguish between the qualities of the governor and those of the government itself.

No class of her subjects were more cordially attached to Elizabeth than the citizens of London. It was this attachment, perhaps, as well as reverence for her administration, which induced them cheerfully to submit to several measures interfering not a little with their chartered rights. Indeed, it is not to be denied, but that some of the proceedings of the civic authorities themselves were hardly to be justified in point of law, a consideration which might reasonably render them less inquisitive into those emanating from a higher source.

Elizabeth exercised the prerogative of impressment as well for land as for sea service. In the assertion of this power, the lord mayor was directed by her letters to keep within the City a standing body of select citizens always well instructed in military discipline. In obedience to this command, that magistrate issued his precept to the respective companies to furnish the required quota, to which they duly attended.[1] On the first intelligence of the Spanish invasion, she required a body of troops to be instantly raised, which demand was readily complied with by the companies, who sent 5,000 men into encampment.[2] She subsequently demanded 10,000 more troops by a letter to the lord mayor; upon which it was resolved in Common Council that the aldermen should raise these soldiers by impressment in their respective wards.[3] In the same way, 38 ships were supplied.[4] Illegal and unconstitutional as these acts were, particularly with reference to the chartered privileges of the citizens, it must be confessed that the occasion furnished an excuse for the measures; and at all events, whatever blame may belong to them, must be shared between the queen and those who put her commands into execution.[5]

[1] Hollingshed, A.D. 1572.
[2] Maitland, vol. i. p. 269.
[3] Act of Common Council, A.D. 1587.
[4] Maitland, vol i. pp. 271, 282. This was but a prelude to many other similar demands.
[5] The practice of impressment both for land and sea service was exercised

154   HISTORICAL ACCOUNT OF LONDON.

BOOK I.
A.D. 1558 to 1603.

The riots in the streets of London, which from various causes, but more particularly from jealousy against foreign settlers, had become common throughout many preceding reigns, grew to a great height in this; and were chiefly fomented by the apprentices.¹ In the early part of it,

as a prerogative right from the most ancient periods of the English history. The latter right, though often disputed as unconstitutional, has been clearly established by many decisions, as founded on immemorial usage and the necessities of the state. The right of impressment for land service, though it may be equally vindicated on the ground of immemorial usage, can hardly be said ever to have been sanctioned by law, except in the cases of civil wars, on which emergencies the state necessarily must supersede every other consideration. These emergencies having happily long ceased to arise, and the military establishment of the nation having been long placed under legislative regulations, all questions upon the subject of land impressments may be considered as practically closed. Both land and sea service are excluded from the obligations of the London citizens, who by their charter are not compellable *to war out of the City* (vide Book II. Ch. IV. p. 344). Neither usage or any other principle of English law, however, gave the sovereign a right to demand a supply of ships, soldiers, or armaments from any class of the people.—Vide Black. Comm. vol. i. p. 240, and authorities; Christian's edition.

¹ No subject of allusion is more common, or more depictive of the riotous state of the City in these times, than that of the disorderly manners of the citizens, and more particularly of the apprentices, on festival days, by the dramatists of the day. It appears that the apprentices formed a sort of confederacy among themselves to resent attacks upon them, or any real or imaginary affronts, and were all provided with *clubs*; armed with which, upon any sudden call from their fellows in the streets, they leaped from their open penthouse shops and rushed to the fray. Thus Shakespeare, in his 'Henry the Eighth,' puts the following words into the mouths of a porter and his man who are defending the palace gate against the influx of the rabble.

'*Man.* There is a fellow somewhat near the door, he should be a brasier. ——That firedrake did I hit three times on the head.——There was a haberdasher's wife, of small wit, near him, that railed upon me till her pinked porringer fell off her head.——I missed the meteor once, and bit that woman, who cried out *clubs!* when I might see from far some forty truncheoneers draw to her succour, which were the hope of the Strand, where she was quartered. They fell on. &c.

'*Porter.* These are the youths that thunder at a playhouse, and fight for bitten apples.'

Again, in a play of the date 1604, a mercer being struck, his servant exclaims—

'*George.* 'Shoot. Clubs! Clubs! Prentices, down with 'em!
Ah, you rogues, strike a citizen in his shop!'
    Decker: *Honest Whore*, 1604.

In another play of the same period, Staines (a young gallant) addresses a citizen thus:—

'*Staines.* Sirrah, by your outside you seem a *citizen*.
Whose coxcomb I were apt enough to break
But for the law. Go, you're a prating Jack.
Nor is't your hope of *crying out for clubs*,
Can save you.'
    Cook: *Greene's Tu quoque*, 1614.

ELIZABETH. STREET RIOTS. APPRENTICES. CLUBS. 155

Elizabeth had found it expedient to issue a joint commission to the lord mayor and several of the courtiers, who were 'to 'devise by all good means to prevent and stay disorders'¹ (such was the undefined quality of their powers). This assumption of jurisdiction was apparently neither complained of nor disputed by the civic authorities. Afterwards, however, the queen ventured upon a much more formidable exercise of prerogative. She issued a commission empowering Sir Thomas Wilford, as provost marshal, to execute martial law instantly upon any persons marked out as disorderly by any justice of peace in London, after examination, by hanging them on the gibbet nearest to their supposed offences." What, in these times, may perhaps excite the highest surprise is, that the lord mayor himself, not unadvisedly it may be presumed, sent to the lord treasurer a letter, distinctly

CHAP. VIII.
A.D. 1558 to 1683.

Again, Gazet (a citizen) is struck, and is made to exclaim—
'*Gazet.* The devil knows off his fingers. If he were
In London among the clubs, up went his heels
For striking an apprentice.'
Massinger; *Renegado*, 1624.

And a young gentleman, quarrelling in the street, thus addresses himself to his antagonist:—
'*Pienty.* Walk into Moorfields, I dare look upon your Toledo. Do not show
A foolish valour in the streets, to make
Work for shopkeepers and their clubs.'
Massinger; *City Madam*, 1632.
In allusion to similar kinds of boisterous merriment, Ralph, a City apprentice, who has been figuring away in the burlesque style in a variety of civic doings, is made to express himself in a sort of dying speech thus:—
'*Ralph.* Farewell, all you good boys of merry London!
Ne'er shall we more upon Shrove Tuesday meet
And pluck down houses of iniquity.
————— I shall never more

Hold open, while another pumps, both legs ;
Nor daub a satin gown with rotten eggs.'
Beaumont and Fletcher: *Knight of the Burning Pestle*, 1613.
In the same vein, Spendall, a young City gallant, exclaims:—
'*Spendall.* I do not think but to be lord mayor. 'Prentices may pray for that time ; for whenever it happens, I will make another Shrove Tuesday for them.'—Cook: Green's *Tu quoque*, 1614.
One, speaking of a morose citizen, a lover of silence, says of him:—
'*Clerimont.* He (Morose) would have hanged a pewterer's 'prentice on a Shrove Tuesday's riot, for being o' that trade, when the rest were quit.'
Jonson: *Epicene*, 1609.
And this morose gentleman himself thus apostrophises some persons quarrelling in the streets:—
'*Morose.* Rogues, Hell-hounds, Stentors, out of my doors, begot on an ill May day.'—Ibid.
¹ Maitland, vol. i. p. 262. City Records, *passim*.
² Stow, An. Engl.

requesting the grant of this extraordinary commission; in pursuance of which no fewer than five persons were executed.[1]

In another attempt of the queen to interfere with the civic government, the citizens evinced a much better feeling, and no small degree of spirit, considering the temper of the times. Elizabeth had lately promoted the recorder, on which occasion she directed the lord keeper to apprise the court of aldermen of her wish to have the names of several lawyers sent to her by them, in order that she might approve one out of them as a successor. The proceeding was, on the whole, insidiously and delicately managed; but the object of engrossing within her own influence the appointment was too plain to be mistaken. Some members of the Common Council having by rumour become acquainted with what was going forward, a Court was on their request suddenly summoned, and an earnest entreaty made to the aldermen, independently, to choose *one man* only, according to ancient custom; which was accordingly done. A submissive letter was then sent to the lord treasurer, stating the name of the person chosen, with an account of the proceedings of the Common Council; and at the same time vindicating this their important and most undoubted privilege.[2] Elizabeth did not deem it consistent with her prudence to insist any further on her pretension; but silently acquiesced in the nomination.

Sumptuary proclamations were not unfrequently made at this time against luxurious extravagance in apparel;[3] and frequent Acts of Common Council passed, deploring in lamentable terms and denouncing the same sinful excess amongst the inferior orders and the apprentices.[4] One, which passed in the year 1582, on this subject, specifies in detail the garments, composed of the coarsest and plainest materials, to be worn by the apprentices; and all others were forbidden upon pain of whipping, fine, and imprisonment.

[1] Maitland, vol. I. p. 278. Stow, An. Engl.
[2] Stow's Survey. Maitland, vol. I. p. 279.
[3] Camden, p. 457.
[4] Hedge's By-laws of the City of London.

CHAPTER IX.

REVIEW OF THE PROGRESS OF TRADE GENERALLY IN ENGLAND AND IN THE CITY.

THE encouragement of trade has been alluded to as one of the main objects of Elizabeth's measures. Indeed, such important advances were made during her reign in this extensive department of national prosperity, that it may be considered an era in the commercial history of the country. Some particulars on this subject have already been mentioned; but it may not be inexpedient to institute a more general though succinct review of our mercantile advancement, in which the civic history and privileges are so materially involved. It is to be observed, however, that such an examination is conducted in reference only to the effects produced on the trade of the City of London; nor can it, indeed, otherwise apply in a work professedly confined to the consideration of its local constitution, privileges, and customs.

Whatever commerce may have been carried on in the earlier ages of British history by foreigners visiting the English shores, it may safely be pronounced, that the *natives* engaged no further in it, than by supplying raw materials to their customers. This may even be gathered from the language of those ancient writers who are lavish in panegyrising the trade of London at various periods under the British, Roman, and Saxon dynasties. They invariably speak of London merely as the frequent resort of merchants from distant nations.

According to Anderson, the English did not begin to build ships until Alfred engaged them in that art for the purpose

CHAP. IX.
A.D. 1558 to 1603.

of opposing the Danes.¹ Afterwards, when the kingdom became tranquil, he let vessels to *foreign* merchants ;² a plain proof how little of the spirit of mercantile enterprise, in the sense of commerce with foreign nations, existed among his own subjects. This inference is still further corroborated by that remarkable law already alluded to,³ as enacted by his grandson Athelstan—by which any merchant who made three sea voyages was to be ennobled. Edgar is said to have possessed a *most enormous* navy ;⁴ but the exaggerations of the monks (the only historians of the age), to whom this prince had endeared himself by his lavish grants, have been sufficiently confuted as well in this as in many other instances.⁵ Not a word, however, is mentioned by any of them, in regard to English commerce. A list of tolls paid by foreign vessels and merchandise in the reign of Ethelred II. is preserved by Howell, which shows that the *imports* were considerable ; but a clause inserted—that 'the 'Emperor's men,⁶ who might buy in their ships, were not to 'forestall the markets from the burghers of London'—evidently implies that their trading was not to interfere with the more local and internal dealings by retail of the Londoners,⁷ which appear entirely to have occupied the attention of the latter.

The system of feudal tenures established at the Conquest was peculiarly unfavourable to mercantile pursuits. The whole community, with the exception of a few towns, may be said under that polity to have consisted of landed proprietors and their slaves, or villeins. It is not to be supposed that men, while subjected to the latter dependent condition, would feel any interest or inclination to embark in commercial avocations ; especially while the accumulation of property was likely to serve only as an allurement to plunder. The first step towards improvement in the national trade and manu-

¹ Anderson's Hist. Comm. Introd. p. 80.
² Ibid. p. 83.
³ Page 21.
⁴ Four thousand ships, say some of the monks.
⁵ Hume, Appendix II.; and note C.

Anderson's Hist. Comm. 93.
⁶ The merchants of the Steelyard, as is well conjectured.—Anderson's *Hist. Comm.* pp. 98, 99 ; vide Ch. IX.
⁷ Anderson's Hist. Comm. p. 98. Howell's Londinopolis.

factures was the emancipation of the greater towns from the thraldom of a tenure strictly in *demesne*, and the acquisition of those local privileges conferred from time to time by which their independence, in arbitrary times, was mainly sustained.

Under these circumstances it is not a matter for surprise that even the exportation of raw materials, as well as the importation of merchandise, had gradually passed into the hands of foreigners and foreign settlers. It is equally certain that the people of England did not, until the reign of Edward I., cultivate any manufactures for the purpose of *wholesale* trade.¹ Most of the manufactured articles, even the woollen (which was the earliest they engaged in), were imported; and it appears that the internal trade in these articles was very largely shared by foreigners.² It is true, that many of the useful arts of life were practised, and necessarily so, by the English. We have notice of the existence of the Weavers' Guild or Company as early as the reign of Henry I.;³ and there is reason to think there were many others at that period.⁴ We have had occasion to observe, that the division of different classes of the people into guilds or associations for various objects, was common in early times.⁵ But it does not appear that any of them ever carried on any particular, and much less any joint, *wholesale* trade. The members of such as were associated for the purposes of trade, it may be believed, confined themselves, for the most part, to the supply of the manufactures required by the immediate necessities of those around them. And during the periods of the Barons' wars, such manufactures were almost altogether superseded by those of foreigners.⁶

In the year 1169 was first formed, as near as can be ascertained,⁷ that association so long famous under the name of the Hanseatic league, a name derived from the Gothic *Hansa*,

---

¹ Hall on Customs. Hargrave's Tracts, part iii. c. 5, 6.
² Stat. Merchant of Winchester. Edward I. which speaks of them as settled in London, York, and Bristol.
³ Howell's Londinop. p. 123, quoting a charter of Henry II. which refers to the Weavers' Company as enjoying privileges under Henry I.
⁴ Vide p. 25, note 2; and p. 59; *post*, 313.
⁵ Ibid.
⁶ Hale's Origination of Mankind. And. Hist. Comm. vol. i. p. 132.
⁷ And. Hist. Comm. vol. i. p. 161.

signifying a *multitude* or convention.¹ It was composed
originally of the number of twelve towns situate on the Baltic
shores, at the head of which was Lubeck; but it subsequently
comprised sixty-four, some say seventy-two, others eighty, of
the noblest towns and cities in Germany, Sweden, and the
Netherlands.² This confederacy, about the year 1200, chose
for their protector the Grand Master of the German Knights
of the Cross or of the Teutonic Order, the governor of a very
powerful republican body settled in Livonia under that appellation; and which subsisted in full strength until the year
1525. The foundation of this association was suggested by
an anxiety for mutual protection against pirates; but in process of time, after their gradual accumulation of riches, the
confederated towns assumed in a great measure independent
governments, and contrived, by the politic employment of
funds raised by common contributions, to gain a firm footing
in most of the nations of Europe. They, at the same time,
acquired such valuable and distinguishing privileges, as to
enable them to engross nearly the whole trade of the countries
in which they were settled.

In the time of Henry III. they obtained a charter, by
which their settlement in England was distinctly authorised.³
There is reason to believe, however, that they were settled in
London before his reign at a place called the Steelyard, from
the nature of the traffic carried on there, and from which
place they derived their denomination of the Merchants of
the Steelyard.³ It is certain that either he or his son Edward
I., not only granted them the liberty of constant residence,
but also the privilege of exemption from any but a specific
and very moderate custom; some say one per cent, others
only a quarter.⁶ The custom, whatever it might be, was
lower than that subsequently paid by the English themselves,
which was a peculiar distinction in their favour; and so continued until these merchants were finally deprived of such
unjust advantages by Edward VI. and Queen Elizabeth.⁴ It
is universally agreed amongst the German writers, that the

¹ Spelm. Gloss. Lye's Gothic Dict.
² Aud. Hist. Comm. vol. i. p. 344;
vol. ii. pp. 35, 134.
³ Ibid. vol. i. pp. 211, 227, and
authorities.
⁴ Ibid. vol. L pp. 421, 422.

grants so obtained were in consideration of services rendered in war by the Hanseatic ships.¹ These confederates were no sooner established, than they drew to themselves almost the whole of the foreign trade of England;² the English neither having then, nor for a very long time afterwards, any vessels of their own.³

There existed at this period another society, composed also entirely of foreigners (who may, however, have been likewise merchants of the Steelyard), called the Merchants of the Staple.³ They were so named from their dealing in particular commodities termed the Staples of England. These staple commodities were the raw produce of the kingdom, as lead, tin, wool, &c.,⁴ but the term came to be applied at last almost solely to wool, which was the chief of them. The reason of such commodities being denominated *staples* was, that fairs and markets were *established* in particular towns and ports from time to time for the sale of these articles, either as the most convenient for intercourse, or for the collection of the king's customs.⁵ In these early times, almost every species of sale, wholesale as well as retail, was conducted in open markets;⁶ which may have given rise to the legal position, that all London is a *market overt*; though for several subsequent centuries, and until late years, the area of it was almost entirely occupied by private retail shops. All *wholesale* trade continued to be so conducted until the reign of Charles II.; the prevalence of which course of traffic, whether by wholesale or retail, may be attributed, not so much perhaps to an anxiety for the accommodation of the dealers, as to the ancient practice of the great barons, as well as the kings, in exacting arbitrary duties on the

---

¹ And. Hist. Com. vol. i. pp. 211, 227.
² Ibid. vol. i. p. 232.—Vide a list of customs paid by the Londoners for half a year amounting only to 76l.; but whether paid by English or settlers does not appear.
³ Ibid. vol. i. pp. 216, 231.
⁴ Ibid. quoting Malyne's Lex Mercatoria.
⁵ Ibid. and vol. i. p. 315.
⁶ Authorities collected in Norton's Exposition of the Privileges of the City of London. This was a pamphlet published in the year 1821, upon the exclusive privileges of trading within the City of London—and of course long ago out of print. The authorities referred to are Acts of Com. Council, temp. Elizabeth, James I. and Charles I. 5 Coke's Rep. 62. Hutchins v. Player, Sir S. Bridgman's Rep. by Bannister, p. 274.

BOOK I.
A.D. 1558 to 1603.

transit of goods amongst their dependent tenants in demesne.¹

Besides these two bodies of foreign merchants, who were regularly associated, as incorporated companies, many others, chiefly Lombards, were settled in different parts of England, and carried on a very considerable trade both external and internal.² The English, and more particularly the Londoners, instead of profiting by the instruction to be derived from these strangers in the arts of manufacture and of commerce, and endeavouring to compete with them, cherished feelings of the most rancorous jealousy and hatred against them. Envious of their wealth, and regardless of the beneficial methods by which it was obtained, they believed that the prosperity of these foreigners was acquired entirely at the expense of the citizens, and, not content with denouncing the special and unjust privileges granted in their favour, they for some centuries endeavoured to procure the most iniquitous and persecuting laws against them.

Edward I. appears to have had in view the encouragement of commerce and manufactures amongst his subjects, though it is too much to say that his mercantile laws were passed for that sole object. In his reign the first statute was passed for the repair of highways,³ the greatest of all steps towards progress of internal commerce. Several statutes also passed to facilitate the internal traffic of foreign merchants of all nations settled in England, particularly in respect to the recovery of debts,⁴ in spite of the remonstrance of the citizens of London and other places. The English company of Merchant Adventurers was formed in London towards the close of his reign, and first attempted the commencement of a woollen manufacture in England. They had a staple allowed them at Antwerp⁵ for raw produce, particularly of wool, to which cloths were also admitted.

It was not, however, till the reign of Edward III. that the woollen manufactures of England arrived at such perfection

¹ Mad. Hist. Exch. passim.
² And. Hist. of Com. vol. i. pp. 236, 253, 295; and quotation from the Charta Mercatoria, p. 258.
³ Stat. 13th Edward I. cap. 5.
⁴ Stats. of Acton Burnell, and of Winchester 2nd.
⁵ And. Hist. of Com. vol. i. pp. 253, 106.

as to produce cloths in any considerable quantity for exportation.¹ At this period the English company of merchant adventurers began in a great degree to supersede the foreign merchants of the staple, by buying up large quantities of wool for their own factories, instead of leaving it for the latter to purchase for the supply of the continent.² The trades with Bruges in English-made cloths largely increased.³ This improvement and increase of our manufactures must be entirely attributed to the great encouragement given by Edward III. to foreign weavers and artificers, great numbers of whom settled in many parts of England, and particularly in London, Norwich, and Worsted—a place in Norfolk, of which not a vestige now remains, but which gave the name to the manufacture of *Worsted*.⁴ They were opposed and insulted by the Londoners with great animosity; but found ample protection in their royal patron.⁵

Notwithstanding these efforts for the extension of commerce, the restraints arising from the assumed and latent powers of the king's prerogative tended to confine it within very narrow limits. The arbitrary authority of the great barons over the property and pursuits of their dependants was somewhat curbed; but still enough remained in the king, at this period and long subsequently, and was so exercised, from motives of caprice and private favour, from mistaken policy, or from motives of extortion, as to occasion the greatest uncertainty and insecurity in all commercial avocations.⁶ He assumed an unlimited discretion in the regulation of all trade, both internal and external.⁷ Permission to engage in it was to be sought at his hands, and usually to be paid for.⁸ He erected what companies and associations he pleased with exclusive privileges of trade, not only with certain places, but in particular articles:⁹ and it was by no means unusual for these companies to be composed

¹ Anderson Hist. of Com. vol. i. pp. 303, 323, 326.
² Ibid. vol. i. p. 342. The merchants of the staple, however, subsequently claimed to compete with the merchant adventurers in the sale of *cloths*, as well as the commodities properly termed staples. Ibid. p. 479.
³ Ibid. vol. i. p. 342.
⁴ Ibid. vol. i. pp. 297, 298, 305, 320, et passim.
⁵ Ibid. vol. i. pp. 317, 355.
⁶ Hume's App. 2nd; and Madox Hist. Exch. ch. xiii. passim.

entirely of foreigners.¹ Tolls on bridges were fixed at pleasure; customs and duties on exports and imports were arbitrary;¹ as well as those which were levied at markets and fairs, until most of the boroughs purchased the liberty of farming them at a fixed rent.² There can be no doubt—whatever may be thought of the policy in regard to the majority of the exclusive privileges granted to many cities—that those which conferred liberties and exemptions from these effects of *arbitrary power*, which form such conspicuous features in many of their early charters, must have very essentially conduced to commercial improvement. It will also appear that the mercantile prosperity of the nation at large increased, as the exercise of these royal prerogatives abated.

Many of the statutes passed for the regulation of trade in these times, and many even of those passed ostensibly for its encouragement, were but little calculated for its benefit. In particular several clauses may be mentioned in the Statutes Staple,³ as they are called, which provided for the sole trade in staple commodities at fixed places, instead of leaving it to that vent which the convenience of those concerned would naturally suggest. These measures were often adopted as means of corrupt favour to particular towns, and sometimes of oppression to others—the private emolument of the king being usually the chief inducement.⁴ With this view a staple for the port of London was erected by Edward III. at Westminster, to the great advantage of the latter and proportionate detriment of the former.⁵ This mart, however, continued there but a few years.⁶

Another statute⁷ was framed, to oblige foreigners to receive staple goods in exchange for their manufactures. Nothing could be more prejudicial than this enactment to the advancement of our own trade, or more partial in its policy. But on the whole, the manufactures of cloth continued gradually to improve and increase; the clothing trade was, at first, chiefly carried on in London; but in the reign of

¹ Hume's App. 2nd; and Madox Hist. Exch. ch. xiii. *passim.*
² Ibid.; and Mad. Firm. Burg. Vide also *supra*, pp. 43, 41.
³ Particularly those of Edward III.
⁴ And. Hist. of Com. vol. i. pp. 326, 497.
⁵ Ibid. vol. i. pp. 333, 334.
⁶ Ibid. vol. i. p. 367.
⁷ Stat. 14th Richard II. cap. 9.

Richard II. it had removed to the adjacent counties, and subsequently to those more remote.¹

At this period we find some English merchants had settled themselves in the Prussian Hans Towns;² and by a statute passed in the reign of Richard II.,³ which provided that English merchants should ship only in English bottoms, we may observe that some attention began to be directed to the shipping trade. It is certain, however, from other authentic records, that this statute could have had but very little operation⁴ in promoting a spirit of foreign commerce amongst the English, and that they had scarcely yet ventured with their ships into the Mediterranean.⁵ Throughout the reigns of Henry IV. and Henry V. mention is made of English vessels trading to France; and as the only ships used in these times for naval warfare⁶ were those belonging to merchants, this circumstance alone may sufficiently explain why the employment of English bottoms should have become a subject of national policy.

In the reign of Henry VI. the list of manufactures had very much increased, particularly in respect to the variety of woollens, which began to be more valued as articles of export commerce.⁶ The merchants of the staple alone paid for customs in one year 68,000l., according to the valuation of that period,⁷ though their share of the trade in staple articles and woollens can hardly have equalled that of the merchant adventurers, and merchants of the Steelyard. In the next reign we find a statute passed, in furtherance of the old mercantile theories presently to be noticed, to prohibit the importation of a vast number of foreign manufactures⁸ as obstructing the sale of our own.

It had been provided by the Statutes Merchant (as they

---

¹ And. Hist. of Com. vol. i. p. 404.
² Ibid. vol. i. p. 384.
³ 15th Richard II. cap. 6.
⁴ Vide the following notes.
⁵ The doge of Venice at this time requested permission for Venetian vessels to trade to London, and promised in return to receive well English noblemen and travellers: he makes no mention of any English trading to Venice. And. Hist. of Com. vol. i. p. 376. The first English vessel which visited Morocco, was in Henry IV.'s time. Ibid. vol. i. pp. 421, 530.
⁶ Ibid. vol. i. p. 445.
⁷ Ibid. vol. i. p. 479, quoting a record in the Exchequer.
⁸ 3rd Edward IV. cap. 4.

were termed) of Edward I., that the mayor of the cities in which foreigners were settled should have exclusive jurisdiction in the recovery of their debts. The merchants of the Steelyard had long enjoyed the privilege of having civil justice administered to them by an alderman of London, appointed by the corporation. In what manner the proceedings before this tribunal were carried on does not appear; but it seems the mode adopted gave much satisfaction; for we find these merchants petitioning the king and Parliament in the time of Henry VI., in consequence of a neglect for some years in the appointment of an alderman for that purpose.

It appears from a statute of Richard III.,[1] passed for the expulsion of foreigners from London, and, in all probability, by way of ingratiating himself into the favour of the citizens, that not only vast numbers of foreigners traded by wholesale and retail as constant settlers, but that the artisans were chiefly composed of the same class. This ill-advised measure was not pursued to any considerable extent; and the policy of Henry VII. imported great numbers of Flemish woollen manufacturers, who were much superior to our own, and settled them at Leeds, Wakefield, and Halifax. Many of the measures of that sagacious prince were directed to the encouragement of trade in his kingdom, though by no means characterised by equal wisdom. One, which enjoined all merchants trading to particular towns to become members of the company of merchant adventurers, which company was in the habit of exacting heavy fines for admission,[2] can hardly be defended on any principle.

Henry VIII. scarcely interfered in the affairs of commerce, except by the exercise of his prerogative in granting monopolies and patents. He did not, however, carry them to such an extent as materially to impede its gradual progress. English vessels began to reach as far as the Levant and Smyrna,[3] and even as far as Guinea.[4] And although the clothing manufacture flourished in a considerable degree, the export of raw wool still continued enormous. Sixty vessels

[1] 1st Richard III. cap. 9.
[2] And. Hist. of Com. vol. i. p. 550.
[3] Ibid. vol. ii. p. 27.
[4] Ibid. vol. ii. p. 62.

laden with that staple, sailed in one year from Southampton for the Netherlands.¹ The English merchant adventurers, neglecting the home manufactures in which they had originally embarked, had directed their trade in that channel for many years, and are said to have maintained 20,000 cloth manufacturers in Antwerp alone.² The policy of giving encouragement to our home manufactures by retaining, instead of forcing abroad, the materials of our manufactures had not hitherto been broached. Henry VIII. was the first founder of a royal navy.³

The time, however, had now arrived, in which the many corporated companies of foreigners, which had from time to time established themselves in London with all their various and distinguishing privileges, were obliged to yield to the universal animosity expressed against them. They had, in the progress of some centuries, dispensed the most important benefits throughout the nation, by the communication of the arts and comforts of civilisation; by the introduction of manufactures of every kind; by their commercial example and instruction; and by their promotion of naval enterprise. The English commercialists had insensibly availed themselves of all these advantages; and, as far as an acquaintance with these arts could conduce thereto, had acquired the full ability of competing with their preceptors. In other respects, in spite of the many partial efforts we have noticed to obtain an equal share, they found the foreigners more than a match for them. Not to mention the many unfair advantages which the foreigners derived from special exemptions in regard to customs and duties, which were long and unwisely continued to them by our monarchs, and which they perverted to fraudulent purposes,⁴ they were almost always enabled, by their superior experience, by their long standing credit in the markets, by the superior management as associated bodies of their mercantile concerns, and, above all, by the adroit employment of their immense capital, to monopolise the markets, to undersell their opponents,⁵ and to stifle all com-

¹ Anl. Hist. of Com. vol. ii. p. 37. Sheridan's Commentaries, lib. 22.
² Ibid. vol. ii. p. 80.
³ And. Hist. of Com. vol. ii. p. 25.
⁴ Ibid. vol. i. p. 497; ii. pp. 90, 91.
⁵ Ibid. vol. ii. p. 90. By *colouring*

petition. These were substantial grievances, which seemed insurmountable while the system was upheld; and the national policy—though narrow when carried to excess or to subserve partial interests—in deference to which these establishments with all their unfair and monopolous privileges were originally founded, had completely effected the object proposed, as appeared manifest in the spirit of trade and navigation which prevailed.[1]

Accordingly, in the reign of Edward VI. all the privileges of the company of the Hanseatic merchants of the Steelyard, which comprised by far the greatest proportion of the foreigners, were declared void, their franchises forfeited, and the corporation dissolved.[2] An over-zealous pursuit of the same policy subsequently dictated a high duty on all their exports.[3] Their trade had become at this time so immensely disproportionate to that of the English, in cloths alone, that they exported in foreign bottoms no less than 44,000 pieces in one year, and in the same year the English exported but 1,000. The good effects of this measure were so immediately apparent, that in the very next year, the English exported 40,000 pieces of cloth.[4] And notwithstanding this large exportation of cloth, raw wool continued to be supplied to Bruges in vast quantities.[5] The most strenuous efforts were made to induce Elizabeth to restore to these foreign associated companies their privileges; but she knew too well the interests of her subjects to comply,[6] and the more strongly opposed them. Owing, however, to these struggles, the company of the merchants of the Steelyard was not in fact finally extinguished till the latter end of her reign.[7]

---

other traders' goods; that is, passing them as their own.

[1] The inconsistency with which Anderson, and indeed many other writers on commerce, sometimes blame and at other times applaud the exclusion of foreign settlers, occasions great confusion in their works. It seems to arise from their not reflecting on the distinction between the *introduction* of these through the medium of artificial support for the sake of instruction and example, and the *retention* of their foreign successors with the same superior advantages after the purposes of the original introduction are fully answered. True policy, however, rejects all artificial support, as well as forcible exclusion, for either purpose.

[2] And. Hist. of Com. vol. ii. pp. 90, 91.
[3] Ibid. vol. ii. p. 93.
[4] Ibid.
[5] Ibid. vol. ii. p. 108.
[6] Ibid. vol. ii. p. 155.
[7] Ibid. vol. ii. p. 192.

The great impulse given to trade in all its departments by this measure, which forms so distinguishing a feature in the commercial history of London, was not sensibly counteracted by the profuse grants of monopolies and trade patents which marked Elizabeth's government; although they were prejudicial as far as they went.[1] The spirit of commercial enterprise was thoroughly roused, and the very flattering countenance which that queen personally gave to it tended to increase it. It would occasion too much digression to trace the many wise measures by which she cherished and improved this grand source of our national wealth; as their application was for the most part general to the whole kingdom, and not peculiar to the City of London. We may remark, however, that the colonisation of America, which was carried in this reign to a large extent, produced a most powerful excitement to every species of mercantile speculation.

The great and continual accession of foreigners for so many ages, had a considerable effect, both on the commercial habits of the Londoners and on the internal administration of the civic government. The rights and customs of the latter, in respect to exclusive trade, were more ancient than the foundation of the earliest of the foreign chartered companies. Those individuals whose introduction into the City they had not the power to prevent, and which comprised the greater portion of their numerous rivals, they never ceased to complain against. Accordingly, until the time of Elizabeth, and for a long period subsequently, the City authorities were chiefly occupied in devising modes of preventing these encroachments. In the earlier ages, as we have seen,[2] foreigners were not allowed to reside in the City more than forty days: they were delivered by magistrates, appointed specifically for that purpose, to particular hosts, who were responsible for their conduct: strict injunctions were laid on their selling their goods within the forty days, by wholesale only, and to none but citizens. The most severe penalties forbade the evasion of these regulations, by the interception

---

[1] For the vast increase of exports and imports during this reign, vide Anil. Hist. Com., and particularly vol. ii. pp. 159, 160, 195, 198.
[2] Vide supra, pp. 20, 75, 120, 159, and post, 371.

of goods on their road to the London markets; afterwards brokers were sworn, and put under rigid control for the due management of all foreign dealing. The seizure of goods foreign bought and sold, according to one of the ancient City customs, was frequently resorted to by the citizens. Officers called foreign takers superintended the traffic in the markets for the same object. Nor can there be a doubt that the depôts of Blackwell Hall and Leadenhall were kept up long after the decline of regular *staples*, more for the purpose of preventing illicit trading between foreigners than for any other, either connected with the requisite fabrication of the manufactures, or the payment of duties upon them.[1]

Nothing contributed so much to allay, and finally to quell altogether, this jealousy against the settlement of trading foreigners in the City, than the persecution of the Huguenots in France and of their Protestant brethren in the Netherlands. The refugees in thousands—and comprising the most industrious and skilful artisans in Europe—were received with sympathetic welcome throughout England, and more particularly in London. They sought no monopolous or distinguishing privileges, they asked no more than protection in common with the people of the land in the pursuit of their beneficial labours. They aimed only at enjoying the condition of fellow-subjects, and gradually they became absorbed as a component part of the English nation, competing for the same national honours, and sharing in all national and local duties. They soon became adopted as amongst the most loyal in the national family; and with them was adopted their superior ingenuity in the arts, and that commercial spirit which was rapidly diffused throughout the country.

The increase of trade had its corresponding effect in increasing the suburbs of London, which Elizabeth and her successor James I. both vainly endeavoured by frequent proclamations to prevent. It is strange that this necessary consequence of the extension of its manufactures as well as trade was not perceived. London, it appears from a list of

---

[1] Norton's Exposition of the Privileges of the City of London: where the authorities are collected, and the subject discussed in detail. Vide note, p. 161.

Customs, exported at this period three times as much as all the rest of England together.[1]

In the reign of James I. the exportation of wool, which had been denied to *foreigners* by Elizabeth, was, in direct contrast to the policy of our early ancestors, forbidden altogether;[2] a policy which has been implicitly followed until late years, with results more than duly advantageous to the advancement of our woollen manufactures and the interests of the woollen manufacturers. The capricious interference of this king in monopolies, licenses, and arbitrary tolls, began now to be not only seriously but successfully remonstrated against as illegal; and many monopolies were abolished by statute. Incorporated companies with exclusive rights of trade fell very much into decay, and we hear the last of the merchants of the staple. The company of Merchant Adventurers continued a short time longer with various fortunes; until at last the facility of admission into it appeased all jealousy against its existence, and, by distributing in all directions, reduced to nothing that strength which could subsist only by combination. We find, in the reign of Charles II., the establishment of them by royal prerogative expressly adjudged contrary to law as monopolous.[3]

It is well known how far the assumption and exercise of the royal prerogatives, in levying arbitrary duties on commerce and in granting monopolies and licenses, by which Charles I. endeavoured to supply his exchequer in defiance of Parliament, tended (among other arbitrary acts) to that civil war which in the result cost that unfortunate monarch his crown and life. The English, and particularly the Londoners, according to Clarendon, made the most lamentable and continual complaints of the ruinous effects of these measures upon their trade; though 'it is evident, both from the assertions of that author and the concurrent testimony of records and public documents, that commerce progressively advanced thoughout the whole of his reign.[4]

---

[1] And. Hist. of Com. vol. ii. p. 260.
[2] Ibid. vol. II. pp. 146, 340.
[3] Ibid. vol. ii. p. 260.
[4] The Customs of England in 1610 amounted to 500,000*l*. Ibid. vol. ii. p. 390. The citizens of London in the civil war agreed to pay 520,000*l*. per annum—a proof of great wealth, considering the time. Ibid. vol. ii. p. 401.

BOOK I.
A.D. 1558 to 1603.

The exertions which characterised the Dutch naval wars with England during the period of the Commonwealth, are sufficient indications of the progress of trade and navigation, and of the importance each nation attached to the dominion of the sea. In one of their earliest engagements no less than a hundred sail of the line fought on each side.[1] To the Parliament of the Commonwealth the nation is indebted for the first establishment of a regular system of maritime policy, which was afterwards brought into full operation under the celebrated Navigation Act.[2] The prejudicial effects produced by this act in destroying the commerce of other nations and advancing the partial benefit of our own commercialists, will be discussed and exposed in a future page; but that all those advantages, which during an age of perpetual warfare attended our nautical superiority, were accomplished by this act, is abundantly testified by the great increase of English shipping and of commercial enterprise which immediately followed it. In the short space of twenty years, it is said by a very competent judge, that the number of ships and merchants were doubled.[3] The Dutch felt so severely the consequences of this policy, that at the treaty of Breda in 1607, they laboured with the utmost anxiety to procure the repeal of the Navigation Act, as entirely destructive of their commerce. They succeeded, however, no further than in obtaining the admission into English ports of all Dutch vessels bringing Rhenish merchandise by way of Dort.

From the expulsion of the foreign associated companies in the reign of Edward VI., as already noticed, to the passing of the Navigation Act, and from that time to the close of the reign of Charles II., the commerce of England, and more particularly that of the City of London, advanced with a rapidity unexampled in the history of the world during those times. Pensionary de Witt, in his work entitled 'The Interest of Holland,' after summing up the causes which had powerfully contributed to the commercial glory of England, at the latter period, uses this remarkable and prophetic lan-

[1] And. Hist. of Com. vol. ii. p. 422. Trade: preface.
[2] Vide post. pp. 186, 187. [1] Anderson's Hist. of Com. vol. ii.
[3] Sir Joseph Child's Discourses on p. 193.

guage:—'So that this mighty island, seated in the midst of
' Europe, having a clear deep coast, and good havens and
' bays, united with Ireland under one king, and now by its
' conjunction with Scotland, being much increased in strength,
' as well by manufactures as by a great navigation, will in all
' respects be formidable to Europe. For according to the
' proverb, a master at sea is a lord on land.'

CHAP.
IX.
A.D. 1558
to 1603.

It would be foreign to the subject of this work to pursue
this examination through all those changes and measures
which have so wonderfully advanced our commercial prosperity throughout the last two centuries. This is a topic
which rather belongs to the History of England, than to
that of the City of London. We have seen that in the
earliest ages foreign merchants, who occasionally resorted to
our coasts from the rising taste for those articles of comfort
and elegance which they communicated, were courted to
continue such intercourse. We have traced the origin of
internal trade and manufactures in the emancipation of the
greater cities from feudal thraldom, and in the free privileges
conferred on them. We have observed the effect of that
policy by which foreign merchants and artisans were encouraged not only to circulate trade throughout the country
by transient visits, but to establish permanent settlements in
all parts of it, and the gradual progress of our countrymen
in the arts and spirit of commerce, in consequence of the
example and instruction thus afforded, impeded as it was by
ignorant jealousies, by impolitic laws, by pernicious prerogatives, and by overbearing rivalry, until a new impulse was
given to trade by the suppression of all these restraints.
There remains, however, a consideration connected with this
topic, which seems to merit a separate and scrutinous discussion.

CHAPTER X.

ENQUIRY INTO THE NATURE AND EFFECTS OF THE EXCLUSIVE TRADING PRIVILEGES OF THE CITY OF LONDON.[1]

BOOK I.
A.D. 1358 to 1603.

THE question about to be examined is one of important concern to the interests of the City of London; namely, how far any franchises of the Corporation—judicial or administrative—for regulating or controlling trade, or any exclusive privileges in its exercise within the limits of the City, may still be deemed beneficial or otherwise, in a public point of view, or even defensible.

This subject has been one of frequent discussion among the more modern and liberal political economists; and the consideration of the quality and influence of these privileges has led to a denunciation from some of them against even the existence of all civic corporations, as maintained from such sources.

It is a question, therefore, which deserves, if it does not call for, some amplitude of examination. Nor will a preliminary enquiry into the origin, the nature, and the effect of exclusive privileges of trade, be thought irrelevant in a work which aims at elucidating the constitution of a corporation, whose prosperity was mainly founded, and must still in a great degree be upheld by them, under due and enlightened regulation, adapted to the spirit of the times.

---

[1] It should be premised that this chapter—first written in 1823 and published in 1829—was composed at a time when the present doctrines of 'Free Trade' now (in 1868) become familiar, were by no means fully recognised, even in England, and are but partially adopted (particularly as regards international free trade) in many enlightened nations. The doctrines, as advocated in this chapter, are hardly, if at all, at variance with those which, not only theoretically but practically, prevail nationally in England; and the author has not found it necessary to revise this dissertation materially.

MODERN PRINCIPLES OF FREE TRADE. 175

The true principles of commerce, both internal and external, have become so clearly established and developed by those great English philosophers who have of late years enlightened the world by their works on political economy, that it would argue both ignorance and folly to contest their doctrines. We may consider the position—that all artificial interference in regulating, directly or indirectly, the course of trade by restrictions, monopolies, or by bounties—is in itself detrimental to the public weal, and prejudicial to the advancement of trade as founded on the imperishable basis of truth and reason. This principle, which had faintly emerged into light under the auspices of some eminent English merchants during the last two centuries, has been placed in the fullest and most conspicuous view by Smith and his able successors; and has been finally adopted as a political maxim by the statesman-like genius of Huskisson and Grant.[1] The fallacy of the old mercantile system, for the support of which mainly these restrictions were imposed, and in defence of which they were advocated, has been exposed almost to demonstration. The liberality of the new doctrines has combined, perhaps, with the credit of the authors of them, to induce an inconsiderate adoption of the proposition of free trade in all its relative applications. It should, however, be recollected that the most liberal of the economists reason upon *general principles* only; they contemplate the *universal* condition of mankind on the scale of empires and nations—as bound together in one social compact of brotherly love and good-will; but they make no allowances for the artificial divisions into separate nations and societies, and the necessary sacrifices which the preservation of national independence or internal liberty from arbitrary usurpation must, under *particular circumstances*, require. Were all men actuated by sentiments of justice, of humanity, or even of enlightened self-interest, the truths which prompt a free intercourse and a free interchange of the benefits of industry amongst mankind would have universal application; but while human nature exists as it is,

CHAP. X.
A.D. 1558 to 1603.

---

[1] It should be remarked that Colsten was a school-boy when this was written.

wrong and violence must be anticipated; and societies must unite, and sacrifice many of the advantages which an universal free intercourse would produce, for the purposes of security and self-defence. There may, therefore, be ulterior objects in the contemplation of a government (as in the case of the navigation laws and the charters granted to the East India Company), which may dictate a devious course in the pursuit of the public welfare. The partial advancement of the few, to the detriment of the many, may, with a view to the general result, be beneficial to all. The restrictions, the impediments, and the exclusions, through the medium of which those partial interests are artificially promoted, may, under certain circumstances, be defensible; and, with reference to those circumstances, the subject of unlimited commerce has not, perhaps, even yet been duly considered under all its bearings.

The two great objects which the mistaken policy of our Government had for a long period in view, when it introduced restriction and monopolies in commerce, were; first, the supply of royal or national revenue; and, secondly, the support of the ancient mercantile system. Both these objects of policy were founded on a mistaken theory, and were both mischievous in their effects.

With regard to the supply of revenue—it may easily be imagined that our early kings, ignorant and unlettered as they were, and bigoted in their attachment to feudal power, would be readily disposed to receive the palpable and present benefit of a bribe from the wealthy classes of their subjects, in remuneration for a mere liberty or privilege granted, which apparently cost the donor nothing. The monopolists would appeal to their exclusive privilege in selling their merchandise, or of acquiring from their neighbours, at a lower rate than the natural market price, the materials for producing their manufactures, as the only source from which they could raise the munificent perquisite they pofessed to pay to their conceding patron. They would represent their merchandise as the source of the Customs, and that without artificial support they must resign their trade, so lucrative to the state, and so necessary for the support of the expenditure directed to the public weal. But, without referring to the futility of enhancing the price of one commodity at the cost of another equally desirable to the public, can anything be more manifest, upon reflection, than that the whole excess of the artificial or enhanced price beyond the natural and regular price, was drained from the public generally; that the monopolising merchants who received this extra price paid but a part, and that a very small one, to the state who protected them, and the rest they put into their own pockets? The enhanced price was therefore, in effect, a tax on the subject, which, instead of being appropriated, as all revenue derived from the people ought to be, to the purposes of the state, was directed into the purses of some few overgrown commercialists; and the king or the nation gained by his grant but a small portion of the sum which he enabled the monopolists to extort from his subjects.[1]

The old mercantile system, which subsisted for ages, and still indeed gasps for life under its death-blow, had a still more prejudicial tendency; because through its influence the public suffered for the benefit of the few, and the state gained not even a partial share in the plunder. This system was founded upon two doctrines—the acquisition of the precious metals, instead of merchandise; and the rivalry, or rather the destruction, of the commerce of foreign nations.

It is almost a superfluous task at the present day to urge the utter absurdity of the proposition, that the possession of gold and silver is of the smallest advantage for the sake of *the metals themselves*; and yet there have been writers, of clear and noble intellect, who have advocated such a principle [2]—whole nations have acquiesced in it; and even now, the sun of science, which has gilded the summits of the intellectual hemisphere, is but faintly descried from its levels

---

[1] The American government still act upon this perniciously absurd system—and with this result, the impoverishment and privation of the bulk of the people—as well as of the government, which is utterly perplexed how to raise an adequate revenue without defrauding the public creditors—in favour of the few commercialists.

[2] During the sixteenth century, this principle was strongly advocated by Mun, Digges, Misselden, and others; all men of genius, and what is perhaps more surprising, men of practical mercantile experience. Their self-interest, it is likely, may have infused something.

and depths. So strong was the impression that the precious metals constituted wealth, that all the exertions of commercialists were directed to the accumulation and retention of them in this country; every incitement was held out by precept and by popular clamour to the same end: and, lest the natural reason of the people, and their own conviction of what was their interest, should not be a sufficient security for the advancement of the principle, the arm of power was extended to *force* what was theoretically considered so desirable upon the people; and grievous statutes passed to prevent exportation of bullion, and to impede, in its favour, the importation of many other products. We have hardly yet ceased to exult in the triumphant excess of our exports over our imports, and to be conscious of the visionary advantage of a *favourable balance of trade*.

To the credit of philosophy, so far back as two centuries ago, the fallacy of this dogma was perceived in England, and attempted to be exposed.[1] It was asked, of what use was the money, but *as a medium* through which to procure real commodities? It became a matter of enquiry and reflection, as to what became of those hoards which a policy so long pursued must have amassed? Nor could it be for ever a secret, that the money did but *represent* those very commodities which were so strenuously denounced; and that it did, in fact, go at last to procure them. Those who possessed the glittering wealth, it was observed, kept it but for a moment, and hastened to dispose of it in exchange for stock or consumable products. The real trade, it was plain, consisted in the *exchange of the commodities*; and the gold and silver was either a mere ware in itself, or the circulating medium to facilitate exchanges. There never was a deficiency of the circulating medium, and more than a sufficiency no force could create. It was found that *paper* was just as valuable as money *in effect*; and that its value depended altogether upon its *credit*, or, in other words, its power of producing *something else*. In the result, therefore,

---

[1] First, and mainly, by Sir Dudley North (whose name and actions in the City will be further noticed under the reign of Charles II.); and afterwards by Sir Josiah Child, Sir William Petty, and Barbon.

all these efforts for the acquisition of the precious metals, by preventing the exportation and encouraging the importation of them, accomplished nothing but a delay and difficulty in procuring those acquisitions which were desirable *for their own sakes*, in consequence of a cumbrous increase of the representative medium through which at last they were to be obtained.

But the destruction of the commerce of other nations, and the engrossment of the whole market of the world free from all competition, was a still more popular scheme for the advancement of our commercial interests, and a still more marked characteristic of the old mercantile theory. The most obvious course which suggested itself to many an ignorant and unprincipled Government, was to plunder the property of mercantile countries, and to put the merchants to death. What else, it may be asked, has been the origin and the effects of the many wars waged between commercial nations?[1] More honourable, but not less futile, expedients have been, either to force, *at the expense of the public at large*, so abundant a supply of the manufactures which are the subjects of competition, as to enable the class of merchants dealing in them *nominally* to undersell their rivals; or to punish ourselves by the self-denial of those commodities which the industry of our neighbours may have produced, for the purpose of impoverishing them.

Before, however, we observe upon the means by which, at so much cost to ourselves, we have laboured to injure our natural friends, let us examine for a moment into the effects produced by our success; to see if any advantage was in truth obtained. The mere *destruction* of the trade, or of some of the benefits of it, whatever loss it might occasion to others, could no way benefit the spoilers. If the preparation of gunpowder, or the secret of preparing the mariner's compass, were lucrative sources of our neighbours' trade, and we should endeavour to effect the abolition of both—the rest of the world would lose much; but what should we gain? It has been urged, that although havoc and waste without some

[1] Particularly the Dutch wars of Charles II.

ulterior motive cannot be defended, it is for the purposes of individual self-interest we lend ourselves to so odious an enterprise; it is for the sake of supporting *our own* industrious manufacturers and merchants, who, dealing in inferior articles, must resign their occupations, if driven from the market by the more beneficial supply of foreigners. But such an argument cannot change the nature of the question. We may substitute bows and arrows for the use of gunpowder, or destroy the mariner's compass for the sake of planetary charts. There is, in fact, no species of useful or agreeable acquisition, for the absence of which we may not console ourselves with an inferior substitute: and if the principle of destroying one article of commerce for the sake of another could hold, we might at last raze the imperial palace for the sake of inhabiting the hut of the Esquimaux.

Clear as the proposition may appear—that the loss of one country can never form the profit of another,—many specious suggestions have been, and perhaps are still, advanced in support of a contrary doctrine. It has been imagined that the destruction of a foreign country's trade would open it to our own; that the profits to be derived from it would then encourage competition among ourselves; until, by industry and talent, we became capable of underselling and thereby engrossing the branch of commerce wrested from the first possessor. Let these notions be examined.

That rivalry in producing the commodities of life tends, in its result, to *increase* and *disseminate* them, and being dependent for its reward upon natural and voluntary demand, is beneficial to a nation—is a truth sufficiently obvious: but that such rivalry is, in the aggregate, either promoted by, or is a consequence of, the destruction of some part of the trade, is contradicted by the very terms of the proposition. The only beneficial rivalry is the free competition of *all*. It is plain, therefore, that so far as such rivalry and competition is destroyed in the aggregate, by so much are the products and the quality of them impaired, to the *aggregate* loss. That the general interest and prosperity of the world, or even of *one particular nation*, is promoted by the withdrawing all foreign competition, is an idea equally fallacious. When the supply of commodities has decreased, by the forcible rejection of that part of them which would be brought from the foreign source, the price is of course *enhanced* in favour of those who produce them at home. The *enhanced* price is, in fact, paid for something that is not wanted, in favour of industry which, to the extent of such enhanced price, is totally useless; and which, but for this fostering, would be directed to another and a more useful channel. The public suffer; and the few, whose claims are preposterously preferred to those of the many, have no real, or, at least, no permanent gain. When by dint of partial and internal competition the price is reduced to its former level, nothing is gained, at the expense of time and industry which might have been profitably applied in different pursuits, beyond the original advantage: and when, at last, ingenious inventions and public sacrifices have reduced the price below the original standard, the nation will but have arrived by a tedious and impeded path at that increase of supply which might have been tenfold more valuable, both in quantity and quality, by the effect of a wider competition. Nor is this all. Insomuch as we impoverish our neighbours by rejecting their merchandise, by so much shall we incapacitate them from receiving or paying for our own manufactures. They may, indeed, direct their attention to other objects of labour or production; but according to this maxim of engrossing their trade, we should but commence our ruinous devastations upon them again, till we left them nothing but the bare earth and the natural gifts of providence peculiar to the climate of their country. This would be the final result of attempting to engross more of the trade of the world than *naturally* falls to our share. In short, devastation and havoc can never be defended but upon one principle; namely, that which dictates the endurance and the infliction of all the accumulated disasters of war, in preference to the greatest of all evils which can visit a nation—its subjugation to tyranny and selfish ambition.

Such have been the commercial objects the influence of which has darkly tinged the stream of ages, and which were long maintained by the councils and policy of the most enlightened country in the world. These were the objects for which so many monopolous and exclusive privileges were created in favour of corporations, and of none more than those of the City of London. It is far from our intention to rank among these injurious privileges, the many chartered grants the effects of which were to exempt the citizens from feudal oppressions and arbitrary laws, and to emancipate them from that state of vassalage under which so large a proportion of the commons of England have formerly groaned. These grants did but secure to them those unalienable rights of liberty under a free government which ought to have been the common property of *all*. They did but confer the power of enjoying freedom themselves, and not that of imposing oppression and restraint on others. The exclusive privileges about to be noticed, are those by which mere commercial associations were cemented together, from a vain desire to improve the revenue or to uphold the mercantile theory. Vain and illusory as the end was, the means were hardly less extravagant.

To force the supply of manufactures, by which bullion might be acquired and foreign rival establishments destroyed, expedients were devised, and rewards were held out to individuals to unite and employ their capital and labour *in the* manufacture of them. They alone were to have the privilege of selling cloth, or leather, or tin, or wool. They were to have the sole right of trading with foreigners or for exportation, in particular places, or admitting others so to trade; and yet the towns where these associations existed were erected into *staples*, at which, only, certain branches of commerce could be carried on. Thus even home competition was paralysed, and the negligence and idleness of our own few overgrown merchants furnished ample incitement to the emulative industry of other countries. Exportation of the raw materials (as they were termed) of the manufactures conducted by these associations was prohibited—that is, in other words, one class of manufacturers (for all exchangeable produce whatever is more or less a manufacture) were obliged to sell to another class of manufacturers their merchandise at a cheaper rate than they could obtain in the natural or general market, for the advantage of the one class over the

INJURIOUS EFFORTS TO ACCUMULATE PRECIOUS METALS. 183

ther. But perhaps the most absurd of all the plans for the advancement of our manufactures was that suggesting the numerous regulations under which the fabric and preparation of them were placed, and the interference of local authorities in conducting the mode of transfer. The public were not supposed to be capable of understanding their own interest, in supplying the most valuable commodities, or in protecting themselves against fraud; and accordingly, weighers, searchers, surveyors, and stampers, were appointed, to the emolument of a few local associations, and to the annoyance and detriment of those whose benefit was professed to be sought. The duty of these officers was to control the breadth, the texture, and the fashion of merchandise. And, lest the demand for commodities which under a free course of trade would be utterly useless, should decrease, the whole population were enjoined to *bury* a large portion of their manufactures along with their *dead*.¹

CHAP. X.
A.D. 1558 to 1603.

Of the restrictions on importations and on their effects enough has perhaps been said. We may consider them, however, as effecting an exclusive privilege or monopoly in favour of particular individuals or associations. Foreign *manufactures* were chiefly denounced; and yet sometimes we were inconsistent enough to denounce *natural products*. Thus cattle, beef, fish, and butter have been prohibited, in favour of the limited number of dealers in those articles: and when the national policy rushed into this eccentricity, Ireland was classed among the foreign proscribed nations. In reference to these measures, an able and celebrated financier asked, 200 years ago,² 'If it be good for England to keep Ireland a 'distinct kingdom, why do not the predominant party in 'Parliament (suppose the western members) make England 'beyond Trent another kingdom? And why may not Eng-'land be *further cantonised* for the benefit of *all* parties?' But the full force of this query has been barely acknowledged by Government within these forty years.³

---

¹ By the statutes which enjoined the burying of the dead in woollens.
² Sir W. Petty, in his Political Anatomy of Ireland.

³ The rigid proscription of foreign manufactures was not, however, always extended to the manufacturers. From the time of Edward I. to that of Alva-

BOOK I.
A.D. 1558 to 1603.

Lastly, we may mention *bounties*—on exportation, or for the encouragement of manufactures; which are raised by taxation from the public, to be given to a few individuals, who have either already engaged in unprofitable labours, or who are thereby to be induced so to employ themselves. To remunerate those who, deceived by public errors, have been led into misfortune, may, indeed, be just enough; but to enable them to persist in the same erroneous course, with advantage to themselves and loss to the community, is a very different consideration. If a particular branch of industry is too unprofitable to induce persons voluntarily to engage in it—either from the articles to be produced by it being already sufficiently plentiful, or else from their being utterly useless, or, which is the same thing, not wanted, like the woollen cloths, which were made solely for the purpose of being buried together with the useless clay of dead bodies—it is evident, that a tax levied on the people for such an object is oppression. To aim at overstocking a plentiful market, in order to occasion still greater cheapness, is a mere absurdity: for it never can be an object to effect cheapness to *foreigners* at our own expense; and while the *home* market is left to be stocked by the free admission of merchandise from every quarter, to make that merchandise cheaper to *our own people* by taxing them first for the production of it, is, in truth, to make them pay dearer for it in the end. The public *demand* —as it is the natural, so it is the most beneficial promoter of the *supply*.

It has sometimes been argued, that there are many commercial speculations which would be highly advantageous to the public, but which persons are unwilling to undertake because the enterprise carries with it too *much risk* and too *large a capital.* And these, it is said, are speculations which a wise and liberal Government should encourage by bounties. Such a course will appear, however, upon consideration to be

persecution in the Netherlands, and from thence to the Revocation of the Edict of Nantes, our wisest kings and our most sagacious ministers did not scruple to harbour and encourage manufacturing refugees; and many eulogiums have been justly passed upon the good effects of that policy—resulting in the introduction of their manufactures into this country.

a kind of joint-trading by Government in conjunction with the individual merchants. *As far as the bounties go*, the Government is speculating for the benefit of the people, and with their funds: it is a kind of state commerce. But experience has abundantly shown, that the worst of all merchants, both in management and projects, are political powers. The self-interest of those personally concerned, when left to its free operation, is by far the most active and effectual agent in ascertaining the most profitable sources of wealth. And, in a natural and free state of things, the profit of one class of traders must always produce a correspondent profit to others.

What then! it may be demanded, are the arts and sciences no longer to be encouraged? Are all associations for the reward of useful genius to be abolished? Are all patents and monopolies to be denounced? Is the invention of the steam-engine, by which millions are enriched, to bring down ruin and neglect upon its individual author only, who has devoted wealth, time, labour, and talent to achieve its construction? Shall the safety-lamp, by which the lives of so many men are saved, and the property of others enormously increased, be an unrequited gift from needy genius? Such a result would, indeed, be a painful sacrifice at the shrine of principle, should it be required at our hands. This is an inference, however, which does not arise out of the positions we have advanced.

The distinction is this. To incite by artificial bounties the future exertions of the *public in general* in one specific branch of labour, is to speculate in one kind of commodity at the expense of the rest; to remunerate *individuals* for services *performed*, is to secure them a proportionate *share* of the profit actually produced. The latter have accomplished their services, and have actually benefited mankind: they have devoted the labour of mind or of body for the introduction or increase of those productions of which the public are in need. The public do, in fact, pay for it, and are contented so to do: the only question is, whether they should pay the ignorant rivals who have possessed themselves of the secret, or those to whom the remuneration is first due. The labourer is worthy of his hire. Nor can those who, in association or otherwise, voluntarily devote a portion of their wealth to the encouragement of arts, be considered otherwise than as benefactors of mankind: they withdraw their contribution from public circulation, which is but little; and they return to the public, through the advancement of the arts, much. The only apprehension is, that one comparatively inferior branch of industry may be advanced by an erroneous direction of labour, to the detriment of another; so that, here also, the principle of *open* competition should be the guide. Mere *reward*, therefore, whether through the medium of patents or otherwise, is not inconsistent with those free principles of political economy which have suggested the impolicy of all artificial restraints and bounties in commerce. It may, indeed, be misdirected; it may be over-estimated. The authors of the sublimest inventions must derive the greater part of their remuneration in the consciousness of having benefited mankind. It is this universal love towards mankind which is the genuine source of all our happiness, as well as of all our virtues.[1]

There may be, however, cases where, for the sake of some ulterior object, the maintenance of such privileges might be justified; but it is certain that such cases must form *exceptions* to a rule sound in its general principle, and be founded on extrinsic circumstances; for all exclusions of competition in trade, either to a small or large extent, are prejudicial in themselves. Whether these exceptions should in justice be allowed, must depend on the nature of the exclusions and the object of them. The object must be useful; the exclusive privileges must be necessary; and not so excessive as to supersede the benefit contemplated.

The purport of one branch of the much-celebrated navigation laws is to provide, that all goods exported from any

---

[1] The author has no wish to disguise that he has borrowed from the writings of Smith, Ricardo, McCulloch, and others, in this attempted exposition of the false and true principles of commercial policy; but he has not quoted his specific authority for all the positions he has advanced, because he has adopted an arrangement of the subject for the purposes of the present work, which has not only blended together the scattered doctrines of these writers, but likewise incorporated with them some observations for which he is alone responsible.

foreign country, except those of the growth of such country, shall only be imported into Great Britain in *British bottoms*. The effect of such a law is most unquestionably to create exclusive privileges: first in favour of the class of shipbuilders and mariners; and secondly, in favour of certain commercialists in England. The general advancement of navigation throughout the world, and the general diffusion of all the benefits to be derived, even to our own nation, from an universal free trade has been by no means attained, though the latter object may have been aimed at by this law. But that by the policy and operation of this statute in retarding the advance of other nations, our own *relative* nautical superiority has been established, if it cannot be absolutely asserted, at least should not be hastily or inconsiderately denied. On our nautical superiority depends our national independence, not too dearly purchased at any cost; and for this extrinsic object we injure by restrictions against foreign nations both them and ourselves. Whether our naval establishment is already too far advanced to fear foreign rivalry, or our liberties too firmly secured to fear foreign opposition—so that some relaxation in the system may now be expedient—is a question which the vital interests of our country require to be deeply considered before a practical decision is made.¹

The old charters of the East India Company conceded to them the monopoly of an exclusive trade in the Indian seas—their charter of 1813 preserved the monopoly of the China trade only. Both the Chinese and the English suffered by this system, as the eastern nations and England did formerly. It was a monopoly, because, but for its existence, others would find their advantage in competing with the Company. The effect of such competition is to increase the quantity of commodities both imported and exported in exchange, to the reciprocal advantage of the two countries. In short, it has been calculated from some official statements of the sales of teas in foreign markets, compared with those effected in our own by the East India Company, that the English pay upwards of two millions sterling per annum for tea beyond the natural market price.² This is, in truth, therefore, a

¹ Vide next page, note   ² Edin. Rev. vol. xxxix. p. 103; vide next page, note.

bounty to that extent, raised from the people for the benefit of this association. The object, however, of these exclusive privileges was, originally, to reward the first speculators, who at great cost and risk had introduced new wealth into the country. That object has been long satisfied. But the monopoly has been continued, partly in consequence of the peculiar and jealous character of the nations with whom the trade is carried on, which renders it expedient, for securing that branch of commerce, that it should be conducted by an organised body and under statutable regulations; and mainly for the purpose of strengthening the hands of that association of merchants which, by a wonderful application of their means, have founded and preserved one of the largest empires in the world. Whether the original objects of the monopoly granted to this Company have at the present day been so sufficiently accomplished as to render it no longer expedient to support its strength through that medium, it is by no means pertinent to the subject of the present work to consider. It may, however, be safely pronounced, that the preservation of associations like these by exclusive commercial rights can no longer be defended than while they conduce to those *ulterior* purposes, whether of territorial government, competent management, or of remuneration, for accomplishing which the existence of such institutions were originally deemed politic.[1]

We now proceed to examine those exclusive commercial privileges which have distinguished the Corporation of London. That it possessed many of those which we have endeavoured to prove were prejudicial in their operation, need but be observed. We must refer to the charters to show the number and the nature of them. There can be no doubt that such privileges produced in the City of London, and indeed generally, the effect of aggrandising a few civic commercialists at the expense of the larger body of the citizens, and of the interests of the public at large; and we may trace these effects in that wasteful magnificence which we

---

[1] The abolition of the Navigation Laws, and of the exclusive trade of the East India Company (and indeed of the Company itself) since this chapter was written, has fully vindicated the commercial principles advocated in the text forty years ago.

have already noticed as characterising the expenditure of the superior citizens. Granted, however, as these privileges were in times of such arbitrary power, to a free and potent body, who continually asserted their own political rights to the advancement of those of the people, it would be wrong to conclude that these means of exalting the few to the debasement of the many, evil as they were *in principle*, may not, by promoting in those times the relative prosperity of the citizens, have ultimately contributed to the common benefit of all. A new and powerful interest was thereby created among the body of the people—that of the commercialists, whose main care it was to oppose lawless and unconstitutional attacks on private rights and public liberties. The progress in wealth of the great traders tended to diffuse the spirit of commerce more generally. The wider that diffusion, the better were the benefits of free trade understood, and the greater became the resistance to undue advantages to be enjoyed by any special classes. It was thus that these privileges—acquired in times of a more arbitrary government, and in the infancy of trade—have themselves contributed to a beneficial reaction. Monopolies and exclusive trading privileges have long ceased to be conferred, or to be maintained, with the exploded view of promoting the public weal. The advance of constitutional rights and liberties, and the development of the true principles of commerce, have effected the proportional retirement of the Corporation of London from the exercise of its more obnoxious mercantile privileges, which, in fact, were never in themselves essential to its maintenance as a political or associated body; and there are few (if any) of this class, which can now be specified as burthensome to the public. The privileges we are about to advert to as still prevailing, will be found to rest on a *distinct basis* from that which supported the system of commercial restraints, and directed to a different object.

The privilege to which we refer, is that which has suggested the present digression; namely, that non-freemen can only deal *by wholesale* with *citizens*, and not in any manner *by retail*, within the jurisdiction of the City. Before we consider the effects of this exclusive franchise of the citizens, it may be as well to enquire shortly into its nature.

That it is a restraint upon competition in trade is not more obvious than its prejudicial quality in the abstract. To exclude the public from that participation in the trade carried on by others, through which participation the general market may be more plentifully supplied, unless payment is made, or a burthen is undertaken, for the liberty of trading, is to tax the majority of the people for the benefit of the privileged class, as far as such restraint extends. This restraint is, however, by no means so extensive as is commonly imagined, or, indeed, such as to produce any sensible effect on the interests of the public. It is not only local, but confined within very narrow limits: neither does it exclude competition in any *particular branch* of industry within London or without. The City of London is no longer a *staple* town, through which the trade in particular articles must of necessity pass. Its exemptions from vassalage and arbitrary power are no longer so peculiar, as to draw the commerce away from districts less favoured in regard to constitutional rights. All other ports are equally competent to emulate its means and its success; nor can the prosperity of the national commerce ever again depend on that of a single city. Whatever may be the tax or the burthen imposed on the participation of civic rights of trade, it is certain they are not such as to arrest the circulation, or to cramp the energy, of commercial enterprise amongst the public in general. Whatever advantages London may hold out to those who trade within it, they are all derived from inherent sources; and the price at which they are purchased, and which may be requisite for maintaining them, is the voluntary tribute of a free judgment exercised in a free country.

If the local advantages of the City of London, as an emporium of trade (independently of those derived through political rights and self-government), were such as would induce heavy sacrifices for the purpose of participation in them, it would be hard to defend the exaction of such sacrifices for no other object than to uphold the emolument and arbitrary authority of a few incorporated individuals. But neither are the local advantages such in their nature, nor are such heavy sacrifices required. The Corporation does, indeed, possess the power of imposing terms for the admission of new members (not entitled by birth or apprenticeship) to the privileges of citizenship—but *numerical strength* is far more essential to the maintenance of the corporate interests than the contributions, or even the quality of new members. Those interests, therefore, suggest what justice demands— namely, that the admission of all applicants for citizenship should be as wide as is consistent with the individuality of the association as a distinct body politic; and, thus, all arbitrary authority in the selection of persons is reduced to a mere shade. Should large payments for full liberty of trade within the City be demanded, and as freely paid, still, as such payments would go to increase a corporate fund to be administered for the common benefit of all the members of the Corporation, it would be but an impolitic and unnecessary expenditure, affecting themselves as members only, while the general advancement of commerce would not be retarded thereby. If, however, having reference to the freedom and facility of commerce throughout the kingdom, such payments were too high to be freely paid, the demand of them would but detach strangers to trade in other places. At the same time it would diminish proportionably the trading of citizens in their own port.

In truth, so liberal is the admission of all candidates for civic freedom, that the exclusion of strangers from the full enjoyment of citizenship, unless they will earn it by service or payment, amounts to little more, in effect (at least with regard to English subjects), than a requisition that all who live within its walls, or exercise municipal rights, should be subservient to its internal regulations, and ancillary to its good government.[1] Moderate, however, as may be the tax upon, or requisitions for this admission, and reasonable as may be the duties which such admission imposes, the justification of their existence must still depend on their efficacy

---

[1] Since the publication of the first edition of this work, the Court of Common Council has, by a resolution passed March 17, 1835, reduced the fee for admission to the freedom of the City from twenty-five pounds to five pounds.

BOOK I.
A.D. 1558 to 1603.

in promoting a *beneficial object*. The question to be considered is, whether a body politic in which such exclusive privileges of trade prevail, is a useful establishment in a state—and if so, whether it can subsist without them.

But few words are necessary to establish the first proposition. It is the very foundation of all society and civil government, that men should unite for the purpose of ascertaining their common interests, and of effecting their common designs. The same principle which attracts individuals of every class and quality into community for the universal object of mutual protection, dictates the distinct association of all those subdivisions of society which possess their own peculiar and subordinate interests to defend or to advance. If we should consider the citizens of London as a mere assemblage of commercialists, it would be impossible not to perceive the advantages of their union into one organised body.

The consolidated existence, and the efficient action, of such a union can only be secured, in a free country, by some form of representation, and no system of representation can be stable and beneficial, in all its just amplitude, unless the representatives are freely elected by those having common interests to be advanced. Now the Corporation of London, acting as the representatives of the citizens at large, is not composed of, and does not emanate from, any one or more classes of the commercial community. If so, it might be concluded that the interests of some classes would be advocated at the expense of the others: but comprising, as it does, in a greater degree than any other in the world, the members of every trading occupation which can be pursued, either within the City or without, the Corporation may be truly said to represent, not only the commercial interests of the City, but, as far as its influence extends, those of the nation itself. Stripped of those monopolous privileges which once separated its own prosperity from that of other cities, it can never advocate its individual interests without advancing those of the mercantile public. It can no longer be urged that the commercial community might, by its selfish influence, become more than a match for the general community of the nation. That apprehension must vanish with the absence of such a cause for it. The public are sufficiently enlightened to know, that the landed or agricultural interest and the commercial interest are, in truth, all one; and depend on their *reciprocal* prosperity. The distinction between the manufacturer of bread and the manufacturer of cloth is *in kind* and not *in principle*. The political influence of great cities, wealthy only by the relative adversity and slavery of other districts, has now sunk to the common level to which, under a constitutional government, all classes may approach, according to their intrinsic merits, in a free state. It is a vain fear to suppose that the owners and occupiers of the soil of a free country will not always possess the real dominion in the end. Their greater reason to fear is, that, by impairing or destroying the representative influence of the commercialists, they may in the result possess but little else than a barren dominion.

That the contribution towards the support of corporate establishments, or the performance of duties imposed by them is *obligatory*, while the concession to the requisitions of other associations is *voluntary*, is obviously an illusory objection. It is impossible that any association can be supported without sacrifices of some sort, either personal or pecuniary. They are none of them absolutely voluntary. All are submitted to for the sake of some ulterior advantage. No combination for the most contracted or private object can be more voluntary on the part of its members, than that which constitutes the Corporation of London. To those who are not members the whole kingdom is open; the participation in the advantages of the civic trade and the civic association, only, is denied. To open that trade to all, without imposing such obligation, is to confer such advantages, without exacting those fair and necessary returns, by which the association itself, and all the benefits to be derived from it, can alone be sustained. No more is demanded, in principle, than the duty which every nation must exact of its subjects who voluntarily place themselves under its government.

Whether the maintenance of this great corporation in all its ancient vigour and splendour is a just object of the public care, may, perhaps, be best decided by attaining a knowledge of the true principles of civil liberty. All the real privileges enjoyed by the citizens at the present day are those only, which, under one modification or another, the free residents of every district in the kingdom *ought to possess* in a free country. As residents of London, they possess the highest constitutional franchises which can characterise any class of the common people: internally, self-government; externally, a voice in the state. As traders, they are endowed with the power of ascertaining and of advocating, as well as in some degree of administering, those regulations by which mercantile intercourse may be best sustained. These are privileges which if they are honourable to the citizens, are certainly not detrimental to the public; and if they are envied by any, are not denied to their participation upon the most easy and reasonable terms.

Of the political use and benefit derived from the existence of the Corporation of London it has been, in some degree, the endeavour of this work to afford proofs, by stating many facts and particulars in the progressive history of our national constitution, the beneficial effects of which are incontestible; and which may serve to instruct the successors of the citizens of London. Should it be intimated, that many restrictions on commerce have from time to time been sanctioned or imposed by it, for its own partial benefit; let it be remembered also, how many arbitrary laws and regulations it has removed for the perpetual advantage of all. Let it be observed, that it is of great importance in a free state to have a regular constituted society, representing the most valuable and vital interests of a country—all the industrious and middling classes of the people; a society, independent enough to maintain the right to an unshackled discussion of political measures, which can claim not only free access to the legislature, but to the throne itself; and which preserves within itself the franchises of self-government, the very seeds of liberty. A serious attention to the distinguishing phenomena of English history, will discover from other events as well as from the seizure of the City charter by Charles II., and its restoration by his successor, that, whenever the rights and liberties of the City of

London are destroyed, those of the nation itself are in no small danger.

This basis of public utility, it is conceived, is that on which the possession of the exclusive civic privileges, as supporting the corporate capacity of the City, may more properly and securely rest, than upon the common plea of a full right of inheritance in the citizens, which has been so favourite a topic of argument with judges and lawyers; as if the rights of an imaginary and artificial essence were indefeasible by the powers which created it, or that private advantages should be fostered, which are inconsistent with the public welfare.

That exclusive privileges of trading are absolutely necessary for the preservation of the Corporation as an active representative body, is so obvious as to require little illustration. The City of London can exist only by its trade; the mass of its useful and productive inhabitants must ever be composed of traders; and it is out of these individuals that the corporators must mainly be chosen, if they are to represent the real interests of the City. The local advantages which distinguish it as a place of commerce, are sufficient to attract inhabitants in vast numbers; and such local advantages will in all probability ever exist. If, however, strangers, who may find emolument in carrying on trade there, are allowed so to do at their discretion, without incurring the expense or burthen incident to the assumption of the civic freedom, the number of non-freemen will go on increasing in proportion to the superior local or natural advantages afforded to commercial pursuits, until the original freemen are nearly, or altogether, supplanted. The Corporation may then still exist, but no longer as the Corporation *of London*, except in name. It will represent no common interests; still less those of the mercantile population of England. The most honourable distinction it can then enjoy will be that of an association of proprietors, or of being a medium of police government. The great City companies have become such associations of proprietors. They have their use. They are supporters of many excellent charitable and scholastic institutions. They are gatherings through whom political sentiments may be circulated, and political influences be brought to bear—to say nothing of the genial enjoyments of good fellowship. But they cannot aspire to the honours, the dignity, the national importance and the public estimation which a great civic corporation is entitled to. It is therefore necessary not only that the London Corporation should possess these exclusive trading privileges on which its organisation rests, but that they should be constantly enforced. The apathy of the citizens in this respect has already produced consequences, in regard to the number and quality of the corporate members, which will deserve their attention.[1]

---

[1] It must candidly be acknowledged, that the views here expressed by the author, as to the expediency of maintaining the exclusive rights of freemen to deal by retail in the City, have been repudiated by the Court of Common Council, in 1856. By an act of the court of that date, this unquestioned privilege has been voluntarily abandoned.

The act (after reciting that this exclusive right was plain and undoubted, and confirmed by sundry Acts of Parliament) provides 'that any person, whether free of the City or not, may sell by retail, or keep any shop,' &c., 'within the City of London, notwithstanding any custom or privilege to the contrary.' It may, however, be fairly doubted how far the citizens at large really were, or can be legally considered, parties to the surrender of this right, and whether, indeed, anything, short of an Act of Parliament, can annul this, or any other, right or privilege of the citizens, resting on the faith of imperial statutes which have explicitly confirmed them. It may be thought that the representatives of the citizens in Common Council were rather entrusted with the duty of supporting their statutable rights, than with any discretionary subordinate power of abolishing them: and it would be too much to infer that, by remaining passive, the constituency of the citizens have acquiesced in the measure, even if they were competent to forego, through their representatives, the rights of their successors. The Charter of Edward III., confirmed by Act of Parliament (which is recited in the act of Common Council), has allowed the corporate authority the liberty 'of amending any customs which might in any part be hard or defective, by ordaining any remedy, so that such ordinances be profitable to the king, and to the citizens, *and to all liege subjects resorting to the City*;' which last expressions may be taken to mean, the *non-freemen wholesale* dealers coming to the public market, where (as has been shown) all wholesale dealing was at this time carried on. It may, however, admit of question, whether such a power of applying a remedy for 'amending a custom hard or defective in any part,' and with such qualification in the exercise of it, extends to the abolition of a valuable and statutable privilege altogether.

Upon the point of expediency, it may be added to the argument in the text, that it must be obvious, that the admission of all comers to the privileges of citizenship, without any requisition to be incorporated as a member of the body politic, must sensibly weaken the chain that binds that community together. If, one by one, all or most of the civic franchises - that of free liberty of trading without being freemen—that of electing

But as, on the one hand, the citizens should be rigid in enforcing these essential rights; so, on the other, if they would preserve their corporate existence in full vigour, they must reduce the price and burthens of the civic franchise to the lowest possible scale,¹ and by no means to allow them to outweigh the local advantages to be derived from it: for on them, after all, must depend the commercial prosperity of the metropolis. These local advantages are such, and so in all probability they must long continue, as to reconcile any interested mind to make considerable sacrifices to acquire. With regard to such as accompany the due discharge of the more dignified offices, no curtailment may appear perhaps to be demanded. Human pride will, in most instances, make such sacrifices agreeable. These offices, as well as those of a more ministerial quality, become lighter in their effects, as the due proportion of freemen is kept up, who are bound to share them. The terms of admission, every policy seems to suggest, should be as liberal and unrestricted as is compatible with the respectability of the new members.

Thus much it has been thought important to advance upon a topic so necessarily and so seriously affecting the interest of the City of London. Whether these sentiments are just and sound, must perhaps be left to experience alone to determine. One conclusion will at least meet with univer-

members of the representative body of the City in Common Council (as conferred by Act of 30 Vict.), without being freemen)—that of electing the City representatives in Parliament (as already conferred on those who may, or may not, be the true citizens of London by occupation, or even by trading therein)—and that of becoming magistrates or common councilmen, as well as members in Parliament of the City—be opened to all the world, without any corporate tie or local interest, the corporation would become a *caput mortuum*. It would become a mere association of individuals, possessing property in common, with or without local or public trusts, as it may happen, and its principle of self-government would, more or less, if not altogether, lose its vitality. A different consideration would be admissible, if the pecuniary tax on the acquisition of the civic freedom was burthensome, and consequently of a monopolous tendency. But this is not the case. The freedom of the City is open to all who are willing to accept the ordinary duties of citizens, in supporting the administration of the civic government, for the performance of which duties the labour which attends public services is, and ought to be, the sufficient and appropriate reward.

¹ The price of admission has been reduced to 5*l.* from 15*l.* Vide p. 191.

sal concurrence; namely, that all restrictions imposed on free commercial competition—by taxes, tolls, monopolies, and arbitrary laws, having for their object, professedly, to contribute to mere individual or class emolument, or tending by unforeseen consequences to that result—must not only retard national prosperity, but, if instituted in favour of a king or of a government, must in the end prove subversive of national liberties also.

CHAPTER XI.

FROM THE ACCESSION OF JAMES I. TO THAT OF CHARLES II.

THE maxim of government, that the king possessed within himself an inherent absolute authority, which from the time of Magna Charta had become gradually weakened, seemed to be revived again by the Tudors, and was maintained with almost unremitting success by Elizabeth. It is manifest that James was disposed to tread in the same paths as his immediate predecessors, and that he conceived his own authority to be despotic and above the law. This may be gathered from the almost uniform language held by him in his own published works, in his speeches to Parliament, and indeed in all his public addresses. His ministers frequently upheld the same doctrine; and it is evident that too much ignorance prevailed on the nature of the Constitution, and of the line requisite to be drawn between the royal prerogative and the rights of the people, to allow of its denial or refutation. What tended, it may be presumed, in no small degree to prevent an actual breach with the monarch on this interesting topic, when the eyes of his subjects were opened to the natural qualities of government, were his constant declarations, not ill-supported by his conduct, that whatever notions he himself entertained of his own inherent authority, his intentions, as well as his inclinations, were to govern according to the law of the land, and the duly ascertained will of his subjects.

The principle of parliamentary independence, which had plainly dawned in the last reign, began fully to shine forth and display itself in this. It had been the practice in preceding reigns for the Crown to assume the privilege of issu-

CHAP.
XI.
A.D. 1603
to 1660.

ing new writs to supply the vacancies of members occasioned by deaths or sickness; and, at last, even by incapabilities adjudged at the discretion of the Crown itself. This had been remonstrated against in the reign of Elizabeth, though with but partial success. James, in summoning his first parliament, issued a proclamation, threatening to fine and imprison anyone who should take on himself the place of a member not elected according to the laws in force, and *according to the tenor of that proclamation*. His chancellor actually proceeded to displace one member, on the ground of his being an outlaw. The Commons, however, not only saw the direct tendency of such an attempt to enslave the House, but so severely remonstrated against it, that the king readily withdrew this alarming claim of jurisdiction.[1]

Such was the first parliamentary step in this reign. In the progress of it, the House testified an anxious resolution to circumscribe the exercise of the royal prerogatives within such limits as to leave the king no longer independent of his parliament, and to relieve his subjects from their dependence on his will for the enjoyment of their common rights and property. Accordingly all monopolies, compulsive loans and benevolences, arbitrary imposts, and rates upon merchandise, were denounced as illegal. Monopolies were finally and in terms abolished by statute; and if all other modes of arbitrary taxation were not expressly abolished, it was only because it was considered every one would be justified in resisting them of his own authority.

The law of proclamations began to be scrutinised with an inquisitive eye; and it was observed that, while such a mode of promulgating laws prevailed, there could be but little security in the constitutional rights of the people, especially while the courts of High Commission and the Star Chamber existed, with powers sufficient to enforce these royal decrees. This was altogether a reign of proclamations. The king delighted in displaying to his people his profound political wisdom, and was never so much himself as when with fond garrulity he was inculcating in the first person his much prized maxims of government. Fortunately for himself, if

[1] Hume's Hist. ch. xlv.

not for his subjects, this ruling passion expended itself for the most part upon trivial objects.¹ To interfere with this dearly-loved branch of his prerogative, was to wound him in the most sensitive part. He defended it strenuously, though with more sophistry than effect;² but succeeded in warding off for a season the discussion of the subject, by candidly acknowledging that his proclamations had no title to be considered on a parity with regular statutes.

At length a rupture took place between the king and his parliament, arising from the claim of the latter, urged with some symptoms of asperity, to discuss freely all matters of state, however personally affecting the former, which drew the attention of the whole nation to the state of their political rights.³ It may readily be concluded that the free privileges of parliament became more and more strengthened by such disputes; and the king must have found, at the close of his reign, that, whatever ostensible concession was tacitly made to his own speculative doctrines in regard to the absolute power of the monarch, he had been gradually deprived of all the substantial means of exercising it. It is of consequence to notice these political proceedings and the feelings which gave rise to them, especially with respect to proclamations; because otherwise it would be impossible to understand or appreciate the constant intermeddling of the king in the civic concerns, and indeed in what might very justly be considered the chartered rights of the citizens.

The courts of High Commission and of the Star Chamber continued to exercise their jurisdiction throughout this reign; the former certainly with mitigated severity, in deference to the king's disinclination to all kinds of religious persecution. It is to be remarked, that the sect of Puritans, which subse-

---

¹ Proclamations against new buildings, against the use of tobacco, for all noblemen to live at their country houses at Christmas, prescribing rules for preaching, &c. &c.

² 'He acknowledged,' he told the Commons, 'that proclamations were not of equal force with laws; yet he thought it a duty incumbent on him, and a power inseparably annexed to the Crown, to restrain and prevent such mischiefs and inconveniences as he saw growing on the state, against which no certain law was extant.'—King James's *Works*, p. 259. ed. 1613. It is plain, however, that proclamations must either have the force of laws or be altogether nugatory.

³ The Commons presented a petition against the Spanish match, which gave great offence.

quently occasioned such convulsions in the government,
began to increase at this period; they rendered themselves
notorious at first by their intolerance of popery; and such
is the effect of religious fanaticism on the human mind, that
this class of persons, who were at all times the most forward
assertors of constitutional liberty, did not hesitate to call
into aid the king's most tyrannical powers, as exercised by
the arbitrary court of High Commission, towards the suppression of difference in religious opinion.[1] The jurisdiction
of the Star Chamber was enforced with less scruple: and
we hear of many persons being censured for their disobedience to the king's ridiculous proclamations against the increase of the London suburbs.[2] While such a prerogative as
this prevailed, of establishing arbitrary courts and commissions of enquiry, there is little cause for surprise that the
citizens of London experienced such continual difficulty in
vindicating their chartered privileges in regard to exclusive
jurisdiction within the City.

The citizens were but once called upon by James to furnish
their quota of soldiers towards a projected war; on which
occasion they supplied only two thousand men; and that, it
would seem, more out of good will than from anything like
compulsion.[3] In an attempt, however, to raise a benevolence, the citizens evinced a more refractory spirit. Twenty
thousand pounds were demanded, but they refused to advance
more than half that sum;[4] a plain indication of the knowledge they had acquired of their own rights in regard to taxation. One citizen upon application refused to contribute
anything; but on its being intimated to him that the king
might require his services to carry a despatch to Ireland, he
deemed it an easier task to comply than to assert his own
rights against the claims of the monarch.[5]

A circumstance which happened in the City at this period
is not undeserving of notice, as illustrating in a remarkable

[1] Remonstrance presented to the king by his last parliament but one against Catholics. Hume's Hist. ch. xlviii.
[2] Maitland, vol. i. p. 289, quoting Stow's Survey.
[3] Stow's Chronicle, A.D. 1624. Maitland, vol. i. p. 298.
[4] Ibid.
[5] Hume's Hist. ch. xlix. note 29, quoting Johnstone's Rerum Britannicarum Historia.

manner the relative pretensions of the king and his people. James had written a work, entitled 'The Book of Sports;' in which he laboured to prove the lawfulness of games of amusement on the Sabbath-day. This book, at the request of some bishops, he ordered by proclamation to be read in all churches; an injunction which gave much offence in the City. The lord mayor, in defiance of the paternal recommendations contained in the royal volume, ventured to stop the king's carriages while passing through the City in time of Divine service. The king was in great wrath, and immediately sent his lordship a warrant to allow them to pass. The lord mayor obeyed; observing, that 'while he possessed 'his power he had done his duty; but that being *taken away* 'by a higher power, he had done his duty in obeying.'[1]

King James conferred on the City of London those possessions in Ireland which became the occasion of founding what is called the Irish Society. It is foreign to the object of this work to detail the nature of these possessions, or to examine the functions of the society in consequence of this grant. It will be sufficient to mention, that the province of Ulster, having become depopulated and for the most part forfeited to the Crown through frequent rebellions, it was judged expedient to colonise it with a body of Protestants. That province, comprising the city of Londonderry and the town of Coleraine, was accordingly granted by charter to the Corporation, who immediately formed a committee (afterwards incorporated into the Irish Society), with powers to raise a sum of money, and to take measures for the plantation of it. For this purpose all the land was divided into thirteen lots: the first, containing the city and town, with the public fisheries, was reserved in the hands of the society; the other lots were disposed of, in conformity with the king's charter of license, to the twelve great livery companies in perpetuity.[2]

A good understanding generally prevailed between the citizens and James, who took pleasure in associating with them. He granted them three valuable charters, the substance and tenor of which sufficiently testified his good-

---

[1] Wilson's Life of King James.
[2] A Concise View of the Origin, Constitution, and Proceedings of the Irish Society. 8vo. 1822.

BOOK I.
A.D. 1603 to 1660.

will to the Corporation, and his anxiety to support its privileges.¹

¹ It may not be thought, perhaps, an unjustifiable use of the license of a note to enquire into the long debated subject of the rank and quality of London citizens, as such, in the scale of society—a subject upon which so much amusing authority is to be found in the scenes of our older dramatists. The term *Barons*, as applied to citizens in very early times, will be the subject of enquiry in considering the charter of William I. We have seen that the citizens assumed much upon that title, at a period so early as the reign of Henry III.; and the great influence which the civic community possessed in the state for ages afterwards, was calculated to foster high notions of their own personal dignity, although their first magistrates never seem to have arrogated any claim to the rank of *nobles*. We may trace, however, plain indications of a spirit amongst the citizens corresponding with the advancement of the age in civilisation; and as soon as *gentility* became an acknowledged grade in society, they resolutely laid claims to it. As *trade* was the criterion of the citizen, so the civic freedom came to be considered, in their own estimation at least, one of the badges of a *Gentleman*. Thus in a play of the year 1607, a City serjeant is introduced with his prisoner just arrested, who sustains the character of a scholar.

'*Scholar.* Nay, use me like a Gentleman; I'm little less.

'*Serjeant.* You a Gentleman! that's a good jest i'faith. Can a scholar be a Gentleman, when a Gentleman will not be a scholar? Look upon your wealthy citizens' sons, that *are* Gentlemen by their fathers' trades. A scholar a Gentleman!'—*Puritan*. Anon. 1607.

Of a rank so vague and so little capable of definition as that of *Gentleman*, comprising as well those who have a superior specific station by birth, as those who, if they possess any at all, possess no other, it is impossible to give a precise idea at any period of English society. For ages after the Norman invasion, and during the period that the feudal principles prevailed in any strictness, the term *Gentleman* was altogether unknown; and the characteristic of *gentleness* was first employed to express the courteous demeanour of nobles and knights, whose profession was arms and the service of the ladies. The only other acknowledged rank of society besides that of nobles, knights, and their esquires, was that of *freemen*. At first the body of independent *freemen* who did not hold by chivalry tenure, was but small, and was probably almost entirely confined to the residents of the few chief cities which were privileged from demesne tenure; for even the serfs or tenants in free socage, were in some degree subjected to the control of proprietary lords. As, however, government improved, and the feudal principle of tenure gave way, through the numerous sub-infeudations and the advancement of the socage tenants to independence, the increase of free proprietors of land, who lived on their own means but who neither directly or indirectly assumed the profession of arms, was proportionably great. The establishment of a constitutional frame of polity and the progress of civilisation, served at once to enlarge their number and to confirm their independence. As they were neither nobles, knights, or esquires, they naturally acquired some other denomination in society, to distinguish them from the general mass of the people, who from the period of Edward III. to that of Henry VII. had gradually, down to the lowest mechanic or labourer, acquired the title of *Freeman*, which had once been a privileged distinction. As nobles and knights possessed a *nominal* dignity, as well as a real rank, which could emanate from the king only, these independent proprietors attained the conventional appellation of

CLAIM OF CITIZENS TO RANK AS GENTLEMEN.

All classes of the people were now animated with feelings of liberty, and a spirit of determination to establish rights

Gentleman or *Esquire*; though at first the former term, as it was the most appropriate, so it was also the more common. The same cognizance was perhaps as soon assumed by, or accorded to, the members of the three learned or liberal professions of divinity, law, and physic.

The freemen of London, who originally had held a rank equal to any class in the kingdom short of the nobility, and who were proud of their own privileged importance, were not slow to vindicate their claim to any new dignity to which their original fellow-freemen had arrived.

By the time of Henry VIII. and Elizabeth, the members of every city and of the meanest boroughs had become, in point of mere constitutional *freedom*, on a perfect equality with the London citizens. At the same time the citizens could hardly contemplate their many chartered privileges, the political influence of the Corporation, the opulence of many of their great merchants, and the legendary splendour of others, without assuming to themselves a decisive superiority over the burghers of other places, who were at the same period almost all engaged in the more mechanical branches of trade. As the wealthiest merchant and the most subordinate shopkeeper equally held their constant residence within the walls of the City, and acquired both the liberty of trading and of such residence by his civic freedom; and as service by *apprenticeship* was in these times the regular course of earning the freedom by *every class* of citizens—it was natural enough that the citizenship should be regarded by the inferior citizens, if not indiscriminately by all, as the common badge of their rank. The civic freedom was in fact gloried in by the very first merchants; and the customs and franchises to which their copies of admission entitled them and their families, were so much a matter of boast, as to form a notorious topic of allusion; although perhaps at the present day such allusions would not be understood in many parts of the City itself. Thus in a play of Massinger's of the year 1632, Lady Frugal, an eminent merchant's wife, is claiming in the presence of her husband and the suitors of her two daughters, the arrangements of the weddings. She says—

'Even so, my Lord,
In these affairs *I* govern.

'*Lord Lacy.* Give you way to 't?
[To *Frugal*.]

'*Sir J. Frugal.* I must, my Lord.

'*Lady Frugal.* 'Tis fit he should, and shall. You may consult of something else; this province

Is wholly mine.

'*Sir M. Lacy.* By the City Custom, madam?

'*Lady Frugal.* Yes, my young sir, and both must look—my daughters will hold it by my *Copy*.

'*Plenty.* Bravo i'faith.'—*City Madam*: 1632.

But whatever respect the London merchants may have enjoyed in public opinion at the period of Elizabeth and James I. (which, after all, must be the only source of conventional rank), it is certain that the *Gentlemen* of that day were very little disposed to concede any superiority to the *mechanical* tradesmen in deference to their civic freedom, over those of any other district in the kingdom. Even the citizens themselves seem gradually to have become conscious of some difference in the degree of their respective claims to gentility. For in the same play which has just been quoted, we find a brother of Sir J. Frugal thus apostrophising his two apprentices.

'*Luke.* Are you *Gentlemen born*, yet have so gallant tincture
Of gentry in you? You are no *mechanics*,
Nor serve some needy shopkeeper, who surveys
His every day takings.

CHAP. XI.

A.D. 1603 to 1660.

which could only prevail under a free form of government; when, in an evil hour and with evil counsels, Charles mounted

'I blush for you—
Blush at your poverty of spirit. You,
The brave sparks of the City!'

In early times Gentlemen had no hesitation in binding their younger sons apprentices to London citizens of almost every quality, both merchants and retailers; and they consoled themselves with the conviction, that although they might not thereby enhance their characters as Gentlemen, they certainly did not debase them. Thus, in the same play, Tradewell, one of the apprentices, speaking of his master, says—

''Tis great pity
Such a *Gentleman* as my master (for that title
His being a citizen cannot take from him).'

And again in a play of an earlier date, upon the marriage of a goldsmith's apprentice with his master's daughter.

'*Golding.* I confess myself far unworthy such a worthy wife, being in part *her servant, as I am your 'prentice*; yet (since I may say it without boasting) I am born a Gentleman, and by the trade I have learn'd of my master (which, I trust, *taints not my blood*), able with mine own industry and portion to maintain your daughter.

'*Touchstone.* Master me no more, son, if thou think'st me worthy to be thy father.

'*Girtred.* Son? Now, good lord, how he shines; and, you mark him! he's a *Gentleman*!

'*Gold.* I indeed, madam, a Gentleman born.

'*Sir Petronel.* Never stand o' your gentry, Mr. Bridegroom; if your legs be no better than *your arms,* you'll be able to stand on neither shortly.

'*Touch.* An't please your good worship, there are two sorts of Gentlemen: there is a Gentleman artificial, and a Gentleman natural: now, though your worship be a Gentleman *natural*—work upon that, now.'—*Eastward Hoe.*

About beginning of James I.

From this we may gather, however, that some suspicion began to be entertained whether a mechanical trade did not, so far from conferring, positively debase the rank of a Gentleman. That this suspicion was not confined to the gallants of the day and the superior classes, but was commonly prevalent within the City also, appears obvious from other extracts. Thus in a play of the date of 1637, an old citizen thus expresses himself:—

'*Bernard.* . . . . . We that had
Our breeding from a trade; *Cits* as you call us,
Though we *hate Gentlemen* ourselves, yet are
Ambitious to make all our children Gentlemen.
In three generations they return again.
We for our children purchase land; they have it
I' the country; beget children, and they sell;
Grow poor, and send their sons up to be 'prentices.
There is a whirl in fate. The courtiers make
Us cuckolds; mark, we wriggle into their
Estates; Poverty makes their children citizens;
Our sons cuckold them. A circular justice.'
The Gamester. Anon. 1637.

And a still stronger instance occurs in a scene of a play already quoted. Touchstone, the Goldsmith, is remonstrating with his apprentice, and exclaims—

'Thou shameless varlet! do'st thou jest at thy lawful master, contrary to thy indentures?

'*Quicksilver.* S'blood, sir, my mother's a Gentlewoman, and my father a Justice of Peace and of *Quorum*; and though I'm a younger brother and a 'prentice, yet I hope I'm my father's son; and

CLAIM OF CITIZENS TO RANK AS GENTLEMEN. 207

the English throne. A concurrence of various circumstances had contributed to foster despotic principles in the mind of

CHAP. XI.
A.D. 1603 to 1660.

by God'slid 'tis for your worship and for your commodity that I keep company.

'*Touch.* (Pointing to his fellow apprentice.) There's a youth of another piece, there's thy fellow 'prentice, as goal a Gentleman born as thou art, &c. [*Exit* Touchstone.

'*Quick.* Marry, phu, goodman Flatcap. 'Sfoot, though I'm a 'prentice, I can give arms. My father's a justice o' peace by descent.'

Addressing himself to Golding, his fellow apprentice, he continues:—

'Wilt thou cry, "What is't you lack?" stand with a bare pate and a dropping nose under a wooden penthouse, and *art a Gentleman*? Wilt thou bear tankards and may'st bear arms? Be ruled, turn gallant.'

It must be acknowledged that the screaming for customers from under a penthouse, the practice of all sorts of petty chaffering artificers, the drawing water from the public conduits, the performing pursuivant to the mistress of the house, and other servile offices which were formerly imposed upon apprentices, were hardly compatible with the nice bearing and sense of honour characteristic of the true Gentleman. Indeed so decided, as well as general, had become this unfavourable opinion of the gentility of mechanical apprentices, that we read in Stow (Strype's ed. book v. p. 330) an account of the terror of an old gentleman in the country, who, in the year 1628, having bound a younger son as an apprentice in London, learned that he had thereby absolutely tainted his blood. His apprehensions were at last pacified by John Philpot, Somerset herald, who proved in a very learned and elaborate treatise, called 'The Cities Advocate, in this case or question of honour and arms, whether apprenticeship extinguished gentry,' that his fears were unfounded. The herald, however, seems to have considered it no part of his duty to collect or refer to public opinion on the subject.

But what marked most plainly the line of demarcation between the mere citizen and the Gentleman, from the period at which the distinctive appellation of *freeman* dropt, to that when the title of Gentleman became an acknowledged grade in society, was the almost exclusive separation of the citizens from all other classes. They lived almost entirely within the walls; they were governed and guided by their own peculiar customs; they were engaged exclusively in trade; their education, manners, and social habits, were all peculiarly civic. Even the lawyers kept themselves in their inns of court as distinct as the divines in their universities. The only other class living near the City were the noblemen and courtiers about the palace. As the buildings of the whole metropolis were not, as at present, blended in one continuous mass, without any distinction between the City and the suburbs, so neither was there the same general diffusion of education, and what may be denominated fashionable manners, which renders it difficult to distinguish the separate links of the social chain which unites the peer and the shopkeeper. The whole society of the metropolis was, in fact, in those times divided into two separate classes —the courtiers and the citizens; and the great criterion of the advancement of the citizens amongst his own class, was his introduction into that of the Court. Numerous are the allusions in the dramas of the day, and in other works depictive of manners, to the visits of noblen and gentlemen 'coming from the Court' to the City, and to the ambitious desire of the more opulent citizens to get introduced 'to the Court,' which will account for the profusion of civic knighthoods bestowed more particularly by James I. Thus, in 'The Puritan,' which has been quoted before

a prince neither imperious nor violent in his natural disposition. His father had carefully instilled into him those

a nobleman who is persuading a City widow and her daughter to marry themselves to two wealthy City suitors, uses this argument:—

'Come, lady, and you, virgin; bestow your eyes and parent affections upon men of estimation, both at Court and in the City.

'Sir Godfrey. Do, good sister, sweet little Frank; these are men of reputation. You shall be welcome at Court — a great credit for a citizen.'

Such being the state of feeling, we may be the less surprised, that, as in France (where citizens never attained, as such, the rank of freemen or Gentlemen in any sense), the *Bourgeois-Gentilhomme* became a term of reproach, so in England the courtiers and wits would feel pleasure as well as policy in degrading the mere citizenship into a *forfeiture* of the title of Gentleman, rather than in exalting it into a claim for such rank; though certainly they were no more justified in doing the one than the other. Towards the latter end of the sixteenth century, the grandeur, the exploits, the opulence, and the *good deeds* of the citizens became a very fruitful source of ribaldry — and the bitterness of the citizens at these jests served to nourish them. In a burlesque prologue to a play of the year 1613, we have the following dialogue.

Enter speaker of the Prologue, and a Citizen.

'*Cit.* Hold your peace. Goodman, boy.

'*Prol.* What do you mean, sir?

'*Cit.* That you have no good meaning. This seven years there have been plays at this house, I have observed you still have girds at the citizens: and now you call your play "The London Merchant." Down with your title, boy, down with your title.

'*Prol.* We intend no abuse of the City.

'*Cit.* No, sir? Yes, sir — if you were not resolved to play the Jacks, what need you study for new subjects purposely to abuse your betters? Why could you not be contented, as well as others, with the legend of Whittington, or the life and death of Sir Thomas Gresham, with the building of the Royal Exchange, or the story of Queen Eleanor with the rearing of London Bridge upon woolsacks.'

Citizens of the more mechanical sort are thus spoken of. Gertred, a goldsmith's daughter, is coquetting herself into a marriage with a needy knight she exclaims—

'*Girl.* For the passion of patience look if Sir Petronel approach. The sweet, that fine, &c. Oh! sister Mil though my father be a lowcapt tradesman, yet I must be a lady, and I praise God my mother must call me *Madam*. Does he come? Off with this gown for shame's sake, off with this gown! Let not my knight take me in the *City cut*.

Afterwards Touchstone, the father addressing the knight, says—

'Sir, respect my daughter: she has refused for you wealthy and honest matches, known good men, &c.

'*Girl.* Body o' truth, citizens! citizens! sweet knight, as soon as ever we are married, take me to thy mercy out of this miserable City, presently, &c.'

Again, Palhantine, a young gallant in great pecuniary difficulties, is addressing his betrothed, and says—

'A foundress thou shalt be, of
A nunnery, Lace, where all the female issue
Of our decayed nobility shall live
Thy pensioners: it will preserve them from
Such want as makes them quarter arms with the City,
And match with saucy Haberdashers sons,
Whose fathers lived in *alleys* and *dark lanes*.'

Davenant: *The Wits*, 1636.

CHARLES I. CITIZENS AS GENTLEMEN.

maxims of divine right and absolute power, which he himself had not the courage or capacity to act upon. Remarkable

CHAP. XI.
A.D. 1603 to 1660.

It may be reasonably supposed that the dramatists in referring to the City Merchants have greatly exaggerated, for the purposes of ridicule, the contempt entertained of them; but we cannot determine, however, that they violated together the common sentiments of the times. A humorous scene of the year 1639 will exhibit some traits of the manner in which young Templars presumed to speak and think of the more opulent merchants.

Enter WAREHOUSE, *a City Merchant, and* PLOTWELL, *his nephew, a young gentleman of the temple.*

(The uncle is endeavouring to persuade the nephew to engage in his rule.)

'*Warehouse.* Think, man, how it may in time make thee of the City senate, and raise thee
To the sword and cap of maintenance.
'*Plotwell (aside).* Yes, and make me
Sentence light bread and pounds of butter on horseback.
'*Warr.* Have gates and conduits dated from thy year;
Ride to the Spittle on thy free beast.
'*Plot. (aside).* Yes, free of your company.
'*Warr.* Have the people vail
As low to his trappings, as if he thrice had fined
For that good time's employment.
'*Plot. (aside.)* Or as if
He had his rider's wisdom.
'*Warr.* When the words
And good deeds of the City go before thee;
Besides a troop of varlets.
Plot. (aside). Yes, and I
To sleep the sermon in my chain and scarlet.
'*Warr.* How say you? Let's hear that,
'*Plot. (aloud).* I say, sir,
To sit at sermon in my chain and scarlet.
'*Warr.* 'Tis right; and be remembered at the cross.

'*Plot.* And then at sessions, sir, and all times else,
Master Recorder to save me the trouble,
And understand things for me.
'*Warr.* All this is possible, &c.'
After the exit of WAREHOUSE, *enter, to* PLOTWELL, BRIGHT *and* NEWCUT *(two Templars).*
'*Bright.* Save you, Merchant Plotwell.
'*New.* Mr. Plotwell, Citizen and Merchant, save you.
'*Bright.* Is thy uncle
Gone the wished voyage? &c.
——what, take thee from the Temple
To make thee an old Jewryman, a Whittington!
'*New.* To transform thy plush to pennystone; and scarlet
Into a velvet jacket, which has seen Aleppo twice, &c. ——In Ovid
There is not such a metamorphosis
As thou art now. *To be turned into a tree,*
Or some handsome beast, is courtly to this;
But for *thee,* Frank—— Oh! transmutation!
Of satin changed to kersey hose I sing.
'Slid! his shoes shine too.
'*Bright.* They have the *Gresham* dye, &c.
'*Plot.* Very pleasant, gentlemen.
'*Bright.* And faith, for how many years art thou bound?
'*Plot.* Do you take me for a 'prentice ?
'*New.* Why then, what office
Dost thou bear in the parish this year?
Let's feel:
No batteries in thy head, to signify
Thou'rt constable?
'*Bright.* No furious jug broke on it,
In the king's name, &c.'
Afterwards Warehouse is rejoiced into the idea of being sought in marriage by an *Irish Baroness,* at which he assumes vast self-importance. Upon being, however, introduced to the lady, the dialogue proceeds thus:—

P

throughout his life for too great a bias towards his advisers, Charles at his accession was entirely swayed, not to say

'*Bancrowright*. I am instructed,
I was mistaken, sir; indeed the lady
Spoke to me for *her gentlewoman*. How
Do you affect *her*, sir? her birth
Not being so high, *she will more suit
with you*.
  '*Warr*. I say, I like her best. Her
lady has
Too much great house with her.'
        Mayne: *The City Match*, 1839.

The following scenes from Massinger's celebrated play of *A New Way to Pay Old Debts*, acted in 1633, may perhaps be considered more genuine samples of the real sentiments entertained of the rank and credit of citizens.

'*Overrreach*. 'Tis my glory, tho' I came
  from the City,
To have their issue whom I have undone
To kneel to mine as bondslaves——
——————— there having ever been
More than a feud—a strange antipathy
Between us and *true gentry*.'

And again, addressing his daughter, he says—

' How like you your new woman
The lady Downfallen——
        Is she humble, Meg,
And careful too, her *ladyship* forgotten?
  '*Margaret*. You know your own
  ways; but for me, I blush
When I command her, that was once
  attended
With persons *not inferior to myself*
In birth.'

A nobleman is rallied on his having proffered himself to Overrreach's daughter, and he replies with indignation—
'Were Overrreach's estates thrice centupled, his daughter
Millions of degrees much fairer than she is,
How'er I might urge precedents *to
  excuse me*,
I would not *so adulterate my blood*
By marrying Margaret, and to leave
  my issue
Made up of several pieces, one part
  scarlet,

The *other London blue*.'

In another play of the year 1614, we have the following dialogue:—

STAINES (*a young gallant, addressing
himself to* SPENDALL, *a young citizen, in
a brawl*).

'Darest thou *resist*? thou art no
  citizen.
'*Spend.* I am a citizen.
'*Staines.* Say thou'rt *a gentleman*,
  and I am satisfied;
For *then* I know thou 'lt answer me in
  the field.
'*Spend.* I say directly, I am a *citizen*.
And I will meet thee in the field, as
  fairly
As the best Gentleman that wears a
  sword, &c.'

It is plain from the drama of the reign of James I., that the manners of the gentry and of the Court were extremely gross and profligate; and it was equally the fashion amongst them to violate the decencies of private life in the City, as to deride the pretensions of the citizens. The wits took their cue from the temper of the gentry; and, not satisfied with exploding the claim of the inferior orders of tradesmen to the rank of Gentlemen by mere virtue of their civic freedom, they were willing to degrade all indiscriminately, while all indiscriminately were the objects of the lowest insults to the courtiers. In the ensuing reign of Charles I., the citizens, by their spirit and their influence, made themselves of important consideration in the state; but it may well be surmised, that, among the cavaliers, or *genteel* ranks of the community, they contracted much more hatred than respect. With the return of Charles II. and his suite from their long French banishment, that animosity broke forth with great violence. Foreign habits had inculcated a contempt for the rank and qualities of their ancient enemies, and the most profligate course of exemplifying it. A feud may be said to

governed, by his minister, the Duke of Buckingham—one of the most presumptuous and self-willed men that ever existed. Dignified, and perhaps haughty, in all his opinions, the king was apt to conceive that the language of complaint and remonstrance from his people savoured of insolence, if not rebellion. Having acquired no small degree of political knowledge in the affairs of his kingdom, he had formed his ideas of the nature of the English constitution, rather from the precedents and practice of his immediate predecessors,

have subsisted between the Court and the City throughout the whole of Charles II.'s reign. It is not possible to refer without a violation of decency to the specimens of the intercourse between the courtiers and the citizens by which their feelings towards each other could be best displayed. The most disgusting profligacy in the invasion of family peace, which passed as a standing joke in the reign of James I., was a fashionable amusement in the reign of Charles II.

These animosities have long passed away; nor does there any longer exist that decided difference in manners and habits which formerly concurred, as much as party spirit, to separate the city and the gentry. With the diffusion of wealth and commerce, that of liberal education and high feeling has kept pace. The City merchant and the City magistrate mingles with the first courtiers and the highest circles of society, upon the same terms and upon the same pretensions. Whatever difference in their relative station, public honour, or influence, or right of precedence, may sanction towards one another—as Gentlemen they acknowledge, or affect to acknowledge, an equality. The qualities of mind and of avocation alone furnish the data upon which social rank is to be accorded. The title of free citizen neither increases or detracts from the personal estimation of its possessors. The laws of society recognise a distinction between the claims of the shop-keeper and those of the merchant to the rank of gentility; although the variety of commercial employment may prevent that distinction being very strongly marked: but we may consider it one proof of the advance of refinement in this age, that as, on the one hand, no civic qualification can ever raise to the rank of a Gentleman the person engaged in base or menial offices, so, on the other, the same qualification will not deprive any individual of such rank, if it has been acquired from other sources.

It is certainly worthy of observation, that the same depreciation of the quality of the citizens, was the fashion with the wits and courtiers of these early times —when many of the dignitaries and merchants of the City ranked among the first statesmen and the most influential men of the day, and became the founders of many of the noblest families of the kingdom—as it since became among wits and gentry of far less consideration. With as little justice, too, in the latter as in the former period; as shown in the forcible evidence of the Hon. Stuart Wortley, the Recorder of London, before the Parliamentary Commissioners who sat in 1854. It has become notorious that most of the greater merchants of London even affect to disdain civic honours, and prefer to seek public and social distinction through other paths. But whether they do not rather lose than follow the surest road, must be left to their own sagacity.

than from its true principles, or the enlightened political opinions universally entertained amongst his people.

Unhappily for this monarch, there flourished at this crisis in the House of Commons men who possessed the most exalted capacities, and who were actuated at the same time by the most generous and patriotic views. These men could not but perceive how dependent the king had become upon Parliament for those supplies, which the alteration of times and circumstances required every year to be more liberal, while the resources of the prerogative had gradually diminished. They resolved to convert the power thus acquired into the means of settling for ever the boundaries between the respective rights of the king and his subjects, and leave no longer in doubt the nature of that free constitution, which they looked to restore, if not to found. With this view the House was induced to pause in the submissive course which had been usual in their grants. The commands of the king —nay, his representations and entreaties on this subject— were met with parsimonious indifference. Remonstrances against grievances and arbitrary measures alone occupied their counsels. Parliament after Parliament was dissolved, in disgust; while Charles in vain endeavoured by the exercise of his prerogative to maintain his absolute independence, until, as he flattered himself, he should collect more subservient members of his legislature. He still, however, found himself doomed to confront the same steady patriots; and these gradually were joined by more turbulent spirits. The list of grievances increased; remonstrances grew bolder. At length, the king conceived that the design of the Parliament was to rob him of all those undoubted royal privileges, without which he could never support the dignity of his crown, if not to overthrow the government altogether. He determined to proceed by what he termed *new counsels*,[1] and to rule independently, as well of Parliament as of every other control but his own will. If, however, we reflect on the characters of the men who composed the first Parliament of Charles; when we see Wentworth, Falkland, and Hyde, joining with Pym,

[1] Hume's Hist. ch. l., quoting the language of the king's message and the vice-chamberlain's speech upon it, as in Rushworth and Whitelocke.

Hampden, and Hollis in the same objects—who can doubt but that this infatuated monarch was as much mistaken in the views of his opponents, as he was in his own power to resist them? Few of the measures taken at this period by the Commons were dictated by any other than the wisest and the most patriotic policy; and, if the example set by them to the nation subsequently led to the subversion, not only of monarchy, but of all just principles of government, we must attribute such consequences not to those great spirits to whom we have alluded, but to that sinister alloy of faction, which but too often is poured into the purest sources of national emancipation and freedom.

To refer, in detail, to the various modes adopted by Charles in prosecution of his *new counsels* would be to recapitulate most of those obnoxious oppressions which spring from the exercise of arbitrary power employed in taxation—oppressions which had all been from time to time denounced; many of which had been actually abolished, and others sunk into oblivion. In the twelve years during which the king persisted in refusing to call a Parliament, it is not too much to say that no measure likely to prove successful in extorting money was left unattempted. At the same time the most odious functions of the Star Chamber were exhausted in avenging the unlicensed ebullitions of popular indignation. The great weight of these sudden and irregular measures fell upon the cities and towns, where capital is chiefly concentrated. London was the emporium of the kingdom; and that City, accordingly, became the chief scene of the royal exactions. Clarendon himself acknowledges that it was too much looked upon as a common stock not easily to be exhausted, and as a body not to be grieved by ordinary acts of injustice;[1] nor had the king yet learned from reason, or been taught by experience, the danger of inflicting injuries on a public body capable of meeting together to promulgate their opinions and discuss their wrongs.

Charles applied to the citizens, in the very first instance, for a loan of 100,000*l*. They well knew the slender nature

[1] Vol. i. p. 372.

BOOK I.
A.D. 1603 to 1660.

of the security offered for the repayment of it,[1] and declined to provide so large a sum; having no power, as they intimated, to *enforce* advances from individuals.[2] The king did not hesitate to imprison twenty of the principal citizens for this refusal,[3] and peremptorily obliged the City to provide twenty ships, although an abatement of the number was solicited in a very submissive manner.[3] On a riot occurring in the City, the lord mayor and aldermen were summoned before the king's Council, and threatened with a seizure of the Charter; they were finally amerced in the sum of 6,000*l*.; and yet it has been doubted whether this was a pretence for extortion.[4] Further, warrants were issued for levying ship-money: the citizens referred to their charter:[4] they petitioned for abatement;[4] they appealed to the courts of law:[5] but all was in vain; and they were expressly told by one of the judges, 'that there was one rule of law, and another of 'government, which latter was not to be controverted.'[5] Four aldermen were imprisoned by the Privy Council for not disclosing the names of citizens who had money, but who refused to advance it to the king.[5] Prosecutions were carried on in the Star Chamber against the Corporation for pretended abuses in the management of the province of Ulster; the City was, after many invitations to compound, condemned to lose its possessions,; and fined 50,000*l*.[6] This sentence was condemned at the very first meeting of the next Parliament, as contrary to the fundamental rights of the people.[6] No limits were set to proclamations; and they were all enforced by scandalous sentences in the Star Chamber. Finally, as if to convince the citizens that the king designed nothing short of completing their degradation and slavery, he forbad their preparing any petition to him for the redress of grievances.[7]

Under these circumstances no apology is requisite, on behalf of the City of London, for their having joined with the famous Long Parliament in a strenuous endeavour to with-

---

[1] Securities for money borrowed of the citizens, it was the practice to avoid on any specious pretences. Clarendon, vol. i. p. 372.

[2] Rushworth, vol. i. pp. 415, 419. Franklyn, p. 207.

[3] Ibid. Maitland, vol. i. p. 299.

[4] Ibid. Kennett's Life of Charles I.

[5] Kennett's Life of Charles I.

[6] Ibid. vol. iii. 1640.

[7] Ibid. vol. ii.

stand the despotic authority of the king, and redress the evils of his government. What man, however prejudiced, could contemplate such a list of oppressions, and at the same time preach submission? Even Lord Clarendon, though he will not justify any of the measures of the citizens, says quite enough to excuse their disaffection to the Court party.[1] There is, however, no reason to believe that, at the commencement of the civil troubles, any party in the Corporation encouraged revolutionary views, or any other than for redress, which would naturally result from a just sense of their wrongs. The king and the citizens long maintained towards each other sentiments of personal good-will; nor were these sentiments confined to professions merely. Charles, in the fourteenth year of his reign, granted them a most ample charter. It confirms all former privileges enjoyed under prior grants, and it confers several additional and important immunities. Parliamentary opposition, if at this crisis it may not with more propriety be termed faction, had already run high, and was fast advancing in the career of disloyalty, when, upon the king's arrival in London after a long absence in Scotland, he was received with a magnificence and universal cordiality which could leave little doubt how personally dear he still continued to the citizens. The Recorder, in the name of the Corporation, pronounced an address full of fervent affection; and Charles, in terms of much sensibility, expressed the contentment he felt in finding that the late tumults and disorders had only arisen from the meaner sort, and that the City had ever been loyal and affectionate to his person and government. The king, after dining in public with the lord mayor, embraced him on taking leave; and desired him to attend with his brethren the aldermen at Whitehall the following day, that he might convince them of his determination to fulfil all those promises of protection in their civic rights, which he had promised in his public address to them.[2]

[1] Vol. i. p. 372.
[2] All the circumstances attending the king's reception and entertainment in the City are detailed in Maitland, vol. i. p. 340, quoting Stow's Survey; Rushworth's Col. vol. iii.; and Nals. Col. vol. ii.

BOOK I.
A.D. 1603 to 1650.

Flattering as these loyal indications were, they were of short duration. It is true that the king assented to many just and popular bills, by which the Courts of High Commission and Star Chamber were abolished, and the more oppressive exercises of his prerogative denounced; but the indiscreet reluctance which he seemed to feel in sanctioning such measures, added continually to the strength and zeal of the republican party in the government; while he gained but few to his side, and those slowly, from amongst the partisans of more moderate counsels. The zealots in the House were unceasing in their efforts to attach the citizens to their cause; and Charles, by his personal animosity and injudicious attacks on the most powerful asserters of the liberties of the people, seemed labouring to estrange them. He attempted, in person, to seize on five of the most popular members of the House of Commons, whom, for their bold conduct in Parliament, he had accused of high treason. The people were generally alarmed; the members threw themselves into the arms of the citizens, and found in them determined protectors. The king in vain presented himself in the Court of Common Council, demanding their surrender in conciliatory terms. A step had now been taken too decisive to be retracted: there was no want of exertion in fomenting the disposition which had shown itself, by every representation that could throw an unfavourable light on the measures of the Court. Former oppressions were not suffered to be forgotten. Parliament denounced the king, as resolved to overthrow the constitution; it declared war against him; and the citizens joined themselves heartily to that cause, for which they saw Essex, Hampden, and Pym, and many of the greatest worthies in England were prepared to shed their blood.

Whoever examines into the nature of these civil disputes, cannot fail to discover that in the prosecution of them there was, as well in the City as throughout the country, as much theological as political acrimony. The progress of the Lutheran reformation had inculcated much reflection and discussion, as well as faith, in religious affairs; and had, consequently, given birth to a variety of sects and opinions. That inseparable union between free sentiments in religion

CHARLES I. RELIGIOUS DISSENSIONS. 217

and free sentiments in government, acting with reciprocal effect, drew the attention of the people at the same time to the consideration, as well of their spiritual as of their temporal welfare; and the sect, so long distinguished under the name of Puritans, were the first who roused the long dormant spirit of liberty in England. While a large portion, if not the majority, of the people were still wavering in their deference to the hierarchy, the bigotry and superstitious practices of the primate Laud, backed by the vindictive inquisition of the Star Chamber and court of High Commission, served to instigate still further that defection, which tyranny never fails to convert into abhorrence. Loud invectives were poured forth against popery and popish ceremonies, to which the primate was accused as more than addicted. Episcopalian government was next attacked, as supported by the same medium. The doctrine of equality in religion, and the reasonableness of lay pretensions to inspiration, began to be relished. Some members of the Presbyterian persuasion arrived in London on a political mission from Scotland: all the enthusiasm of the self-inspired votaries of the kirk was poured forth in the City, to the amazement and delight of their new auditors. The churches were left desolate; and happy was he who by timely exertion in obtaining a seat in the Scotch congregation, was at length blest with the edification bestowed in a ranting sermon of three hours' length.[1] The reign of fanaticism began, and was characterised by the usual blindness and zeal which actuates religious faction. The City abounded in schismatical congregations. Without any standard of faith to which common allegiance was attracted, every man not only followed, but was anxious to preach his own system. Some proposed a religious community of goods, others declaimed against tithes and lawyers; some laboured to establish a dominion of saints, others expected the second coming of Jesus Christ to govern the world in person.[2] The great majority of the people were united in one feeling of hatred to episcopacy and church government; and as Charles was not only religiously but

CHAP. XL
A.D. 1603 to 1660.

[1] Clarendon's Hist. vol. i. pp. 189, 190.
[2] Hume, ch. lx. et passim: Reign of Charles I.

politically attached to the principles of the Church, he shared but too largely the prevalent detestation of them.

Such were the circumstances which concurred in arming the citizens against their sovereign. Throughout the civil war their influence was great, indeed almost decisive; and the troops they contributed proved the best and bravest in the field. Both sides used the most anxious exertions, the one to acquire, the other to retain, their support. Numerous were the delegations by the Parliament of their most prominent members to address them on their successes, and on the hopes entertained of finally accomplishing their views.[1] And as frequent were the messages of the king, expostulating with them and appealing to their loyalty.[2] The Corporation, however, continued true to the parliamentary interest, until very near the end of the war and the destruction of the king.

Before that period a radical change had taken place in the quality and objects of those at the head of government. It is needless to specify the series of arts by which Cromwell had arrived at a complete command of a powerful and victorious army, or the manoeuvres by which he had lulled the suspicions of that Parliament by whose support he had risen, and which he was at length able to overthrow. As soon as the House perceived the loss of their authority with the army, it made a fruitless effort to oppose those views of regal authority, at which it then became notorious Cromwell aimed. The City sided openly with the Parliament.[3] That assembly, however, could make but a feeble stand against the force under which the nation was about to fall. It already abounded with many partisans of Cromwell; and on the arrival of that general in London, those who opposed his views were unceremoniously ejected by that clearance of the House of Commons by Colonel Pride, which commonly passed by the name of *Pride's Purge*. The House then submitted to the government of Cromwell and his generals.

This was a state of things on which the citizens had never calculated; and they made no hesitation in breaking both

---

[1] Maitland, vol. i. p. 358.
[2] Clarendon's Hist.
[3] Hume, ch. lix. Maitland, vol. i. p. 390.

with Cromwell and the newly packed Parliament.[1] The former, however, prevailed. At the trial of Charles several of the citizens were appointed as the king's judges;[2] and the autocrat was by no means deficient in paying court to his ancient freinds. Yet, although he succeeded in great measure in apparently attaching the Corporation to his interests, he never truly secured their good-will. Several of the aldermen absolutely refused to proclaim a commonwealth;[3] and during the many subsequent civil dissensions, the City juries, by their acquittals of public offenders, more than once taught the Protector on what a precarious foundation his interests rested amongst the citizens. At his death the citizens were early in their defection from his son Richard; and some of them complained, not without reason, that the *good old cause* had been long entirely neglected.[4] When Monk applied to the Common Council to join him in restoring king Charles II., nothing could exceed the universal joy with which his invitation was accepted; and Charles was received by the citizens with such abundant marks of cordial welcome, that he wondered 'where his enemies were concealed, 'and why he had delayed so long in repairing to his friends.'

[1] Hume, ch. lix. Maitland, vol. l. p. 390.
[2] Hume.
[3] Maitland, vol. i. pp. 347, 355, 419.
[4] Hume, ch. lxii.

CHAPTER XII.

FROM THE ACCESSION OF CHARLES II. TO THE CLOSE OF THE REIGN OF GEORGE II.—SURVEY OF THE MEASURES OF CHARLES II.—SEIZURE OF THE CITY FRANCHISES BY A WRIT OF QUO WARRANTO—SURVEY OF THE MEASURES OF JAMES II.—CONFIRMATION OF THE CITY'S CORPORATE RIGHTS, FRANCHISES, AND PRIVILEGES BY THE STATUTE OF 2 WILLIAM III.—NATURE AND EFFECT OF THE STATUTE OF 11 GEORGE I. FOR REGULATING THE ELECTIVE FRANCHISES—SUMMARY OF SUBSEQUENT LEGISLATION AND OF THE CIVIC ELECTIVE FRANCHISES AT THE PRESENT TIME—CONCLUSION OF THE FIRST BOOK.

BOOK I.
A.D. 1660 to 1724.

It had been well for the ill-fated family of the Stuarts, if those constitutional doctrines comprised in the Bill of Rights, and which have at once served to confirm the dignity of subsequent monarchs and the liberties of the people, had been openly asserted at the Restoration; at such a crisis Charles II. would not have been able, nor perhaps disposed, to have disputed their establishment. But such was the headlong zeal of the people, and the triumphant loyalty of the victorious party, that although the Convention Parliament, on whom this important task fell, was chiefly composed of the liberal party, yet it was deemed either no longer prudent or safe ostensibly to profess any such design.[1] That national party, however, resolved to accomplish, by covert and indirect means, the great scheme of liberty to which the eyes of the people had been gradually opened. Charles, neither nurtured in the free principles of a limited monarchy, nor fairly apprised of the prevalence of them among his people, may be said in some degree to have been unwarily led into those arbitrary measures which have rendered the events of his reign too remarkable

---

[1] Lenthal, a member, declared in the House his opinion, that those who first took up arms against the late king were equally guilty with those who condemned him to death. This declaration was resented, and Lenthal was reprimanded by the Speaker. Parl. Journ. vol. viii. p. 24. This, however, was the only open indication of the assertion of free principles.

in the annals of the City to be passed over slightly; the prosecution of which, in the end, mainly conduced to expel his family from the English throne.

The first Parliament summoned by Charles contented themselves with not restoring any of the most obnoxious royal prerogatives; and it must be confessed that the king did not in his early measures evince any design of assuming them contrary to the inclination of his subjects, or of exerting any independent power of taxation. A charter granted in the year 1663 to the City of London, which confirmed in the most ample terms, by name and by recital, their preceding charters, as well as their ancient privileges and customs, sufficiently exemplified his deference to popular rights.[1] Subsequent Parliaments, however, manifested no disposition to encourage in the king a confident reliance on their financial support, by granting supplies adequate to the reasonable necessities of the monarch; and Charles may be at least excused, if not justified, in harbouring the disgust such conduct was calculated to raise. He began to suspect, not without cause, that the Parliament designed to render his political measures subservient to their views: but to what extent that design might be carried, and what was the ultimate object of the popular party, he had no means of ascertaining.

Notwithstanding the untoward suspicions generated by this backwardness in regard to supplies, it is clear, from the conduct of Parliament, that in reality it intended neither to intrench on the just authority of the king, nor to deprive him of any of his requisite and constitutional prerogatives. In all other respects every indication of loyalty, and even of subserviency, was manifested. Although the republican army was disbanded, a body of about one thousand horse and five thousand foot was suffered to be retained without reproach;[2] and this was the first establishment of a regular standing army in the nation. Many acts were passed calculated to crush the smallest seeds of rebellion; all legislative power in

---

[1] This charter, dated June 24, 1663, contains almost all the previous charters recited at large in the way of Inspeximus, and is usually referred to as the text of the City charters. It does not, however, contain the whole of them.

[2] Hume, ch. lxiii. James's Memoirs.

the Houses *alone* was specifically renounced. A commission was authorised for the expulsion from corporations of all magistrates who held principles dangerous to the constitution; that is, who did not disclaim the Scotch covenant, and abhor the position that the king could on any pretence be resisted by force of arms¹—a position which it was subsequently found impossible altogether to explode. Even two or three proclamations, which assumed the character of statutes, were allowed to pass without any direct remonstrance against their validity.² It is but reasonable, therefore, to suppose that this Parliament, like the earlier ones of the preceding reign, meant no more by such parsimony than to establish a check on the conduct of the king, and to ground the government on a constitutional basis: nor can there be any doubt that if Charles had persisted in a just and liberal course of administration, and in appealing to his Parliament or to his people for the requisite financial support to his government, he must have eventually succeeded, both in strengthening his own power and in obtaining the reverence and love of his subjects. Several causes contributed to recommend more impolitic and disgraceful measures.

One of these causes, and that not the least, arose from the state of religious parties. At the Restoration the majority of the sectarians, if not of the people, were Presbyterians; and as few besides the Royalists were high-churchmen, the nation at large was far from zealous in returning to episcopacy.³ As, however, the high-church party, which comprised the king's ministers, were at the head of affairs, there was no hesitation, on the part of government, in establishing the prelatical rights and forms of ecclesiastical government; and as soon as the Royalists had found their exertions successful in acquiring a considerable majority in

---

¹ Corporation Act.
² Such as those regulating the national worship, issued at the commencement of the reign; and one or two in respect of the buildings after the great fire of London.
³ This is apparent, not only from the king's early ecclesiastical proclamations, in which he pays the Presbyterian party the utmost deference, but also from the conferences at the Savoy, in which both Presbyterians and Episcopalians stoutly maintained their respective dogmas, but without making any progress towards convincing their opponents.

the House of Commons,¹ they endeavoured to fix the exercise
of the national religion according to those tenets which
they conceived most primitive and correct. The Presbyterians, in the meanwhile, partly attracted by the love of
power, and partly impelled by distaste to any coalition with
the other sectarians, declined in number; the Independents
and others, who were distinguished by their republican
principles, were not averse to any severities inflicted on the
Presbyterians, by whom they conceived the national interests
had been betrayed. The Catholics, who although powerful
at court had very little influence in the country, were disposed to encourage any schemes for dividing the Protestants;
so that it was with something like a general concurrence that
the Royalists in Parliament were enabled, in the early part of
the reign, to pass the famous Act of Uniformity, by which all
dissenters from the Church of England were forbidden, under
heavy penalties, the exercise of congregational worship.² As
the differences which divided the various Protestant sectarians
were rather in mere forms than in their fundamental tenets,
they soon began, as the force of enthusiasm expended itself,
to draw again towards each other, and their animosities
gradually subsided into the ancient and united detestation
of Popery; the principles of which they were disposed, as
much politically as religiously, to abjure. The tenets of this
faith the king unhappily both believed and patronised in
secret:³ while his brother James, duke of York, on whom
most of the cares of government fell, as well as the apparent
succession, did the same openly; and the people became,

---

¹ There were but fifty-six Presbyterian members in the first Parliament
after the convention, says Hume, quoting
Carte's Answer to the Bystander, p. 79.

² This account of the circumstances
which led to the passing the Act of
Uniformity, is taken from Hume. It
seems not only to tally with the party
pamphlets of the day, but is the only
consistent explanation of the great and
sudden change which then took place in
the religious principles of the great
majority of the nation.

³ This point was formerly much
disputed; but after the publication of
James's Memoirs, who, in stating the
projects of the king in the French alliance, declares *that Charles wept for joy
at the prospect of re-uniting his kingdom
to the Catholic Church,* no reasonable
doubt can be entertained on the subject.
He died in the presence of Catholic
priests; and James published two post-
humous papers in his brother's own
handwriting, wherein he argues in favour of the Catholic faith.

accordingly, the more united and resolute by the consciousness of a common cause.

It was a conflict of religious zeal which occasioned the first breach between Charles and his Parliament; a breach that was never afterwards entirely closed. He saw that a considerable body of his subjects were scandalised by the Act of Uniformity; and he fondly hoped that, by evincing a deference to their conscientious scruples, he might open the path for the admission of the Catholic religion. He published a declaration of *Indulgence*, as it was called, by which he claimed the power of dispensing with the penalties against dissenting congregations. The people were alarmed, not only at this assumption of prerogative, but at the object of it. The secret intention of introducing Popery by these means did not elude the vigilance of Parliament. The Houses passed no express remonstrance against the declaration itself, but made their sentiments sufficiently apparent by a concurrent denunciation against all Catholics.

With this experience of the opinions of his people—becoming more and more bigoted to the Popish faith and principles—straitened in his circumstances (which were not likely to improve under his indulgent habits of life)—Charles had recourse to an entirely new plan of administration. He discharged all his old and honourable advisers, and took to his counsels a set of men long known under the appellation of the Cabal, who possessed neither honourable principles or the credit of them; by whose suggestion he proceeded upon as scandalous a course of government as ever disgraced the ruler of any nation in the world.

Louis XIV. of France, a man bigoted to the Catholic religion, of considerable talents and of unbounded ambition, and commanding in men and money enormous resources, openly aimed at the dominion of Europe. Charles was cajoled into the chimerical hope of establishing, through his assistance, an independent and absolute power over his own subjects in England, and of overturning for ever the faith of ninety-nine hundredths of his people.[1] Actuated by these

---

[1] Hume, chaps. lxv. lxvi., quoting Appendix. D'Estrade's, July 21, 1667. James's Memoir. Sir J. Dalrymple's Temple, vol. ii. p. 179.

views, he secretly sold himself to the interests of France for a paltry annual pension; and engaged by every measure in his power to promote her schemes of conquest, and to prosecute her aggrandisement, although at the sacrifice of every dictate of sound policy, of many engagements of honour, and even at the imminent risk of eventual ruin to his kingdom.[1]

The first measures taken in the advancement of this wild and shameful enterprise, was a coalition to subdue the Dutch—a valuable and easy prey, as it was presumed; against whom, however, there not only existed no cause of complaint, but with whom there subsisted a treaty of the closest alliance. The people of England received the intimation of this war with equal amazement and indignation: insomuch that it was suspected the sailors were ashamed to do their duty in battle.[2] The king, fearing that his Parliament might scrutinise his measures, and perhaps by its interference render them abortive, had recourse to continual prorogations; in the meanwhile he encouraged the vain hope either of finding that assembly more subservient, or of ruling in defiance of it. To obtain those supplies which no foreign resources could sufficiently afford, various devices were put in force. An effort was made, though unsuccessful, to intercept a Dutch fleet of valuable merchandise, before that nation was fairly apprised of the intended hostilities. The merchants, bankers, and goldsmiths of London, with whom it was the practice to lodge capital, had been invited to deposit these funds in the king's exchequer at interest, from which the principal could be withdrawn as might be convenient. This practice had become habitual, when on a sudden, Charles was advised to shut up the exchequer and seize on the deposited capital for his private use; and this measure was carried into effect, to the dismay and ruin of thousands.[3]

Not content with these direct efforts at establishing an

---

[1] Hume, chaps. lxv., lxvi., quoting James's Memoirs. Sir J. Dalrymple's Appendix. D'Estrade's 21st July, 1667. Temple, vol. ii. p. 179.

[2] Hume, ch. lxv.

[3] Anderson's Hist. of Com. vol. ii. p. 519. Hume says the king advertised for some expedient among his courtiers, at the price of the treasurer's staff; that Shaftesbury dropped the hint to Clifford (both members of the Cabal), and that the latter at once proposed it, and gained his reward. Ch. lxv.

independent power, Charles proceeded to issue arbitrary proclamations, dispensing with the statutes of the realm—a prerogative which, thus exercised, it was easy to foresee would draw after it all other absolute authority. One of these forbade, under bitter menaces, all undutiful expressions against the king's measures;[1] another gave unwonted facilities to impressments;[2] another announced martial law among the troops, although not in actual service;[3] and another suspended the Navigation Act.[4]

What might have been the eventual success of such proceedings on the part of government is a subject of some doubt, so prepossessed were the people in favour of a monarch gifted with the most winning and agreeable manners. But an attack on the *religious* prejudices of his subjects served at last to deprive Charles of all prospect of enslaving them. He made a second declaration of indulgence to all Dissenters. The apprehensions of the nation had been before warmly excited; the people viewed this stretch of prerogative as a direct introduction to a forcible change in the national religion, and it was resented with the most violent animosity.

When the king was at last obliged to summon a Parliament, he found in it a steady determination to oppose his counsels—a determination which continued to actuate every Parliament to the end of his reign. It was in vain that he employed the arts of corruption, which now first began[5] to smooth the way to that sinister influence of the crown in Parliament which its most strenuous advocates can only defend as practically useful, though theoretically injurious. In vain he pretended deference to their opinions; and laboured to obtain the means of carrying on his views, and indulging his extravagances, by entreaties, and even by passing his *royal word* to employ the sums voted according to their intentions[6]—a promise which at the very time of making he fully intended to break.[7] Parliament had become altogether distrustful of his designs.

---

[1] Hume's Hist. ch. lxv.
[2] Ibid.
[3] Ibid.
[4] Ibid.
[5] Ibid., ch. lxvi. Temple's Memoirs.
[6] Message to Parliament. Session 1677.
[7] Temple's Memoirs. Dalrymple: Appendix, p. 103.

Every proceeding which emanated from the Court party seemed fraught with Popery. Popular hatred was directed with unremitting virulence to this point of dissension; and it became a complete mania. The king was obliged to annul the declaration of indulgence.¹ The Test Act was passed, which closed the doors to all public offices against Papists; and it was soon after attempted to pass the Exclusion bill, by which the succession of the Duke of York, who had the credit of governing the king, was to be set aside. The kingdom was divided into the Court and Country parties. The latter acquired the name of Whigs, and the former that of Tories. There was much political, but more religious, zeal on both sides.

Just at this crisis of public feeling broke out the rumour of the famous *Popish Plot*. It is not intended here to discuss the merits of this much disputed question of treason. It is certain that, whether there ever was any real foundation for the charge or not, many designing men were found base enough to make a political use of it, and to convert it to the distraction of their opponents. The belief of its genuineness and of its horrible malignity was industriously fomented, and there were villains who laboured to gain wealth and credit by administering in the most scandalous manner to the public credulity. Accusations, supported by the grossest perjuries, were levelled at many members of the Court party. A universal alarm prevailed amongst the people that a general massacre of the Protestants, and the establishment of Popery and despotism, was intended; and the design was without scruple fixed on the partisans of the king and the Duke of York.

Of all the believers and propagators of this alarm, none were so conspicuous as the citizens of London. And hence began a course of memorable proceedings in the City, which, though disgraceful to them in the beginning, carried much more of injustice towards them in the end. The citizens were the least disposed to submit to the baneful policy of Charles, the effects of which, in the stagnation of trade and in the

¹ Hume's Hist. ch. lxv.

pressure of taxation, weighed most heavily upon them. The shutting up of the exchequer, and the many arbitrary proclamations, had excited in them no small disgust. The favour shown to Catholics was particularly unpopular in a district where religious zeal had long been conspicuous, when the infatuation produced by the terror of the Popish Plot transported the citizens beyond all bounds. Many victims had already fallen before this bloody idol: the appetite of the people for sacrifices of this nature began to grow satiated; and the king thought he might venture to exert some influence in arresting the fearful course which marked the administration of justice. Two or three acquittals took place, to the great disappointment of the citizens; who attributed them solely to court intrigues, for the purpose of preventing the full detection of the much dreaded plot.

At this period the administration of justice in the courts of law was a disgrace to the age. It is impossible to peruse the State Trials without indignation at the venality and party zeal of many of the judges,¹ and at the pusillanimous bigotry of the juries. Much discretion was improvidently left in the hands of sheriffs in regard to their returns of jurors; and the courtiers had not been inattentive to the importance of having these officers firm in their interests. The Whig party among the citizens, not less alive to the same advantage, resolved to elect such persons for their sheriffs as they could rely upon for their distaste to the Court and their abhorrence of the plot, in order that by their means juries might be secured thoroughly inoculated with the prevailing prejudices.² Accordingly, two gentlemen, by name Bethel and Cornish, distinguished for their zeal against Catholics and the plot,³

---

¹ There is no topic on which Englishmen dwell with greater pride and admiration than the sacred integrity of their judges. It is indeed a just tribute which they pay to qualities which form one of the firmest bulwarks of their rights both political and private. Let us not ascribe, however, to mere human nature those principles of upright justice in the judicial character which are preserved at least, if not caused, by the unrelaxing control of a free government and a free press.

² Maitland, vol. i. p. 468. Burnet's History of His Own Time.

³ These sheriffs, when the innocent and venerable Lord Stafford, convicted by Oates's perjury of participation in the Popish Plot, was to be brought to the block, sent to the Houses of

CHARLES II.   CONTESTS IN APPOINTING SHERIFFS.

were set up against two others of the Court interest; and their election was carried by a large majority, with great acclamations of triumph.¹ The king evinced the utmost dissatisfaction;² and the sheriffs were not backward in manifesting their animosity against the Court.³ The following year two others of the same political character were elected, in spite of great efforts made against them; and the king went so far as personally to declare to the citizens how unwelcome to him that election was.⁴

It was now plain that, whatever confidence might be reposed in the time-serving activity of judges like Scroggs, North, and others, an insurmountable bar was placed against all further progress in quelling the spirit whether of liberty or of faction in the City, through the prostitution of legal forms. The Whig party had gained a complete, though a dishonourable, ascendency; and Charles was determined in his turn to make another struggle to acquire judicial dominion. The conduct of one party may perhaps be in some degree excused, as the effect of an unhappy infatuation, partly justified by the apprehension of unconstitutional designs; but that of the other can be considered in no other light than arising from a deliberate resolution to overthrow the liberties of the people, in open defiance of law, justice, and humanity. The means adopted were as illegal as the end was disgraceful. The king resolved to trample on the ancient right of free election in the City, and to nominate a sheriff devoted to his own will.

The right of choosing sheriffs from among themselves is one of those as clearly appertaining to the citizens at large, as the language of a charter and long subsequent usage can demonstrate.⁵ It seems, however, that a practice had originated as early, according to the best authorities, as the reign of Edward III., for the lord mayor, and occasionally the court

CHAP. XII.
A.D. 1660 to 1725.

Parliament to know whether the king had authority by his prerogative to insist on their executing that nobleman by decapitation, instead of hanging and quartering, as usual in cases of high treason. --Hume's *Hist.* ch. lxviii.; Ken. *Eng. Hist.*

¹ Burnet's Hist. Ken. Eng. Hist. Maitland, vol. i. p. 467.
² Ibid. Each. Hist. Eng.
³ Vide note 2, p. 227.
⁴ Ken. Eng. Hist. Each. Hist. Eng. Maitland, vol. i. p. 473.
⁵ Charter of Henry I.

of aldermen, to *nominate*, usually one citizen, but sometimes more, to the office of sheriff; and tender such nominee to the Common Hall for election. This mode of nomination began in the reign of Elizabeth to be exercised by the ceremony of the lord mayor's *drinking* to some person at a festival, which took place a few weeks before the day of election; and it was then first held, that the person so *drank* to was not merely *nominated*, but *ipso facto* elected. This opinion had crept in during times when magisterial authority had almost undisputed sway, and elective franchises were but little valued. But in the year 1641 this usurpation was stoutly disputed; and though no final decision was formerly made by authority, the Common Hall succeeded in tacitly regaining the privilege of at least exercising their discretion in regard to confirming the person drank to, and latterly, on the election of Bethel and Cornish, of *choosing* whomever they thought proper. It is unnecessary to pursue in detail the merits of this controversy, especially as, upon a thorough enquiry and discussion, the free and full right of election in the citizens was completely established; but whoever has the curiosity to investigate the nature and progress of the dispute, will find ample materials in the authorities quoted.[1]

It was under these circumstances that the lord mayor, Sir John Moore, was induced by the court to exercise the claim of an absolute choice of one of the sheriffs by the ceremony of drinking to him. Sir Dudley North, more honourably known at the present day for his able tracts on the true principles of trade, and the enlightened and liberal views with which he explained and advocated them, was prevailed on by his brother the lord keeper[2] to undertake the office so to be

---

[1] Lib. P. & S. Town Clerk's Office. Harg. MSS. Nos. 136, 140. Brit. Mus. Acts of Common Council, 30 Hen. VIII., 24 Eliz. Strype's Stow, vol. ii. pp. 76, 90, 439. Maitland's Hist. vol. i. pp. 208, 229, 268, 473. And Northouck's Hist. of London, pp. 168, 247, 251. Also an excellent pamphlet published in the year 1683-4, called The Modest Enquiry, in which the subject is fully discussed, and the authorities collected.

[2] The circumstances of Dudley North's taking office are detailed in the Life of Lord Keeper North, by whom that measure was suggested. It is impossible to refer to a more correct portrait of a low-minded and cunning lawyer than is drawn in the above work; and it is not a little curious, that the character is drawn in panegyrical traits, by a near relation. The lord keeper died in retirement of chagrin; which Burnet (no very reliable authority) explains by saying he was at last universally despised.

conferred. Accordingly, previous to the election, instead of the usual precept being issued to the livery, requiring their attendance *for choosing sheriffs*, they were called on to attend for the *confirmation* of one, *who had been chosen*, and the election of another.[1] What the nature of the right of confirming a person already appointed could be, if the lord mayor's choice was *absolute*, it is not easy to comprehend. The citizens fully understood the design, and assembling in great numbers on the day of election, insisted on putting up as candidates *two* of the Country party, Papillion and Dubois. The show of hands being decisively in their favour, a poll was demanded on behalf of North and Box, the latter being also a Court candidate. Great confusion ensued; some few of the Court party insisting on a distinct poll book for those who chose to vote for a confirmation of one candidate as well as the election of another; but as the design of that was obviously to furnish the lord mayor with a pretext for declaring the legal election to have fallen on North at least, if not on both North and Box, the demand was rejected as unusual and preposterous. The polling had proceeded for some time, when the lord mayor, clearly foreseeing the result, first endeavoured in vain to stop the polling, and then adjourned the Hall. The sheriffs, however, continued the poll until very late at night, and then adjourned the Hall, of their own authority, to the same day to which the lord mayor had previously adjourned it.

In the meantime the two sheriffs who had managed the election were summoned before the Privy Council, and sent to the Tower; but on being bailed, they attended the next Common Hall held by adjournment. The lord mayor immediately sent to adjourn the Hall again; but the sheriffs disregarded the message, and the poll having finished, declared Papillion and Dubois duly elected. It is to be observed that, on reference to the Recorder upon this occasion by the court of aldermen, he declared, without hesitation, that the full right of election was in the livery. The mode of taking

---

[1] Maitland's Hist. vol. i. p. 474. For a detailed account of the proceedings at this election, vide Ken. Eng. Hist.; Ech. Hist. Eng; and Burnet's Hist. of His Own Time.

the poll and of adjournment by the sheriffs was strictly consonant to ancient usage.

An order of the king's council was produced on the next adjournment day appointed by the lord mayor, by which he was required to begin the proceedings *de novo*, the last election being alleged to be altogether irregular. In professed obedience to this order, the lord mayor declared to the Common Hall that North *was elected* (in other words, appointed by himself), and he proceeded to take votes for Box. No opposition was made on behalf of Papillion and Dubois, as no one was disposed, by voting for candidates assumed to be already elected, to depreciate the regularity of such election: the lord mayor, accordingly, declared North and Box to be sheriffs. The latter fining, Mr. Rich was substituted, and elected after the same fashion. Papillion and Dubois in vain petitioned to be sworn into office; and by this barefaced outrage on the civic rights, the Court eventually succeeded in their object.

The effects of this triumph soon became apparent. Juries were found who gave a verdict with 100,000*l.* damages against Alderman Pilkington, one of the late sheriffs, for scandal against the Duke of York; and convicted Sir Patience Ward, a late lord mayor, of perjury, for swearing that, although he was present at the time of the alleged uttering of the scandal, he did not hear it. He was sentenced to the pillory.

The Court party, however, conscious that to accomplish their purpose a fresh struggle was to be encountered every year, resolved to strike a blow that should at once obviate all future disturbance in their progress, that should prostrate Parliament altogether, and leave the lives and liberties of the subject entirely at the mercy of the Crown. Their project was to seize the charters of all the corporate boroughs in England. Sawyer, the attorney-general, with a previous understanding in the proper legal quarters, intimated that he could undertake to prove a forfeiture of the City charters and liberties.[1] A writ of *quo warranto* was authorised to be prosecuted; and Charles well knew that a victory over this stronghold of liberty would be followed by the implicit surrender of all other

---

[1] Maitland, vol. i. p. 177. Burnet's Hist. of His Own Time.

corporations, where the establishment of the Court influence might be thought necessary. The pretence of forfeiture was, first, an act of Common Council, passed nine years previous, by virtue of which a new rate of tolls had been levied on persons using the public markets which had been rebuilt after the great fire; secondly, a petition presented to the king two years before, in which it was alleged, that, by the king's prorogation of Parliament, public justice had been interrupted, —and which petition the court of Common Council had caused to be printed.[1] Whether any corporation *could* forfeit its existence, *as a corporation*, by any abuse of its powers, or even by voluntary surrender, was not at this time clearly settled, nor indeed is it now.[2] Whether the *representatives* of a corporation, such as the court of Common Council, could effect a forfeiture of the rights of their constituents (which would imply that they could, by an act of their own, defeat the trust reposed in them, and alter the *essential constitution* of the body at large), may be still more reasonably doubted; and ample authorities may be referred to, showing that it cannot.[3] But that a by-law, if bad or doubtful, or a disrespectful address to the king, however reprehensible, could legally produce any such effect, is a position hardly requiring to be confuted; especially when it is known, that by one of the City charters it is specifically provided, that none of its liberties or franchises are to be forfeited by any abuse of them whatever.[4] The case was argued at great length, and with peculiar ability, on both sides. The Crown lawyers were forcible in their appeals to precedents sought out from troublesome and tyrannous times; the City advocates were more successful in their references to reason and principle. The judges, however, who were partisans in the cause, and some of them thought, with good reason,

---

[1] Quo warranto case.
[2] Kyd, on Corporations, vol. ii.
[3] The cases of Dr. Bonham, Co. Rep. vol. viii. p. 118; Calvin, Co. Rep. vol. vii. p. 17; and Co. 4th Inst. p. 42, in which this principle is discussed. And Coke lays it down that even an Act of Parliament against natural equity and the rights of the subject would be invalid. (Vide 3 Burr. 1827; Term. Rep. vol. iii. p. 196; Term. Rep. vol. iv. p. 810; & Harg. MSS. Brit. Mus. No. 135. p. 209; Vide also Kyd, vol. I. p. 259, & Comp. Rep. p. 26–29.) From which it may be gathered that the *corporation at large is not the same as the delegated representation of it by a selected number.*
[4] Charter 7th Richard II.

to have been raised to the bench for the express purpose,¹ gave judgment against the City. This decision seems to have excited but one opinion; namely, that whether we consider the conduct or the object of this proceeding, it deserves to be denounced as one of the most scandalous acts of this reign.

This violent act of power was followed, as was expected, by the surrender of the charters of most of the corporations in England, who could entertain but little hope of retaining their privileges after such an example. In London, all the obnoxious aldermen were displaced, and others appointed in their room by royal commission. A new lord mayor and recorder, and new sheriffs were appointed, in the same manner, to act during pleasure.² Secured against failure, the Court seemed now disposed to set no bounds to judicial iniquities. The juries selected were completely subservient. All who had evinced a spirit of opposition, and particularly the chief citizens engaged in the late elections, were convicted of seditious or libellous offences, in most instances on extremely frivolous evidence, and heavily fined. Amongst these was Oates, the infamous suborner of the Popish Plot, who was sued for scandal against the Duke of York: but the satisfaction that would naturally spring from his conviction is marred by the consideration of the vindictive nature of the verdict, in reference to his offence, which was to pay 100,000l. damages. No proceeding, however, raised such general and lasting indignation as the trial and execution of Russel and Sydney. There is no doubt that these noble persons, with no dishonourable or selfish design, were participators, to some extent, in a conspiracy to alter the course of government, or at least to change the king's scandalous measures. There is reason likewise to believe, that some understanding existed between them and a much more guilty party, who had amongst themselves gone so far as to discuss the subject of assassination. The general and just hatred of the Court measures—the illegal and tyrannical modes adopted to procure a conviction not warranted by the evidence on the trial—the many virtues and great qualities of the individuals, and their popularity throughout the nation—

¹ Burnet's Hist. of His Own Time. ² Ken. Eng. Hist. Ech. Hist. Eng.

have combined to sanctify their memory to posterity; and even to acquire for them, amongst many, the credit of martyrs to a good cause. Russel, in his dying words, attributes his destruction to the means used in packing his jury.¹

Having succeeded thus far in crushing his domestic enemies, Charles was enabled to look round on a temporary, though delusive, appearance of popularity.² It is said,³ with some degree of probability, that he had resolved to make an effort substantially to secure it, by relaxing in that cruel and vindictive course which, it must be allowed, was not consonant to his natural disposition; by dismissing his unpopular ministers; by summoning a free Parliament; and by throwing himself entirely on the good-will of his subjects. If such were his genuine intentions, it is to be regretted that an unexpected death should have prevented his thus clearing in some degree the stains on his memory. As it was, he left a fatal example of an apparently successful issue of arbitrary counsels to a successor every way disposed to follow it.

It has not been judged expedient to break the thread of the narrative by alluding to the great Fire of London, which happened at the beginning of this reign. By this conflagration the whole of the City was consumed, except a narrow circle round its boundaries. Although many accidental sources of this calamity were apparent and natural, in the closeness of the streets, the wooden structure of the houses, the accumulation of families in the same tenement, and in the common use of wood for fuel—yet they were all overlooked in the greedy anxiety to fix the charge of it on some unpopular party, which prompted the public to confide in accounts teeming with the greatest improbabilities. It was first attributed to a republican party;⁴ then to the Dutch,⁵ with whom we were then at war; without a shadow of proof in either case, except that some Republican con-

---

¹ Burnet's Hist. of His Own Time. Maitland, vol. i. p. 176.
² Addresses came from all parts, full of loyal and submissive expressions.— Hume's Hist. ch. lxix.
³ James's Memoirs. D'Avaux's Negotiations, Dec. 11, 1684.

⁴ Ken. Eng. Hist. Each. Hist. Eng. Maitland, vol. i. p. 433, quoting the Gazette of April 1666, containing an account of the trial of the republican conspirators, published with that view.
⁵ Ibid.

BOOK I.

A.D. 1660 to 1725

spirators had been hanged for treason the same year, a that a Dutch boy of ten years old had declared himself father, and his uncle, to have been the authors of the fir not a word of which the lord chief justice, upon further i vestigation, believed. But lastly it was fixed with zeal acrimony on the Papists, upon no other evidence than t single confession of Hubert, a poor mad Frenchman, wh related a story of himself and some Popish conspirators, ridiculous in itself, and so inconsistent in its several par that it must have required an uncommon degree of credulity which nothing but the temper of the times can explain, have gained any belief.¹ The miserable creature was, ho ever, executed upon this confession. It is remarkable, th in a case of such importance no corroboration was ever sub stantiated of this man's story: though most of the particular were abundantly capable of it, had they been true; and is the main instance he was positively contradicted, it being proved by one witness that Hubert was on board a ship a the time of his own alleged activity in raising the fire.² Burnet, indeed, relates a corroborative circumstance, as told to him,³ but that has been since satisfactorily disproved.⁴ Notwithstanding which, the record of this slander was sought to be perpetuated by an inscription on the monument erected in memory of this fire.⁵

In the rebuilding of the City, which was entirely com pleted in the space of seven years, many inconveniences arising from narrow streets and wooden houses were avoided: considering, however, the immense traffic carried on, which

---

¹ Ken. Eng. Hist. Each. Hist. Eng. Maitland, vol. i. p. 433, quoting the Gazette of April 1666, containing an account of the trial of the republican conspirators, published with that view; and Jour. Ho. Com. 1666.

² Maitland, vol. i. p. 437. Each. Hist. Eng.

³ Hist. of His Own Time.

⁴ Maitland, vol. i. p. 436. Mr. John Graunt, supposed to be a Papist, who, it is said, designedly got himself made manager of the New River waterworks, stopped the water from flowing into the pipes on the night of the fire, to prev its being used in quenching it.

⁵ This inscription had outlived it credit as early as the time of Pope's Epistles, who writes:—
'Where London's column pointing to the skies,
Like a tall bully, lifts its head and lies.'
It was erased when James came to the throne, but placed up again after the Revolution. It was finally erased again.

was then rapidly increasing, and the prevalence of all sorts of vehicles, the City was not so much improved as it might have been. Two plans of a very superior description were proposed, by the great architect Wren,¹ and by Evelyn ;² both of them of such beauty and convenience, that it has been a subject of great regret that the interested opposition of those citizens who owned the sites of the houses and buildings destroyed should have defeated their accomplishment.³ It was provided by statute,⁴ that a quay of forty feet breadth should be left vacant from the Tower to the Temple ; but this provision was very soon neglected, and much of this land was built on. This statute was repealed by that of 1 Geo. IV. ch. xl.⁵

CHAP. XII.
A.D. 1680 to 1725.

For settling all disputes which might arise on the subject of the new sites, a commission was issued to the twelve judges,⁶ who in seven years' completed their task with singular success, and gave general satisfaction. The Court of Common Council were empowered by Acts of Parliament to make the requisite regulations in laying out the streets and markets.⁷ The management of paving and cleansing the City was, by the same statutes, first entrusted to a commission of citizens denominated the Commissioners of Sewers.

The counsels which disgraced the reign of Charles ceased not at the accession of his brother, whose immediate conduct confirmed the justice of those suspicions, which attributed their former prevalence to his influence. Almost his first act was to wreak his vengeance on Alderman Cornish, who was with Bethel appointed sheriff in opposition to the intrigues of the Court, and who had shown himself a zealous supporter of the Exclusion Bill. The proceedings which marked the trial of Alderman Cornish were such as to shock every feeling of justice and humanity. He was sud-

¹ Parentalia.
² Evelyn's London Restored.
³ Parentalia.
⁴ 19 Charles II. cap. iii. s. 33. 22 Charles II. cap. xi.
⁵ The Thames Embankment Acts have at last carried out in the most magnificent style this original design, which forms one of the glories of the reign of Victoria.
⁶ 19 Charles II. cap. ii.
⁷ 25 Charles II. cap. ii. & x.
⁸ 19 Charles II. cap. ii. 22 & 23 Charles II. cap. xvi. 25 Charles II. cap. x.

denly thrown into prison, and after lying there a few days
was apprised on Saturday, at noon, that an indictment for
high treason was prepared against him, and that his trial
would take place on Monday. His children applied to the
king for time to prepare his defence, and for a copy of the
indictment (for the nature of the treason of which he was
accused was perfectly undisclosed to the prisoner). It was
urged, that his witnesses were at a distance, and that he was
therefore altogether incapacitated from proving his innocence.
The crafty tyrant referred his petition to his venal judges.
who rejected it. He was accordingly tried on the Monday.
and convicted on the sole evidence of two pardoned traitors;
one of whom saved himself from prosecution for a second
treason by the merit of this very accusation. He was
executed within a week after his first imprisonment; and a
few days after, his innocence and the perjury of the Crown
witnesses were made so abundantly clear, that James was
constrained by a sense of shame to return his forfeited
estates to his injured family.[1]

This execution following immediately upon the bloody
career of the infamous Jefferies in trying the rebels concerned
in Monmouth's invasion, was sufficient alone to alienate for
ever the minds of his subjects, never cordially well affected
to his person. But James lost no time in evincing that he
was determined to overthrow the liberties of the people, and
to govern altogether by force of prerogative. His bigotry
led him to apply these political maxims in a manner the most
offensive which could be adopted to the sentiments of the
nation; almost all his measures being pointedly directed to
encourage the exercise of the Popish religion, contrary to the
then existing laws, if not to restore it to its ancient pre-
eminence. He had, before his first summons of a Parliament,
levied by prerogative authority the duty of excise,[2] which
passed without complaint. He now levied forces at discretion,[3] and demanded, rather than requested, from Parliament supplies to maintain them.[4] He dispensed with the

[1] Ken. Eng. Hist. Each. Hist. Eng. And Burnet's Hist. of His Own Time.
[2] Hume's Hist. ch. lxx.
[3] Ibid.
[4] Ibid.

operation of the Test Act, and, in defiance of the laws as well as the sentiments of the people, promoted several Catholics to public appointments.¹ This last assumption of prerogative caused some discussion in the House, and a submissive address was presented against it.² The king gave an imperious and violent answer;³ but finding he had still some spirit to contend against in that assembly, he first prorogued, afterwards dissolved it, and never called another.

Freed from this ungrateful control, James gave full scope to his designs. He arrogated the right of dispensing with all statutes at discretion,⁴ and actually did dispense with many; among which were the penal statutes against Catholics.⁵ He issued compulsory directions with regard to preaching in churches.⁶ The Court of High Commission was re-established, in which he tried and suspended those who disobeyed his mandates.⁷ He published a declaration of indulgence, which he ordered to be read in all churches.⁸ Seven bishops presented a remonstrance against it; and their trial for this offence (called a libel), and acquittal, so famous in English history, served to detach the whole body of the people from the interests of James, and suggested the resolution of expelling him from the throne by inviting the Prince of Orange to come over and head the nation.

No sooner was the king apprised of his danger and of the landing of the Prince of Orange, than he sent for the mayor and aldermen, and informed them of his determination to restore the City charter and privileges.⁹ His great legal adviser, Jefferies, accordingly came to Guildhall and delivered the charter with two grants of restoration to the court of aldermen.¹⁰ The king had hardly left London with an intention of encountering his opponents, when the lords of Parliament assembled at Guildhall, and in the court of aldermen made a solemn declaration in favour of the Prince

---

¹ James's Speech to Parliament. Hume's Hist. ch. lxx.
² Ibid.
³ Ibid.
⁴ Hume's Hist. ch. lxx. Sir Edward Hale's case. Sir Robert Atkyns, p. 41.
⁵ Hume's Hist. ch. lxx.
⁶ Ibid.
⁷ Ibid.
⁸ State Trials. Case of Seven Bishops.
⁹ Each. Hist. Eng.
¹⁰ Repertorium, 1688. Town Clerk's Office. Maitland's Hist. vol. i. p. 485.

of Orange.¹ This declaration was followed by an address from the Court of Common Council, in which they implored the prince's protection, and promised him a welcome reception.² James, finding himself universally deserted, fled the kingdom, and the Prince of Orange shortly afterwards arrived in London; when the Corporation waited upon him with an ardent address of congratulation delivered by the Recorder.³

The Prince issued a proclamation, desiring a convention composed of the House of Peers, and of all the members of the House of Commons who had served during the reign of Charles II., together with the lord mayor, aldermen, and a committee of fifty of the Common Council, to meet as a Parliament for the purpose of settling the nation.⁴ From this convention proceeded the declaration, that James had abdicated the throne: and by it the crown was settled on the Prince and Princess of Orange, under the title of William III. and Mary; and, in default of their issue, on Anne Princess of Denmark and her issue. It is well known that during the reign of the latter princess, Queen Anne, the crown was settled on the House of Brunswick.

The nation, having completely succeeded in emancipating itself from tyranny, resolved to perpetuate, at this opportunity, that free form of government and those constitutional maxims which had so long and so passionately been sought, and which have since distinguished it above all the empires of the earth. This was accomplished by that memorable statute which passes under the name of the Bill of Rights. It was conceived that the security of the City of London, in all its rights and privileges, was an integral ingredient in the national welfare. With an intent, therefore, to secure for ever the prosperous existence of this great Corporation, it was declared by statute,⁵ that the judgment obtained upon the late *quo warranto*, and all the proceedings thereupon, were illegal and arbitrary; and it was enacted, not only that such judgment should be reversed, annulled, and made void, but that the mayor, commonalty and citizens should for ever

¹ Ken. Eng. Hist. Maitland's Hist. vol. i. p. 487.
² Ibid. vol. i. p. 489.
³ Ech. Hist. Eng. Maitland's Hist. vol. i. p. 188.
⁴ Ibid. vol. i. p. 490. Ken. Eng. Hist.
⁵ 2 Will. & M. sess. 1. c. 8.

thereafter remain a body corporate and politic, without any seizure or forejudger, or being thereof excluded or ousted, upon any pretence of forfeiture, or misdemeanour, whatsoever, theretofore or thereafter to be done, committed, or suffered.

CHAP. XII.
A.D. 1660 to 1725.

The citizens now, fully impressed with the importance and value of their political rights, began to be more than ever desirous of attaining civic distinctions; and their elective franchises, accordingly, occupied an increased proportion of their attention. The rights and forms of election by the common hall and by the wardmote, were not at this period so clearly ascertained as such constitutional privileges should have been. The ancient customs in this respect had, in early times, been often invaded; the law had been several times altered by the citizens themselves; and contradictory enactments had from time to time been made. The seizure of the charter, by which so many corporate dignitaries and officers had been displaced, and its sudden restoration, together with some provisionary clauses in the Act of William, tended, still further, to increase the confusion. Disputes arose almost immediately after the passing this Act; and severe contests for office, continually occurring, served to enhance them. The Court of Aldermen exercised the right of adjudicating, in the first instance, on the election of their fellows, subject to the jurisdiction of the Court of King's Bench; the Court of Common Council assumed that of deciding contests in regard to their own members, and even in regard to the returns of aldermen—a right which they certainly did not possess in either instance. Several acts of Common Council passed from time to time declaratory of the rights of voting, and regulating the modes of proceeding at elections. The disputes, however, were by no means allayed, and appeals were made to the courts of law both in the cases of aldermen and in those of common councilmen, one of which was carried up to the House of Lords.[1]

[1] For a detailed account of these disputes and contests, and the many opinions in regard to the elective qualifications, vide Maitland, vol. i. pp. 491, 495, 499, 521, 522, Journals. Stamps, pp. 144, 211. Misiner, p. 219. Lawes, pp. 3, 5, 22. Town Clerk's Office. Harg. MSS. Brit. Mus. No. 1305, pp. 209 et seq., 285; No. 139, pp. 485, 557, 599; No. 142, pp. 353, 354; No. 309, pp. 285, 290.

242   HISTORICAL ACCOUNT OF LONDON.

BOOK I.
A.D. 1680 to 1725.

To settle these controversies, to regulate the order of election at wardmotes, and finally to decide upon the qualifications of the voters and candidates, a committee of the Court of Common Council was formed, who were instructed to draw up an act for that purpose.¹ They were proceeding to effect this object, when, in the year 1725, an enquiry having been instituted in the House of Lords relative to the proceedings on disputed elections in the City of London, a bill was brought into the House of Commons calculated to supersede their labours, and to provide a legislative decision on these much contested points. The citizens were naturally jealous of this interference, and the Court of Common Council petitioned strenuously against it.² Notwithstanding which, the Bill (11 George I. ch. 18) passed, after considerable opposition and many protests;³ but certainly without a due consideration of the original and genuine constitution of the Corporation. One proviso of this Act, however, which confirmed a privilege claimed by the aldermen of negativing any question carried in the Common Council, the citizens still persistently resisted; and after much contest, both in the Common Council and the Common Hall, the clause was at length repealed by the Act of 19 George II. ch. 19.

Under the statute of 11 George I., ch. 18,—combined with the previous ordinances and ancient customs of the City unaffected by it—the elective franchises of the citizens continued to be exercised, without any modification, for the space of one hundred and seven years; that is, until the great parliamentary Reform Act of 1832. They continue, indeed, to be so exercised to the present day as regards the elections in Common Hall of the lord mayor, sheriffs, chamberlain, and some other minor officers, by electors possessing the mere title of liverymen of companies and being freemen of the Corporation, with the proviso of residence within twenty-five miles of the City. Under subsequent statutes and an act of Common Council—beginning with the great parliamentary

¹ Journal, Lewen. Town Clerk's Office, p. 23, which contains the appointment of the committee, whose proceedings are continued from time to time in the subsequent journals.
² Ibid. Maitland's Hist. vol. i. p. 554.
³ Ibid.

Reform Act of 2 William IV. ch. 45—modifications have been introduced with respect to the qualifications of the other two classes of civic electors, namely, those for electing members of Parliament in the Common Hall, and those for electing aldermen, common councilmen, and ward officers at wardmotes.

These are the last legislative interferences with the political privileges and the constitutional government of the City. It may be expedient, therefore, at the close of this historical account of the City, to bring under a summary review the rules which govern the qualifications for citizenship and for the exercise of the elective franchise, as modified from time to time by custom and by the civic ordinances (noticed in preceding pages according to periodical sequence) and by subsequent acts of the imperial legislature. In this review, the bearings of the statute of George I.— superseding the legislative powers of the Common Council, and serving to perpetuate the right of election to corporate magistracies and offices by the liverymen of companies in Common Hall—will have to be examined. It will, further, be requisite to advert to the more recent imperial acts which have conferred on others these elective franchises in Common Hall for choosing representatives of the City in Parliament, and for choosing aldermen and common councilmen at wardmotes, in respect of mere *occupation* in some capacity, which statutes have superimposed *residence* also within certain limits as an additional qualification for voting for the former.

We have seen that usage, from the earliest periods of the civic history, required only *residence* or *occupation* and *payment of scot and lot*, as a qualification for the enjoyment of *all* the rights and privileges of citizenship. Under this only qualification, and according to the same ancient usage, the citizens, as soon as they obtained the liberty of appointing their own magistrates, elected the aldermen and their councillors and officers of the various *soes*, or *leet gilds* (afterwards called *wards*), which had theretofore been held in propriety, or from grant of the crown, by the owners of these socs; and also elected the chief magistrates bearing rule over the whole

City generally. Subsequently, in the reign of Richard I., upon the incorporation of the City as one associated body, enrolment as a *freeman*, or member of the Corporation, was further prescribed. In the reign of Edward II. an ordinance was passed which required, in addition to this qualification of residence and enrolment, that each citizen should become a freeman, or member of one of the *misteries*, or (as these misteries were afterwards more commonly termed) *companies*.

The citizens thus qualified as residents paying scot and bearing lot, and freemen both of the Corporation and of the trading companies, continued, as theretofore, to meet at large both at the Common Hall, or Hustings court, as a deliberative body for legislative and administrative purposes, and also as electors for the purpose of choosing corporate magistrates and officers and representatives in Parliament. But the confusion arising from the great increase of numbers assembling on these occasions, led to two new ordinances by the general body of citizens, passed—one on the 20th and the other in the 49th year of the reign of Edward III.—for separating the meetings of the citizens into two classes, and regulating who only should attend as a deliberative body, or *Council*, of the City and who should nominate them, and also regulating who only should attend as voters at elections for the lord mayor, sheriffs, chamberlain, and other minor officers and representatives in Parliament at the *Common Hall*. These ordinances proved unsatisfactory as regards the constitution of the representative or deliberative body ; and, accordingly, in the 7th year of the reign of Richard II., another ordinance was enacted by the ' *immensa communitas*' of the citizens, by which the *court of Common Council* was instituted specifically under that designation as the representative body of the citizens ; and by which it was provided that the members of it should consist of citizens elected by the wards at their wardmotes—that is, by the same electors who in their wards, according to ancient usage, elected the aldermen and their councillors and officers : namely, by the freemen occupiers paying scot and bearing lot. On this basis the government of the City, in its legislative and administrative capacity, rests at the present day (except that, under the statute of 30 Vict. ch. 1, presently to be noticed, the voter need not be a freeman of the Corporation); and this representative body, together with the aldermen, and the lord mayor as president, alone represent the Corporation of the City of London.

The last of these ordinances of Edward III., however (that of the 49th year, which declared what citizens should be entitled to attend at the *corporate elections in Common Hall* of the lord mayor, the sheriffs, the officers of the Corporation, and the members to serve in Parliament), remained, in that particular, unrepealed and unaffected by that of 7th Richard II. By this ordinance of 49th Edward III., it has been shown that the *trading companies* were to nominate the persons who only (being freemen of the City) should vote for these administrative functionaries. An usage had, however, grown up for the lord mayor to summon, out of these so nominated by the companies, only those whom he pleased to come to those elections, and that usage of selection still continued to prevail for eighty years longer. The irregularities and abuses arising out of this usage probably suggested an ordinance, passed in the 15th year of Edward IV., by which the nomination of these voters at Common Hall was transferred altogether to the companies; and it was provided that the *liverymen* of the companies (that is, those freemen of the companies to whom a particular distinctive clothing was assigned by them) should alone (being freemen of the City) possess this elective franchise in the Common Hall.

Under these two purely civic ordinances of 7th Richard II. and 15th Edward IV.; the constituent and the elective franchises of the citizens at their wardmotes and at the Common Hall, were regulated up to the period of the statute of 11th George I. ch. 18 (1725); the effect of which we proceed to consider.

It is plain to account for the controversies which arose upon the restoration by James II., previous to his abdication, of the chartered rights which had been seized into the king's hands by the judgment in the *quo warranto* case at the close of the reign of Charles II., and upon the reversal of that judgment by the statute of 2nd William and Mary. Those controversies have already been adverted to. Had the Corporation, however, been left to introduce reforms by exercising their chartered and customary rights in self-government through their legislative powers in Common Council according to the ancient custom of the City, it may be assumed that the elective franchises would not have been allowed to remain on the then existing basis, at least as regards the elections in Common Hall, and on which they were then fixed by the Imperial Legislature. The basis settled by the old ordinances, as respects elections in the Common Hall, did not, at the time of their enactment, materially conflict with the constitutional and customary rights of the citizens, any more than the basis on which the election of members for the Common Council was settled did, or now does. But this was no longer the case.

Up to the time of Edward IV., and long after, the members of the City companies were all traders, and they could hardly carry on their trades in the City without being householders paying scot and bearing lot. Very few—hardly any, it may be said—of the freemen of the City or of the companies, whether traders or not, had their residences beyond the City walls. The City was almost isolated from the west, or court end, of the general metropolis, and from the villages round about. The City gates and bank of the river were closed at night, and rigorously guarded against both egress and entrance. The delegation, therefore, to the companies (over whom the Corporation used to exercise an almost unlimited authority of regulation and of conferring the power of granting liveries) of the choice of electors to attend at common hall, amounted to little more than entrusting them with the charge of selecting from the trading householders those to whom, as being the superior class of the freemen of such companies, those bodies had granted *liveries*—citizens who for these purposes were termed, and were therefore summoned, as the '*probi homines*' or ' of the 'discreeter sort.' The same class were probably designated in Athenian history under the term *kalokagathoi*, which may perhaps be best translated as *the aristocratical party*.[1]

[1] No two translators would be likely to agree in construing the term *kalokagathoi*, and least likely perhaps those who studied the subject most. The word ..... may be thought to apply mainly to men of high birth, and especially if combined with personal beauty, which always throughout Greece attracted

But long before the reign of George I., not only the municipal authorities of the City had ceased to interfere much in regulating the companies, but the companies also had ceased to interfere in regulating the mode of trading within the City. The companies admitted to the freedom of such associations, and eventually to the rank of a liveryman, whomever they thought fit, without regard to his being either a tradesman or a householder either within the City or elsewhere; and, upon such admission, the chamberlain, with the sanction of the Corporation, admitted any such freeman, whether householder or trader or not, to the civic freedom, as entitled to it by purchase, or *redemption*, as it was termed. The consequence was that a large bulk of the freemen and liverymen of the companies no longer represented the true citizens as householders within the City paying scot and bearing lot, or often even as traders. In the mere capacity of *liverymen of a company* and freemen of the City, without being householders or occupying as traders, they had no more real connection with the City of London than with that of Liverpool or any other city. It is obvious that those who were neither householders nor traders in London derived no better qualification as citizens of London through their admission into the City companies as liverymen (which is usually by purchase) than if they had purchased with the same money so much Government stock.

This result has become still more conspicuous in these later times. The companies having altogether ceased to concern themselves about any trading avocations of their members, it may be questioned whether a majority of their number are householders, or carry on trade, either in the City or elsewhere. The companies, as such, have ceased to be much concerned with the City's municipal affairs, further than by contributing their quota of men to parade in civic processions, and by attending at civic feasts. They are still

peculiar admiration. Alcibiades gained his influence as much by this latter quality, as by his waring spirit and mental abilities. The term ἀγαθοί had also a double meaning, as applied to men of influence through wealth and political ascendency, combined with high moral worth.—Vide two instructive notes in Grote's *History of Greece*, vol. ii. p. 68; and vol. iii. p. 62.

influential associated bodies, but only as possessors of much corporate property, and as governors of many noble scholastic and charitable institutions, and from the social position of many of their members.

It is not within the author's province, or that of this treatise, to discuss the question whether this mode of exercising the elective franchise in Common Hall—adverse, as it certainly is, to the chartered rights and ancient customs of the City—should be permanently acquiesced in, as most expedient on public grounds. The object of the various ordinances and regulations of the City was, that householders, or occupiers, only—and out of them those only who had the most interest in the good government of the City, and best qualified to select those dignitaries and functionaries who could best assist towards that end—should be the electors; at first through the summons of the lord mayor, and afterwards by delegating the choice of such electors to the companies. The Act of George I., passed after inhabitancy had, through the change of times and of the habits of the people, ceased to be a necessary qualification, and had become only partially so, still maintained the right of the companies to decide who should be the '*probi homines*' as electors, without regard to their being inhabitants, or traders, or not.

The subsequent policy of the Imperial Legislature—and, it may be added, of the Corporation itself—in regulating the elective franchises in and for the City, has certainly taken a different tendency, and one more in conformity with the original constitution of the City government, than that so heedlessly adopted by the statute of George I. None of the subsequent acts have, indeed, interfered with the important right of the liverymen of the City companies, being also freemen of London, of electing on such bare title the *corporate magistrates and officers* in Common Hall. But, as regards the election of *representatives in Parliament*, the first Reform Act of William IV. ch. 45, has provided against the manufacture of voters, by requiring that no freeman of London (or of any other city or borough) shall possess the elective franchise unless his title to the civic freedom has accrued through servitude, or through birth derived from an original freeman by servitude. Next, it has provided that every such elector for members of Parliament shall *reside* within seven miles (subsequently by Act of 30 and 31 Vict. ch. 102, extended to twenty-five miles) of the City boundaries. These, it must be acknowledged, were steps in the right direction, although the thread connecting such voter with the City and its interests by residence within twenty-five miles is but slender. In reality, such residence, though coupled with mere enrolment on the books of the Corporation and of a City company, but without any connection with the City by occupation as an inhabitant, or trader, or in any other capacity, can supply no more rational qualification for electing parliamentary representatives for the City, than for those of Windsor, or any of the great parliamentary metropolitan divisions around the City of London. But, further, this Act of William IV. introduced another large body of electors for members of Parliament—who, in truth and in fact, were, and still ought to be, the real citizens of London, before artificial qualifications, founded on other considerations than connection by interest, or trade, or habitancy, were introduced. Electors under this Act are the sole *occupiers* of separate tenements of *any quality* of 10*l.* annual value, or joint occupiers of the annual value of as many sums of 10*l.* as there are occupiers—such occupiers paying scot and bearing lot, and residing within seven miles —without any reference to their freedom of any company, or even of the Corporation itself. By the recent parliamentary Reform Act of 1867 (30 & 31 Vict. ch. 102), this elective franchise is still further extended, and comprises, in addition to the above classes of electors, every male person, being the sole occupier inhabiting any separate *dwelling-house*, rated to the poor, and having paid his rate, and also every male *lodger* in part of a dwelling-house whose lodging is of the annual value of 10*l.*, unfurnished.

Next, with regard to the election of aldermen and common councilmen as a representative body of the citizens in Common Council, and the ward officers in the wardmotes of the several wards. The Act of 12 & 13 Vict. ch. 94, conferred the right of voting upon every sole occupier (being a freeman of the City) of any house, warehouse, office, chamber, counting-house, or shop rated to the annual value of 10*l.*, and upon all joint *occupiers* of such premises so rated to as many amounts of that sum as there are occupiers; and the Act further established the same qualification for a common councilman. The Act of 30 Vict. ch. 1, has conferred the elective franchise upon all such occupiers, without any requisition for their being freemen of the City. The same Act confers this elective franchise upon all occupiers entitled to vote for representatives of the City in Parliament, and therefore comprises, additionally, inhabitants of *dwelling*-houses rated to the poor, to any amount, having paid such rate; and also *lodgers* of a part of a dwelling-house of 10*l.* annual value, unfurnished, as above stated. It must be observed, however, of these recent Acts exempting the occupiers in the City, in the capacity of inhabitants or traders, from the qualification of the civic freedom, as one important—and perhaps the most appropriate title of citizenship, that they have (like that of the exemption of the retail trader from any such requisition, which has been heretofore noticed) still further weakened the chain which binds the City community together as a body politic—while, at the same time, it may be considered as the natural consequence of the concession by the Common Council of this essential privilege of trading to a numerous class of occupiers declining to have any connection with the Corporation as a body politic, that the Imperial Legislature should adopt the precedent in further granting to the same persons the franchise of electing members of the municipal government of the City under which they live and trade, without requiring that these electors should themselves become citizens, and pay scot and bear lot in that capacity. The question still remains whether, by these measures of admitting to the most valuable of the civic chartered rights and privileges, those who are under no common bond in protecting the interests of the Corporation, the difficulties of the citizens in maintaining the influence and constitutional rights of the Corporation, or even its existence—are not greatly increased, should those rights, and even its existence, be again and again assailed. But on this subject of upholding the right, under due modification, of exclusive trade, and of the necessity of preserving it, too much discussion perhaps has already been expended in previous pages. The question, however, is a national one.

It may give the reader a clearer view of the various elective franchises exercised in or for the City of London, if summarised under distinct heads, omitting prescribed particulars as to registration, time of possessing the qualifications, &c., and other minor details.

Election of the Corporate Offices of Lord Mayor, Sheriffs, Chamberlain, or other Minor Offices in Common Hall.

The qualification of electors under this head, is that of being barely a liveryman of a livery company, and an enrolled freeman of London, without any requisition of residence, or of occupation for the purpose of trade or otherwise, either within the City or any limited distance.

Election of Representatives in Parliament for the City of London in Common Hall.

Under this head there are four distinct classes of qualifications for electors:—1. The first qualification is that of being a liveryman and freeman of London by birth or servitude, with the additional proviso of residing within twenty-five miles of the City. 2. The second qualification is that of *occupying* 'any 'building' of 10*l.* annual value, paying scot and bearing lot. 3. The third qualification is that of being a male person and sole occupier, inhabiting a *dwelling-house*, rated to the poor-rate to any amount, and having paid such rate; with an equivalent provision in favour of joint occupiers. 4. The fourth qualification is that of being a male *lodger* in part of a dwelling-house, whose lodging is of the value of 10*l.*, unfurnished. For neither of these last three classes of voters is civic freedom requisite.

Election of Aldermen, Common Councilmen, and Ward Officers in the Wardmotes.

Under this head there are three classes of qualified electors: —1. The first qualification is that of being a sole *occupier* of any house or other premises (though not a dwelling-house) rated to the annual value of 10*l.*, with an equivalent provision in favour of joint occupiers. 2. The second qualification is that of inhabiting a *dwelling-house* rated to the poor at any amount, the rate having been paid. 3. The third qualification is that of being a *lodger* of part of a dwelling-house of 10*l.* annual value, unfurnished.

None of these electors (except those voting for the corporate magistrates and minor officers and for representatives in Parliament in Common Hall upon the bare title of liverymen as well as freemen) are required to be freemen of the City.

Between the reign of George I. and the passing of these Acts regulating the elective franchises of the occupiers and freemen of the City, no memorable event or measure affecting the civic rights or constitution has occurred; except that the Court of Common Council has, by a resolution carried March 17, 1835, exempted applicants for the civic freedom from the necessity of becoming previously free of one of the City companies, and that an act of Common Council of 1856 has authorised retail trading by non-freemen—upon which act so much comment has been made. It is true that many events, exciting intense temporary interest of a political nature, have from time to time, within the last century and a half, agitated the City; but, as none of these (with the exception of the measures just detailed) have produced any lasting effect, if any, on its corporate rights and constitution, or on its system of municipal government, it is conceived the history of them may be properly left to those volumes which have treated of them at large.[1]

This historical account of London is therefore here brought to a conclusion. In dismissing a subject which long ago, and for many years, engaged the author's labours and reflections, he cannot but invite the reader, who may have followed his researches and acquired any resulting information, to share also with him the conviction that the Corporation of London has fairly done its duties by the state, and earned its position as a serviceable national institution. Whoever may be at

[1] They are to be found in Maitland and Northouck's Histories of London.

the pains of tracing its history though its thousand eventful years, whether as superficially treated of in these pages, or more scrutinously examined in many voluminous chronicles, or in the City archives, will be, it is believed, the more disposed to acknowledge its honourable career as the chief of our subordinate bodies politic. It has supplied to the service of our country a long list of able statesmen and distinguished politicians, intelligent financiers, eminent judges, and the greatest of merchants; to say nothing of those citizens who have been the founders of many of the noblest families of Great Britain and Ireland. Among them may be named Gresham, Bernard, Sir William Petty, Sir Dudley North, Lord Chancellor Sir Thomas More, Lord Chief Justice Coke, Lord Chancellor King, and other names, as well of ancient as of more modern distinction—names of men ever to be honoured, if they are never to be emulated. The citizens of London have always been on the side of our constitutional liberties, and have often been foremost in the triumphant vindication of them. If they have been strenuous in asserting their own municipal rights, they have always been liberal in admitting their fellow-subjects to share in them. They may have often erred in judgment—never in patriotism.

BOOK II.

OF THE CHARTERS OF LONDON

CHAPTER I.

CHARTER OF WILLIAM THE CONQUEROR — THE PORTREVE — THE BOROUGH-BARONS — CITIZENS TO BE LAW-WORTHY — RIGHT OF HEIR-SHIP.

IT will be the attempt of this book to detail and explain the charters of London[1] — a task which obviously comprises a considerable discussion of the legal and constitutional rights of the citizens. A full dissertation on this subject would involve nearly all that concerns the civic rights and privileges,

---

[1] It has not escaped attention, that an explanatory exposition of the charters of London may, on a superficial consideration, be liable to objections; as compromising by possibility the private rights and privileges of individuals as citizens. With respect to any other Corporation this objection might be entitled to some weight; but with regard to that of London, it is confidently submitted that the following observations are sufficient to refute any such idea. 1st. The rights and privileges of the citizens of London are hardly to be considered of a *private* nature: the public have a general and a national interest in them, and the preservation of them is, or ought to be, a national object. 2nd. The charters have been already published by various hands; and the substance of them has become easily accessible and notorious. 3rd. The erroneous translations of them, together with the barren and ignorant commentaries of all who have hitherto undertaken the task, have done the City all *the harm* which could possibly arise from the publication of them, while *the good* has been hitherto unattained. Under these circumstances it will be readily acknowledged that the chartered rights of the citizens cannot be enlarged by being fully and properly understood. The author is unable to furnish an accurate or corrected translation of the City charters, as none at present exists; but he may be justified in mentioning that, as such a labour would be both extensive and responsible, the Corporation would consult their real interest by undertaking, as a public object, to acquire one, for their own use. The following abridgments are taken from the common printed translations, but have almost all been corrected either from the originals themselves or copies recorded in the Town Clerk's Office, or in the British Museum.

and occupy several volumes. It would therefore exceed the general scope and object of this work, to examine all the minute details of the charters; although few points will be left altogether unnoticed. One object will be more peculiarly kept in view, which is, to explain those terms and passages which are likely to be least understood or most liable to misconstruction.

The use of sealed charters, and indeed the term itself as applied to seignorial grants, though not absolutely unknown to the Anglo-Saxons, may be said to have been introduced into England by the Normans.[1] The original nature of a charter amongst those nations who first adopted the term was, in all probability, nothing more than the grant of such lands or other property, as the grantor might claim a proprietary control over; or of privileges to individuals who were subject to the almost absolute dominion of their lord. But in the progress of regal assumptions, a royal charter came to have a much more extensive operation; and in England, from the time of the Conquest until the establishment of a Parliament on its present constitutional basis, in the reign of the first Edwards, a charter of the king was considered as declaratory at least, and often dictatory, of the law of the land. Thus we find Magna Charta at the head of our statute-book: and in the earlier charters, and particularly those of London, many clauses are introduced which the present system of our constitution will not allow to be conferred, except by legislative authority; and many privileges granted would not at present be considered valid, unless they had been confirmed in a Parliament, or that such confirmation could be implied from immemorial prescriptive usage. The learned antiquary may perhaps reconcile charter grants of this extensive kind, conferred in early times, with that legislative stamp of validity, which at present the law of the land requires, by a reference to the attestations usually affixed to them; and which appear to have been so affixed by those who might be considered as members of the great national council; without whose concurrence, it has been argued, the king could not make laws:

[1] Spelman's Gloss.: 'Charta.' Madox's Hist. Exch. pref. p. 15 et seq. Seld. Janus Angl. lib. 2, s. 2, quoting Ingulphus.

but the distinction in quality between charters strictly proprietary in their nature, and those which may be termed legislative, is certainly very evanescent.¹ The nature and operation of a royal charter, as at present settled after the full establishment of the principles of the constitution, may be succinctly described—as the grant of such powers and privileges, only, as specifically emanate from the royal prerogative.

The first of the City charters was granted by William the Conqueror very soon after his accession, and is an obvious illustration of the preceding remarks. It runs, according to the Saxon dialect, in these words :²—

Wiłłm kyng ȝret Wiłłm biſceop ⁊ ȝoſfreȝð porȝnreran, ⁊ ealle þa burhþapu binnan lonðone freneiſce ⁊ enȝliſce freonðlice. ⁊ ic kyðe eop þ ic pylle þ ȝet beon eallra þæra laȝa peorðe þe ȝyt pæran on eaðpertðeſ dæȝe kynȝeſ. ⁊ ic pylle þæt ælc cylð beo hiſ fæðer yrfnume æfter hiſ fæðer dæȝe. ⁊ ic nelle ȝeþolian þ æniȝ man eop æniȝ pranȝ beoðe. ȝoð eop ȝehealðe.

The literal translation is as follows:

'William the King greets William the Bishop and Godfrey 'the Portreve, and all the Burghers within London, French 'and English, friendly. And I make known to you that I 'will, that ye be law-worthy, as ye were in the days of King 'Edward. And I will, that each child be his father's heir 'after his father's days. And I will not suffer that any man 'command you any wrong. God keep you.'³

---

¹ Lands were often granted in the Saxon times *with the consent of the witenagemote*.—Turner's *Anglo-Sax.* vol. ii. p. 183.

² It is preserved with great care in an oaken box amongst the archives of the City. This charter is likewise copied into Liber Albus, and is recognised in the Inspeximus Charter of Charles II.

[The Saxon charter above has been collated with the original in the Town Clerk's Office.—Edit.]

² There is another charter of the Conqueror preserved in the same box with the above. It is without date; and it does not mention *to whom* the grant is made. It is directed to the Bishop and Sweyn the *Sheriff* of *East Saxony*, and merely states that he has granted to *his dear men or men* (friends) a certain piece of land at Gyddesdon, according to his agreement; and that he will not suffer the French or the English to hurt them in anything.

³ Editor of the first edition, Mr. Edward Tyrrell, Barrister-at-law and afterwards Remembrancer.

The import of this short charter has been already, to some extent, explained.[1] It grants nothing new, nor does it confer any specific or *distinguishing* privileges. It merely declares that the Conqueror will not reduce the citizens to a state of dependent and slavish vassalage. It is granted to French and English indiscriminately, in their simple quality of residents within the City. The terms of it are such as rather characterise *a law* made by an absolute prince, than a grant made with relation to private property; they refer to rights strictly constitutional. At the same time they imply at least *a claim* of proprietary title in the donor; and, simple as these conceded rights may appear to us at the present day, the remission of the exercise of the power to reduce the City to the condition of a demesne appanage of the crown, must, at the time of granting this charter, have been appreciated by the citizens as an invaluable boon. In making the citizens *freemen*, or rather *free tenants*, this charter forms the appropriate and stable basis of all the subsequently acquired franchises of the citizens, whether political, corporate, or private.

PORTREVE.—The Gerefa, or governor of the port, to whom, with the bishop, this charter is addressed, was an officer whose functions and authority it is now impossible accurately to define. As, on the one hand, it is probable he possessed some powers beyond that of the sheriff of a county; so, on the other, it is certain the sheriff exercised functions in his district which the portreve did not. As governor of the *port*, and of the metropolis in which the king himself resided, it may be reasonably conjectured he possessed a fiscal, as well as magisterial, authority of larger extent than the sheriffs: and perhaps as the head of all the London wards, or guilds, when assembled in the general *folkmote*, or grand hustings court, he might exercise some municipal prerogatives beyond those of the sheriff in his folkmote or *shiremote*. But neither the City folkmote or the hustings court were ever known to exercise the judicial functions of a *criminal* court, as conducted by the *shiremote*; nor had the portreve any jurisdiction in the separate City leets, as the sheriff had in each

[1] Vide *supra*, pp. 17, 41, 101.

hundred in turn: but leet courts were always held distinctly and independently by the reve or alderman of each ward or guild. Indeed, in the time of Athelstan there does not seem to have been any such municipal chief as the portreve, or any magistrate executing his functions; for in that prince's reign we find the great legislative assembly of the citizens composed of a congregation of reves, eorles, and ceorles, together with the bishop.

The term *gerefa* is of Gothic origin, and was applied throughout Europe to dignitaries of various distinctions; such as *landgrave, margrave, palsgrave, shirereve,* borough-reve; the prefix (Ge) being merely expletory in this and many other Gothic words. Literally, the word signifies a *companion,* or attendant, and, no doubt, was originally applied to those noble youths who, as we learn from Tacitus, allied themselves in peace and in war to the persons of the ancient Germanic princes, and formed the main support of their dignity and authority.[1]

When this officer was appointed to preside over a whole county in England, he seems originally to have borne the same rank and duties as an *earl* or *ealderman*. In the early Saxon times, and perhaps still earlier, all governors of counties and provinces were termed *ealdermen*, or *aldermen—quasi*, the *olderman*. And the title of *reve* seems to have been subsequently applied by the Saxons as another appellation for the same person.[2] Thus we find Alfred appointing an alderman over all London.[3] In the time of Knut, and not before, *eorles* came also to be called *ealdermen* or *aldermen*; though, according to Selden, the *eorle* or *earl* was, originally, a higher dignitary than the *ealderman*, and literally signified *etheling*, or noble.[4] It was at this period that the term *eorle* was first translated by *comes*, in Latin, and thus became synonymous with the term *reve*. Accordingly we learn from Selden, that, when the term *vice-comes* was first used as the Latin translation of 'sheriff,' in the Saxon times,

CHAP.
I.

[1] Tac. de Mor. Germ. caps. 13, 14. The historian terms them 'comites;' which is precisely the Latin name applied to the earls who succeeded the original reves in their authority in England.

[2] Seld. Tit. Hon. p. 630 *et seq.*
[3] Ibid. p. 630.
[4] Ibid. p. 639 *et seq.*

it did not signify *deputy-earl*, but rather one invested with the functions *of* an earl, in a district where there was no earl appointed by the crown—as one '*vicem comitis supplens*.'[1]

There is no reason to think that the reves, or the aldermen, were in the earlier Saxon times appointed by the king; although he had, unquestionably, the power to displace them for misconduct; but it rather seems that they were elected by the people of the county or the district over which they presided.[2] The appointment of earls over counties, when that term first came to be applied to governors of that description, although it probably sprung from the king's authority, yet seems neither to have been general throughout all counties, or to have superseded the ordinary functions of the more ancient reve. At the same time it is certain that, when by degrees a distinction arose between the titles of earls and reves of counties, the latter held a rank considerably inferior: for we find that the *were* (or price) of an earl's head was 8,000 thrymsas, and that of a high-reve or sheriff was but 4,000.[3]

These changes in the relative rank of earls and reves appear never to have been applied to London; for the reve of London, passing under the various denominations of portreve, provost, bailiff, and custos, not only always appears to have held the same authority and functions as the earl of a county;[4] but in the time of Richard II. we find the lord mayor taxed as an earl:[5] and it is difficult to discover any principle upon which this magistrate ought to have an inferior rank assigned to him at the present day.

BURGHERS.—Literally, *burhwaru*, i.e. boroughmen; from

---

[1] Seld. Tit. Hon. p. 615 *et seq.*

[2] Black. Comm. vol. iv. p. 413; and Robertson's Charles V. vol. i. note 10 *ad fin.*, and the authorities there quoted. Blackstone insists that all magistrates were in the Saxon times elected by the people themselves. However, towards the latter end of the Saxon dynasty, the earls of counties, and even an officer called the alderman of all England, seem to have taken their authority under the crown (vide Turner's Anglo-Sax. vol. i. pp. 93, 94). There are no traces of the sheriff or of any other inferior magistrates being so appointed. So Heywood (on Borough Elections, p. 10) calls the head officers of boroughs, who hold by prescriptive *election, the Common Law officers*, as their notorious denomination.

[3] Turner's Anglo-Sax. vol. ii. pp. 232, 234.

[4] Vide *infra*, Cb. III. p. 315 *et seq.*

[5] Northouck, p. 76. Maitland, vol. i. p. 128. Gough's Lond. Triumph, p. 347.

bur, *burg*, or *burgh* (Sax.), a city or fort, and *war* or *wara*, a man.¹ This Gothic term *war*, it is considered by Spelman, was the original etymon from which that of *baron* was derived,² the letters *b* and *w* being very capriciously and indiscriminately used by the Saxons.³ The word *baron*, in its original import, signified no more than a *man*;⁴ as we say to this day, in legal language, *baron* and *femme*, for man and wife; and as the Scotch still term a child a *bairn* or *barn*, which expression originally meant any *man child*, and probably sprang from the same derivation.⁵ So also 'varon' is the Spanish for a *man*. In denominating the citizens, therefore, *burhwara*, although the term is equivalent to that of *boroughbarons*, or, in more modern language, *barons of London*, yet nothing more is meant than the appellative men, or citizens, of London.

As applied to a particular class of subjects, the denomination of *barones* seems first to have been adopted in the earlier ages of the German Empire, as the Latin translation of the appellative *freyen* or *freon*, signifying *freeman* simply; and in progress of time, as the translation of that of *freyherren* and *herren*, signifying, more especially, *lord of a district*.⁶ The word was introduced into England, in the latter sense at least (if indeed it was ever previously known in any other), by William the Conqueror; and by him it was appropriated to designate, according to the doctrines of feudal law, those who held lands immediately from himself as his *tenants in*

---

¹ Lye's Gothic Dict.: 'Burgh.'
² Spelm. Gloss.: 'Baro;' and Hist. Eech. vol. i. pp. 197, 198. It is possible that the earliest etymon of the word is to be found amongst the Oriental languages, the acknowledged roots of the Gothic and Scandinavian tongues. Thus *wa*, *walla*, *waris*, and *war*, all signify 'man,' and sometimes 'lord,' in the Sanskrit and modern languages of Hindostan. From these words we draw the derivatives 'pooh-wa,' the *foreman*, 'guik-war,' *the man of the cow* (the most sacred of animals among the Hindoos), which are titles of royalty in the East. When Europeans first came to settle in India they were called *Toper-wallahs*, *men of the hat*. Latterly the civil servants selected upon literary competition, were called 'competition-wallahs.'
³ Lye's Gothic Dict. Let. 'B.'
⁴ Spelman's Gloss.: 'Baro.' Hist. Eech. pp. 1197, 1198. Seld. Tit. Hon. p. 461. So *weregild* means the *price* of a *man*; that is, the compensation to be made by way of fine for his murder.—Vide *infra*, ch. ii. Turner's *Anglo-Sax.* chapter on *weres*; Spelman on *Feuds*, p. 15.
⁵ Lye's Gothic Dict.: 'Barn.'
⁶ Spelman's Gloss.: 'Baron.' Seld. Tit. Hon. pp. 178, 479 *et seq.*

capite, possessing at the same time the rights of criminal jurisdiction within their respective domains.¹ These tenants were often distinguished by the name of *barones regis*.²

It was in this capacity of tenants of the king *in capite* in free burgage, that burgesses of that quality acquired the title of barons; and the term was not confined to the citizens of London in particular, but those of many other boroughs were greeted with the same style, in deference to the same right.³ These barons, or king's tenants, as the persons most concerned in the political interests of the state, were summoned by the king to form the great or parliamentary council of the nation;⁴ and this is sufficient to account for the constant attendance of some of the citizens of London in that assembly.

In consequence of the gradual transfer of estates and the parcelling out of the royal demesnes, the number of barons under the Norman dynasty greatly increased; and included amongst them many chief tenants whose property was, comparatively, very insignificant.⁵ The practice likewise of *sub-infeudation* produced many other free tenants of estates, who, possessing in virtue of their property the right of criminal and civil jurisdiction, or of holding courts leet and courts baron, which was deemed the distinguishing qualification of a baron,⁶ attained by custom the same denomination, though improperly; for, according to feudal tenures, this secondary class of free tenants was composed of such as were anciently termed *varasours*,⁷ and had not any claim to be summoned to the king's great council.⁸ This increase in the number of barons gave occasion to the division of them, by some ordinance now unknown, into the two classes of *greater* and *lesser barons*, about the latter end of the reign of King John,⁹

---

¹ Selden, Tit. Hon. pp. 478, 479 *et sq.*; and 719, 732. Madox's Hist. Exch. vol. i. p. 107. Heywood's Dissert. p. 218. The rights of *sac* and *soc* compared the *baronial* jurisdiction.—Vide *Domesday Book*; Ellis's *Introd.* p. 87; Lambard's *Archaion*, LL. Ed. 21.

² Domesday Book. Ellis's Introd. p. 14.

³ Selden's Tit. Hon. p. 717. Spelm. Gloss. Madox's Hist. Exch. vol. i. p. 198.

⁴ Selden's Tit. Hon. p. 729 *et sq.*

⁵ Ibid. pp. 738, 739 *et sq.*

⁶ Lambard's Archaion. LL. Edw. and vide note¹.

⁷ Selden's Tit. Hon. p. 743; and Spelm. Gloss.: 'Vavasours.'

⁸ Selden's Tit. Hon. p. 743.

⁹ Ibid. p. 730 *et sq.*

not with reference to the quantity of their estates or knights' fees (as was once commonly but erroneously supposed¹), but rather, as it is conjectured by Selden, in consequence of the opposition of the more ancient and powerful barons to the introduction of so numerous a body of newly-erected free tenants to an equal dignity with themselves. The former class included all those tenants *in capite* who were summoned to the great council, *singulatim*, by the king's own letter, and who were to pay a certain sum of one hundred marks for their whole barony, however numerous the knight's fees might be within it.² The latter comprised, not only all the other tenants *in capite* who were directed to be summoned to the council *by the sheriff*, and who paid, as anciently *vavasours* did, 5*l.* for every knight's fee, but also those who merely held manors, and were termed barons in virtue of their juridical franchises.³ In the higher class of this subdivision it would seem that the barons of boroughs, or at least those who represented them in state affairs, were anciently entitled to be ranked; unless we are to suppose that the common *borough-barons* formed a distinct class among themselves. The aldermen of London, however, would at all events, in respect of their jurisdiction in wardmotes, be entitled to at least an equal rank with the barons of manors;⁴ but it does not appear that they ever changed their earlier title, whether it was reve or alderman, for the specific appellation of baron. They were buried with the same ceremonials as were customary at the funeral of barons of the highest order;⁵ and in the time of Richard II. they were assessed at the same amount.⁶

After this distinction of the *greater* and *lesser* barons, the name, as applied to the latter, grew gradually into disuse; and it is to be gathered that, by the reign of Richard II., it had altogether ceased, and the title was used as the general designation of the *greater* barons only. The citizens of

¹ Selden's Tit. Hon. p. 766.
² Ibid. p. 739.
³ Spelm. Gloss. Selden's Tit. Hon. p. 739.
⁴ Lambard's Archaion. Ll. Edw. Thus we find they are termed *barons* of

ares in Henry I.'s charter.—Vide *supra*, p. 62; and *infra*, p. 330.
⁵ Strype's Stow, book v. p. 138.
⁶ Northouck, p. 76. Maitland, vol. i. p. 138.

London were commonly termed barons, in charters and other public documents, down to the reign of Edward I.; but there is no trace of such distinction in subsequent reigns. Richard II. first created barons by letters patent;[1] and the title then, and not before, became a name of dignity;[2] for previous to that period, a baron could not plead or be impleaded by that addition, but simply by that of a knight or esquire;[3] nor, indeed, were they permitted to wear coronets till the reign of Charles II.[4] After the creation of barons by letters patent had raised the term to a title of dignity, all lesser barons of course lost every real pretension to that name; and finally, by the abolition of chivalry tenures in the reign of Charles II., every vestige of claim to that denomination, in any sense, became obliterated. It has been thought pertinent to enter into some detail in explanation of this term, as its ancient application to citizens of London has sometimes occasioned a mistaken conception of their dignity.[5]

LAW-WORTHY.—That is, the citizens were to enjoy the privileges of *freemen* in courts of justice; for by the Saxon as well as the feudal system of law, none but *freemen* were entitled to the privileges of trial according to any recognised judicial form, either in civil or criminal suits.[6] It has been remarked that the administration of criminal law during the Saxon dynasty was very imperfect and irregular.[7] There were various modes of trial, however, recognised amongst them for the investigation of public and private wrongs, the adoption of which, in each particular instance, seems to have

[1] Selden's Tit. Hon. p. 774. Lord Raymond's Rep. vol. ii. p. 859.
[2] Selden's Tit. Hon. p. 774. Davis's Rep. p. 60. Bro. Ab. 'Amercement,' pl. 52. 8 Henry VI. 9, 22. Jenk. Rep. p. 209.
[3] Selden's Tit. Hon. p. 774.
[4] Ibid.
[5] Although in this explication of the quality and dignity of ancient barons some confidence of opinion may have been expressed, yet the best authorities have been studiously consulted on the subject. At the same time it is acknowledged that the subject is one of considerable difficulty; and has occasioned not only doubts, but palpable errors among several learned men. The suggestions of Sir William Temple with reference to the German and Italian *buiarmi* seem very fanciful, and unsupported by authority.—Vide his *Treatise on Heroic Virtue*.
[6] Selden's Janus Angl. 1023. Ibid. Notes upon Fortescue, 1895. Spel. Gloss. liber 'Lagamannus.' This was the law amongst all the ancient nations of Northern Europe.—Vide *Edin. Review.* vol. xxxiv. p. 196.
[7] Vide *supra*, p. 35 et seq.

depended, sometimes on the caprice of the defendant, and, at others, on the custom of the place. Among these, appeals to the interposition of the Deity, so general among all barbarous nations, by some ceremonial—such as the *ordeal*, the *corsned*, and many other devices—were by no means uncommon. But the most frequent modes of trial seem to have been that by jury, and that by wager of law, or purgation, i. e. by the oath of the party denying the act, together with that of some prefixed number of men, termed *compurgators*, who swore they believed in such oath of the defendant.[1] To these forms of trial, the Normans added that by wager of battle. A person entitled to appeal to any of these forms of trial was declared to be '*rectus in curia*,' and was called '*liber et legalis homo*;' terms which were deemed synonymous, and were used indiscriminately.[2] But villeins, and those who were not free tenants, or at all events those composing the numerous class of slaves or bondmen amongst the Saxons, had no right to appeal to any of these acknowledged modes of trial, and their oaths were in no respect to be taken.[3] So a person attainted of perjury was adjudged *to lose his law* or his *free law*; or, as Glanvill expresses it, *loses the law of the land*, and was to be no longer oath-worthy.[4]

HEIRSHIP.—Literally, *beo yrf-nume*, be the taker of his inheritance. The right of heirship amongst free tenants was a general common-law right during the Saxon times,[5] and is plainly derived from their ancestors the Germans.[6] The right, although not strictly consistent with pure feudal principles,

---

[1] Selden's Notes upon Fortescue, 1895. Spelm. Gloss.: 'Jurata,' 'Lada,' legem 'vadiarre.' It is by no means clear whether the trial by jury, and by wager of law, was not originally *the same*. But certainly trial by jury was during the Saxon period in a most crude and imperfect state.—Vide Turner's *Anglo-Sax*. vol. ii. ch. ix.; and *infra*, ch. ii.

[2] Spelm.: 'Legalis,' 'Liber.'

[3] Seld. Janes Aug. 1025. Wright's Tenures, p. 215 *et seq.*; and Robertson's Hist. of Charles V. ch. i. note 9. The district was not liable to the usual fine in case of his murder and the non-production of the murderer (Dial.' Scac. lib. i. s. 11). He could hardly be more completely out of the pale of the law's protection.

[4] Selden's Notes upon Fortescue, 1895, and authorities quoted. So according to the laws of the Scandinavian nations, which may be said to be almost identified with those of our Saxon ancestors, a person disgracing himself in a court of justice *lost his law, and could no longer be a witness*.—*Edin. Rev.* vol. xxxiv. p. 196.

[5] Ll. Edw. Lambard's Archaion.

[6] Tac. de Mor. German.

seems to have been engrafted into that system before the arrival of the Conqueror in England.¹ The law of descent, however, in regard to real property, was different amongst the Saxons and the Normans. The latter introduced into England the feudal rule of primogeniture; though it appears that, by the ancient common law, all the males shared alike.² Whether the latter was the rule or not amongst the citizens of London cannot now be distinctly ascertained; but it is reasonable to conclude that in the Saxon times the rule of descent in London was in conformity with that which governed other free tenures in England. This rule of descent by partition very soon gave way to that by primogeniture throughout all the free socage tenures, with very few exceptions,³ as well as throughout those which had been converted into military feuds; and the change might have taken place with greater facility amongst the citizens, as they retained the ancient Saxon privilege⁴ of devising their lands by will according to their own pleasure.⁵ With regard to their *personal* estate, the customary law of London would not allow of a bequest of more than one-third; one of the other two-thirds being the property of the widow, as her dower, and the other that of the children in equal shares by right of inheritance.⁶ *Villeins*, or strict tenants in demesne, having neither estates real nor personal, but belonging, themselves, their children, and their effects, to the lord of the soil, like the rest of the stock or cattle upon it, could have no heritable rights whatever.⁷

¹ Wright's Tenures, pp. 73, 74, in not.
² Ibid. p. 174 et seq.
³ Such as gavelkind, and borough English. Ibid. pp. 176, 177.
⁴ Ibid. p. 171 et seq. Seld. vol. vi. p. 1666.
⁵ Seld. vol. vi. pp. 1666, 1667, 1914.

⁶ Priv. Lond. Index 'Custom,' 'Hotchpot.' Calthrop's Rep. pp. 30, 155 et seq. This is now altered by 11 Geo. I. c. 18, and the citizens have the free disposal by will of *all* their effects.
⁷ Wright's Tenures, p. 215 et seq. Turner's Anglo-Sax. vol. ii. p. 90 et seq.

CHAPTER II.

CHARTER OF HENRY I.[1]—HOLDING MIDDLESEX TO FARM—CITIZENS TO APPOINT THEIR OWN JUSTICIAR—NOT TO PLEAD WITHOUT THE WALLS—EXEMPTIONS FROM SCOT, DANEGELD, AND MURDER, AND FROM WAGING BATTLE—COMPURGATION—LODGINGS FOR THE KING'S HOUSEHOLD—TOLL, PASSAGE, AND LESTAGE—CITY SOCS—AMERCIAMENTS AND WERES—MISKENNINGS AT THE HUSTINGS—ATTACHMENTS FOR ILLEGAL TOLL-TAKING, AND FOR DEBTS.

THE king directs this charter to the dignitaries composing the Great National Council *nominatim*, and to all his subjects generally. By it he grants that the citizens shall have Middlesex to farm of him and his heirs for 300*l.* yearly rent; and that they shall appoint their own sheriff for Middlesex:[2] that they shall appoint their own justiciar to keep the pleas of the crown, and none other shall be justice over them: that they shall not plead without the City walls in any plea: that they shall be exempt from scot, danegeld, and murder; and that they shall not wage battle: that they shall have the privilege of purging themselves by oath: that they shall not be compellable to receive the members of the king's household or others into lodgings within the walls, as guests: that they and their goods shall be free from all manner of customs, tolls, passage, and lestage, throughout all England and the seaports: that the church, the barons, and the citizens shall have their *socs* in peace; so that no guest tarrying in any *soc* shall pay custom to any other than him to whom the *soc* belongs: that they shall not be mulcted or amerced, in pleas appertaining to money, beyond their respective *weres*, i. e. one hundred shillings: that *miskennings* shall no longer be suffered in the

---

[1] This charter has no date. It is to be found at large in the Inspeximus Charter of Charles II., and in Liber Albus.

[2] That this grant included the farm and sheriffwick of *London*, also, or at least that such franchise was held as of right by the citizens, vide *supra*, p. 60, note 2.

hustings, or in the folkmote, or in other pleas within the City: that the hustings court shall sit every Monday: that the king will cause the citizens to have their lands and their debts, both within the City and without. He also grants, that they shall have right adjudged to them in respect of lands, which they shall have put in suit before the king, according to the law of the City: that, if toll or custom be taken from a citizen in any borough, that citizen shall take as much from such borough, as will compensate the damage received: that they shall have the right to take the goods of any debtor, who will not pay or appear to disprove the alleged debt, which may be in the city or in the county where such debtor lives as pledge: that they shall have their hustings as their ancestors had, to wit, in Chiltern, in Middlesex, and in Surrey.

MIDDLESEX TO FARM.—That is, the citizens are to exercise the shrieval custody and power over Middlesex, and to have the collection of the king's demesne revenues arising within it: but this right should not be confounded with the tenure by which the citizens held freely their private landed possessions in their borough. The royal revenues derived from counties, cities, and demesne districts were extremely numerous; and the farming of them was a very honourable and, it may be believed, a very lucrative grant.[1] It was sometimes bestowed on favoured individuals of the court at a stated sum; though ordinarily, in the counties and larger cities, it was the proper duty of the sheriff to collect and account for them in the king's court, according to his actual receipts.[2] In the Saxon times the royal revenues were chiefly derived from the demesne lands of the king; and the free tenants at large of counties and other districts were very little burthened by demands for fiscal contributions. But, upon the introduction of the feudal system by the Normans, the whole commonwealth had not only to submit to the various exactions incident to feudal tenure, but likewise to many of the modes of taxation which had previously been enforced only against demesne tenants of the king. These taxes, or issues, the king claimed

---

[1] Madox's Hist. Exch. passim; and Firma Burgi, ch. xi. ss. 3, 6. From many records it appears that large sums were paid by individuals for the office of Custos or Farmer.

[2] Firma Burgi, ch. xi. ss. 3, 6.

as by seignorial title to the whole kingdom; and they consisted of a great variety of tolls, customs, and duties at bridges, ferries, markets, towns, ports, &c., which constituted the issues let to farm; besides the numberless fines, amerciaments, and forfeitures which accrued to him from the penal provisions of the forest laws, and from the extension of the jurisdiction of the royal courts throughout his dominions.[1] The fiscal powers of the sheriff became, therefore, in the aggregate, of vast interest to the crown; and the king no longer intrusted the appointment of so responsible an officer to the people,[2] who would of course be anxious to evade as much as possible the burthen of his exactions. At the same time it is easy to conceive, that, besides the anxiety which all sheriffs appointed by the crown would naturally feel to acquit themselves to the satisfaction of their master, many would be actuated also by motives of self-interest and views of peculation in the collection of the royal revenue. If, however, these public and accountable officers of the crown were urged to extortion by such obvious inducements, the individual farmer of these regular demesne issues of a district at a stated sum could regard his appointment in no other light than as a license for rapacity; and, indeed, such grants were commonly made for the purpose of enriching those on whom they were bestowed.[3] We have seen that the exactions and abuses of all kinds practised by the sheriffs formed some of the heaviest charges in the people's complaints when Edward I. began his work of reformation; and were amongst those which were first to be redressed.[4]

In the meanwhile, all those cities and towns which possessed any influence with the crown, exerted it with great zeal to have their farmer, or bailiff, appointed from amongst themselves; and to account for the more regular demesne issues at a stipulated farm rent.[5] The applications for such valuable grants are very numerous in ancient records; and there are frequent instances of very large sums being paid for them.

[1] Firma Burgi, ch. xi. ss. 3, 6.
[2] Ibid. ss. 5, 6, et passim; Hist. Exch. vol. i. p. 17.
[3] Madox's Firma Burgi, ch. xi. ss. 3, 6.
[4] Vide supra, p. 78 et seq. Blacks. Comm. vol. I. p. 339: and stat. 28 Edward I. cap. 8.
[5] Madox's Hist. Exch. p. 397 et seq. et passim. Firma Burgi, ch. xi. et passim.

BOOK II.

This privilege of a bailiff holding the shrieval authority over cities and towns, and of accounting for the demesne revenues arising therein at a stipulated farm, became common to most of the great cities and towns before the time of Edward I.:[1] but, although it was not unusual for the king, as a special favour, to choose a sheriff over counties, and occasionally over towns, from amongst the inhabitants, there is scarcely an instance to be found of his delegating the former appointment to their own election.[2] Still less can any instance be adduced of the king granting to one district the privilege of appointing so high an officer over another; although a notorious one exists of the shrievalty in fee over a county having been granted to a particular individual.[3] The franchise bestowed on the citizens of London, of farming the sheriffwick of the county of Middlesex at a stipulated rent, must, therefore, be considered as a very distinguished mark of the royal favour. It is probable that the many interests which the citizens possessed throughout the county of Middlesex, in the detection and arrest of malefactors, in lands, in goods, in the fairs and markets, in their privilege of hunting, and in their continual trading occupations, as well as in the dispensation of justice in the county court, would render the shrieval authority over that district, not only of intrinsic value to them in itself, but almost a necessary adjunct to the secure enjoyment of their more peculiar civic franchises—circumstances quite sufficient to account for their zealous importunity in obtaining and preserving this singular privilege: and for those unceasing complaints whenever the king, for arbitrary purposes, seized the shrieval authority into his own hands by appointing a custos or farmer over the City.

APPOINT THEIR OWN JUSTICIAR TO KEEP THE PLEAS OF THE CROWN.—This was a privilege of the utmost importance. We have had occasion to remark that, in the Saxon times, all criminal suits proceeded in the courts leet, which were held by

---

[1] Madox's Firma Burgi, passim.
[2] Except the statute of 28 Edward I. cap. 8, enacting that the men of each county should elect their own sheriffs, being such as would not burthen them; but it was repealed by 9 Edward II. cap. 2, and, apparently, but little regarded in the interim.
[3] The shrievalty of the county of Westmoreland was hereditary in Lord Thanet.

the sheriff or other officer in his hundred, or by the lord over his demesne district.¹ Very few of the mulcts and forfeitures arising from such suits then belonged to the king, but generally to the owner of the jurisdiction, or *soc*, as it was called, or else to the people of the district for specific purposes of their own;² the king interfered very little in any other legal proceedings than those arising between such nobles as owed deference to no other authority.³ Amongst the continental nations also the great proprietors of estates and the barons under the feudal system possessed, and long preserved, both civil and criminal jurisdiction over their vassal tenants.⁴

It had been the policy of the foreign feudal powers, before the arrival of the Conqueror in England, to curtail those juridical privileges of the barons, and to engross into their own hands as much as possible such important prerogatives;⁵ and an instance occurred of the appointment of a royal officer in this country holding the title of alderman of all England during the Anglo-Saxon period.⁶ But, whatever may have been the extent and quality of that officer's functions, and whatever indications might have been manifested in the latter years of the Saxon dynasty of the crown's assuming a general jurisdiction, it appears certain that the Conqueror was the first monarch who introduced into this kingdom the officer so long afterwards known by the name of the *capital justiciar* of all England.⁷ In the establishment of this judicial authority, it may be easily believed that the king was not so much actuated by a desire to curb the independence of his barons, as by an anxiety to establish the feudal system of policy, to appropriate

---

¹ Vide *supra*, p. 34 *et seq.*
² Robertson's Hist. of Charles V. vol. i. Illustrations, note 23. That many of the mulcts and forfeitures were to be paid to the king, may be gathered from several of the Saxon laws (*LL. Sax.* pp. 2, 12). At the same time, in many of the gilds, the mulcts were by their own regulations paid to others, and often to the lord of the district (Turner's *Anglo-Sax.* vol. ii. pp. 104, 105, 214, 240). The lords, too, had the forfeitures incurred within their own respective *socs*.—Ibid. and p. 181 ; Madox's *Firma Burgi*, *passim*.

³ Turner's Anglo-Sax. vol. ii. p. 212. Hist. Exch. vol. i. pp. 92, 93.
⁴ Robertson's Hist. of Charles V. vol. i. Illustrations, note 23.
⁵ Ibid.
⁶ Doddridge on Parliaments, quoting Ingulphus. Spelm. Gloss. 'Aldermannus.'
⁷ Spelm. Gloss: 'Justiciarius.' Madox's Hist. Exch. vol. i. pp. 36, 37, 92. The office was an ancient one in Normandy. Ibid.

OF THE CHARTERS OF LONDON.

to his own revenue the numerous fruits arising out of the new tenures; and to secure to himself the valuable proceeds which were made to spring from the administration of the law

Originally, the term *justiciar* was often applied by the Normans indiscriminately to any inferior magistrate who held a court.[1] After the establishment of the *aula regis*, the functions of all inferior courts began rapidly to decline, and were superseded by those of the royal court: the consequence of which was, that the *chief* justiciar, who officiated in that court with regal authority, became eventually the only magistrate recognised by that name. The *aula regis* was, in fact, the king's supreme council of the realm, known previously under the name of the witenagemote.[2] But in the Saxon times this court was only appealed to as the last resort by the common people, and decided, as an original court, the claims of the nobles only.[3] The Conqueror laboured with successful anxiety to render it the common source of law and justice throughout the whole kingdom. The chief justiciar sat in it as his representative and viceroy.[4] It followed the person of the king wherever he might go; and instantly suspended the jurisdictions of all the inferior courts in the district in which he might happen to be.[5] As early as the reign of Stephen, if not before, it was the custom for the chief justiciar to send judges into the different counties to try causes arising within them, to receive appeals from the judgments of other courts, to punish crimes, and to exact the forfeitures of every kind which had been incurred.[6] And, finally, Henry II. appointed certain persons to be regular justices itinerant.[7] So that the *aula regis* became by degrees a court, not only of general authority, but, in actual practice, the first and last resort in almost all cases both criminal and civil.

The evils arising to the body of the people from these innovations were neither few nor inconsiderable. The burdens

---

[1] Spelm. Gloss.: 'Justiciarius.'
[2] Turner's Hist. Anglo-Sax. vol. ii. pp. 229, 261. Hist. Exch. vol. i. p. 12.
[3] Vide supra, p. 41.
[4] Hist. Exch. vol. i. pp. 31, 32, 36.
[5] This was the case in London until 1755, when the statute 25 George III. cap. 18, was passed to remedy the inconvenience.—Edit.*
[6] Ibid. pp. 15, 35, 36, 93, 103, 116.
[7] Ibid.

* Mr. Tyrrell, who edited the first edition.

arising out of the feudal tenures, if not the tenures themselves, were as novel as they were slavish and oppressive. The laws, under which justice ought to have been administered, were neither understood in principle nor practice. Ancient customs, both general and local, and the ancient forms of judicial trial, were for the most part either disregarded or unintelligible to judges of foreign extraction and habits. Delay and uncertainty began to pervade the whole system of the judicature. The appeal to legal justice was made the subject of a pecuniary fine to the king.[1] Grievous as these oppressions were, they were easier to be endured than the practices of exaction introduced into the dispensation of the criminal law. The judges being entirely dependent, and mere creatures of the crown, strove, with great zeal, to collect for the royal treasury a rich harvest of mulcts and forfeitures. This it was, in the language of the day, *to keep the pleas of the crown*, or rather to exact the fines and forfeitures arising out of pleas of the crown;[2] and this kind of jurisdiction was easily converted, as we have before had occasion to remark,[3] to the most oppressive purposes.

It became, therefore, a great immunity to be exempted from these new, uncertain, and arbitrary jurisdictions. Thus, it was a privilege confirmed to the nobility by Magna Charta, that they should be amerced only by their peers in the great council or parliament.[4] The barons and officers of the king's exchequer were privileged likewise from the judicial interference of any other court;[5] and some few counties and districts, under the denomination of *palatine*, preserve to this day all the royal rights of judicature.

It was also a privilege granted to the citizens of some favoured cities to elect their own judges, and to be exempted from any other judicial authority. The value of such an immunity was very soon appreciated by them. It preserved the benefits of their ancient laws and customs, and secured, in some degree, talent and integrity upon the judgment-seat: it relieved them from that system of peculation and bribery

[1] Madox's Hist. Exch. vol. i. p. 155 et passim.
[2] Dial. Scac. lib. 2, cap. 12. Hist. Exch. vol. i. p. 210.
[3] Vide p. 77 et seq.
[4] Hist. Exch. vol. i. p. 529.
[5] Ibid. vol. ii. pp. 13, 18, 19.

which, under the name of fines, poisoned the very sources of justice; but, above all, it prevented the numerous extortions for which corrupt motives could always invent a pretext as long as judicial penalties formed the most productive branch of the royal revenue.

In the City of London, in which so large a portion of the personal wealth of the whole nation was concentrated, independent courts of judicature were most desirable; for as, on the one hand, the subdivision of property, both real and personal, and the general distribution of it through various ranks, would render their legal rights and liabilities more various and difficult of adjudication; so, on the other, greater facilities and temptations would be held out to the cravings of arbitrary rapacity. The numerous seizures of the civic franchises, in early times, were resorted to as the readiest means to effect that which was on such occasions invariably accomplished—namely, the supply of the royal coffers by the exactions of the custos, or other magistrate, into whose hands the government of the City was entrusted. It is probable that, for many years after the Norman Conquest, all criminal trials were held in the wardmote or alderman's court leet, in each respective *soc* or *gild* within the City of London, as they had been during the Anglo-Saxon period in the other courts leet.[1] The practice of superseding these petty local courts by the general jurisdiction of the chief justiciar, throughout whatever district he might happen to sit in, or by that of the king's commissioned justices, naturally led to the establishment of different and superior courts of judicature, as well in the City as elsewhere: and we may accordingly trace to the period of this charter the gradual conversion of the wardmote court leet into a mere court of *inquest*, as far as respects the purposes of *criminal* proceedings. At the same time we have no certain grounds for asserting that the *soc* or *leet* courts of the aldermen were absolutely and at once superseded in this branch of their functions by the grant of the justiciarship; but it is probable that the justiciar at first exercised his authority only by superintending and control-

---

[1] Vide *supra*, pp. 34 *et seq*. and *post*, 289. in this charter as to Socs, or Sokes, and the quality of those jurisdictions.

ling the proceedings of the leets. By Magna Charta, the leet courts were deprived of all jurisdiction over *pleas of the crown*; and, as long as their jurisdiction continued in practice afterwards, it was confined to those petty offences which were the subjects of amercement upon the leet jury presentment, without any trial.

The person alluded to as the justiciar in this charter, there is every reason to believe, was the *portreve*, or whoever at this period held the highest authority within the City: for there never was any officer known by the specific denomination of justiciar for London; and it has already been mentioned that the Normans originally applied that term to magistrates of every quality.

The charter proceeds, in this grant of the justiciarship, to add, that '*none other shall be justiciar over the citizens.*' These exclusive words seem to imply, that the king has no authority to issue commissions to other justices to hold pleas of the crown within the City; and yet we find, in practice, that such authority is constantly and regularly exercised by the crown with respect to all offences committed within the liberties. The state of the law, and of the constitutional rights of the people, have been long so much changed, that it has become a principle in the supreme courts of judicature to discourage as much as possible all exclusive jurisdictions, as endangering impartiality and correctness in the administration of justice.[1] In conformity to this maxim, as well as to the rule of law which inculcates the utmost caution in depriving the king of any of his constitutional prerogatives,[2] it would no doubt be now held that the grant in question must be construed most strictly; and that the office of justiciar, and the pleas of the crown submitted to his jurisdiction, must refer to that particular magisterial authority and those identical pleas of the crown subsisting at the time of the grant, and would not include various other powers, and various other offences, since created by royal and legislative ordinances[3]—as the statute of 5 Elizabeth, cap. 4, which disables

---

[1] Wilkes's Reports, p. 223. Wilson's Rep. vol. ii. p. 110. Bur. Rep. vol. v. p. 5820.

[2] Black. Com. vol. ii. p. 346.

[3] 14 Henry IV. cap. 20.

persons from exercising trades without first serving an apprenticeship, has been scrupulously restricted to such trades as at that time were pursued.¹ There is also reason to believe, that the privilege granted would be deemed merely *personal* to the citizens; and therefore an *exclusive* cognizance over pleas of the crown, like that which is granted specifically to certain authorities in the universities, could not be claimed by *the Corporation*, which did not then in fact exist, either as one united mercantile guild, or as a representative community. The consequence would be, that, to take advantage of this privilege, the citizen must personally plead it, and show himself to be a citizen, *re, facto, et nomine*—that is, a householder paying scot and lot, commonly resident, and admitted to his corporate freedom.² And, after all, such a plea could avail him nothing, as being merely productive of a short delay and a more unsatisfactory trial.

In truth, however, as the courts of criminal law are at present constituted within the City, there seems every reason to conclude that such a plea would be invalid; and that such courts have an indisputable authority, under the commissions creating them, to try offences arising within the City, of every description. According to the better opinions, although by a grant to citizens to hold pleas of the crown, and to appoint their own judges for such purpose, all other courts are excluded from any concurrent jurisdiction;³ yet the court is still the king's court, and the judges, when so appointed, become the king's judges;⁴ and it by no means follows that the king may not have occasion to issue his commission to such judges confirmatory of their functions and authority. So, in the two universities, although the members are not only privileged, *individually*, from the jurisdiction of the ordinary criminal courts, but an exclusive *cognizance* is granted by statute to particular individuals on behalf of the whole society; yet, when offences are to be tried under such special jurisdiction, the

---

¹ Saund. Rep. vol. i. p. 312, n. I.
² Case of prisage of Wine-Calth. cases, p. 31; and the numerous cases quoted in Mayor of London v. Liverpool; in note to Mayor of Lowdon v. Lynn

Regis, Ros. & Pul. Rep. vol. i. p. 498.
³ Hardres. Rep. p. 509. Palmer's Rep. p. 456.
⁴ 20 Henry VII. 6. a.

king not only exercises a right of approval of the appointed judge, but issues his commission to invest him with the delegated functions.¹ So likewise, in case any indictment is removed out of the City court into the King's Bench by writ of *certiorari*,² a commission necessarily issues, if it is to be tried by the latter court, appointing the judges who are to try it. But when the king issues his commission for the trial of offences, although he cannot change *the court* as established by law or statute, unless for some special reason, such as partiality in the mayor or constituted judges, yet he may *add* and *associate* whomever he thinks fit in the same commission to be judges;³ and he may further give authority in the same or another commission to any number of them to proceed without their fellows.⁴ Accordingly, all that appears necessary for the due establishment of the City court, according to the charters, is that the justiciar should at least be of the *quorum*;⁵ and so it is with regard to the Admiralty jurisdiction, which properly is under the administration of the Lord High Admiral, or his deputed judge; yet the court is always composed, in fact, of various dignitaries, at the head of whom is placed the Judge of the Admiralty.⁶ And in like manner the Mayor of London is still always placed at the head of the commissions which create the criminal jurisdictions in London.⁷

SHALL NOT PLEAD WITHOUT THE WALLS IN ANY PLEA.—This is the same immunity granted to the citizens, with reference to civil suits, which had been secured to them by the preceding clause in respect of criminal prosecutions; and although, under the present pure administration of the law, it happily no longer confers any advantage, except in regard to the prompt and cheap adjudication of *small causes*, yet, in ancient times, it was a privilege highly and justly appreciated. The circumstance of the *aula regis* being ambulatory, and following the king's person, until, by Magna Charta, it became stationary, was, in itself, a perpetual source of annoyance,

---

¹ Black. Com. vol. iv. p. 277.
² Chitty on Criminal Pleadings, vol. i. p. 374, and authorities quoted.
³ Fitz. Nat. Brev. 'Writ of Oyer and Terminer.' Hale's Pl. Cr. pp. 2, 23 et seq.
⁴ Ibid. Ibid.
⁵ Ibid. Ibid. p. 32.
⁶ Black. Com. vol. iv. p. 269.
⁷ Ibid.

particularly to the inhabitants of cities; who were, consequently, obliged to leave their avocations for an indefinite period, and often at grievous expense, delay, danger, and difficulties, to assert their rights in the midst of strangers. Nor were these the only grievances to be endured. They had to plead their causes before judges who neither knew nor regarded their laws or peculiar customs, nor even their language. They were compelled to pay fines, exacted with shameful rapacity, even for permission to litigate:[1] and, in case of failure, were amerced, at almost an arbitrary discretion, as for a false complaint.[2]

The evils thus enumerated were probably never sustained by the citizens of London. But that they oppressed the inhabitants of most other towns may be collected from the frequent applications for this internal and exclusive jurisdiction, and the sums of money paid for the grant of it.[3] If the citizens of London escaped the exactions of the king's supreme court, they owed it altogether to their early charters, which secured to them their ancient independence. So sensible were they of the advantages derived from this immunity, that they took great care to have it repeated in many subsequent charters, for which they often paid considerable sums of money. In their jealousy of judicial encroachments under royal authority, they were often involved in obstinate disputes with the Crown; and, although they as often suffered in consequence, they still maintained their claims with the same resolution. They interdicted all pleas between citizen and citizen out of the jurisdiction, under pain of fine and disfranchisement;[4] they inserted a clause in the freeman's oath, that he would not so plead;[5] and even to this day, part of the oath of their common pleaders, or City counsel, is 'to plead 'no *foreign* plea, whereby the City should be ousted of its 'jurisdiction."[6]

---

[1] Mad. Hist. Exch. *passim*; and vide vol. i. C. II. pp. 396, 429.
[2] Ibid. p. 529.
[3] Ibid. p. 397, *passim*.
[4] Order of Com. Coun. 17 Henry VIII. cap. 21. Hodges's Bye Laws. Calthorp's Rep. p. 170. Calthorp's Usages,

p. 4 *et seq*.
[5] This clause in the freeman's oath was annulled by stat. 11 Geo. I. cap. 18.
[6] A *foreign plea* is one which alleges, by way of defence, some fact of a *local* nature occurring out of the jurisdiction; that is, a fact which cannot be tried but

But in the progress of legal reformation, both the grounds and reasons for the City's peculiar exclusive cognisance of suits between citizens have long ceased to operate. Judicial corruption and extortion are unknown—the civil courts have long been stationary—the language of the law and the modes of trial have become uniform—all issues of fact have been rendered determinable twice a year at the suitor's own doors;[1] and the customary rights of the citizens are better ascertained in the supreme courts than even amongst themselves. In former times, the pleas of a *personal* kind between citizens for debts or damages were neither many nor important. Most of the suits were of the quality called *real actions*, affecting the tenures, property, and possession of lands and houses, and which were *local* in regard to the jurisdiction of trial. But with the decline of the feudal system, the cumbrous forms of litigating in real actions were gradually disused, and new and more commodious processes were devised by legal ingenuity for the adjudication of real property questions, until at last the ancient methods of suing by real action have altogether ceased. It would now be as useless as laborious to explain in detail the variety of *real suits* formerly used in the hustings court, as distinguishing the judicial rights of the citizens from those of common feudal suitors. Those who may take the pains to inquire concerning them in the meagre dissertations, ancient and

in another county in which it is alleged to have taken place: as, for instance, a plea of judgment recovered in the Court of King's Bench, by way of a justification of an assault charged, and a plea of acting in the alleged assault under authority of process issuing upon that judgment and extending through a particular county, with a denial of any assault in *the county alleged by plaintiff*. Such foreign pleas, however, were common in *real actions*; as where the tenant, being sued for land in an inferior court, vouched a foreigner to the jurisdiction to warrant his title; which, in case he was the vendor to the tenant, he was bound to do, at the peril of assigning land of equal value instead. By these foreign pleas the court was ousted of its jurisdiction, as the limited court could not try facts of a *local* nature like those arising out of its bounds; consequently, they were often resorted to for mere purposes of delay and vexation. To restrain such practices the defendant was obliged to swear to the truth of his plea; but it does not appear how early the date of that requisition is. Another method, adopted for the same purpose within the City, seems to have been that mentioned in the text; but it must be understood to refer to such foreign pleas as were pleaded *falsely*, and merely for delay.

[1] Four times a year in the City of London, viz., in and after every term.

modern, which have been produced about the obsolete writs of *right patent*, *ex gravi querela*, of *dower*, of *gavelet*, of *waste*, &c., will be convinced that the writers did not themselves understand their subject, and that they have succeeded only in making themselves incomprehensible.

With regard to *personal* actions, it was held by very early authorities, that the exclusive jurisdiction of the City does not extend to them when they are in their nature *transitory*;[1] that is, where the cause of action may be laid as arising in any place, at the will of the plaintiff, as in actions of debts and contracts: the maxim of law being that debt and contract are of no place, but that the liability follows the person, and raises an implied stipulation of payment, wherever the debtor may be.[2] The consequence is that the *Corporation* cannot, in such cases, itself claim to have cognisance of the suit; although, if the plaintiff alleges in the body of his declaration, or plaint, that the cause of action did actually arise in London, the *defendant* may, in his personal right, plead to the jurisdiction.[3] If, however, the defendant should so plead, he must aver that he dwells within the City, or has some local property therein, whereby he may be distrained to appear, and to answer for the judgment recovered.[4] In analogy with other similar cases in principle, it would probably be held, that he must aver himself to be such a citizen as is contemplated in the charters, viz., one by residence. It has been likewise ruled, that the plea would not be allowed, if it should by any means appear that a failure of justice would follow;[5] as in cases of personal interest or prejudice. And, further, that the privilege is to be considered as altogether *personal* to the *defendant*; and that, consequently, he may waive it, if he thinks fit, and remove his suit into the superior court.[6] An Act of Parliament has also passed whereby the clause as to pleading a citizen

---

[1] Tidd's Practice and Authorities, vol. i. p. 634.
[2] Chitty on Pleading, p. 373; and authorities.
[3] Ibid. p. 431; and authorities.
[4] Ibid. pp. 432, 433. Tidd, vol. i. p. 633.
[5] Ibid. Ibid.
[6] Salk. Rep. p. 148. Lord Raymond, Rep. vol. ii. p. 836.

EXEMPTION FROM *SCOT.*

out of the jurisdiction has been expunged from the freeman's oath;[1] and it may be reasonably inferred, that so to plead can no longer amount to a civic offence.

Any claims by which it is sought to deprive the superior courts of their jurisdiction, are extremely disfavoured;[2] and the party attempting to avail himself of his privilege will be found to establish it *strictissimo jure*. The courts have with a laudable object somewhat strained the law, perhaps, to establish this doctrine. But as they scrupulously preserve to the citizens an exclusive jurisdiction in all *customary* legal proceedings and in all *customary* rights[3] which are peculiar to them, it would be mere cavilling to dispute upon what is clearly for their own as well as for the general advantage. At the same time it may be allowed, with reference to the great delays and expenses attending suits in the superior courts, that a most valuable benefit would be secured to the poorer citizens, by strictly confining all causes of a trivial amount to the City courts; supplied as they are, and ever must be, by learned and experienced judges, and by intelligent juries, as well as by an efficient bar. They would thereby obtain cheap, prompt, and satisfactory justice; the beneficial effects of which would be experienced in establishing credit, in encouraging industry, in extending the tradesman's dealings and prosperity, and in repressing dishonesty and dissipation.[4]

SHALL BE EXEMPT FROM *SCOT.*—Great uncertainty has prevailed amongst the learned with respect to the precise import of this word.[5] In its etymology it seems to signify a *rateable contribution*: and it is plain that the term was applied as well to taxes of a general and national quality, as to those of a peculiar and limited nature.[6] In the present charter it no doubt refers to taxes of the former description, and in all probability to those levied by royal, or, in other

---

[1] 11 George I. cap. 18.
[2] Willes's Rep. p. 233. Wilson's Rep. vol. ii. p. 440. Burr. Rep. vol. v. p. 2820. Tidd. vol. i. pp. 635, 638, 639.
[3] Tidd, pp. 469, 470, and authorities.
[4] This reform has been established since the text was written.
[5] Douglas on Elections, vol. i. p. 140. Male on Elections, pp. 16, 204.
[6] Spelman's Gloss. Douglas on Elections, vol. iii. p. 126.

words, arbitrary authority, for public purposes.¹ The ancient Chronicles testify sufficiently the unjust and burthensome effect of these levies.²

But the contributions under the denomination of *scot*, to which townsmen were more especially liable, were those which were levied by their internal authorities, for the common purposes of the borough; and the citizens were so far from being able to withdraw themselves from such liability, that the paying scot became, and continues to this day (except where usurpations have intervened), the distinguishing criterion of a full and complete citizen.³ In London it was a very early requisition, 'that all who pretended to 'enjoy the privileges of free citizens should be in scot and lot, 'and participant in all burthens according to their means."⁴ So their oath prescribes that ' they shall be contributory to all ' manner of *charges within the City*, as summons, watches, con-'tributions, taxes, talliages, *lot* and *scot*, and all other charges.' And the records are very numerous which prove that the paying scot was the distinguishing characteristic of a genuine and complete citizen.⁵

What these ancient *scot* rates in cities specifically were it would now be in vain to inquire: for when, in the reign of James I. and in subsequent reigns, the nature of these rates first began to be a question, in order to establish the common law rights of voting, Parliament could not discover their precise meaning.⁶ Lord Glenbervie, in his valuable work

---

¹ Spelman's Gloss. Douglas on Elections, vol. iii. p. 126.

² Ibid. 'Omne injustum *Scottum* interdixit' (scil. William II.).

³ Mad. Hist. Exch. vol. i. p. 422, in notes; and vide Heywood, Male. Doug. on Elections, Index, 'Scot.' The usurpations alluded to are those of Corporation claims derived from parliamentary decisions and statutes; and vide Book I. Ch. XII.

⁴ Articles of Edward II. Rec. Tow. Pat. 12 Edward II. p. 2, M. 2.

⁵ Harg. MSS. No. 150, p. 89. Rec. of Reign Edward III. lib. G. fol. 173. Lib. Alb. fol. 200, 234. Rec. of 39 Edward III. lib. Dunthorne Ret. Parl. 11 Henry IV. vol. iii. p. 616. Ros. & Pul. Rep. vol. i. p. 498, as to what citizens are exempt from tolls. lib. K. fol. 125, and vide ibid. fol. 64. Jorn. Stockton, fol. 14. lib. M. fol. 173. lib. Q. fol. 138. Waller's cases quoted in Ros. & Pul. vol. i. p. 498. Vide also Lord Hale's 'Preparatory Notes touching Rights of the Crown;' and many records to the same effect in Town Clerk's Office, as per indices, 'Scot;' and vide Book I. Ch. 1.

⁶ Douglas on Elections, vol. iii. p. 126.

on Elections,' states it as his opinion that no such *specific* rate existed; but that the scot meant all sorts of contributions to which citizens were liable.' And it has been long settled in parliamentary committees on contested elections, that paying the *poor rate*, though that tax originated so late as the reign of Elizabeth, came within the meaning of paying scot;' and not only so, but that it was the criterion of the scot-man. This decision can only be accounted for from the circumstance of all other rates having become obsolete, or from this tax being, in fact, the *chief* local one paid in the district. In the City of London many other local or *scot* taxes still continue to be paid; in reference to which, the statute of 11 George I. cap. 18, s. 9, in enacting who, as paying scot, shall be entitled to vote as a corporate elector, declares the scot to be—' rates to the church, to the poor, to the ' scavenger, to the orphans, to the rates in lieu of watch and ' ward, and to such other annual rates as the citizens of ' London, inhabiting therein, shall hereafter be liable unto, ' other than and except annual aids granted by Parlia-' ment.'

DANEGELD.—This was a well-known tax, originating in the demand of a national contribution for the purpose of expelling and resisting the continual invasions of the Danes.' It continued long after the occasion for which it was created had ceased, and became a kind of regular revenue, so common as to pass by the general name of *geld*; nor was it, in fact, abolished until the reign of Henry II.' It was levied from lands and tenements, being fixed at a proportion of so much per *hide*.'

MURDER.—This was likewise, in effect, a tax, and a general and very burthensome one.' By the ancient Saxon laws, all who were in frankpledge were sureties for each other's good behaviour; and were bound to produce every malefactor, or

---

' Douglas on Elections, vol. iii. p. 126.
' So, *Scotale, Romescot*, &c. were contributions of the same genus.
' Heywood on Elections, p. 181. Male, p. 204. Doug. vol. iii. p. 129.
' Dial. Scac. lib. l. s. 11.
' Madox's Hist. Exch. vol. i. p. 585 *et seq*. Spelm. Gloss. 'Geldum.'
' A hide of land contained, it is thought, 100 acres. Spelm. Gloss.
' Madox's Hist. Exch. vol. i. p. 543.

pay his *were*, as a compensation to the person wronged.¹ By many other Saxon ordinances, districts were also compelled to pay a fine for the escape of malefactors,² and particularly murderers; and the mulct so paid by them was termed *the murder*. According to Gervase of Tilbury,³ the assassination of the Normans immediately after the Conquest, occasioned by the violent hatred which the Anglo-Saxons bore towards them, was very frequent. To remedy this, the Conqueror levied from the hundred in which such assassinations took place, a fine, according to the circumstances, in case the malefactor was not produced. This custom soon became a general law, applicable to all the king's subjects, except the villeins or slaves. This ancient author is, however, mistaken if he means to suggest, which appears to be the case, that this fine first originated with the Normans, although it is probable that they carried the ancient laws in this respect more systematically into effect.

Whatever may have been the real origin of this fine, as levied by the Normans, it became a regular source of revenue, and was accounted for at the king's exchequer with the other fruits of the criminal courts.⁴ These fines were extremely numerous,⁵ and in all probability the source of injustice and oppression. At all events, they must have been a real hardship upon populous and prosperous towns, where the offenders were often strangers, and had so many facilities of escape. It became, accordingly, a common privilege in towns to be exempt from this penalty.⁶

THAT THEY SHALL NOT WAGE BATTLE.⁷—Of the trial by combat, or judicial duel, the learned Selden has treated at large in an express treatise on the subject.⁸ The Lombards, who are said originally to have migrated from Scandinavia, first introduced this mode of trial into Italy, from whence it spread throughout most parts of Europe. It was introduced into England by the Normans, and it was resorted to both

---

¹ Lambard, Archaion, LL. Edward. The *were* was the estimated price of a man, to be paid as a mulct or compensation.
² Ibid.
³ Dial. Scac. lib. 1. c. 10.
⁴ Madox's Hist. Exch. vol. i. p. 539 et seq.
⁵ Ibid.
⁶ Ibid.
⁷ Vide *supra*, p. 20.
⁸ 'The Duello,' from which the following account is extracted.

in criminal and civil suits. In the former, if *anyone* charged another with any *treason*, or if the *party injured*, or his relations, charged another with *murder*, *felony*, or other *capital* offence, he was said to *appeal* him, and was termed an appellant; and the party charged was at liberty either to put himself upon his country for trial, or *to defend himself by his body*. If the defendant chose the latter mode of defence, the appellant was bound to meet him on an appointed day, in marshalled lists; and the parties fought armed with sticks shod with horn. The party vanquished was adjudged to death, either as a false accuser, or as guilty of the charge. If the defendant could maintain his ground until the stars appeared, the appellant was deemed vanquished: if the defendant called for quarter, or was slain, judgment of death was equally passed upon him. In civil suits, the judicial combat took place in *real actions* only, wherein the mere right to land was sought to be established; and was conducted on somewhat different principles. For the parties, demandant and tenant, as they were called, substituted their champions to fight for them—who fought with *plain* sticks; and the party vanquished was adjudged to perpetual infamy, not doomed to death.

It does not appear that these trials were, in fact, of frequent occurrence,[1] although there are several instances of them reported with much particularity in the Year Books. Ridiculous and barbarous as they were, they were not totally abolished until the Act of 59 George III. cap. 46, which repealed both appeals and trials by battle, and which passed in consequence of a memorable attempt to appeal a man of a murder of which he had been previously acquitted by jury.[2]

MAY PURGE HIMSELF BY OATH IN PLEAS OF THE CROWN —THAT IS, IN LEGAL LANGUAGE, BY WAGER OF LAW.[3]—The trial by purgation on oath was of a very ancient origin, and was very common throughout Europe, being expressly established by the ancient laws of various nations.[4] In England we find it distinctly recognised by the laws of

[1] The Duello.
[2] Case of Ashford and Thornton: Barn. & Ald. Rep. vol. i. p. 405.
[3] Vide *supra*, p. 261–5.
[4] Vide Spel'm. Gloss. 'Jurata.'

INA.¹ The manner of this purgation was for the accused to present himself, with certain others called his compurgators, before the court; in which the former, on oath, denied his guilt, and the latter swore they believed in his innocence.²

None, however, but those who were free and *law-worthy* were admitted to this purgation.³ The number of compurgators varied according to the quality, or rather wealth, of the accused party;⁴ for it was a maxim, that the richer the person, the more credit was to be given to his oath:⁵ the usual number, however, was twelve.⁶

From this rude semblance of a judicial trial, it has been aptly conjectured, the trial by jury was derived.⁷ For, in fact, it is only the appointment of compurgators *by the sheriff*, instead of their being produced *by the party*, who are to deliver a verdict upon oath, according to the testimony of *others*, instead of by the oath of the *party*;⁸—a reformation which the obvious inducements to perjury in purgation trials would naturally suggest.

Under whatever modifications the trial by jury might prevail among the Anglo-Saxons and under the first Norman kings, it seems clear that this mode of judicial investigation was not generally adopted on its present established principles until the time of Henry II.⁹ Before that period trials by battle, by various ordeals, and by wager of law, were the most frequent: and the latter appears in some cases to have been a matter of indulgence; for we find, so late as the reign of Stephen, a record of a fine paid to the king by an individual for liberty to purge himself from a criminal charge by oath, instead of by judgment of the hot iron.¹⁰ It is probable,

¹ Lamb. Archaion. LL. Inæ. fol. 11.
² Ibid. Iterum et Verbor. Explic. voce 'Vades.' Spelm. Gloss. 'Jurata,' 'Lex.'
³ Lamb. Arch. ibid.
⁴ Ibid. et fol. 11, 42. Spelm. Gloss. 'Jurata,' 'Lex.'
⁵ Lamb. Arch. Rer. et Verb. Explic. voce 'Vades.'
⁶ Ibid. et Spelm. Gloss. 'Jurata.'
⁷ Ibid. vide supra, p. 36, note; 265, note.
⁸ Ibid.
⁹ Glanville, lib. 2, cap. vii. et ibid.

It appears from an ancient tract, in Latin, entered in the Liber Albus, explaining how the citizens were to demean themselves at the eyre held by the king's justices at the Tower, that down to the reign of Edward I. (if not later) the citizens, when presented individually before the court for any crimes committed, always purged themselves by their jury of compurgators, varying in number according to the quality of the crime charged—the highest number being 36.
¹⁰ Mad. Hist. Exch. vol. i p. 497

herefore, that this ancient customary privilege, granted, or rather confirmed, to the citizens by the present charter, was an object of no small consequence. It is singular that defendants in actions of debts, detinue, and account, are still at liberty, both in the City and in the supreme courts, to wage their law; though, as these actions are almost entirely superseded by others of more convenient nature, this kind of defence has fallen into disuse.

SHALL NOT BE COMPELLABLE TO RECEIVE THE MEMBERS OF THE KING'S HOUSEHOLD, OR OTHERS, INTO LODGINGS AS GUESTS.[1]—So in several other charters it is expressed that none shall take lodgings within the City by force, or by 'delivery of the marshal.' The king's marshal was a great officer of state, one of whose duties was to *provide lodgings* for the king's household on his journeys.[2] In early times the king was constantly attended by an enormous retinue, for whom, in his various progresses, he was unable to provide by any establishments of his own. The accommodation of himself and his household was accomplished by the system of purveyance—which has elsewhere been alluded to.[3] The marshal presided over a court, denominated 'The marshalsea ' court of the king's household,' in which all discussions appertaining to these matters were decided.[4] The abuses to which this system of providing for the royal necessities gave rise, became a continual topic of complaint from the people for several reigns.[5]

TOLL, PASSAGE, AND LESTAGE.—*Toll* is the generic term, of Gothic derivation,[6] for every species of tribute levied upon the transit of commodities or persons throughout the realm. That of *passage* was for passing over ferries.[7] That of *lestage* was a custom, of variable amount, levied to the king's use, upon every *last* of leather exported.[8]—In ancient times these tolls were very numerous: such as, toll *thorough*, toll *traverse*,

---

[1] Vide pp. 108, 355, and in notes.
[2] Spelm. Gloss. 'Marescballus.' Mad. Hist. Exch. vol. i. p. 48.
[3] Vide *supra*, p. 108.
[4] Coke's 3rd Inst. pp. 132, 165. A particular Court was afterwards established by stat. 36 Edward III. for these causes.
[5] Coke's 2nd Inst. pp. 33, 170, 542. And. Hist. Com. rol. i. pp. 256, 364.
[6] Lye's Saxon Dictionary.
[7] Co. Rep. part viii. Webb's Case.
[8] Mad. Hist. Exch. vol. i. p. 793.

tolls for markets, those of passage and lestage, stallage, pickage, wharfage, pavage, tronage, cranage, package, murage, &c. &c., many of which still remain in market towns. They are all payable on the principle of some consideration, expressed or implied, such as the establishing and maintaining a market, a wharf, a beam (trone or scale) for weighing, erection of stalls, walls, &c.[1] With regard to toll *thorough* and toll *traverse*, some consideration must be *expressly* shown; such as, in the former case, repair of the street or highway over which the people pass, and in the latter, that the land was originally private property.[2] Most of these tolls were collected in the king's towns and demesnes, ports and markets.[3] To many cities and towns, however, as well as to individual lords, the king granted the right of collecting toll; and such a grant is always implied to such as claim them from prescriptive usage. The privilege of exemption from toll was occasionally granted to particular individuals,[4] and in some few instances to whole cities. But it is said that such grant of exemption extends only to tolls taken on the king's property,[5] and not to tolls granted to others; though an exemption *throughout all England*, as conferred in the present instance, would no doubt be valid by a charter *in parliament*. It has, however, been finally settled, after much discussion, that such a privilege cannot be claimed by or on behalf of *non-resident* citizens; nor can it be claimed against any tolls created by statute for new purposes, such as turnpike tolls. The effect of this privilege of exemption was unquestionably of important value in a commercial point of view; for the abuses in collecting tolls had become so notorious and oppressive in the time of Edward I., that they were expressly restrained under the severest penalties by statute.[7]

---

[1] Co. Rep. part viii. Webb's Case. Term Rep. vol. iv. p. 520. Ibid. vol. i. p. 660. Cowp. Rep. p. 48. The reason of weighing seems to have been to secure the king's and other customs (Madox's Hist. Exch. vol. i. ch. xviii.) as well as for securing just dealing between merchant and merchant.

[2] Comyn's Dig. 'Toll.'

[3] Vide *supra*, pp. 64, 66 in note.

[4] Hist. Exch. vol. ii. p. 19.

[5] Coke's 2nd Inst. p. 221.

[6] Mayor of London v. Liverpool quoted in notes to Mayor of London Lynn Regis. Bos. & Pul. Rep. vol. 1

[7] Stat. West. Prim. cap. 31. Coke 2nd Inst. p. 219.

THE CHURCH, BARONS, AND CITIZENS TO HAVE THEIR *SOCS* IN PEACE—GUESTS TO PAY CUSTOM ONLY TO THE OWNER OF THE SOC.—The subject of this clause of the charter has already been fully discussed.[1] The soc or soke was that district in the demesne of the lord over which he possessed judicial authority, both criminal and civil.[2] And in boroughs and cities, those departments over which the citizens or their delegated magistrates exercised the same functions, received the same denomination. Thus the districts under the government of aldermen were termed socs or sokes; *gilds* were another, and perhaps the more ancient title of them; and both these denominations afterwards gave way to that of *ward*. The soc was, in fact, the modern manor,[3] in which the court leet was held; and we find the *wardmote*, which is a City court leet to all intents and purposes,[4] now held at stated periods by the aldermen; though most of the numerous subjects of criminal enquiry in this court have, in the progress of time, been transferred to the judicial control of other tribunals.

Of the dominion of the lord over his soke, and of the profits and services exacted from the tenants living within it, according to their quality of tenure, we have before treated.[5] It remains merely to add a few observations with regard to the *customs* here spoken of, as payable to the owner of the City *soke*.

In country *sokes*, it is probable that the lords or their officers did not interfere much, if at all, in regulating the reception or lodging of strangers. They came in most instances for purposes of traffic; and could hardly appear in the *soke* without incurring some toll or duty payable to the lord, who was satisfied with the receipt of his customs, and the knowledge of the quality and objects of the parties paying them. But in populous cities it was more necessary to observe restrictive rules, with regard to the reception of strangers. They were liable to become the continual and convenient

---

[1] Vide supra, Book I. Ch. vi.
[2] Lye's Saxon Dict. Heywood's Dissert. p. 145. Vide also pp. 358, 359, note 1. Madox's Hist. Exch. vol. i. pp. 724, 725. Spelm. Gloss.
[3] Spelm. Gloss.
[4] Vide the exact corresponding articles of Levi Inquiry. Strype's Stow, book v. p. 413.
[5] Book I. Ch. vi.

refuge, not only of runaway slaves and malefactors[1] of all kinds, but also for those who, in these times, were regarded with even still greater hatred and jealousy—the foreign traders,[2] whether aliens or denizens; who, migrating from various manufacturing districts, had become, by superior industry, talent, or education, more than able to compete with the regular *scot-and-lot men* of the boroughs into which they intruded, and at the same time contrived to avoid any participation in the civic burthens required for the public welfare. For the purpose of detecting and repressing such offenders, it was provided, that the names and occupations of every individual within the soke should be noted by the constable:[3] every host was to give notice within three days of the guests staying with him;[4]—the guests were to appear before the aldermen for their sanction to such residence;[5] they were required also to give sureties for their good behaviour,[6] and to put themselves in frankpledge.[7] It was likewise a custom, and apparently a very ancient one, for the aldermen or magistrates to assign lodgings for all newcomers;[8] and this custom seems to have been prevalent throughout all the towns in England, with reference to merchant strangers, as late at least as the reign of Henry VII.[9]

It is reasonable to infer—and, indeed, it may be in some degree substantiated, as well by the present charter as by other authorities—that strangers paid to the lords of the civic soke not only the tolls and duties levied on their traffic, but likewise other customs, in consideration of liberty to reside within the soke, and of the lodgings assigned to them; although it is perhaps impossible at this period to specify

---

[1] Articles of Edward I. Lib. Horne, fol. 272. Strype's Stow, book v. p. 365. Vide also Letter of Edward II. to the mayor, quoted by Stow, book v. p. 314.

[2] Ibid. and ch. xix. and xx. *passim*. And numerous records quoted in Norton's Exposition of Laws relative to Wholesale Dealers in the City; long ago out of print.

[3] Articles of Wardmote Inquest. Strype's Stow, book v. p. 313.

[4] Ibid.

[5] Ibid. p. 365, quoting Articles of Edward I. Lib. Horne, fol. 272.

[6] Articles of Wardmote Inquest. Strype's Stow, book v. p. 313.

[7] Ibid.

[8] Vide *supra*, p. 130 and notes; and authorities referred to. And. Hist. Com. *passim*.

[9] Stats. 3 Henry IV. cap. 9; 4 Henry V. cap. 5; 18 Henry VI. cap. 4; 17 Edward IV. cap. 1; and 3 Henry VII. cap. 7.

BARONS AND CITIZENS TO HAVE THEIR SOCS.   291

what these particular payments were.¹ We may collect CHAP. also from the same sources, that the jurisdiction exercised II. by the City magistrates was often encroached upon and disturbed by the intrusion of the royal prerogative.²

The charter alludes to sokes belonging to the *church* and to *barons*. In fact, several of the City sokes belonged at this period to religious establishments; of which the ward of Portsoken and the soke of Aldgate, which belonged to the priory of Holy Trinity,³ and the liberty of St. Martin's-le-Grand, which appertains to this day to the abbey of Westminster, are instances. By the *barons* are meant the aldermen, who were so styled in virtue of their ward or leet jurisdictions, when such jurisdictions were expressly alluded to, although they never permanently changed their ancient title of aldermen.

The system of national police, exercised through the medium of frankpledge and the soke court, has, in the lapse of many ages, entirely disappeared. The practice of providing lodgings for strangers, and of deriving customs for their liberty of residence and traffic, has, with that system, long since ceased also. Payments of this description were, upon the establishment of a Corporation in the City of London, transferred from the ward to the Corporation fund; and many compositions, paid on the credit of such customary duties to the Corporation, may be still traced in their early records.⁴ But in the progress of civilisation great changes have gradually appeared, both in the quality of our commerce and in the arrangements of mercantile intercourse. The ancient jealousies against foreigners have given way to more liberal policy; they have long had full and free liberty of residence for their commercial pursuits, and the City has become the

¹ Northouck's Hist. of London, p. 59. Rymer's Fœd. vol. v. p. 105. And Hist. Com. vol. I. pp. 291, 502, et passim. Maitl. Hist. vol. i. pp. 83, 184. From which it appears that many payments were made to the City by foreign merchants for liberty to reside and trade; and that all non-freemen, whether aliens or denizens, were, and still are, equally termed foreigners.

² Strype's Stow, book v. p. 591, quoting from Lib. Horne. fol. 230. And vide *supra*, under the heads of this charter, referring to the exclusive jurisdiction of the City in civil and criminal suits.
³ Vide *supra*, pp. 25, 35; and Strype's Stow, vol. i. 'Aldgate Ward.'
⁴ Vide authorities quoted in note 1 *supra*.

U 2

greatest emporium of the whole world. The Corporation gradually resigned these customs, which they had derived from the aldermen's sokes; and so completely have these claims become antiquated, that the precise quality of them can no longer be specified, and it would now be impossible to revive them.

NOT TO BE AMERCED OR MULCTED BEYOND THEIR WERES.—It has been before observed,[1] that all crimes, of whatever magnitude, were in the Saxon period to be expiated by pecuniary compensation; and in default of payment, only, the punishment of death was awarded. The estimated price at which wrongs, such as robbery or murder, were computed by way of compensation to the party injured, or to his relatives in case of his murder, was denominated the party's *were* or *weregild*[2]—in other words, the price of his head: and this *were* varied according to the rank of the criminal. The price fixed by this charter of one hundred shillings seems very moderate; for it was something less than that of a *ceorl*, who was of the inferior order of husbandmen; and it was probably deemed a privilege for a citizen to have his *were* estimated at this low sum, as the admeasurement of the extent at which he should be liable to *amerciament* in courts of justice.

The amerciament was the pecuniary penalty imposed for offences, and also for those kinds of inferior delinquencies of which the courts of record took summary cognisance, considering them in the light of contempts of court—such as making false complaints, defaults, non-appearances in the progress of suits, neglect of duties by ministerial officers,[3] &c. The term has long given way to that of *fine*, except as applied to defaults in civil suits; though the fines originally signified the stipulated sum agreed to be paid to the king for *ending*, or settling by his interference, subjects of litigation, both criminal and civil.[4] It was no uncommon thing to pay a *fine* for the remission of an *amerciament*.[5] When the party

---

[1] Vide *supra*, p. 37, and notes pp. 283, 331 *et seq.*

[2] Vide *supra*, p. 261, note 4, and authorities quoted.

[3] Madox's Hist. Exch. vol. i. ch. xiv. Black. Com. vol. iv. p. 397.

[4] Madox's Hist. Exch. vol. i. ch. xi., xii., xiii. and record, vol. ii. pp. 290, 291, in which accounts are given 'tam de finibus quam de amerciamentis.'

[5] Ibid. vol. i. p. 527 *et seq.*

delinquent was subjected to amerciament, he was said to be *amerced* or *amercié* (in the original Latin, *amerciatus*, and sometimes *admensuratus*),¹ which term was in process of time confounded with the term *in mercy* (latinized *in misericordia*), though the *misericordia*, or being *in mercy*, was altogether a distinct thing.² The true derivation of the word amerciament seems to be from *merces*, and not from *misericordia* (the application of which appears peculiarly inappropriate to a mulct actually levied); and its genuine signification is, some mulct *admeasured*,³ or, as the expression was, *affeered* against the party, which it always was; and ought to have been so in all cases, except where the court amerced as for a contempt, upon oath of the freeman doing service at the court, though often, in fact, affeered by the king's justices, commissioners, and others.⁴

The charter adds, by way of explanation to this clause, 'I 'speak of pleas appertaining to money.' But it is to be understood that although *plea*, in its primitive sense, meant a *suit* or action (*pleoh*, Sax.), yet it was in very early times used to signify the pecuniary *mulct* arising out of pleas of all sorts.⁵ In fact, it signified precisely the same as *amerciament*, and so is to be taken here, and does not merely refer to pleas of personal actions.

The system of punishment by pecuniary amerciament began after the Norman Conquest gradually to grow into disuse, with reference to the more atrocious offences; but in regard to all those for which they continued to be imposed, and particularly to what may be called civil delinquencies, they were made the means of great oppression and abuse.⁶ It was accordingly provided by Magna Charta, upon the same principle which suggested the clause now under discussion, that no man should be amerced but according to his

¹ Madox's Hist. Exch. vol. i. pp. 526, 527.
² Ibid. Individuals were often said to be *in mercy*, and to be subject to a *misericordia*, which *misericordia* was afterwards *amerced*, and so became an amerciament.
³ Ibid. vol. i. pp. 526, 527.
⁴ Ibid. vol. i. p. 61; and vol. ii. pp. 65, 66.
⁵ Dial. Scac. lib. ii. cap. 13. 'Placita autem dicimus *poenas pecuniarias* in quas incidunt delinquentes.'—Madox's Hist. Exch. vol. i. p. 210.
⁶ Madox's Hist. Exch. particularly the chapters on Fines and Amerciaments; and *supra*, p. 102 *et seq*.

offence, and *not so as to deprive him of his land or of his stock in husbandry or trade.*[1]

By another clause in Magna Charta,[2] all offences, except those of common nuisances,[3] over which the leets still retained jurisdiction, were remitted to trial before the king's judges, instead of the sheriffs and lords of courts leet; and the affeerment of amerciaments in those courts almost entirely ceased. Amerciaments were reduced by subsequent provisions to 100*l.* for an earl, 100 marks for a baron; and, lastly, to 10*l.* for a duke, and 5*l.* for an earl.[4] We may trace by records that, by the time of Edward I., the term *fine* was used to signify the pecuniary penalty imposed by the king's judges, instead of by the affeerment of the jury, for the punishment of particular crimes passing under the denomination of misdemeanours;[5] and it is said by Coke, with regard to such newly-introduced mode of punishment by judicial sentence, that the law of amerciaments does not apply.[6] These impositions, however, lingered some time longer, as penalties imposed in courts leet for nuisances, and for defaults, &c. in the superior civil courts; but they have now become merely nominal, and the practice of levying them has long ceased.

MISKENNINGS TO BE NO LONGER SUFFERED IN THE HUSTINGS OR FOLKMOTE.—*Miskenning* is a very ancient word, of rare occurrence, and now totally obsolete. It seems to have been derived from *ken* (Sax.), which is a term precisely synonymous with *con* (Sax.), *to know, to commit to memory.*[7] From *con* appears to spring the French word *conto*, a *narration* or *account*; and it is certain that from this word is derived our expression *count*, as applied to pleadings and indictments;[8] those who pleaded professionally at the bar of the superior courts were, in early times, denominated *countors* and *serjeant countors.*[9] *Miskenning*, therefore, appears to have the same signification

---

[1] Cap. 14: and Coke's 2nd Inst. p. 27 et seq.
[2] Cap. 17.
[3] Bro. 'Leet,' 26. Dyer, p. 234. Fitzh. 'Torn,' l. 4.
[4] Coke's 2nd Inst. p. 27 et seq.
[5] Madox's Hist. Exchequer, vol. ii. pp. 65, 66.
[6] Coke's 2nd Inst. p. 27.
[7] Lye's Sax. Dict.
[8] Doct. Plac. 83; Coke Litt. 17. a.
[9] Mirror des Just. lib. 2. Cap. 'des loiers'; Coke's 2nd Inst. pp. 213, 214.

MISKENNINGS IN PLEADINGS PROHIBITED.

as *miscounting*, and it has always been taken in the sense of false or mispleading.[1]

Anciently, all pleadings, both civil and criminal, were delivered, *ore tenus*, at the bar of the court, and taken down by clerks, who at more convenient leisure reduced them into a formal record.[2] This was a practice well suited to the simplicity of the times.[3] It is obvious, however, that by such a course, an unlimited, and in many cases a most pernicious, power might be assumed by the court which made up the records; and that the litigant parties were always reduced, not only to depend altogether on the court's integrity,[4] but also on the impartiality, accuracy, and skill of its officers. The skill and correctness of the officers became more heavily taxed as the law became a professional and scientific pursuit; and it is well known that the Normans imported with them into England a considerable proficiency in jurisprudence, and a mischievous dexterity in special pleadings, by which the rights of suitors were often made to depend on the ingenuity of the *countors*, rather than on the real merits of the case.[5] A practice, therefore, soon arose of granting to the suitors, under the name of an *imparlance*, time to consider of the nature and purport of the opposite party's pleading, and of the form to be adopted in reply. This concession naturally led, as the art of writing grew more and more diffused, to the filing complete pleadings, written out by the party's own legal advisers, instead of by oral delivery at the bar of the court; and, finally, to the service of copies to the respective litigants;[6] though it is remarkable that, in the City courts of London, the service of copies is dispensed with, and the parties are required to search at the record office, at the expiration of the time limited for filing the several pleadings.

The practice of reducing the pleadings to writing by the

---

[1] So in the charter of 20th Mer. (52nd Henry III.) Miskenning is explained as meaning 'not having *declared* well.'

[2] Black. Com. vol. iii. p. 293. Com. Dig. 'Pleader,' a.

[3] This course is pursued in India, in the Adawluts, or Native Courts, superintended by British judges.

[4] That the integrity of the judges was often sacrificed for private and sinister purposes in these early times, may be plainly seen in Britton, Proem 2, 3.

[5] Coke's 2nd Inst. p. 213. Stat. West. prim. cap. 29. Stat. Gloster. cap. 11. Stat. West. secu. cap. 36.

[6] Black. Com. vol. iii. p. 293.

pleaders themselves, may certainly have relieved the suitors from those evils which resulted from the errors and corruptions prevalent in the court itself; but, at the same time, by introducing a much wider scope for the refined chicanery of the lawyers, it probably tended, on the whole, to pervert in a greater degree the administration of justice. One of the most common subtleties was, to plead some matter which, although apparently a valid answer, did in truth involve some fact immaterial to the real question, in order to ensnare the opposite party into joining issue upon some irrelevant subject.¹ The consequence of this was an award of a *repleader*, and of course a harassing delay and expense. But this abuse was of trifling importance when compared with those arising from false and foreign pleas; a great number of which are noticed with indignation by Lord Coke, as defrauding the people of their property, and as scandalizing the legal proceedings, before the age of Edward I., and particularly those which prevailed in the London courts.²

The prohibition contained in the present charter is of a general character, and seems to suggest no other coercion than that which might spring from the authority of the courts themselves, exercised by fine and amerciament, or by penal regulations. By the time of Edward I. these grievances had arrived at such a height, that several severe statutes were passed for the express purpose of repressing them.³ In furtherance of this object, the pleaders, on their admission to practice in the City courts, were required to swear ' that they ' would change no quarrel out of its nature, according to their ' understanding ; and that they would neither plead, nor suffer ' to be pleaded, any foreign matter, to put the courts out of ' its jurisdiction ; nor any other matter but such as they might ' find rightful and true by the information of their clients, whose ' information upon their oath and conscience they should be- ' lieve to be true ; and that they would neither inform nor in- ' force any man to sue falsely against any person by a false or ' forged action.' And so late as the reign of Elizabeth, ' for

---

¹ Black. Com. vol. iii. pp. 294, 395.
² Coke's 2nd Inst. Stat. West. prim. cap. 29; Stat. Gloster, cap. 11; Stat. West. secu. cap. 36. Vide supra, p. 278, note 6.
³ Stat. Marlebridge, cap. 11.

'the purpose,' as it is declared, 'of avoiding foreign and 'dilatory pleas,' it was ordained by the court of aldermen, 'that no special pleas should be received, unless signed by a 'common pleader.'¹ As the administration of justice improved, special pleading grew more and more discountenanced; and many matters of defence were allowed to be given in evidence by the courts, without being specially pleaded, and many more by particular statutes; while in the meantime all formal and clerical errors were cured by various other statutes.² It is often made a subject of reproach against the English law, at this day, that the refinement and prolixity of the pleadings serve very much to delay and enhance the price of justice. It will be found, however, upon a more intimate acquaintance with that branch of the law, that although many unnecessary forms are still suffered to remain, the system of judicial pleadings, as established on its present principles, is, on the whole, admirably calculated to secure correctness of decision upon the rights of the suitors.

By the Hustings and the Folkmote we are to understand all the judicial courts in London. The former court has been already slightly alluded to:³ it was and still is the highest civil court in London, in which were held all pleas which concerned lands or real property, which pleas were the chief subjects of litigation in early times. The ancient and tedious modes for suing in what were termed *real actions* has long been disused, in favour of the more expeditious course by personal actions: but though the jurisdiction still subsists in law, the legal practice in the husting court has nearly expired; except that wills are sometimes, by custom, proved in this court, fines levied, and *recoveries* suffered, for the sake of cheapness and facility. The Folkmote or Assembly (literally, Consultation of the People) was the general name for all kinds of courts, judicial and otherwise; and was applied in common to the husting court, the general or common assembly of citizens, the county courts, the leets, and the wardmotes.⁴

¹ Lib. Y. fol. 192, City Records, Town Clerk's office.
² The Statutes of Jeofails.
³ Vide supra, p. 35.

⁴ Coke's 2nd Inst. pp. 69, 70. 4th Inst. cap. 60; Bohun's Privilegia Londini, p. 239; Freeman's Comp. p. 27; City Liberties, p. 66; Emerson on City

THAT IF TOLL BE TAKEN OF ANY CITIZEN IN ANY BOROUGH, THAT CITIZEN SHALL TAKE AS MUCH FROM SUCH BOROUGH AS WILL COMPENSATE THE DAMAGE RECEIVED; AND THAT THE CITIZEN SHALL TAKE THE GOODS OF ANY DEBTOR, WHO WILL NOT PAY OR DISPROVE HIS DEBT, WHICH MAY BE IN THE CITY, OR IN THE COUNTY WHERE SUCH DEBTOR LIVES.—Both these clauses must be construed to refer to the seizure of goods by process of law. With regard to the seizure of goods within a borough for illegal toll there taken, it must be understood that, both before and after the incorporation of towns, the property of the inhabitants—sometimes that of particular individuals who answered for the rest, and sometimes that of all or any of the inhabitants indiscriminately—was liable to the king or superior lord for the common debt, such as the farm or tallage of the town.¹ The illegal taking of toll in the name of the lord of the borough, or in right of the borough itself, which might pretend to that franchise, would be a common liability of the borough, and in most instances it would be vain to seek redress from the party by whose immediate hand such illegal toll was levied. It would seem, therefore, that by special favour of the crown the citizens were supplied with the same remedy against boroughs as were exercised by superior lords. When towns came to be represented by a community or corporation holding distinct corporate property, and the individual inhabitants became more independent in their persons and possessions, the process was naturally directed against the specific effects of the party actually committing, or authorising the commission of, the wrong complained of. The seizure, however, was made only as *a distress*, in order to compel an appearance in court; which was the sole process allowed by the ancient law for this purpose, in cases of civil injury without force; and so the law remains to this day, in all suits against corporations.² But this difference is to be observed, that by the usual process in common cases, a certain *small portion* only of the debtor's

Courts, p. 1; Maitland's Hist. vol. I. p. 29; Northouck's Hist. p. 49; Strype's Stow, vol. ii. p. 378; Lib. Alb. fol. 9, 10; LL. Ed. 'De Meretrichiis;' Lambard Archaion, 'Explicatio,' &c. 'County Tare.'

¹ Madox's Firma Burgi, Contents of chapters.

² Kidd on Corporations, vol. I. p. 272.

goods could be distrained; and further distresses were to be made from time to time, which upon eventual default were to be forfeited to *the king*.[1] In the cases in question the *whole* amount of the damage sustained might be taken at once, and condemned eventually *to the use of the party* aggrieved.

The latter clause has an evident allusion to the very ancient custom of foreign attachment, which is nothing more, in principle, than a law providing, by distress, for the appearance of debtors in court to answer legal demands;[2] comprising, likewise, provisions for the condemnation of property so distrained in satisfaction of the debt. The clause may be properly said *to allude* to the custom of foreign attachment; for it does not profess to set it out, nor does it, in fact, set it out fully or correctly. The custom did not originate with this charter, nor does it in any degree depend upon it; but whatever effect might at this day be legally grounded on the terms and language of the clause (which it is impossible, perhaps, now to decide), it is certain that this customary proceeding by attachment was never held to operate, except in respect of debts and effects existing *within the civic jurisdiction;* and not in respect of debts which could never be said to have arisen within it, or to effects existing altogether within some *other* city or county.

To explain the law as applicable to this custom would occupy too much space for the present work. The origin of it is so completely buried in antiquity, that its legal operation can only be deduced from tradition and usage. All customs in the City of London are to be certified, when in dispute, by the mouth of the recorder; and this custom, valuable as it is to the citizens, has been many times so certified to the superior courts.[3] These certificates, though not inconsistent with each other, are not equally precise, nor do any of them state the nature and effect of the custom in full detail; which is to be learned only in the practice pursued in the lord mayor's and sheriffs' courts, sanctioned as it is in every particular by recorded decisions of the superior courts. Without affecting a

---

[1] Black. Comm. vol. iii. p. 280.
[2] Jones's Reports, vol. ii. p. 222.
[3] Bohun's Priv. Lond. p. 254; Lord Chief Justice King's Commonplace Book (who was a recorder of London); Harg. MSS. Brit. Mus. No. 135, p. 1 *et seq.*,

complete definition, which can hardly be relied upon, except as proceeding from the mouth of the recorder, the nature and quality of this custom, as resting upon the authority of reports and accustomed practice, may be attempted to be described to the following effect:—That, if a plaint is filed against any debtor for any debt, which can be legally deemed to have arisen within the City, and such debtor cannot be found within the City, and the officer returns that he has nothing within the City by which he can summon him; then, upon suggestion of the plaintiff that any person *within* the City has chattel effects of, or owes any debt to, such debtor—such effects or debt (if a liquidated one) may be attached in his hands; and in case such debt or effects are proved in court, upon issue joined, to be in the hands of such person due to the defendant; or, in case such person will not appear and deny it; or, in case the defendant himself does not appear in court to answer the plaint— the debt or effects may be condemned to the use of the plaintiff, provided he gives security to refund to the defendant the money condemned, in case, within a year and a day, he appears and disproves the debt alleged by the plaint against him.¹ The beneficial effect of this custom in a city of such a commercial character as London, which enables the citizens to recover their debts against fugitive and fraudulent debtors, is very obvious, and can be amply testified by those at all experienced in the City courts; and many thousands of pounds are annually recovered, which, but for this cheap and easy process, would be irremediably lost to the creditors.²

quoting Praxis Utriusque Banci, p. 164 et al.: Year Book, 22 Edward IV. 30.
¹ Roll. 551.

² For the outline of the law relative to foreign attachments, vide Barn. & Ald. Rep. vol. iv. p. 649.

CHAPTER III.

CHARTER OF HENRY II.—PLEAS OF FOREIGN TENURES—THE KING'S
MONEYERS—PORTSOKEN WARD—BRIDTOLL—CHILDWITE—JERESGIVE
—SCOTALE — FIRST CHARTER OF RICHARD I.— SECOND CHARTER OF
RICHARD I.—WEARS TO BE REMOVED FROM THE THAMES—FIRST
CHARTER OF JOHN—SECOND CHARTER OF JOHN—SHERIFFWICK OF
LONDON AND MIDDLESEX—BLANK MONEY—REMOVAL OF SHERIFFS—
PRESENTATION OF SHERIFFS — SHERIFFS' ACCOUNTS — SHERIFFS'
AMERCIAMENTS—THIRD CHARTER OF JOHN—FOURTH CHARTER OF
JOHN—WEAVERS' GILD EXPELLED—FIFTH CHARTER OF JOHN—THE
MAYORALTY—PRESENTATION OF THE MAYOR—CHAMBERLAINSHIP
RESERVED TO THE KING.

CHARTER OF HENRY II.[1]

This charter is directed nearly in the same manner as the last. It is likewise almost to the same purport. With regard to the exemption of the citizens from pleading without the City walls, an exception is added of 'pleas of foreign 'tenures, and also of the king's officers and moneyers.' To the clause of acquittal from *murder* within the City, it is added, 'and in the *portsoken* thereof.' The citizens are privileged to discharge themselves of pleas of the crown 'according to the old usage of the City.' With respect to the taking of illegal toll from the citizens, it is provided, in more accurate terms, that 'after the party so taking it *shall 'fail of right*, the sheriff of London may take goods *thereof* at '*London*.'

This charter further grants that the citizens shall be free from *Bridtoll, Childwite, Jeresgive,* and *Scotale*; so as the sheriff shall no longer levy scotale. It concludes with a general confirmation of all the ancient customs and liberties enjoyed in the time of Henry I., when the citizens might have held them more freely and advantageously; and declares

CHAP. III.

---

[1] This charter is without date, and may be found at large in Lib. Alb. and in the Inspeximus charter of Charles II.

OF THE CHARTERS OF LONDON.

that such liberties and customs are to be held as of inheritance from the king and his heirs.

EXCEPTING PLEAS IN FOREIGN TENURES.—By 'foreign 'tenures' are meant lands held without the jurisdiction of the City; and it is a maxim in law that, in all pleas which affect real property, the cause of action shall be alleged to have arisen within the county in which the land is actually situate; and that it shall be there also tried. Therefore no pleas in foreign tenures could, by the ancient law, have been held in London; which may be inferred from what has been already noticed in regard to foreign and false pleading:[1] and the clause to that effect in the present charter must be considered as merely explanatory. With respect to his foreign tenure, the citizen would be considered as a tenant in the manor or district in which such land lay, and as owing suit and service either to the local or king's general court.

EXCEPTING ALSO THE KING'S OFFICERS AND MONEYERS.—The personal privilege of the king's servants and officers, to be sued in the king's courts only, has been already mentioned.[2] There were special royal courts established for cognisance of all matters in which the king's immediate officers were concerned, according to their respective characters and employments; the chief of which seems to have been the Court of the Marshalsea.[3] These officers, and particularly the moneyers or officers of the Mint, were continually engaged in their duties within local jurisdictions;[4] and some misunderstandings with regard to their liabilities may probably have led to this express exception of their persons from such judicial control.

AND IN THE PORTSOKEN THEREOF.—The *portsoken* of the City was a certain district without the walls appended in very early times to the civic jurisdiction, and in all probability was the same as that which is now called Portsoken Ward. This ward was anciently called Cnightengild, as belonging to certain knights and their successors, burgesses

---

[1] Vide supra, p. 278 note.
[2] Vide supra, pp. 41, 272.
[3] The nature, prerogatives, and jurisdiction of the various special courts are treated of in Coke's 4th Inst.
[4] Madox's Hist. Exch. Index, 'Moneyers.'

PORTSOKEN WARD. CHILDWITE. JERESGITE.   303

of London, by gift from the crown.¹ After possessing this   CHAP.
territory, or soke, for several generations, they conferred it,   III.
in the reign of Henry I., with all its appurtenances, on the
priory of the Holy Trinity of Aldgate; which priory had
been founded about seventeen years previously by Matilda,
queen of Henry I., and who had endowed it with the adjoining
soke of Aldgate, which she possessed, as it is said, as of
demesne.² The priory thus becoming lord of two sokes, that
of Aldgate (which was within the walls) was occasionally
termed the *inner soc* or *soke*;³ and that of Cnightengild
changed its name to the *Portsoke*, one extremity of it being,
in fact, part of the port of London which was situate without
the walls. The recent change of the name, and a possibility
of doubt under the circumstances as to whether this district
still formed part of the civic jurisdiction, may have occasioned
the express mention of it in this and several subsequent
charters. It appears that some contention formerly
took place on the subject, which however was entirely
and finally allayed in the reign of Edward III.⁴

BRIDTOLL.—Toll for passing bridges, called also *pontage*.⁵

CHILDWITE.—The *wite* (Sax.) was, under the Saxon system,
the forfeiture payable to the *king* or *magistrate* for offences,
as the *were* was that paid in compensation to the *party
injured*.⁶ It was a discretionary fine, and, unlike the *were*,
imposed only on the lighter class of offences.⁷ There were a
great number of *wites*, which took their distinguishing names
from the respective offences for which they were inflicted.
This of *childwite* seems to have been the penalty for begetting
a bastard on a lord's female bondslave.⁸

JERESGITE, a word of very doubtful signification.⁹—As no

¹ Strype's Stow, book II. ch. i. 4.
² Ibid.
³ Ibid.
⁴ Ibid.
⁵ Vide p. 287 et seq.
⁶ Turner's Ang.-Sax. vol. II. p. 240. Index, 'Wite.'
⁷ Spelm. Gloss.
⁸ Strype's Stow, book ii. p. 107. So *Lairwite* was the penalty for adultery or fornication. Spelm. Gloss. 'Lairwite.'

⁹ In 'The City charters' and Bohun's 'Priv. Lond.' the same explanation of this word is adopted; and it is stated to mean, 'A toll or fine taken by the king's officers on a person entering into his office; or rather a sum or bribe given to them to connive at extortion in him that gives it.' No authority is quoted for this strange position; and it is difficult to conceive how payments of

sufficient authority can be discovered, either for the word itself or its meaning, it probably has been miswritten or misprinted for *heregeat* or *heregeld* (for both terms were in use), a tax common amongst the Danes and Saxons, and being in fact the well-known *heriot*.¹ The *heriot* is derived from *here*, an army, and *geatten* or *geldan*, to pay or contribute; and the tax was, in its origin, a stated contribution of military stores such as horses, spears, armour, &c. by the vassal, according to his rank, on occasion of a war. In process of time it became a regular and customary fine, on the death of every tenant, out of his goods—usually the best beast; and so it continues to this day in most copyhold manors. The heriot was not, however, properly a feudal or a demesne burthen, though usually so considered.

SCOTALE.—Whether this was a general and national tax, and signified no more than the scot; or whether it had a more specific sense, referring to some tax upon *ale*, is doubtful. It is certain that the Saxons had their convivial meetings, called *beorscipes* or *beerships*;³ and, in imitation of their German ancestors,³ it appears that at such meetings subjects of a public and political nature were discussed.⁴ But that any common scot was levied in shape of a tax, or arose out of such original contribution to the beership, cannot now be ascertained. Manwood says that the scotale was an extortion demanded by certain *forest officers* living in the king's forests, and who there *kept alehouses*, by forcing the people of the neighbourhood to attend them, for fear of their displeasure:⁵ but such sort of scotales (if there really were any, which is doubted by Spelman)⁶ could hardly be the scotale mentioned in the present charter, which was a public tax *levied by the sheriff*. That the king's foresters levied a tax called *scotales* is certain, for we find it forbidden by the twelfth clause of the Forest charter. It is equally certain that they demanded

---

this kind could ever be recognised as a regular toll with a specific name, or that an acknowledged offence should be expressly legalised.

¹ Spelm. Gloss. and Spelm. Fewds, ch. xvii. xviii; and Lye's Sax. Dict.
² Ll. Ine. Lamb. Archaion. Bode.
³ Hist. lib. 4, cap. 24. Cædmon. 74, 15. Lye's Saxon Dict.
⁴ Tacit. De Mor. Germ. cap. 22, 23.
⁵ Ibid. and Ll. Ine. Lamb. Archaion.
⁶ Spelm. Gloss.
⁷ Ibid.

for themselves, until forbidden by express statute,[1] a supply of provisions and liquor when on their forest eyres, which passed by the name of *potura* or *putura*;[2] but it is by no means clear that this toll was the same as the scotale mentioned by Manwood; or, if it was, that the scotale here spoken of, which the London sheriff is prohibited from levying, was the same. Spelman considers the word scotale as a general term for all sorts of taxes payable under the name of scot, and grounds that conjecture on the various modes in which scotale was spelt. It is remarkable that the word is never spelt *scoteale*, though the English *ale* seems to have been only known to the Saxons by the term *eale*.[3]

FIRST CHARTER OF RICHARD I.[4]

This charter is merely a recapitulation of the charter of Henry II.

SECOND CHARTER OF RICHARD I.[5]

This charter is directed to the same dignitaries as the several preceding charters; but amongst them are also enumerated all 'stewards, castle-keepers, constables, and bailiffs.' It grants, that all *wears* shall be removed from the Thames; and a remission of the claim of the king for any annual proceeds received on account of such wears by the constable of the Tower. And it adds that this charter is granted on sufficient advice of such wears being greatly detrimental to the City of London and to the whole realm.

ALL WEARS SHALL BE REMOVED.—The wears, called in Latin *kidelli*, were obstructions in the Thames formed by damming up the river on each side, so as to leave a narrow outlet only for the passage of the water, across which a net

---

[1] 25 Edward III.
[2] Coke's 4th Inst. p. 307.
[3] Lye's Sax. Dict.
[4] This charter is to be found at large in the Inspeximus of Charles II., and was granted in the fifth year of the reign of Richard I.
[5] This second charter is to be found at large in the Inspeximus of Charles II., and also in Liber Albus: it is dated in the eighth year of Richard's reign.

was extended to intercept the fish.¹ The extreme nuisance thereby occasioned, both to the navigation and to the fishery, it is quite unnecessary to dwell upon. Of such public detriment were these obstructions, that their removal was expressly provided for by Magna Charta,² and by many of the City charters. The reason of their continuance for any period may be plainly gathered from the fact alluded to in the present charter—that payments were levied for keeping them by the constable of the Tower, on behalf of the king. The constable claimed and enjoyed, formerly, many personal privileges in the waters of the Thames;³ and, indeed, the jurisdiction over them was sometimes claimed by him, and sometimes by the Lord High Admiral.⁴ After several controversies on the subject, the jurisdiction (or conservancy, as it is termed), of the Thames was finally decided, in the reign of James I., to belong by immemorial prescription⁵ to the City; and for the purpose of settling all further doubts on the subject, such conservancy was confirmed in express terms by a charter of that king, as extending from Staines to Yenleet, and in the river Medway, since which period it has never been called in question.

FIRST CHARTER OF JOHN.⁶

This charter is precisely in the same words as that of Henry II.

SECOND CHARTER OF JOHN.⁷

This charter has a similar direction to the last. It grants and confirms to the citizens the sheriffwick of London and Middlesex, with all customs thereunto belonging, both within the City and without, at the rent or farm of 300*l.* blank sterling money—that they shall make amongst themselves sheriffs whom they will, and amove them when

---

¹ Spelm. Gloss.
² Coke's 2nd Inst. cap. 23, p. 38. Strype's Stow, book i. pp. 33, 34, 70 et seq.
³ Maitland's Hist. vol. i. p. 59 et seq.; Howel. p. 14; Calthorpe's Usages, pp. 8, 9.
⁴ Ibid.
⁵ Ibid. Calth. Rep. p. 167.
⁶ This charter is to be found in Lib. Alb., and in the Inspeximus of Charles II. It is dated the 11th of June in the first year of John's reign.
⁷ Ibid.

they will—that they shall present such sheriffs to the justices of the Exchequer, to answer for those things appertaining to the sheriffwick for which they ought there to answer; and unless they shall answer and satisfy, the citizens themselves shall answer and satisfy the amerciaments and farm—that if the sheriffs shall commit any offence whereby they incur any amerciament, they shall not be condemned at more than 20l., and that without damage to the other citizens, in case the sheriffs are not able to pay such their amerciaments; but if the sheriffs commit any offence, whereby they incur the loss of life or limb, they shall be adjudged according to the law of the City. It then declares that this grant and confirmation was made for the amendment of the City, and because it was in ancient times farmed for 300l., and confirms the grant of the sheriffwick in general words.

SHERIFFWICK OF LONDON AND MIDDLESEX.—Sufficient has already been said in explanation of the meaning and effect of this clause;[1] but it may be observed, that this is the first grant or recognition of the right of the citizens to the sheriffwick of *London*. That such franchise was the ancient and prescriptive right of the citizens, may not only be collected from circumstances already noted,[2] but from the express language itself of the present charter. It says that the king *confirms* the sheriffwick of London; and in a subsequent clause, it declares that such confirmation and grant is made, because it was in ancient times held by the citizens; and further, that the accustomed farm of 300l. was paid for *both* sheriffwicks.

BLANK STERLING MONEY.—*Blank* money was silver melted down, or *blanched*, in order to ascertain its fineness, and freedom from alloy. So that a payment in blank money meant a payment of so many pounds of tried and genuine silver. This mode of insuring the just payment of accounts existed while coin was scarce and of rude manufacture.[3]

AND ABOVE THEM WHEN THEY WILL.—Doubts have been entertained, whether any authority exists within the City for

---

[1] Vide *supra*, p. 268 et seq. [2] 'Middlesex to farm.' [3] Vide *supra*, pp. 23, 79. [4] Madox's Hist. Exch. vol. i. p. 275

the removal of sheriffs without cause;[1] and it must be confessed that the extreme rarity of such a measure tends to countenance, in some degree, such a supposition. The charter, however, is express to the point: and many City records can be quoted, which recognise the existence of such an authority.[1] There are, indeed, several instances of the actual removal of the sheriffs;[2] but they took place at such early periods and under such circumstances, as hardly, perhaps, to furnish a decisive precedent on the subject. Express legal decisions with regard to the amotion of sheriffs by corporations, from the extreme rarity of such an occurrence, cannot be found; but it may be sufficient for the purpose to refer to cases of town-clerks, recorders, aldermen, common-councilmen, and others.

In the case of a town-clerk, a distinction has been taken between the power of amoving, under the authority of a charter giving a right of appointment *durante bene placito*, and one giving authority to *remove at will*: and Justice Twisden hazards the position that, in the latter case, a removal could not be, except for sufficient cause.[3] Another distinction taken has been, that where the office was *judicial*, or concerned the administration of justice, there could not be a removal without cause, under either of such chartered authorities.[4] A third distinction, taken to the same effect, has been, where the office was a fee,[5] or the officer was a *component part* of a corporation.[6] Now it is certain that the two first objections will apply to the amotion of the sheriffs of London. The first distinction, however, certainly seems nice; and the second does not seem borne out by the case itself then under discussion, which was that of a town-clerk, whose office not only concerns the administration of justice, but is in many corporations judicial, and anciently was so in London; and yet the simple return of amotion without cause

---

[1] Strype, in his edition of Stow (book v. p 95), states that after they are sworn they cannot be removed; but quotes no authority.

[2] Ordinances and Acts of Common Council, quoted in Strype's Stow, book v. p. 95; and Lib. D. fol. 146, Lib. Lee. fol. 70; Lib. G. fol. 54; Lib. H. fol. 92, Town Clerk's office.

[3] In John's reign, Northouck's Hist. Lond. p. 38; also in Edward I.'s reign, Lib. C. fol. 70; and in Richard II.'s reign, Lib. H. fol. 92.

[4] Dighton's Case: Ventris's Rep. p. 82.

[5] Ibid. p. 77.

[6] Ibid. p. 302; Jay's Case.

[7] Ibid. p. 82; Dighton's Case.

shown, was held to be sufficient.¹ In an earlier case, the steward of Reading, who had been removed, applied in vain, under the circumstances of a similar charter, for restoration;² and in a still stronger and later case, the recorder of Cambridge was held to be bound by a mere return of amotion, without cause alleged, where the charter gave authority to appoint *ad voluntatem*.³

It must be recollected that the sheriffwick of the City of London does not belong to the sheriffs, but to the City, who executes the office through the medium of these two officers: but the City is liable for the account to be rendered by their sheriffs; and the goods of the citizens, or at least of the Corporation, are liable to be seized for their default:⁴ and great opposition was formerly made to their being sworn to the king, before the justices of the Exchequer, duly to fulfil their office. The power of appointment is the same as, or rather substituted for, that of the king; and it would naturally seem to follow, that the citizens possess the same authority to discharge from office. The reasonableness of the power may also be considered as rather a favourable argument for its existence; for it would appear strange that, possessing and exercising the office, and being bound by the conduct of their appointees, the citizens should not have an unlimited discretion as to the persons by whom they will think fit to officiate. In fact, the Corporation has not only constantly exercised from the earliest times a perfect authority over the election, the duties, the conduct, the courts, and the officers of the sheriffs, and the appointment of them,⁵ but has actually proceeded to the length of dismissing them, without any resistance having been made to such prerogative.⁶

A more doubtful question seems to remain, as to what

---

¹ S. C. Siderfin's Rep. p. 451.
² Ibid. Hagrave's Case, p. 40.
³ Pepis's Case: Ventris's Rep. p. 342.
⁴ There are many City ordinances directing and regulating in what manner the office of sheriff shall be conducted in London; and some of the regulations are ordained on pain of dismissal in case of disobedience.
⁵ The earlier records of the City are full of ordinances on these points; by which it may be seen, that the Corporation continually exercised many of the ordinary functions of the sheriffs.— Vide Letter Books, Indices, title 'Sheriffs.'
⁶ Vide p. 307 and preceding note 5.

BOOK II.

branch of the Corporation possessed the authority in question. By the language of the charter, it appears to have been the original intention to delegate both the power of election and that of removal to the same body—viz., the commonalty of the citizens of London. It is well known, however, that both the original and the present representative commonalty of the citizens are quite a different body from that which at this day exercises the *elective franchises* in Common Hall. The original commonalty were the *whole body* of borough residents.[1] The system of selecting at discretion a *representative body* from the respective wards, by the lord mayor or aldermen, first began to prevail in the reign of Edward I.; and so continued, without any distinct enactment or regulated plan, until the reign of Edward III. In the 20th year of the reign of that monarch, the system of election by the medium of ward representatives, or, in other words, by the Common Council, was established by a specific law made by the whole commonalty.[2]

Until this period, and for some years after, the sheriffs and all other dignitaries of the City, including members of parliament,[3] were elected either by the original full commonalty of citizens, or by their ward representatives;[4] all of whom, both representatives and represented, were required to be scot-and-lot men.[5] But in the 49th year of Edward III., an enactment of the whole assembled commonalty passed, by which the right of election was transferred from the ward representatives to the trading companies, a few members of which were directed to be selected by the masters or wardens to come to the hall for election purposes.[6] In them it has in fact continued ever since—only that, by an Act of Common Council, the right of election was opened to

[1] Vide *supra*, Book I. Ch. vi. and p. 276.
[2] Vide *supra*, pp. 114, 126.
[3] Lib. C. fol. 23; Lib. E. fol. 22, 137; Lib. L. fol. 287 b; Lib. M. fol. 184 b.
[4] Ibid.
[5] All who voted for, or who could be elected into, corporate offices at wardmotes, were, according to ancient and, indeed, general common law, free tenants, or rather occupants or householders; in other words, scot-and-lot men. (Vide *supra*, Book I. Ch. vi.) The general meetings of citizens to elect, were nothing more than the meeting of the citizens at the hustings or folkmote, instead of in their wards. Elections by the Common Council were, of course, elections by householders.
[6] Vide *supra*, pp. 114, 126.

all the liverymen of Companies, generally; and that right has been finally confirmed to such liverymen, being freemen of the Corporation of London, by statute 11 George I. c. 18. For the purpose of exercising this elective franchise, it is not required of the elector that he should be a *resident* within the City, nor indeed was it required of him that he should be a freeman of the Corporation, until the statute of George I. But even as a freeman of the Corporation, he is not that full and genuine free citizen, contemplated by the original charters as entitled to the many immunities thereby conferred, or as a component member of the true and original commonalty of the City of London.[1]

The true commonalty of the City are the *resident householders*, represented by their mayor, aldermen, and common-councilmen in common council assembled,[2] all of whom must have passed the ordeal of an election by the householders of the several wards. The constitution of this assembly has never, from the time of its first establishment by the common assent and law of the whole body of genuine free citizens, been changed, except for the short space between the 49th of Edward III. and the 7th of Richard II.

---

[1] Vide *supra*, Book I. Ch. vi. and pp. 276, 288 in notes. Vide also p. 243 *et seq.*, explaining how these elective franchises have been changed and regulated by the Legislature as regards Members of Parliament for the City, and aldermen, and ward officers.

[2] In early times, and down to a comparatively modern period, the *Common Councilmen*, as representing the Commonalty, were called the *Commoners* of the City; and were the persons who presented, by the wardmote, or leet at its *inquest*, which always was the duty of the resident scot-and-lot members of the district. Thus, in an old play of the year 1605, founded expressly on City manners and customs, the following dialogue occurs between a tradesman and his son-in-law, who had lately been his apprentice:—

Golding. It hath pleased the worshipful commoners of the city to take me i' their number at *presentation of the inquest*; and the alderman of the ward, wherein I dwell, to appoint me his deputy.

Touchstone. How!

Golding. In the which place I have had an oath ministered to me since I went.

Touchstone. Now, my dear and happy son! let me kiss thy new worship, and a little boast mine own happiness in thee. What a fortune was it (or rather my judgment indeed) for me first to see that in his disposition, which a whole city conspires to second! Ta'en into the Livery of his Company the first day of his freedom! how! (not a week married), *chosen commoner* and alderman's deputy in a day! sought but the reward of a thrifty course—the wonder of his time! Well, I will honour Mr. Alderman for this act as becomes me; and shall think the better of the Common Council's wisdom and worship while I live.—*Eastward Ho.*

As representing the entire body of full and perfect citizens, to whom the appointment and removal of sheriffs was originally granted, it is to this assembly, it might at first appear, we should look for that power of removing them: but as neither the Common Council nor the Livery in Common Hall assembled are courts of record, the cause for amotion cannot legally be enquired into by either of these bodies; and it is therefore probable that this power can only be exercised by the mayor and aldermen in the Court of Hustings, being a court of record before which the sheriffs are sworn and admitted into office.

THEY SHALL PRESENT THE SHERIFFS TO THE JUSTICES OF THE EXCHEQUER, TO ANSWER, &c.—It has been for many ages the custom to present the sheriffs at the Exchequer, as persons whom the citizens have elected into that office, and for whom they will be answerable.

It may seem unnecessary for the sheriffs of London to present themselves at the Exchequer to render any account, as the sheriffwick is farmed at a stipulated sum. It is to be observed, however, that the farm is paid in lieu of, and arose entirely from, certain regular and well-known issues, or *locata*:[1] but there are likewise many other irregular and uncertain levies and receipts coming to the hands of the sheriffs, for which they have to account, and which were not included in the farm—such as tallages and assessments, escheats, debts to the king or estreats, amerciaments, customs paid by foreigners, waifs, treasure trove, royal fish, &c.[2]

AND UNLESS THE SHERIFFS SHALL ANSWER AND SATISFY, THE CITIZENS THEMSELVES SHALL.—This was perfectly consistent with ancient usage, both before the date of this charter and afterwards. For in case the sheriffs could not make up their accounts of the proceeds of any privileged town, the king resorted to the principals; and either seized the liberties of the City into his own hands, and levied indiscriminately upon the goods of any of the towns-

---

[1] Madox's Hist. Exch. vol. ii. ch. xi.; and vide *supra*, pp. 43, 44, 69.
[2] Madox's Hist. Exch. vol. ii. ch. x. *passim*; and p. 385. Vide also ch. xxiii. and p. 162. The sheriffs often made payments by order of the king, which were to be allowed on account.—Ibid. p. 385.

men; or he authorised the sheriff to seize any property of the inhabitants, by way of distress, until the dues were forthcoming; and sometimes imprisoned the sheriffs for not having enforced payment.¹

WITHOUT DAMAGE TO THE OTHER CITIZENS, IN CASE THE SHERIFFS SHALL NOT BE ABLE TO PAY THE AMERCIAMENTS INCURRED BY THEM.—That is, the citizens are not to be punished, or amerced, for the personal offences of their sheriffs, but that the sheriffs shall bear the penalty of their own misconduct. It has elsewhere been noticed as a great abuse, that whole districts were amerced in common for the offences of individuals²—an abuse which, in these times, seems to have required the special clause of a charter to abolish. It became at length the express subject of one of the reforming statutes of Edward I.³

THIRD CHARTER OF JOHN.¹

This charter is precisely in the same words as the second charter of Richard I.

FOURTH CHARTER OF JOHN.

This charter² is directed as the last. It states that at the request of the mayor⁴ and citizens of London, the king grants that the gild of weavers shall no longer be in the City; but that, as that gild was accustomed to pay the king eighteen marks per annum, the citizens shall pay twenty marks in lieu.

This charter in some degree explains and proves that the gildated or incorporated companies of tradesmen neither

---

¹ Madox's Firm. Burg. ch. x. and xi.; and vide Mad. Hist. Exch. vol. i, pp. 708-9.
² Vide supra, p. 79 et seq.
³ Vide supra, ibid.
⁴ This charter is to be found at large in the Inspeximus of Charles II., and in the Liber Albus. Date 17th of June, first year of John's reign.

⁴ Inspex. Chas. II. Lib. Alb. Date 20th March, third year of John's reign.
⁵ Mention is here made of the mayor; although the privilege of electing a mayor, eo nomine, was not granted until the sixteenth year of John. The name, if not the office, of mayor of London was known in the reign of Richard I.

became, by virtue of such incorporation, the true original citizens, nor could claim the rights and privileges of citizens. These mercantile associations were created, or, if not originally created, certainly subsisted, by royal prerogative alone, and they usually paid a fine or rent to the king for their liberties. So far from becoming incorporated citizens, or even bearing an affinity to them in character, their existence was at variance with the rights of the latter. Their trade was usually a monopoly;[1] although it is well known that by ancient right the citizens of London may change their trade, as far as respects buying and selling, at will;[2] but even the trading of such associated companies at all, without being regular enrolled citizens, was an encroachment. This will sufficiently account for the request of the citizens for the abolition of this gild.[3]

From very early times, and probably soon after the establishment of the oldest of the City merchant gilds or companies, the City authorities claimed and exercised a kind of visiting jurisdiction over them.[4] They compelled the companies to bring their charters to be enrolled amongst the City records; they exercised a discretion as to admitting the members to the civic freedom; and in later times this jurisdiction has been testified by their conferring on companies the liberty of granting a livery,—in effect, the rights of liverymen. But it is plain that the authorised participation of any of the members of these companies, whether liverymen or not, in any of the civic franchises, has arisen from those laws and regulations of the Common Council conferring the privilege of election, to which allusion has already been made.[5] Nor can it be

---

[1] For an account of the farms paid by gilds, vide Madox's Hist. Exch. vol. i. p. 237 et seq., and p. 399 et seq.

[2] Calthorp's Rep. pp. 9, 48; Rolls Abridg. vol. ii. p. 573; Barr. Rep. Harrison v. Cro. Car. pp. 371, 372, 516. This point was lately clearly decided on in the Mayor's Court. The author was of counsel.

[3] The citizens paid 60 marks for this charter. Madox's Hist. Exch. vol. i. p. 405.

[4] It is impossible to refer more specifically to the very numerous authorities on this subject, than to the City Records generally, and the returns of the various Companies to orders of the House of Commons of the dates 1724, 1735, from which returns and records the positions in the text abundantly appear.—Vide Northouck's *History of London*; Maitland's Hist. vol. i. p. 486; stat. 3 Henry V. Cotton's *Abridgm.* p. 545; Houlgr's *Bye Laws of London*, passim; and Riley's *Memorials of London*, passim.

[5] Plumbe's case.—Ever since the de-

MAYORALTY GRANTED IN TERMS.   315

doubted that such regulations, for the purpose of so transfer- CHAP.
ring the rights of election, were originally in contradiction to III.
ancient custom, and that such transfer owes its permanent
validity at the present day to the statute of 11 Geo. I. c. 18.

FIFTH CHARTER OF JOHN.

This charter[1] is directed as the last. It declares that the king
has granted and *confirmed*[2] *to the barons*[3] of London the right
of choosing a mayor every year, and *at the end of the year*[4] of
removing him and substituting another, if they will, or electing the same again. He is to be presented to the king, or
his *justice*, in his absence, and is to swear to be faithful to
the king. The charter proceeds to confirm to the said barons
all their liberties generally, 'as well in the City as without,
and as well by water as by land—*saving to the king his
chamberlainship.*'

TO CHOOSE A MAYOR.—Some uncertainty has prevailed with
regard to the first creation of this magistrate. It seems clear
that a magistrate over London did exist under that title during
the reign of Richard I., for we find Fitzalwyn recognised by
that name at the period in question.[5] Before that reign, the
only lay magistrates bearing rule in the City from the time
of Athelstan, who are to be found mentioned in records, are
the reve, the portreve, the sheriff, the provost, the custos, and
the bailiff.[6]

---

cision in this case, several companies have uniformly used to refuse to attend at any meetings of Common Hall, except for *elective* purposes; and the wardens used not to issue precepts for any attendance for other purposes. But since the new regulations of the elective franchises (detailed in pp. 213 *et seq.*) this usage has, of course, changed.

[1] Dated 9th May, 16th year of his reign, to be found at large in the Inspeximus of Charles II., and in Lib. Alb.

[2] This word shows that the right was not now *originally* conferred, but existed before both in name and functions. This, indeed, is made clear by a MS. in Brit. Mus. Harg. MSS. 153, fol. 113.

[3] This grant to the *barons* to choose a mayor, sufficiently shows that the *aldermen* were not meant by the term, as some have supposed; for the aldermen have never had the exclusive right of electing the mayor.

[4] There is a material difference in this clause of the charter, with reference to the removal of the mayor, and that in the charter conferring the sheriffwick, with regard to the removal of the sheriffs.

[5] Spelm. Closs. 'Maior;' Tract by Petyt; Appendix to Strype's Stow, p. 19; Strype's Stow, vol. ii. p. 100.

[6] Ibid.; and Maitland's Hist. Index, 'Mayor.'

The denomination of *mayor* can be traced as of very early antiquity amongst many nations of the Continent, and particularly the German and French, where that magistrate was well known.[1] He seems originally to have presided over a small associated body, and answered to our Saxon borsholder, or more properly, perhaps, the *alderman*;[2] for as our Saxon ancestors used to entitle the president of a society the *alderman*, so it seems the German and Gallic mayor was thus termed, as being the *major natu*. When, in the eleventh century, town communities first arose in France,[3] the chief governor of such civic bodies was likewise denominated the mayor.[4] Town communities did not commence quite so early in England; and as the Normans did not bring with them any political devices of erecting town communities, so had they no occasion to change the titular denominations of the ancient common-law functionaries.

In the reign of Richard I. and towards the latter end of the twelfth century, we find the first mention of the citizens of London as a community.[5] Indeed, an express grant is made that it should have a community. The citizens had for ages before that period been used to assemble together for common purposes in the husting assemblies;[6] and they had likewise their separate soke, or gild jurisdictions, over which the reves or aldermen respectively presided. To act however in concert, and for any specific object, without any head or representative body, must, as the population increased, have presented almost insurmountable difficulty. The independent jurisdiction of each alderman in his soke would likewise occasion much confusion, unless the control of some superior should be supplied for the purpose of uniting their authority. Under these circumstances it was that John, who governed the kingdom as regent in the absence of his brother Richard in the Holy Land, and who in fact designed to usurp his throne,—knowing the nature of the French town communities, and their influence in resisting constituted autho-

---

[1] Spelm. Gloss. 'Maior.'
[2] Ibid.
[3] Vide supra, p. 27.
[4] Spelm. Gloss. 'Maior.'
[5] Vide supra, p. 27.
[6] Vide supra, pp. 19, 61, 74; Bohun's Priv. Lond. p. 239; Strype's Stow, vol. ii. p. 370.

rities, and labouring by every machination to increase his power and popularity in the kingdom,—first established the commonalty of the City of London, as a corporate body, by express grant; though in so doing he did but confirm many corporate privileges which had been prescriptively exercised by the citizens before.

PRESENTED TO THE KING'S JUSTICE.—This clause is annexed as a condition of the grant of the mayoralty. The justice here meant probably was the chief justiciar; though all the king's judges of the *aula regis* were occasionally denominated his justices, in whatever branch of its jurisdiction they might sit.[1] The presentment was for the purpose of *admission*, and of being *sworn* into office before the king;[2] the former deference to the royal prerogative seems rather to rest on an implied construction of the language of this charter, than on any express stipulation. It is certain that from the date of the present charter the mayor was constantly presented, as well for admission and for the royal assent, as for the purpose of taking his oath of office:[3] and in a charter of the 37th of Henry III., it is further explained that the mayor is to be presented, *that he may be admitted*. Very few instances can be adduced of an absolute rejection of the mayor chosen; yet there are repeated indications, both of assumption on the one hand, and of acknowledgment on the other, that the king possessed the prerogative both of admission and rejection.[4] This presentation of the mayor was directed, by charter of the 37th of Henry III., to be made before the barons of the Exchequer, in case of the king's absence from London or Westminster; but that he should be presented again before the king upon his return, and so admitted; and thus it has continued to be ever since, for the purpose of the mayor being *sworn in*: but a custom has of late prevailed of presenting the mayor for the royal approbation to the *Lord Chancellor*, who signifies on that occasion, that

[1] Madox's Hist. Exch. vol. ii. p. 312; also John's second charter, '*Justices of the Exch.*'
[2] Madox's Hist. Exch. vol. ii. p. 92 et seq.
[3] Ibid.
[4] In early and unsettled times there have been some instances of rejection on presentation, and particularly in the reign of Henry III.—Fabian's Chron. part 7.

he has it in command from His Majesty to intimate his approbation. An old book entitled 'City Liberties,' of an uncertain date, declares this to be a new practice, and asks by what authority it was introduced.[1] However, there seems nothing really objectionable, either in law or reason, that the king should express his approbation of the choice of the citizens through the highest judicial dignitary in the kingdom.

SAVING TO THE KING HIS CHAMBERLAINSHIP.—It needs not the testimony of this charter to prove that in ancient times the chamberlain of London was an officer of *the king*; that the chamberlain's treasury belonged to the king; and that payments made to the chamberlain were made on behalf of the king, until the greater portion of them by subsequent charters were granted to the corporation. The records are very numerous which explain the nature of the receipts of the chamberlain of London, and that they were all accounted for at the Exchequer.[2] He collected all maritime customs from foreign merchants coming to London; all fines for liberty granted to them and others to trade in specified articles, and to export or import them; prisage of wines; produce of the sale of captures from enemies; of forfeitures for contraband trading, and of escheats also in many instances.[3] He also took to the king's use the duties on tronage, scavage, tolls for passing through the City gates, and even, on some occasions, the forfeitures incurred for breaches of the City liberties[4]—such as for goods foreign bought and foreign sold, all of which are now appropriated to the chamber of the City of London for the use of the corporation. Entries of these accounts may be found in the Rolls of the Exchequer down to the reign of Edward I., and perhaps much later; and there is certain proof of the king's prisage of wines being collected by the chamberlain during the reign of Edward III.[5]

---

[1] Page 107 in that work.
[2] Madox's Hist. Exch. vol. 1. pp. 765, 766, 776 et seq.; vide post, p. 377.
[3] Ibid. and Lib. B. fol. 38, City Records.
[4] Madox's Hist. Exch. Ibid.—The duty of scavage, and the forfeitures for goods foreign bought and sold, seem, however, to have been paid by the king's officers, as *custodes*; consequently it may be inferred that, of right, they belonged to the commonalty.
[5] Hargrave's Tracts (British Mus.), p. 118.

CHAPTER IV.

FIRST CHARTER OF HENRY III.—SECOND CHARTER OF HENRY III.—THIRD CHARTER OF HENRY III.—FOURTH CHARTER OF HENRY III.—FIFTH CHARTER OF HENRY III.—WARREN OF STAINES—SIXTH CHARTER OF HENRY III.—QUEENHITHE GRANTED—SEVENTH CHARTER OF HENRY III.—ALLOWANCE IN THE SHERIFF'S ACCOUNT FOR THE LIBERTY OF ST. PAUL'S—EIGHTH CHARTER OF HENRY III.—NINTH CHARTER OF HENRY III.—PLEADING WITHOUT THE WALLS—SWEARING ON GRAVES—PRISAGE OF WINES—MAKING ATTORNEYS FOR PLEADING IN THE COURTS—DEBTS OF CITIZENS ENROLLED—FIRST CHARTER OF EDWARD I.—SECOND CHARTER OF EDWARD I.—FIRST CHARTER OF EDWARD II.—ARTICLES FOR THE BETTER GOVERNMENT OF THE CITY, AND FOR REGULATING THE CITY CONSTITUTIONAL FRANCHISES, CONFIRMED—SECOND CHARTER OF EDWARD II.

THE FIRST CHARTER OF HENRY III.[1]

THIS charter is a recapitulation of the second charter of John, to which it refers as granting the sheriffwick.

CHAP.
IV.

THE SECOND CHARTER OF HENRY III.[2]

This charter grants the mayoralty in the same words as the fifth charter of John, to which it refers.

THE THIRD CHARTER OF HENRY III.[3]

This charter prohibits wears in the Thames, and is the same as the second of Richard I. and the third of John, to which it refers.

[1] Dated 18th of February, 11th year. To be found in the Inspeximus of Charles II., and in Lib. Albus; also in the Inspeximus of 7th Richard II.

[2] Dated as the last. To be found in the Inspeximus of Charles II., and in Lib. Alb.

[3] Dated, and to be found as the last.

THE FOURTH CHARTER OF HENRY III.[1]

This charter is in the same language as those of Henry II and the first charter of John, to which it refers.

THE FIFTH CHARTER OF HENRY III.[2]

This charter is directed in the same manner as those preceding, except that, in addition to the other authorities, 'the 'king's Foresters' are named. It can hardly be considered as one of the charters of London; for it is granted *to all the free tenants of the county of Middlesex* of every rank, and does not specify the citizens of London by name, though they were much interested in the immunity conferred. It declares, that the Warren of Staines, in Middlesex, is unwarrened and disafforested for ever; so that all such free tenants may have liberty of warren and forest therein, and to till lands, cut their woods, and dispose of them at their will, without view or contradiction of any warreners or foresters; and that neither they nor any justice of the Forest shall meddle with their lands or woods, nor with their herbage, or hunting, or corn; nor shall by any summons or distress, cause such free tenants to come before such justices of the Forest in respect of their tenements situate within the warren; but that they shall be free and quit from all exactions whatever in regard to forests.

It is foreign to the object of this work to enter into an account of the oppressions of the ancient *forest laws*. They may be fully ascertained by consulting the many excellent works on the History of England and of the English Constitution; and are particularly adverted to in Blackstone's Commentaries and in the Institutes of Lord Coke. The disafforesting of the royal forests was one of the great national objects of the barons' wars; and the Charter of Forests, as it is called, was scarcely less esteemed than Magna Charta

---

[1] Dated 12th March, 11th year. To be found as the last; and also in the Inspeximus of 7th Richard II.

[2] Dated 18th August, 11th year. To be found as the last.

itself. The invasions of private property and of personal liberty, to which the forest laws gave rise, are in some degree shown by the present charter. The citizens by this charter secured their liberty of hunting—so long a favourite pastime—which was granted to them by many charters over Middlesex, and which they took especial care to have often confirmed.¹ The great and obvious interests the citizens had in the subject-matter of this charter no doubt occasioned its having been included amongst the charters of London.

SIXTH CHARTER OF HENRY III.²

This charter is directed in the same manner as the preceding. It is the first charter which mentions the mayor and *commonalty* of the City of London, and recognises their corporate acts under their common seal. This charter is a confirmation by the king of a certain covenant, to which it refers as having been executed between the mayor and commonalty on the one part, and Richard earl of Cornwall, the king's brother, on the other. It appears that this prince was the proprietor of the petty port or landing-place of Queenhithe,³ and in virtue of that proprietorship claimed certain tolls and customs. For the consideration of a farm-rent of 50*l*. per annum, Richard granted it *in fee* to the commonalty of London by a deed of indenture; to one part of which the earl set his seal, and to the other of which the mayor and commonalty affixed the City seal.

By the possession of this property the citizens gained a right to all the customary duties or tolls payable by those who used the quay: and these payments were probably dedicated by them, together with the other common *locata* from which profits were derived, to the satisfaction of their farm rents.⁴ These duties during the occupation of the king and

---

¹ Vide *supra*, p. 64.
² Dated 26th February, 31st year. To be found in the Inspeximus of Charles II., and in Lib. Alb.
³ *Hith* (Sax.) signifies a small port or quay, such as are formed in rivers. (Spelm. Gloss. 'Heda.') Thus we find *Rotherhithe* Queen*hithe*, Lamb*hithe* (Lambeth), and many others.
⁴ After being thus granted to the citizens, the issues were collected by the *sheriff*. So fines and amerciaments

earl appear to have been numerous and strictly enforced; and no doubt must have much impeded the commerce and supply of the City, and have greatly harassed the citizens. By this transfer to the citizens, the duties were not only adjusted upon a certain and fixed scale, and the public and merchants secured against arbitrary extortions, but the quay itself, it is probable, was better maintained for the general accommodation, which was the legal consideration for which the duties were paid.

The king by the feudal law had the prerogative property of all ports, quays, and havens, both on the sea shore and in navigable rivers.[1] By virtue of that title, he assigned at discretion what particular spots should be used as ports and quays, and received his customs there, by way of compensation for his care in maintaining them.[2] This quay had been in the continual occupation of the king or his grantees.[3] It had been assigned by Henry III. to his queen (whence the hithe derived its name), and subsequently to several other grantees before it finally came into the possession of Richard earl of Cornwall, who granted it with the king's consent to the citizens.[4]

Queenhithe was anciently much resorted to as a quay both from below and from above London bridge, which formerly had a drawbridge over the centre arch, for the purpose of giving passage to vessels.[5] The citizens, who were themselves exempt from all duties and tolls, derived a very considerable income from the issues of Queenhithe. It appears that by ancient custom all corn was, under penalties, to be landed there, whether it came from the east or the west,[6] and also a proportion of vessels with fish: but the resort to this quay had so much diminished, or the tolls were so remissly gathered, that in Henry VII.'s reign, Fabian says, they amounted barely to 15*l.* per annum.[7] This may be attributed partly

---

collected by the sheriff were granted to the City, for the purpose of assisting in the payment of the farm rent. Vide Charter of Edward III. *post.*

[1] Blackstone's Commentaries, vol. i. p. 261 *et seq.*

[2] Ibid.

[3] Strype's Stow, vol. i. b. iii. p. 214 *et seq.*

[4] Ibid.

[5] Ibid.

[6] Ibid. divers inquisitions.

[7] Ibid.

to the inconveniences in passing London bridge from the eastward, and partly to the many more convenient wharfs, both private and public (particularly that of Billingsgate), which from time to time had been constructed in various situations on the river.¹

SEVENTH CHARTER OF HENRY III.²

This charter is directed to the same parties as the last. It confirms, in general words, 'to the mayor and citizens,' all former liberties and customs, as they had them in the time of Henry II., and as granted by former charters. It also grants, that the citizens may present their mayor for admission to the barons of the exchequer, in the absence of the king from London or Westminster, so as notwithstanding, he shall be presented to the king again for admission, upon his return. It further grants, that 7*l*. per annum shall be allowed, in deduction upon the sheriff's account of the City farm, in regard to the liberty of St. Paul's. And, lastly, it confirms the civic exemption from tolls and customs throughout all the king's dominions.

ALLOWANCE IN THE SHERIFF'S ACCOMPT FOR THE LIBERTY OF ST. PAUL'S.—The soc, or liberty, vested in the deanery of St. Paul's is one of the most ancient in the kingdom. We find it confirmed in the usual terms of *sac and soc, thol and heame, infanghthefe and outfanghthefe*, by William the Conqueror.³ 'All the issues of this soc would belong to the Church, and not to the City; and the deduction in the sheriff's accompt is an indulgence granted, accordingly, in respect of this privileged exemption from his jurisdiction.⁴

---

¹ Strype's Stow, divers inquisitions, and book i. p. 21, book ii. p. 19, book v. p. 281.
² Dated 18th of June, 37th year. To be found as the last, and also in the suspentions of 7th Richard II.
³ Strype's Stow, book iii. p. 142.
⁴ Maitland (Hist. vol. I. p. 88) states his deduction from the sheriff's accompt to be in consideration of *a piece of land* formerly belonging to the city, and then lately annexed to St. Paul's; and quotes Fabian, page 7. Fabian, however, vouches only as stated in the text. But supposing the citizens did possess this piece of land, what could the transfer of it to the Dean and Chapter of St. Paul's have to do with the king's farm rent, paid upon an entirely different consideration?

EIGHTH CHARTER OF HENRY III.[1]

This charter grants that the citizens *may traffic* with their commodities and merchandise throughout the king's dominions, without interruption and exempt from tolls and customs; and that they may abide, for purposes of trade, wherever they will: adding, however, 'until such times as it 'may be more fully ordered by the king's council, touching the 'state of the City.'

The immunities granted by this charter are only such as the citizens clearly possessed before under former charters; and the origin of such a charter can only be accounted for by the supposition, that some of the many aggressions on the chartered rights of the people, which characterised this reign, had been committed against the citizens. The last clause is an assumption of an illegal authority to deprive the citizens of their vested rights, which it does not appear the king subsequently attempted to enforce.

NINTH CHARTER OF HENRY III.[2]

This charter was granted by way of remission after a seizure of the City liberties. It is directed as the preceding charters, and contains, with considerable variation of language, a recapitulation of most of the particulars comprised in them, together with some few additional and explanatory clauses.

Reference is first made to the king's pardon of trespasses and forfeitures. It then proceeds to grant, that the citizens shall not plead without the walls; but adds two more exceptions to those specified in the former charters: viz. 1st, for things done against the king's peace; and 2nd, the pleas concerning merchandise; which, it says, were wont to be decided by *law merchant* in the boroughs and fairs, by four or five of the citizens there present. It expressly re-

---

[1] Dated 11th January, 50th year. To be found in the Inspeximus of Charles II., and in Liber Albus.
[2] Dated 26th March, 52nd year; and to be found in the Inspeximus of Charles II.; in that of 7th Richard II.; and in Liber Albus.

ABSTRACT OF NINTH CHARTER OF HENRY III.

serves to the king the amerciaments arising out of these pleas. It then proceeds to grant acquittal of murder; exemption from trial by battle; and the liberty of discharging themselves from pleas of the Crown, according to the ancient custom of the City: but adds this remarkable exception, 'that the 'citizens shall not be allowed to swear *upon the graves of the* '*dead*, precisely to what such deceased would have declared 'had they been living: but that, in the stead of such deceased 'who might have been selected to discharge those who had 'been appealed or arraigned on pleas of the Crown, other free 'and lawful men should be selected, who without delay should 'perform what the persons defunct would have been called 'upon to perform in case they had lived.'

With reference to the exemption of the citizens from all tolls and customs, an exception is introduced of the *prisage of wines*; viz. one tun before, and another behind the mast.

It grants, that the hustings shall be held but one day in the week, or at furthest its sitting should not be protracted beyond the following morning, in case any causes should remain undetermined as of the preceding day;—that right should be done, in regard to *lands* and *tenures* within the City, according to the custom of the City; so, nevertheless, that foreigners as well as all others may make their attorneys to plead and defend, as elsewhere in the king's courts;—and that they are not to be questioned for miskenning, 'that is to say, if 'they had not counted or declared altogether well.'

It is then granted, that for *debts* and *promises* the pleas are to be held according to the ancient custom of the City; also an exemption from childwite, heargeat,¹ and scotale: and further, that no merchant shall meet another coming towards the City and buy his merchandise to sell again, upon pain of forfeiture and severe imprisonment; and that no merchant shall expose his merchandise for sale before due customs are levied; or buy or sell the same before they are weighed by the king's *trone*, or beam (in case they are such as ought to be troned), under the same penalty.

Further it is granted, that debts due to the citizens may be enrolled in the king's exchequer for their greater surety

¹ Called *Jereagive* in the usual translations. Vide *supra*, p. 303.

upon recognizance of those who shall stand bound to them; so that no such recognizances shall be taken of any persons who may not be themselves known at the Exchequer, for the purpose of enrolling them as debtors, unless six or four lawful men make it manifest by their testimony concerning the identity of the persons so enrolled upon such recognizance, and which lawful men shall be sufficient to answer any damages received by any persons, in case of such recognizance being entered against them falsely; and that a penny in the pound shall be paid for enrolling debts.

It proceeds to confirm, in general terms, all just and reasonable customs, not contrary to right and justice. It reserves the liberty of the Church of Westminster, as granted by the king's predecessors and himself; and declares, that with regard to Jews and merchant-strangers, and other particulars not included in that charter, which may concern the king or the City, he and his heirs will provide as may seem expedient.

NOT LIABLE TO PLEAD WITHOUT THE WALLS, EXCEPT FOR THINGS DONE AGAINST THE KING'S PEACE.—It is a well known maxim in the English law, that all criminal matters must be tried in the county in which they arose. This exception in regard to the exclusive jurisdiction of the City courts over the citizens not having been particularised in former charters, may, perhaps, have occasioned some doubts as to the extent of the civic judicial powers; especially as strong contests prevailed, in the early periods of English history, on the subject of local jurisdictions.

EXCEPT FOR PLEAS OF MERCHANDISE, WHICH ARE WONT TO BE DECIDED BY LAW MERCHANT IN THE BOROUGHS AND FAIRS BY FOUR OR FIVE OF THE CITIZENS THERE PRESENT.—This clause adverts to a very ancient custom, under which *law merchant*, as it was called, or the law according to the usages of merchants, was administered throughout all the boroughs of England (in which places alone, by an ancient law, mercantile sales or dealing by wholesale could take place),[1] amongst foreigners to the borough jurisdiction who might happen to

[1] LL. Gul. Emend. Lamb. Archaion. Coke's 2nd Inst. p. 58; and vide *supra*, pp. 161, 170.

be trading within it. The judges in these mercantile courts were ordained by statute 1 Edward I. to be the mayor, bailiff, or chief municipal authority: but, with regard to London, the citizens exercised of old the privilege recognised in the present charter, of appointing certain wardens of their own to adjudicate on all litigated points.[1] Thus we find, also, that the citizens were used to appoint one of the aldermen to administer law merchant to the merchants of the Steelyard.[2] These commercial jurisdictions have long ceased to exist; but the law merchant, incorporated as it has ever been with the Common Law, and considered indeed a part of it, has been dispensed through the medium of the king's supreme courts.

CITIZENS SHALL NOT BE ALLOWED TO SWEAR UPON THE GRAVES OF THE DEAD, &c.—To understand this clause we must refer to the ancient mode of trial by compurgation[3] of which so much has already been said. The citizen was at liberty to discharge himself from all pleas of the crown by the wager of law, or, in other words, by the oath of his jury of compurgators. As, however, in the progress of such criminal plea, some of his selected compurgators might die, a custom (which, as far as can be collected from the language of Selden,[4] seems to have been peculiar) prevailed in the City of London, for the accused party, or perhaps others, to testify solemnly on oath upon the graves of the deceased, who had been summoned as compurgators, precisely as to their intended verdict.[5] From the language of the common translations of the City charters it is by no means easy to deduce this explanation, or indeed any meaning at all; it would appear from them, that the subject matter testified was rather the evidence of the deceased in the character of a witness, than that of a compurgator's verdict. Upon reference, however, to the original Latin charter,[6] illustrated as it is by the characteristics of a compurgation trial, it is evident that the latter species of testimony is the one alluded to. The charter speaks of the liberty granted to the citizens of discharging,

[1] Calthorpe's Usages, pp. 12, 13. Liber Albus, fol. 40.
[2] Vide supra, p. 166.
[3] Vide supra, pp. 36, 265, 285 et seq.
[4] Selden, Marm. Arund. Ad Smyrn. Fœdus, vol. ii. tom. 2, p. 1550.
[5] Ibid.
[6] Ibid.

or acquitting (*disrationare*) themselves, *according to the ancient custom of the City*: it then refers to these deceased individuals as chosen (*electi*) to discharge or acquit (*disrationare*) those arraigned (*rectati*) or appealed; and provides that other *free and lawful* men shall be *chosen* (*eligantur*), who shall do that without delay, which, &c. All these phrases apply perfectly well to the oath or *verdict* of the compurgators, according to the ancient and accustomed trial by purgation, but are utterly inconsistent with the *testimony of witnesses*, which could not by possibility be supplied by any *choice* of other freemen, as is suggested.

EXCEPT PRISAGE OF WINES.[1]—Prisage of wines was an ancient prerogative appanage of the crown, and formed one of its chief flowers. It was a custom of one tun before and one behind the mast, payable as a duty from all vessels coming into an English port laden with wines,—and was one of what were called the *great* customs.[2] It has been seen that by a series of charters the citizens were exempted from *all* tolls and *customs*; but it is to be understood that there were two sorts of customs, the *great* and the *petty* customs;[3] the latter of which, as Lord Hale says, though commonly so called, were not so much to be considered customs, as *tolls* or dues in regard to territorial propriety.[4] Consequently it has been ruled, that the citizens were not by these charters exempted from the great prerogative customs, but only from those of a petty nature, which were originally due as upon a proprietary title,[5] and the exemption from which might be claimed by prescription; which is not the case with regard to the greater customs.[6] This charter does not therefore contravene former grants; though, as will be subsequently observed, an exemption from this custom also was granted by a charter of Edward III.

FOREIGNERS AS WELL AS ALL OTHERS MAY MAKE THEIR ATTORNEYS TO PLEAD AND DEFEND, AS ELSEWHERE IN THE KING'S COURTS.—Originally the plaintiffs and defendants

---

[1] Vide post. Ch. V. p. 367.
[2] Hale's Dissertation concerning the Customs Harg. Tracts.
[3] Ibid.
[4] Ibid.
[5] Ibid. ch. iv.
[6] Ibid.

were bound to appear personally at the bar of a court of
justice in all suits, whether criminal or civil.[1] This rule,
which began to be relaxed by a clause in the statute of Merton,
20th Henry III., was altogether abrogated by the subsequent
statutes of Westminster 1st (3rd Edward I.) and of Gloucester (6th Edward I.), and attorneys were admitted to represent
the parties in all civil suits.[2] The practice of appearing by
attorney, it is evident, had crept in before such direct sanction
by the legislature, since this clause in the charter under consideration seems to have no other object than to *extend* the
privilege to such individuals as by the custom of the City
had been previously excluded.

WEIGHED BY THE KING'S TRONE.—Of the toll or duty of
tronage we shall have hereafter occasion to speak.[3] It may
be sufficient here to observe, that the word *trone* literally
means *a scale*, from which we derive our term *troy weight*,[4]
sometimes spelt *trone* weight. For the purpose of ensuring
the just weight of the chief staples of the kingdom, and good
faith among merchants, the king erected his trone in all the
staple towns of the kingdom, by which the respective weight
of these goods was adjusted, and a duty paid by way of compensation for the trouble incurred.

DEBTS OF THE CITIZENS MAY BE ENROLLED IN THE KING'S
EXCHEQUER.—The practice of entering acknowledgments of
debts upon the records of the king's supreme courts, under
the denomination of recognizances, was of a very early date,
and prevailed at common law before any statute.[5] The court
of exchequer was that department of the *aula regis* in which
these enrollments were the most common; and so it continued long after the separation of the different jurisdictions
of that supreme tribunal,[6] although recognizances might be
enrolled in any of the other courts.[7] No doubt the object of
this practice was to secure the most conclusive evidence of
the existence and justness of these debts; and a considerable

---

[1] Tidd's Practice, vol. i. pp. 51, 52. Co. Litt. 128ª.
[2] Coke's 2nd Inst. pp. 99, 224, 249, 312.
[3] Vide *post*, chap. vi. p. 376.
[4] Barrington on Statutes.
[5] Tidd's Practice, chap. xl.
[6] Madox's Hist. Exch. vol. ii. p. 85 *et seq*.
[7] Tidd's Practice, chap. xl.

advantage accrued to the creditor in obtaining, through the medium of these enrolled recognizances, a more immediate and effectual process for compelling payment in case of default.

It is to be remarked, that at the period of the present charter, parties who obtained judgments in any *inferior* courts could not take out execution on the property of his debtor, except in the way of *distress*, to compel payment; but a recorded judgment in the king's supreme court would support an execution at once for the whole money recovered.[1] Accordingly it became of obvious advantage to have debts as of record in a *superior* court, rather than that they should be left to the ineffectual jurisdiction of local courts.

At common law no execution could issue against the *lands* or the *body* of the debtor in case of *contract*, except where the king was a party, or by virtue of an express recognizance enrolled of record in a supreme court;[2] in which cases the sheriff might, under a writ called the *levari*, take into his hands the party's lands, until he had levied out of the profits of them the whole amount of the judgment.[3] It was not until the statute of Westminster 2nd (13th Edward I.), that this mode of seizing the lands was altered by the introduction of the more commodious writ of *elegit*; under which writ of execution the recoverer of any debt, or the recognizee of a recognizance, was at liberty to *elect*, to take into his own hands the *moiety* of the lands of his debtor until he should have paid himself his debt.

The advantage of a recognizance consisted not only in its affording a more effectual, but likewise a more immediate process: for the debt being made by this course a debt of record, execution could be taken out at any time within a year and a day, without further litigation; and as was subsequently provided by statute Westminster 2nd, by process of *scire facias* after the lapse of that period.[4] The prevalence, therefore, of the practice of recording debts is sufficiently accounted for. But as this right subsisted at common law, it may possibly

---

[1] Gilb. Law of Exec. p. 1 et seq. Comm. vol. iii. p. 417 et seq.
[2] Ibid. [4] Tidd's Practice, ch. xl.
[3] Gilb. Law of Exec. and Blacks.

excite some surprise why it should be inserted as a special privilege to the citizens of London in a royal charter. The truth is, that at this period many plain common law rights, from the frequent violation of them, grew to be considered *privileges* when actually exercised and respected; and none were so fundamentally secured as not to be deemed fortified by the express acknowledgment of the monarch. It may be also noticed, that the taking recognizances by the chief judicial magistrates was a privilege in the City of London by *custom*;[1] and although the process and security acquired by such enrollments in London might not be so available (which in fact they were not) as those registered in the king's courts, yet it might have been held that such customary enrollments only were open to the citizens.

This *common law* recognizance grew almost immediately after the passing this charter into general disuse. The beneficial results of the improved method of securing debts became so obviously important to the trading part of the community, that so early as the 11th and 13th years of Edward I.[2] statutes passed, by which, in favour of *merchants*, these recognizances were made available against the *body* as well as against the lands and goods of a debtor. These recognizances were to be taken by the chief authorities in most of the cities and towns in England, and were called *statutes merchant*. Other recognizances were by statute 2nd of 27th Edward III. c. 9, ordained for similar objects to be taken in *staple* towns only, and came thence to be termed *statutes staple*. The benefits of these statutes were still further extended by 23rd Henry VIII. c. 6 (amended by 8th Geo. I. c. 25), by which any person, *though not a merchant*, may secure his debts by recognizance *in the nature of statute staple*; which recognizances were directed to be taken by the Chief Justice of the King's Bench or Common Pleas, or in their absence from town by the Lord Mayor and Recorder of London jointly. The practice of enrolling debts upon recognizance, though still subsisting, has become almost obsolete; and has been superseded by the security of a warrant of attorney to enter up

---

[1] Ibid. and Authorities. [2] Statutes of Acton Burnel and De Mercatoribus.

judgment; which from the extension of the process of execution to the *body* on judgments in debt, as well as to goods and half of the lands, has become in most cases equally efficacious: and requiring no process by *scire facias* after the lapse of a year and a day to revive its effects and, being a transaction altogether between private individuals, it has become an easier and cheaper resource.

The precaution against personation and collusion in enrolling a recognizance in the name of an unconscious person, which is provided in this clause of the charter, forms no ingredient in the subsequent statutes by which the original common law recognizances were superseded by those of statute merchant and statute staple. That such omission gave rise to occasional frauds, the special writ prepared for such cases by process of *audita querela* sufficiently shows: but it may be reasonably concluded, that the gradual amendments in the administration of the criminal law, and the facilities given to remedy such injustice by summary application to the courts, as well as by the writ of *audita querela*, may have been sufficient to check any very general prevalence of such malpractices.

FIRST CHARTER OF EDWARD I.[a]

This charter grants, that for the greater convenience of the citizens, they shall present the mayor and sheriffs to the constable of the Tower, in case neither the king or the barons of the exchequer should be at Westminster or in London. It also grants, that the citizens shall be free from passage, pontage, and murage,[b] throughout all the king's dominions. Also that the sheriffs, when they shall happen to be amerced

---

[1] Gilb. Law of Exec. p. 103. Blackstone's Commentaries, vol. iii. p. 406. Fitz. Nat. Brev.

[a] To be found as the last. Dated 18th April, 20th of reign.

[b] Of these tolls some explanation has been already given, vide p. 364 *et seq.* The first mentioned is usually termed *passage* or *passagium* in transmission of the City Charters, which was a sum paid for liberty of *depasturing* hogs. The author has preferred the more obvious reading, *passage*, the exemption from which toll was an ancient immunity. Pontage was a contribution or tax for building or repairing bridges, and levied on the passengers.

in any of the king's courts, shall be amerced according to the measure and quantity of their offence.¹ And lastly, it confirms former free customs in general terms.

SECOND CHARTER OF EDWARD I.²

This charter contains a recital by *Inspeximus* of the last of Henry III., which it confirms, together with all free customs, in the same general terms as expressed in the last clause of the former charter of Edward I.

FIRST CHARTER OF EDWARD II.³

This charter first refers to certain articles agreed upon by the citizens, and submitted to the king for confirmation; out of which he had been pleased to ratify the following:

1st. 'That the mayor and sheriffs be elected by the citizens, 'according to charters granted.'

2nd. 'That the mayor remain but one year in office.'

3rd. 'That the sheriffs have but two clerks and two ser-'jeants, for whom they will be responsible.'

4th. 'That the mayor hold no other civic office besides the 'mayoralty. Nor draw suits irregularly before him from the 'sheriffs' courts, or otherwise beyond his jurisdiction.'

5th. 'That the aldermen serve but for one year.'

6th. 'That the tallages after being assessed in the several 'wards by those deputed for such purpose, be not afterwards 'increased at the discretion of the mayor and commonalty; 'and that the sums raised be delivered into the hands of four 'of the commonalty, who shall account for the disposal of 'them.'

---

¹ Vide p. 292 and notes.
² To be found in Liber Albus, and in the Inspeximus of 7th Richard II. Dated 17th April, 27th year.
³ This is a confirmation of certain articles originally prepared by the citizens for their better internal government, rather than a charter. It was, however, incorporated in the general Inspeximus charter of 15th Edward III. and subsequently in that of 7th Richard II.; it is also referred to as a charter by the 3rd charter of Henry VIII. It is to be found in the Tower Records, Pat. 12 Edward II. p. 2. m. 2., and was granted 18th June, 12th year. The articles are to be found at large in Strype's Stow, book v. p. 363, and Maitland's Hist. vol. i. p. 115.

7th. 'That no stranger be admitted into the freedom of the
'City at the hustings court. That inhabitants to be admitted
'shall be of some mystery or trade, six members of which
'shall be sureties to indemnify the City in respect of them.
'That strangers¹ who are members of any trade or mystery
'shall, upon being admitted at the hustings court, give the
'same security; if they are members of no trade or mystery
'they shall then only be admitted by full assent of the com-
'monalty assembled. That all who have been admitted con-
'trary to these forms, as well as they who have acted in such
'admission contrary to their oaths and the law of the City,
'shall, on lawful conviction thereof, lose their freedom. This
'clause, however, is not to affect the admissions of apprentices,
'who are to be admitted according to ancient form.'²

8th. 'That every year, if need be, inquiry shall be made if
'any freeman exercise merchandize of the goods of others
'not being freemen, by calling them his own, contrary to his
'oath. And upon conviction thereof, such freeman shall lose
'his freedom.'

9th. 'That all who are of the Liberty of the City, who
'would enjoy the liberties and free customs of the City,
'should be in *scot and lot*, and partake of all civic burthens
'according to their oath, under penalty of disfranchise-
'ment.'

10th. 'That all who are of the Liberty of the City, but
'who, living without it, exercise by themselves or their
'servants merchandize within it, be in *scot and lot* for their
'merchandize, like the commoners, under pain of disfranchise-
'ment.'

11th. 'That the City seal shall be put under the custody
'of two aldermen and two commoners, to be chosen by the
'commoners. That the use of the seal be not denied to those
'who may have just occasion for it, and that nothing be taken
'for putting to of the seal. That judgments, especially on
'verdicts after inquisitions taken, be not unnecessarily de-

---

¹ *Strangers* are here spoken of as contradistinguished from *inhabitants*; not as in the preceding sentence, entire strangers both with regard to resiancy and a trading company. Entire strangers were to be admitted only at the general folkmote, and not at the hustings court.

² For a full explanation of the meaning and effect of this article, vide *supra*, pp. 91 *et seq*.

ferred; and if difficulties arise upon the judgments, that still they be not deferred beyond the third court.'

12th. 'That the weights and scales of merchandize to be weighed between merchant and merchant, the issues of which belong to the commonalty, be in the custody of honest men expert in the office of weighing, who are to be chosen by the commonalty.'[1]

13th. 'That the sheriff shall commit the charge of collecting toll and customs belonging to their farm, to competent persons, for whom they will be responsible. And that any such persons collecting undue custom, or otherwise misconducting themselves, shall be removed.'

14th. 'That non-freemen shall not sell, by retail, wines or other wares within the City or its suburbs.'

15th. 'That there shall be no brokers but those chosen by the merchants of the mysteries, in which the brokers may exercise their office; and that all brokers shall be sworn to this effect before the mayor.'

16th. 'That common harbourers within the City and suburbs, though they may not be citizens, shall nevertheless be subject to the civic burdens for maintaining its state, like other inhabitants, in respect of their dwellings. Except the merchants of Gascoigne and other foreign parts.'

17th. 'That the keeping of the bridge be intrusted to others of the City than aldermen; and be chosen by the commonalty, to whom they shall be responsible.'

18th. 'That no serjeant of the chamber of Guildhall take a fee, or do execution on the citizens, except he be elected by the commonalty; that the chamberlain, the common (town) clerk, and the common serjeant be chosen by the commonalty.'

19th. 'That the mayor, recorder, chamberlain, and common clerk, be content with their just and ancient accustomed fees.'

20th. 'That the property of the aldermen be taxed in aids, tallages, and other contributions, by the men of their wards, as the property of all other citizens.'

[1] Vide first charter of Henry IV.; second charter of Edward IV.; and the first and third charters of Henry VIII. *post*.

BOOK II.

These articles the king confirms for perpetual observance. He further grants, that the mayor, aldermen and commonalty, may by common consent, for the common necessities and profit of the City, assess tallages upon their own goods and rents, and upon the mysteries; and levy the same without impeachment. And that the money so levied shall remain in the hands of certain commoners, to be chosen by the commonalty, to be laid out for the common benefit of the City, and not otherwise.

Articles 1 and 2.—It has been already noticed that, from the early part of the reign of Edward I. down to the Act of Common Council of 20th Edward III., great confusion and irregularity prevailed in the elections of the mayor and sheriffs, and much uncertainty with regard to the elective rights of the citizens at large.[1] This may be obviously attributed to the gradual increase of the civic population and the diffusion of independence. For as, on the one hand, the zealous exercise of these important franchises was calculated to introduce popular tumult and disturbance, so, on the other, the repressing and regulating such occasions of violence by the civic authorities would naturally lead to usurpation and contests. In fact, the whole period alluded to was occupied in continual struggles between the citizens at large and their municipal governors, upon the subject of their municipal elective rights.[2] It appears that the general community could hardly maintain their just rights without disorders and excesses, nor could the higher powers refrain from making encroachments on the popular franchises, which they appear at times almost to have established as legal. The proclamations against the attendance of electors not specially summoned by the mayor were counteracted by popular resolutions against illegal usurpation of the civic dignities, until the acts of 20th and 49th Edward III., by raising qualifications and a system of election by the representatives of the whole civic body, first laid a basis for reconciling the exercise of a general elective right with the preservation of peace and good order.

The first two articles of this charter advert to both subjects

---

[1] Vide *supra*, pp. 61, 74, 115.   [2] Ibid. and Strype's Stow, book v. pp. 71, 363.

of complaint. In the former, the ancient mode of election according to the charters is enjoined; which, although it would appear to suggest the general election by the community *at large*, yet had for its object the election by a select body, specially summoned, and the prevention of the tumults of a popular election: for the election by the select body had, only four years before the passing of this charter, been proclaimed by royal authority to be the genuine ancient and customary mode;[1] and that practice, though continually interrupted by the citizens asserting their original independent claims, had been recognised by numerous entries on record, both before and after the charter under present consideration. In the second article the unauthorized usurpation of office by the mayor, either without any election or by a factitious one, is forbidden. The language of the charter seems, literally, to imply that the same mayor was not to be elected two years successively; but the repeated instances of such successive elections from the earliest period, has sanctioned the more legitimate construction, that it was the practice of *holding over*, without a regular election, which was prohibited.

Article 3.—The clerks here spoken of were probably the chief or only officers in those early times for conducting the proceedings in the sheriffs' courts; although since, and at present, these officers are much more numerous, and pass under various other titles, as Secondaries, Prothonotaries, &c. The Serjeants (*servientes ad clavam*) are only another, and the original, denomination of bailiffs, or officers who were appointed to carry into execution the process of the courts.[2] The abuses practised by these officers, and more particularly by the Serjeants, seem to have been frequent and various. At a time when bailable process could be taken out for the most trivial debts, it may easily be conceived that it became a ready means, in the hands of the inferior orders of tradesmen, and of these officers, to harass and oppress the humble and the distressed. It must be confessed that the citizens, by their ready employment of these people against their debtors, and their jealousy of all interference with the

[1] Strype's Stow, book v. pp. 74, 363.   [2] Spelm. Gloss.

exclusive legal jurisdiction in the City, fostered these abuses, as well as a spirit of self-importance in those who might commit them almost with impunity.¹ It is certain the sheriffs formerly made their account in the delegation of this odious branch of their authority; and equally so, that the citizens suffered much grievance by the unrestricted and indiscreet appointment of such officers.² An Act of Common Council of the reign of Edward III. provides that the sheriffs retain but three or four serjeants at the most, *that the people be not oppressed.*³ And many similar civic ordinances passed from time to time, to regulate the conduct and restrict the number of these and all other sheriffs' officers.⁴

¹ In allusion to this topic, a gallant of the year 1636, in a play of that date, making answer to a proposition started, exclaims:—
'I'll sooner kill a Serjeant, choose my jury in the City, and be hang'd for a tavern bush!'—The Wits: *Davenant*.

² As specimens of the City Serjeant's estimation and character, taken from genuine sources of the manners of the age, we give the following quotation from old plays:—

A Cyprian sees a person with whom she has made an appointment, and thus expresses herself:—

Enter MOLL (*like a man*).

'Noll. Oh! here's my gentleman: if they would keep their days as well with their mercers as their hours with their harlots, no bankrupt *would give threescore pounds for a Serjeant's place*; for, would you know, a catchpole rightly derived, the *corruption of a Citizen, is the generation of a Serjeant.*'—The Roaring Girl: *Middleton*. (About the beginning of James I.)

In another play, a lady of the same vocation is under arrest; whereupon the scene thus proceeds:—

FRANCES *under arrest*, SERJEANT, *and* DRAWER.

Draw. Three Serjeants feed on very good venison.

On capons, teals, and sometimes on a woodcock,
Hot from the shrieve's own table; the knaves feed well.

Fran. Come, let's pay and be gone; the arrest, you know,
Was but a trick.

Serj. True; but I have an action
At suit of Mistress Smellsmock your quondam bawd;
The suit is eight good pound, for six weeks' board,
And five weeks' loan of a red taffata gown
Bound with a silver lace.

Fran. I do protest,
I got her in that gown in six weeks' space
Four pound——

Rat, honest Serjeant,
Let me go, and say thou didst not see me;
I'll do thee as great a pleasure shortly.
—Ram Alley: *Barry*, 1611.

³ Hedges's Dye Laws, p. 5. So sheriffs of counties swore that they would have but a needful number of serjeants.—Vide Madox's Hist. Exch. vol. I. p. 147.

⁴ Ibid. *passim.* The ordinances themselves are to be found at large in Lib. Legum. Lib. II. fol. 286. Lib. I. fol. 32. Lib. K. fol. 257. Lib. L. fol. 221. Lib. M. fol. 180, 198. Lib. N. fol. 245.

The following ludicrous scene from

Article 5.—There is no trace when the term *Alderman* was first applied to the presidents of the London gilds or wards; the probability is, that it was introduced after the Conquest. The denomination was common in the Saxon times to various judicial dignities and officers, from the highest to the lowest rank,[1] but there is no record of it as applied to the

An old play of the date of 1607 will best illustrate the subject of this article:—

Puttock (arresting Pyrboard, a scholar). They say you're a scholar. You'll rail against Serjeants! you'll tickle their vices!

Pyrb. Pray do not handle me cruelly. I'll go whither you please. Pray give me so much time as to knit my garter.

Putt. Well, we must be paid for this waiting upon you. ——'s foot, how many yards are in thy garters, that thou'rt so long tying them? Come away, Sir.

Pyrb. Troth, Serjeant, I protest you could never have took me at a worse time; for now at this instant I have no lawful picture about me.

Putt. 'Slid, how shall we come by our fees then?

Ravenshaw. We must have fees, sirrah.

The prisoner here proposes to go to some gentleman in the neighbourhood on whom he has a claim for the five pounds, for part of which sum he is arrested.

Putt. Why, how far hence dwells that gentleman?

Rav. Ay, well said, Serjeant; 'tis good to cast about for money.

Pyrb. The next street.

Putt. 'Slid, we have waited upon you grievously already. If you say you'll be liberal, and give us double fees and spend upon us, why we will show you that kindness.

Pyrb. Troth it shall be all among you. My hostess shall have her four pounds five shillings, and the other fifteen shillings I'll spend upon you.

Rav. Why, now thou art a good scholar.

Putt. I'faith,——has behaved very well of late.

While *Pyrboard* withdraws with the gentleman to receive his 5l. the officers proceed:—

Rav. Where shall us sup to-night? Five pounds received—let's talk of that. I've a trick worth all. You shall bear him to the tavern, whilst I go close with his hostess, and work out of her. I know she would be glad of the sum to finger money, because she knows 'tis but a desperate debt. What will you say, if I bring it to pass, that the hostess shall be content with *one half* for all, and we share *t'other 50 shillings*?

Putt. Why, thou should'st be king of Serjeants; but I think he receives more money, he stays so long.

Rav. That would be rare, we'll search him.

Putt. Nay be sure of it, we'll search him; and make him light enough.

The prisoner escapes by the assistance of the gentleman, while thus the dialogue proceeds:—

Rav. Vengeance dog him!

Putt. But if e'er we clutch him again the Counter shall charm him.

Rav. The *Hole* shall rot him.

[*Exeunt Serjeants.*

Gent. So; vex your lungs without doors.

Alas, poor wretch! I could not blame his brain
To labour his delivery, to be free
From their empiring fangs.—Puritan *Anon.* 1607.

[1] Heywood's Dissertation, pp. 53, 54, 57. Doddridge, quoting Ingulphus, p. 50. Spelm. Gloss. 'Aldermannus,' 'Maior.'

heads of particular districts in London during that period: and there is reason to believe that the appellation was not used in that sense until the reign of Henry II.[1] Alfred, we have noticed, appointed one alderman over *all* London:[2] in Athelstane's reign, the aldermen are not mentioned amongst the civic authorities who met for the purpose of passing penal regulations for the good government of the City.[3] Neither the Conqueror nor any of his immediate successors mention them in the early charters; but we find the presidents of *socs* (an ancient name for the ward jurisdiction) called in Henry I.'s charter *barons*. Aldermen of London are first mentioned in the reign of Henry II. as presiding over gilds, some of which were territorial and others mercantile.[4] In the reign of Henry III. *aldermanries* had become a common term for a civic district comprised within a leet jurisdiction, as well in London as in other cities.[5]

Until the time of the Conqueror, there is every reason to conclude that the president of the soc or gild, under whatever name he exercised his authority, held his office by election, like most other of the Saxon dignitaries.[6] It is certain, however, that by the time of Henry III. the aldermanries in London and other cities had become property in fee, and hereditary[7]—most probably in consequence of the introduction of the feudal system. The ordinances of the charter under consideration show that they did not long continue so, and that such proprietary titles were usurpations on the genuine constitutional rights of the citizens. The aldermen continued to be *annually* elective until the 28th year of Edward III., when an ordinance was passed by the king in council to render them irremoveable without cause;[8] a regulation which was afterwards established on a more legal basis by a statute passed in the 17th year of Richard II., and which has ever since continued.[9]

---

[1] Fabian asserts that they were first chosen in the twenty-fifth year of Henry III. (part 7).
[2] Vide *supra*, p. 19 and notes.
[3] Vide *supra*, p. 10.
[4] Madox's Firma Burgi, p. 26; and vide *supra*, p. 76 et seq.
[5] Madox's Firma Burgi, book xiv.
[6] Vide *supra*, p. 259 *in notis*.
[7] Madox's Firma Burgi, p. 14. Vide *supra*, p. 93.
[8] Bohun's Priv. Lond. p.57. Howel's Londin. p. 35. Strype's Stow, book v. p. 81. Lib. Cust. fol. 192.
[9] Noorthouck, p. 81. Maitland's Hist. vol. i. p. 181. Strype's Stow, book v. p. 81.

Article 8.—This and the 14th and 15th Articles relate to the ancient privilege of exclusive trade in the City, which has always been justly considered as a prescriptive right. It is referred to in the most ancient books of collections of the laws, privileges, and customs of the City of London, and existed in the reign of Henry III.¹ This privilege did not originate from any charter, or out of the commercial character of the civic community; but from the Saxon principles of municipal polity, which prohibited the residence of strangers, *for any purpose*, without their becoming enrolled in frankpledge—which was, in fact, to become a freeman in the primitive sense. The right of exclusive *trade*, considered as a distinct and specific privilege, was rather an emanation from the chartered mercantile privileges of the citizens, than a positive and distinct original law of the civic constitution.²

The *colouring* or falsifying the ownership of non-freeman's goods has always been a subject of great jealousy within the City; and the regulations for the purpose of preventing this fraud are the most numerous, and amongst the most ancient of the Corporation.³ This is the oldest recorded allusion to the subject; and although the freeman's oath is referred to as previously forbidding the practice, we may infer, from the express penal prohibition here ordained, that both the oath and the practice itself were matters of recent occurrence.

Article 10.—This clause establishes a most important point —namely, that by the ancient law of the City it was not necessary that the householder, who, paying scot and bearing lot, represented the full citizen, should continually reside, sleep, and diet within the walls (a qualification which has been sometimes insisted on), but that *any* residence as a personal

---

¹ Lib. Horne, fol. 60, 230.

² Vide *supra*, pp. 75, 120 *et seq.* 169.

³ It is almost impossible to enumerate the many laws and bye-laws directed to this object; they may be traced in nearly every page of Hudgin's Bye Laws of the Corporation, and their nature and meaning are ably discussed in Sir O. Bridgman's judgment in the case of Player *v.* Hutchins, MSS. Harg. MSS. Brit. Mus. No. 56, fol. 26. The whole subject has been drawn into one view in Norton's Exposition of Privileges of the City of London in regard to wholesale dealing. Besides an invasion of the civic right of exclusive trade by *colouring* strangers' goods, the king's customs on aliens' and non-freemen's goods were defrauded.

occupier, by day or night, was as much as could be required.¹
A contrary doctrine, as much at variance with the ancient
common law principles of the civic freedom as with the
direct corporation ordinances, could not fail, by disfranchising the great body of wholesale merchants and the higher
orders of retail shopkeepers, to entail the most disastrous
consequences on the interests of the City and on its political
influence.

Article 11.—Corporate bodies can act only by their seal;
and it need not be here explained on how many important
occasions individuals have a private interest in its testimony.² The history of these times sufficiently shows the
unjust bargains and extortions which from time to time were
ratified through the medium of the public seal.³ The assured and responsible custody of it became absolutely necessary, as well for the repression of public fraud as for the
security of private title. The City Seal is seldom now affixed
to any other documents than those for the transfer or assurance of proprietary rights; but there can be little doubt that,
in earlier times, its testimony was often required to certify
many other particulars, which were of the utmost moment
to the citizens—in questions which concerned their tenures,

---

¹ Some late cases go far to establish distinctly this proposition. Vide Rex *v.* Hall. Barn and Cres. Reports, vol. i. p. 123 ; Rex *v.* Poynder, ibid. p. 178.

The author had once occasion to draw up an exposition, in the shape of a legal opinion, on the qualifications of citizens as wardmote electors ; and the result of a laborious search into the authorities on the point was, that the position in the text was sanctioned by the principles of Common Law, by uniform usage in the City, by the City Records, by the contemporaneous opinion of many great lawyers taken expressly on the point, and by the language of the statute (11th George I. c. 18) regulating wardmote elections. The cases quoted above were decided soon after that exposition was drawn up, and appear fully to corroborate the same principle. Vide pp. 281 *et seq.* 334, art. 9 ; and also

supra, p. 98 *et seq.* Vide also *supra*, pp. 213 *et seq.*, reviewing the various recent Reform Statutes which have restored and confirmed the ancient elective franchises, in virtue of occupation.

² Kyd. on Corporations, vol. i. s. 2, parts 2 and 3.

³ Most of the bargains for relief from toll for assent to royal ordinances, pardons, fines, &c. passed under the sanction of the City Seal, and seem to have been numerous. Vide Fabian *passim*, and under title 'London,' Index. The Commons also continually complained of the City Seal being placed to grants of City lands, without due authority, by the mayor and aldermen. Vide Ordinances of 14th Edward III. Lib. F. fol. 34 b ; 50th Edward III. Lib. H. fol. 45 ; 3rd Edward II. Lib. D. fol. 145 ; and also *supra*, p. 71, note 0.

their legal proceedings, their privileges, and their exemptions before the king's courts and throughout various parts of the kingdom.

Article 18.—By this clause we find that the chamberlain, who is the City treasurer, and who has many other important functions to sustain, was in ancient times elected by the *commonalty* in Common Council, in the same manner as the Common-serjeant and Town-clerk. The latter officers continue to be elected by the Common Council to this day, but it is well known that the former is now elected by the free liverymen in the common hall. Nor is it surprising that the same mercantile influence of the companies which established the trading qualification of the freemen, should also be powerful enough to remodify their elective franchises, as far as regarded the chief civic dignitaries. With respect to the mayor and sheriffs, we have already traced the course of usurpation on the ancient franchises of the commonalty.[1] It even became a common impression, that the former must belong to one of the twelve great companies, as they are called, though it would be difficult to assign any ground for such a dogma.[2] The transfer of the elective franchise from the commonalty to the liverymen, in regard to the appointment of chamberlain, was perhaps of more modern origin. Whether it originated in some Act of Common Council, or was obtained by gradual custom, is not very apparent; it is probable, however, that the election of chamberlain, though not mentioned in those various ordinances which, beginning in the reign of Edward I., finally established the elective claims of the liverymen in that of Edward IV., soon followed the course observed in that of the mayor and sheriffs. That the Common Council should retain the right of electing their Common-serjeant and Town-clerk may be easily accounted for from the nature of the duties of these officers; which were chiefly connected with the proceedings of that assembly, and were, in these times, for the most part of a ministerial nature. But those of the chamberlain being not only of a magisterial

---

[1] Vide *supra*, pp. 74, 114, 126, 243 *et seq.*

[2] Strype's Stow, book v. p. 173; Howel's Londin. p. 41. There is a precedent, however, of the lord mayor being elected from the Coopers' Company, which is not one of the twelve chief companies, as early as 1712.—Maitland's Hist. vol. i. p. 629.

quality, but of infinitely greater importance to the citizens (particularly in regard to his control over apprentices, and his admission of freemen), the companies would be proportionably anxious to secure his appointment by themselves. It seems certain that he was elected by the livery so early as the 7th of Henry VII., when an Act of Common Council passed, enabling the mayor and aldermen to nominate two, out of whom the *commonalty* should elect one; which Act was repealed in 1643,[1] and the election was ordained to proceed *according to the ancient custom.* It is remarkable that the election of the chamberlain by the livery was never *expressly* sanctioned until the statute of 11th Geo. I. c. 18, as far as can be discovered, even by Act of Common Council; it being clear, supposing it had, that the regulations of the Court of Common Council cannot legally change the constitutional rights of those whom they represent; but although no real distinction was originally intended, or ought, strictly speaking, to exist between the election of this officer and that of the common-serjeant and town-clerk, such distinction has now perhaps become too firmly established, both by long usage and the statute above referred to, ever to be shaken.

SECOND CHARTER OF EDWARD II.[2]

This charter recites the military services of the citizens in besieging the castle of Leeds in Kent, and in divers other parts of the kingdom; and grants that such military service shall not be drawn into precedent.[3]

---

[1] Hodge's Bye Laws; Strype's Stow, book v. p. 373.

[2] Dated 15th December, 12th year. To be found in the Inspeximus of Charles II. and Liber Albus.

[3] Because it was an ancient privilege that the citizens should not go to war out of the City. This privilege was of no small importance in an age when wars and warlike disturbances were but too common, both within England and the king's continental dominions, and when almost every individual was compellable in such cases to bear arms.

Judge Foster, in his Discourse on Crown Law, shows that the king in all such cases has a prerogative *right* to impress. But the supply of soldiers is now systematically provided for by the Mutiny Acts.

The real origin, however, of this exemption from warring out of the City was, that by the condition of *burgage tenure*, the citizens were, according to the feudal system, bound only to defend their own walls.— Vide Wright's Tenures, p. 203; Baron's Hist. of English Government, p. 298.

CHAPTER V.

FIRST CHARTER OF EDWARD III.—INFANGTHEFT AND OUTFANGTHEFT—BEQUEATHING IN MORTMAIN—AMERCIAMENTS OF SHERIFFS FOR ESCAPES FIXED—CUSTODY OF THOSE ESCAPING TO SANCTUARIES—THE KING'S CLERKS OF THE MARKET TO HAVE NO JURISDICTION IN THE CITY—THE MAYOR TO BE ESCHEATOR—CITIZENS TO BE EXEMPT FROM PRISES OF VICTUALS TAKEN BY THE CONSTABLE OF THE TOWER—RECORDING OF CHARTERS IN THE KING'S COURTS—CITIZENS TO BE TAXED AS A COMMONALTY, AND NOT INDIVIDUALLY—KING'S OFFICERS NOT TO TRADE IN THE CITY—LANDS OF CITIZENS WITHOUT THE CITY AS WELL AS WITHIN LIABLE FOR CITY OFFICER'S DEFAULTS—CRIMINAL INQUISITIONS TO BE HELD ONLY AT ST. MARTIN'S-LE-GRAND, BESIDES THOSE AT THE TOWER, AND AT THE GAOL DELIVERY AT NEWGATE—SECOND CHARTER OF EDWARD III.—GRANT OF SOUTHWARK—THIRD CHARTER OF EDWARD III.—EXCLUSIVE TRADE—FOURTH CHARTER OF EDWARD III.—POWER OF MAKING BYE-LAWS—FIFTH CHARTER OF EDWARD III.—CITY MACES.

FIRST CHARTER OF EDWARD III.[1]

THIS most important charter, which is directed *nominatim* to all dignitaries and magistrates of the realm, and to all the king's subjects generally, begins by declaring, that the liberties referred to and enumerated in it have been then lately confirmed by the king in parliament. It proceeds to state, that the citizens possessed many ancient liberties both by custom and by express charter, all of which were confirmed by Magna Charta; but that these liberties had been occasionally invaded: it accordingly annuls all statutes and judgments contrary to their liberties, and confirms them as secured by the Great Charter of England. It then grants, That the mayor for the time being shall be one of the justices at the gaol delivery at Newgate; That the citizens shall have *infangtheft* and *outfangtheft*, and chattels of felons attainted at Newgate; Also that no more than the legal sum

---

[1] Dated 6th March, 1st year. To be found in the Inspeximus of Charles II. and that of 7th Richard II., and in Liber Albus.

rent for the sheriffwick of London (viz. 300l.) shall be taken at the Exchequer. Further, That the citizens may bequeath their tenements in mortmain or otherwise, as of ancient time. Referring then to the charter of Edward II., by which it was granted that the sheriffs of London should only be amerced, according to their offence, like other sheriffs, and reciting that other sheriffs on this side Trent were used to be amerced but 100s. for the escape of thieves,—it declares that the City sheriffs shall not be otherwise amerced; and also, that the City shall be charged only as of old was accustomed for the custody of those who fly to the churches for sanctuary. Further, that they may remove wears in the Thames and Medway, and have the fines for conviction of offenders.

It further grants, That all foreign merchants shall sell their merchandise within 40 days, and shall lodge with freehosts appointed for them, and not in societies of their own;[1] that the marshal, or clerk, or steward of the market of the king's household, shall exercise no official jurisdiction in the City, nor draw the citizens without the City to plead.[2] That none other but the mayor shall be *escheator* within the City, who shall be sworn duly to execute that office; that the citizens shall neither do nor provide for military service beyond the City; that the constable of the Tower shall take no *prises* by land or by water of the citizens' victuals or other like goods coming to the City, nor shall he arrest ships or boats laden therewith; and that their ancient custom to hold pleas concerning the citizens at fairs is confirmed.

It proceeds to grant, That the sheriffs shall only be required to be sworn on yielding their accounts.[3] Alluding then to some question pending before the judges regarding the liberties and free customs of the City—which, contrary to their privileges, the citizens had been compelled to claim at the eyre held at the Tower in the last reign,—it confirms all such liberties, and allows of their being recorded as was of old accustomed, notwithstanding any judgments or statutes to the contrary; and that for the future but one writ shall be required for the allowance of the charters in each reign.

[1] Vide supra, pp. 20, 97, 290, and notes.
[2] Vide supra, pp. 108, 257.
[3] Vide supra, p. 312.

It then grants, That process shall be executed in the City by the City officers only; That the sheriffs shall, according to the tenor of the charters, have all forfeitures incurred towards payment of their farm; That the citizens shall be dealt with, at the eyres held at the Tower, by the same laws and customs which prevailed in the times of King John and King Henry, and that nothing done at the more recent eyres shall prejudice them.

It further grants, That the citizens shall contribute to all taxes and subsidies like the *commonalty* of the realm, and not as *men of a city*, and that they shall be quit of all other tallages; that the liberties shall not be seized or a custos appointed for the delinquency of any minister of the City, but that such minister shall suffer individually for his individual offence; that purveyors shall not seize the goods of the citizens against their will;[1] that they shall be quit from prisage of wines; that the king's officers shall not trade in the City in the merchandise about which their offices are concerned; that the lands of the City magistrates lying without the City, as well as their tenements within it, shall be liable to the king for matters concerning their offices; that no market be held within seven miles in circuit of the City; that all inquisitions of the City taken by the king's justices and ministers, shall be held at St. Martin's-le-Grand, except those at the Tower and those of gaol delivery at Newgate; and, lastly, it grants that the citizens shall not be impleaded, at the Exchequer or elsewhere, except in matters which concern the king or his heirs.

INFANGTHEFT AND OUTFANGTHEFT.—Great doubts and differences of opinion exist with regard to the precise meaning of these terms. Some explain them as meaning a criminal jurisdiction over thieves arrested *within the liberty*, and also over those who, being originally members of the liberty, are seized *without it*. But this construction seems far too wide to be consistent with the best authorities on this particular subject, and on that of ancient criminal jurisdictions. The words literally signify, *jurisdiction over a thief taken both with-*

---

[1] Vide *supra*, p. 109, as to Purveyors and their practices.

in and without. It appears clear from all authority, as well as from principle, that this jurisdiction never extended to those offending, as well as seized, *out of* the district; and we must consequently understand it as extending only to those who *belonging* to the district were seized within it, and to those also who might happen to be so seized, though belonging to another district. Later authorities, with much probability, limit the nature of the jurisdiction still further, and restrict it to a course of criminal proceeding peculiar to the circumstances of the times.[1]

It is well known how vague and unsettled the administration of criminal law was during the Saxon era. The infliction of summary punishment without any formal trial, in certain cases of offenders seized by means of *hue and cry*, upon their flight, by the members of the gild and *borhoes* in which the offence was committed, may be clearly traced in the older Saxon laws;[2] and such a course does not seem inconsistent with the simplicity of those ages, nor with that principle of rendering pecuniary satisfaction for crimes, which was either to be made by the party himself, or by the *borhoe* in failure of detection. This summary mode of conviction is particularly recognised by the laws of all Northern nations with regard to offenders taken *in the mainour*, that is, in the actual possession of the plunder.[3] The term Fang does not signify, as has been supposed,[4] 'plunder *in hand*;' but merely something seized, or *a capture*, that is, of the offender. Yet we have the most decisive authority, not only that a summary course of convicting persons seized in the *actual possession* of goods stolen, or in the *mainour*, was taken throughout England, but also that such course was the characteristic of the jurisdiction of the infangtheft and outfangtheft,[5] although the etymology of the word does not *sua vi* imply so much. Bracton says, that by common law summary justice was done on those thieves taken Ðonðhabenð (hand-having), and those Bacbepenð (back-bearing), upon their being pursued and

---

[1] Spelm. Gloss.
[2] LL. Athelstan. Wilk. Jud. Civ. Lond. Coke's 2nd Inst. p. 172.
[3] Barrington on Stat. Index, 'Manner.'
[4] By Barrington, ibid.
[5] Spelm. Gloss.

seized by the Saccabop (inhabitants of the leet¹), without any judicial trial: he adds, that this was the peculiar jurisdiction of the infangtheft; but that, if there was no such seizure of the offender in actual possession of the plunder, the party was to be indicted formally in the king's court."

The exercise of this jurisdiction, there is reason to believe, had altogether ceased before the time of the present charter. The mention of the privilege in conjunction with the grant of chattels of felons convict, would imply that these ancient terms, like that of *pleas*, had been adopted as signifying the forfeiture and fruits of the criminal jurisdiction.

MAY BEQUEATH IN MORTMAIN,—that is, to a body corporate, which, rendering no services of a personal kind to any superior lord, and not being liable to forfeiture or escheats, hold its possessions, as it were, in *a dead hand*.³ The bodies corporate here referred to, were ecclesiastical and not civic; for it is worthy of remark, that all the earlier statutes forbidding alienations in mortmain to this period, solely respected ecclesiastical corporations and the devices of the religious fraternities to accumulate landed property, and did not relate to lay or town corporations.⁴ By the ancient law of the land, and that which prevailed in the City, alienations of land were unrestricted; and though it is said that a licence from the king was necessary in the Saxon times ⁵ for any transfer to an ecclesiastical body, that position does not seem very clearly made out,⁶ and can hardly be said to apply to the citizens of London, who owed to the king none of those personal services from which, if they could be demanded, this prerogative control over alienations arose. The licence in question seems rather to be of a pure feudal origin, and prevailed for the purpose of securing to the lord of the fee—whether ultimate as the king, or immediate as the person holding as feudal

---

¹ This translation is but conjectural. The express explication of this word has puzzled the most learned. Selden. (Tit. Hon. add. 999) explains the Saccabor as the accuser or appellant of the leet jurisdiction. The literal meaning of the word is, *baron or man of the sac*. Lord Coke's derivation (3rd Inst. p. 69) is plainly erroneous.

² Bracton, lib. 3. Tract. 2, Ca. 32, 34.
³ Kyd. on Corporations, vol. i. p. 95.
⁴ Or, according to Blackstone, being composed of monks, who were dead men in law.
⁵ Selden, Jan. Ang. 1, 2, s. 452.
⁶ Kyd. on Corp. vol. i. p. 88.

tenant to another, and subinfeudating to a third—the military and many other personal services which could not be rendered by a corporate body. This licence, though never absolutely resigned by the Crown, was gradually, by the contrivances of the monks, almost superseded in effect; and entirely so, as far as regarded the mesne lord of the fee: so that, in the time of King John, there was scarcely any other restriction from alienating to a corporate body than to a private person.[1]

The evils which flowed from thus withdrawing the personal services of tenants from national calls, from the stagnation of property, and from the overgrown influence of the clergy,[2] became in the reign of King John so apparent, that a clause in Magna Charta was provided for the purpose of preventing these mortmain appropriations. But so great was the ingenuity of the monks, that it required the force of several statutes, passed in the reign of Edward I., to defeat the many fraudulent devices by which they contrived, notwithstanding the statutory restrictions, to get landed property into their hands; and by their invention of *uses*, under the sanction of which lands were conveyed to trustees *for their use*, they still managed to acquire almost all the benefits of estates not absolutely conveyed to them in fee; until by the statute taking away all *superstitious uses*,[3] and that regulating the disposal of property to *charitable* uses,[4] the mischief consequent upon alienations in mortmain was at length prevented.

The citizens of London holding, by free burgage tenure, a tenancy equally distinct from feudal as from a demesne tenure, were neither within the letter nor spirit of the statutes of mortmain. As far as respected personal services, and every other seignorial interest, except that of forfeiture, which was not of feudal origin,[5] the City, with its rights, privileges, and property, was, by ancient exemptions, already in *a dead hand*; and no alienation could in a further degree deprive the lord of his rights. The king was, indeed, still immediate lord of the fee, but not according to feudal principles; and

---

[1] Kyd. on Corp. vol. i. p. 88.
[2] Barrington on Statutes, pp. 24, 76.
[3] 1st Edward VI. c. 14.
[4] 9th George II. c. 36.
[5] Vide post, p. 356.

SHERIFF'S AMERCIAMENT FOR ESCAPES.   351

as he could claim no feudal services, he could claim no feudal CHAP. right of licence. The nature of the civic constitution and V. the liberties enjoyed by the citizens will sufficiently explain, therefore, the origin of that which has been considered an ancient custom [1]—viz., that they should be free to bequeath in mortmain; a privilege confirmed by this charter, as of ancient right, though probably in some degree impeached by the construction of the then recently enacted statutes of mortmain.

That this privilege should have been considered of any value in these times, still more that it should be prized so much as to become the subject of this charter, may serve to show the influence of superstition and of a rapacious clergy on the minds of the people. With the abominations of the Catholic hierarchy, the monastic establishments have long since perished; every trace of the feudal system has been obliterated; charitable and religious donations and bequests have been put by the legislature under regulations as favourable to the pious feelings of individuals of all classes, as to the advancement of the general welfare;[2] so that the statutes of mortmain, and the civic privilege here discussed, have become, in practice, almost a dead letter.

SHERIFFS TO BE AMERCED FOR THE ESCAPE OF THIEVES AT ONE HUNDRED SHILLINGS.—Something has already been said in explanation of the nature of *amerciaments*;[3] but this passage of the present charter suggests some further observations on a topic of such universal importance in the administration of justice throughout this kingdom during every reign of the Plantagenets.

Under the Saxon dynasty, when all crimes might be expiated by a pecuniary ransom, which was fixed, except in a few instances, it is probable that an *amerciament*, or mulct *admeasured by the suitors* of the leet, was inflicted in cases of crimes for which no fines were settled by positive law under an express name — such as *weregild*, *bloodwite*, *childwite*, *danegild*, &c., which were only different denominations of the same kind of punishment. As by degrees the specific punish-

[1] Bulst. Rep. vol. ii. p. 187. and 9th George II. c. 36.
[2] By statutes 1st Edward VI. c. 14 [3] Vide supra, pp. 292 et seq. and p 32.

ments of death, of mutilation, of scourging, of exposure, of imprisonment, of forfeitures and of fines, came to be assigned to various offences respectively, *amerciaments* became less generally applicable; and we find, by a long current of authorities,[1] that after the Conquest they were applied only to that class of offences and defaults which were deemed too trivial to have express punishments provided for them, and which were sometimes termed *parva delicta*.[2]

According to modern principles of law, every illegal act of commission or omission of a public nature, not coming within the special construction of a contempt of court, amounts at least to a misdemeanour, subject to a judicial sentence; and no man can be convicted of any *misdemeanour* without a regular trial. But, according to earlier doctrines and practice, a remarkable distinction was observed between great and small offences (in which latter class were comprehended several offences now commonly punished as misdemennours), both in respect of the conviction and mode of punishment. All the greater offences were, or ought to have been, regularly *tried* upon an issue between the king and the party of 'guilty' or 'not guilty;' and upon conviction, the presiding judge passed a sentence, which, when pecuniary, came to be called a *fine*:[3] the smaller offences were reserved, according to ancient practice, for punishment by the *affeered amerciament* of the suitors; and the party was convicted without any *trial* upon an issue joined, upon the mere *presentment* of an inquest jury.[4] The greater offences were all ranged under the class of *pleas* of the Crown; and the smaller under a class of charges, or more properly convictions, especially designated by the term *presentments*.[5] Thus by Magna Charta the jurisdiction over

---

[1] Coke's 2nd Inst. Index. 'Amerciament,' 'Eyre.' Hale's Pleas of the Crown, vol. i. ch. 52; vol. ii. ch. 19.
[2] Magna Charta, ch. xiv.
[3] Fines are distinguished, as imposed *by the court*, or by force of some statute; —amerciaments, as imposed arbitrarily *by the country*. (Termes de la Ley. Kitchin's Jurisdictions, p. 214. Coke's Rep. part viii. pp. 39, 41, 80a). The fines imposed by the court of their own inherent authority, as for contempts to officers, or by suitors in their pleadings, were also called amerciaments originally.
[4] Hale's Pleas of the Crown, vol. i ch. 52; vol. ii. ch. 19. Hill's edition of Coke's Rep. 21st Edward III. 5th Henry VII. fol. 9. 18th Edward III. fol. 8 Dyer's Rep. fol. 13.
[5] Hale's Pleas of the Crown, vol. ii chap. 19; Coke's 2nd Inst. p. 738.

AMERCIAMENTS—NATURE OF. 353

pleas of the crown was taken away from all courts leet; but those courts still continued to punish, by disgraceful exposure and by *amerciament*, for a variety of petty offences, upon *presentments* by the leet inquest:[1] and towns, hundreds, and frankpledges continued to be *amerced* by the king's justices in eyre, although these bodies seldom, if ever, in the earlier times, traversed or *pleaded* to the presentments.[2] It is scarcely possible to draw the line between what at any one period were considered the greater, and what the smaller offences; but there is no doubt that during the period in which the punishment by *amerciament* prevailed, many misdemeanours, which ought to have been prosecuted by way of indictment before a petty jury, were treated either as contempts of court, and fined at the discretion of the judge, or as of the smaller kind of offence, and amerced by affeerment of a jury.[3]

The crimes punishable by amerciament were, or ought to have been, of the most trivial sort; as such a course of conviction for this class of offences, during the latter period of its existence, was tolerated only upon the legal maxim of *de minimis non curat lex;*[4] yet, as we have had occasion to notice, owing to the nature of the royal revenue, the punishment by amerciament formed, in the earlier ages of our history, one of the most fruitful sources of oppression.[5] Not only were these exactions numerous and severe throughout all the petty courts of the kingdom; but the king's judges, and more particularly the justices in eyre, levied *amerciaments* with unsparing zeal, to supply the royal necessities—imposing them for every possible default in public duty or in private litigation.[6] A particular sort of *amerciaments* passed by the name of *royal*; arising chiefly from the defaults of magistrates, public officers, and chief tenants,

CHAP.
V.

---

[1] Greenwood on Courts: charge to leet jury. Scrype's Stow, book v. Coke's 2nd Inst. p. 738.
[2] For the variety of amerciaments, see Madox's Hist. Exch. chapter on Fines and Amerciaments.
[3] Ibid. The numerous subjects of amerciament.

[4] Hale's Pleas of the Crown, vol. I. ch. iii.
[5] Vide supra, pp. 32, 77 et seq. and 292 et seq.; and Madox's Hist. Exch. passim, and particularly the chapter on Fines and Amerciaments.
[6] Ibid.

who, subject to no other superior control, were visited by the king's judges, and more especially by the justices in eyre,[1] whose commissions were sometimes solely issued for that object.[2] It was under this jurisdiction that sheriffs were amerced for escapes: for although any escape, whether negligent or voluntary, was perhaps from the time of the Conquest an indictable offence, subject to punishment by the sentence of the court, and consequently, as Lord Hale observes, the charge was traversable,[3] and ought to be substantiated by trial,—yet that position of the learned judge must be rather understood to relate to the law as it stood in his own time, and not to the practice, or perhaps the law, as it stood before the reign of Edward III.; for the present charter and many other records and authorities sufficiently testify, that the king constantly levied his amerciaments for escapes[4]—such offences being treated either as contempts, or as of the smaller kind of offences, and sufficiently substantiated by mere presentment.

How these amerciaments were restrained, until, under new principles in the dispensation of criminal justice, they have at length entirely sunk into neglect, has been noticed in a former part of this work.[5]

CHARGED ONLY AS OF OLD ACCUSTOMED FOR THE CUSTODY OF THOSE WHO FLY TO SANCTUARY.—The old law of sanctuary was, that any person guilty of felony might fly to a church or consecrated place, and there remain in security for forty days, after which he was to be allowed no food. Within the forty days he was at liberty to abjure the realm; which was to submit to perpetual banishment by forswearing the kingdom, upon a public confession of guilt before the king's coroner or bailiff at the church-door.[6] Sanctuaries have long since been abolished by statute.[7]

---

[1] Termes de la Ley.; and also the first charter of Charles I., where *issues royal* for the misconduct of magistrates are spoken of.

[2] Madox's Hist. Exch. vol. i. pp. 140, 141.

[3] Hale's Pleas of the Crown, vol. i. ch. lii., and Coke's 2nd Inst. p. 165; and also p. 28, where judicial and ministerial authorities are shown to be subject to amerciament for escapes.

[4] Hale's Pleas of the Crown, vol. i. ch. lii.; and Madox's Hist. Exch., chapter on Amerciaments.

[5] Vide *supra*, p. 292.

[6] Termes de la Ley. Blacks. Comm. vol. iv. p. 332. Coke's 3rd Inst. p. 216.

[7] 21st James I. ch. xxviii.

SANCTUARIES.   CLERK OF THE MARKET.   355

When any person fled to a sanctuary, the vill in which it was situated was charged with the custody of such person until he left the kingdom under adjuration, or was brought to justice.[1] The old reports and authorities refer so often to amerciaments levied for escapes of felons from sanctuary, that we may plainly gather this privilege of sanctuary gave frequent occasion to extortion and abuse.

MARSHAL OR CLERK OF THE MARKET OF THE KING'S HOUSEHOLD TO EXERCISE NO JURISDICTION WITHIN THE CITY, NOR DRAW OUT THE CITIZENS TO PLEAD BEFORE HIM.—The king's market, held at his palace gate, we have already noticed.[2] This market of the king's *household* had been disused for ages; but a similar jurisdiction to that which the clerk of the market of the king's household possessed was exercised by him at most other markets throughout the kingdom, as incident to the market itself;[3] and it subsists with diminished authority to this day. His office was to punish deceit in false weights and measures; and for that purpose he held a court, and tried by jury.[4] His power being continually abused for the purpose of extorting fines, in which he was interested as a sharer, this jurisdiction became a constant subject of complaint and of legislative restriction.[5] So late as 1607, Lord Coke, in his charge to a grand jury of Norwich, says: 'The 'clerk of the market will come down and call before him all 'weights and measures: if there is a fault, he and the informer 'share the penalty, but never redress the abuse. It was once 'my hap to take a clerk of the market in these tricks; *but I* '*advanced him higher than his father's son by so much as from* '*the ground to the top of the pillory.* If you of the jury, there-'fore, will present these offences, by God's grace they shall not 'go unpunished; for we have a coif, which signifies a skull, 'whereby in the execution of justice we are defended against 'all oppositions.'[6]

The clerk of the market of the king's household, and the

[1] Hale's Pleas of the Crown, vol. I. p. 605.
[2] Vide *supra*, pp. 108, 112, note 2.
[3] Coke's 2nd Inst. Articuli super Chartas, pp. 541, 542, 3rd Inst. p. 273; and Black. Comm. vol. iv. p. 275.
[4] Ibid.
[5] Ibid. and Barrington on Statutes, p. 340.
[6] Barrington on Statutes, p. 340.

other king's officers who held courts at Westminster, were continually harassing the citizens by assuming a jurisdiction over them, contrary to their chartered privileges :[1] and we have sufficiently explained how obnoxious such authority was. By Edward IV.'s first charter, the clerkship of the market in London was conferred upon the City.

THAT THE MAYOR SHALL BE ESCHEATOR.—Escheats are of feudal origin. The term signifies *something fallen*,[2] and is applied to lands fallen, or reverting into the hands of the lord or original owner, for want of heirs of the tenant. The term was applied generally, after the Norman Conquest, as well to all lands and tenements coming to the king's hands *under the ancient Saxon law*, whether accruing to him by way of forfeiture for offences or as belonging to him when there was no other owner, as to lands reverting to the king as *lord of the fee*, under the feudal system, for want of heirs; which want of heirs might occur either by natural or legal defect, as corruption of blood in consequence of treason or felony committed by the tenant.[3] There was this difference, however, between forfeitures under the Saxon law and escheats under the feudal law—that in cases of *treason* only, the lands vested *by way of forfeiture* to the king *for ever*; and in cases of *felony*, the king only enjoyed the profits of the land *during the felon's life*, and for one year after his death: but as by the feudal law any felony worked *corruption of blood*, and consequently a failure of heirs, the Norman kings claimed, *by way of escheat*, an absolute right to the land of convicted felons *for ever*, as ultimate lord of the fee.[4] This latter kind of escheat, properly so called, can hardly be considered as legally arising in the City of London; the citizens being, by their ancient customs and charters, lawworthy as they were in King Edward the Confessor's days, and consequently exempt from all feudal burthens, and enjoying their property under the Saxon or common-law tenure. It is probable, however, that the king did, in fact, as considering himself chief lord of the fee, assume lands and tenements *forfeited*

---

[1] Vide supra, p. 112, note 2. Pleas of the Crown, vol. ii. ch. xxiii.
[2] From *Eschoier Fr., excidere*. [4] Coke's 4th Inst. ch. xliii.; and
[3] Coke's 4th Inst. ch. xliii. Hale's Blackst. Comm. vol. iv. p. 381 et seq.

by the citizens, as well for felony as for treason, as coming to
him by way of escheat for want of legal heirs.

These escheats, arising to the king both in his regal capacity, and as lord of his various fees, were most extensive throughout England in the earlier Norman times.[1] Those which arose by way of forfeiture were held to apply as well to *interests* in land as to the land itself; nor were they confined at all times to cases of treason and felony, but sometimes included trespasses and misdemeanours.[2] For the purpose of ascertaining and securing these royal rights, officers called escheators were commissioned, whose duty it was to manage and account for the proceeds of escheats, and to adjudicate, by the intervention of a jury, upon the title of the crown in respect of them; though, with regard to smaller escheats, the sheriffs occasionally exercised both these official capacities, particularly where estates escheated by forfeiture.[3] Sometimes the king constituted courts by especial commission to enquire into escheats; but it became, like all other prerogative claims, more prominently a subject of the inquisitions by the justices in eyre.[4]

When it is recollected with what rigour and zeal all claims of the crown were enforced, we shall be at no loss to appreciate the importance of the office of escheator, or the value of that privilege by which the citizens, for their greater security from oppression, executed that office by their own appointed magistrate.[5]

CONSTABLE OF THE TOWER TO TAKE NO PRISES OF VICTUALS, &c.—*Prisage* was a term applied to various maritime and port customs; but it was usually intended to signify custom levied upon wine,[6] from which the citizens were not exempted by the ninth charter of Henry III., but are exempted by a subsequent clause in this charter. As prisage of wine was called a *great* custom, the mere *general* exemption from sea-customs granted by previous charters would not include that,[7] but was understood merely to comprise all other prisages,

CHAP.
V.

[1] Madox's Hist. Exch. vol. i. ch. x.
[2] Ibid.
[3] Ibid. and Coke's 4th Inst. ch. xliii.; and Hale's Pleas of the Crown, vol. i. ch. xxiii.
[4] Madox's Hist. Exch. vol. i. ch. x.
[5] Charter of Edward IV. post.
[6] Hargrave's Tracts. Hale concerning Customs, chaps. i., ii., & iii.
[7] Ibid. and vide 9th Charter of Henry III. Prisage of Wines, p. 328.

such as those taken by the constable of the Tower upon victuals coming up the river in the smaller craft, which were considered as *petty* customs, or, more properly speaking, tolls.¹ Accordingly, this charter does not profess to *grant*, but rather to *confirm*, the exemption from prises or customs of the inferior kind. In respect to the prisage of wine, or prisage absolutely so called, the charter declares in a distinct clause that they *shall be quit of it.* So highly was the prisage of wine considered, that a grant in general terms of prises, even by name, would not convey the former custom; because, there being many smaller sorts of prises or customs, they were rather considered to be intended by such general grant than this more important prerogative duty.²

The smaller prises were levied upon every sort of provision coming by water to London, by the constable of the Tower,³ either for the king's use or that of the king's grantee; and the places for levying them were at Billingsgate and Queenhithe, which were at one time almost the only quays in London.⁴ It is probable that such customs became due only in respect of the quay, for the *constable* is forbidden to take any prises; but the *citizens* after the purchase of Queenhithe certainly did take them from foreigners down to a very late period. If these customs were due in any other right than by way of toll at the quay, the exemption of the *citizens* from petty customs would not interfere with the constable's authority to levy them from others; but if they were due in right of the quay, the prohibition to the constable from levying them from all persons, strangers as well as citizens, would be consistent with the chartered transfer of this quay, which we have already mentioned.

It was the practice of the constable of the Tower to arrest ships and boats coming to London, when he suspected any attempt to avoid the quay customs.⁵ Afterwards, although the right may perhaps have ceased, yet it would seem the practice was still continued of taking prises, and arresting the vessels for the purpose of enforcing payment.⁶

---

¹ Hale concerning Customs, ch. iii.
² Ibid.
³ Strype's Stow, vol. i. book iii. p. 211 *et seq.*
⁴ Ibid. and vide *supra*, p. 321 *et seq.*
⁵ Ibid. Fabian, part vii. fol. 33.
⁶ Ibid.

PRISAGES FORBIDDEN. REGISTRY OF CHARTERS.   359

Whatever may have been the justice of the claim, the injurious effects of it in lawless times must have been most serious upon the prosperity and traffic of the City, whether such claim was enforced upon the citizens or only upon strangers. This clause in the present charter must, therefore, have been of great importance, though without doubt the peculiar exemption from so heavy a duty as that of prisage of wine, being at the rate of one-fifteenth of the whole cargo,¹ was rated much higher. This latter privilege, however, great as it was formerly,² has now become of very inconsiderable importance, since the national revenue has become almost altogether statutable, and made to bear with more equal pressure on all classes of the community.

ONE WRIT TO SUFFICE FOR ALLOWANCE OF CHARTERS IN EACH KING'S REIGN.—The justices in eyre were used to require all who claimed any franchises or chartered privileges to present such claims before them for allowance and registry of record, whenever they came; and, notwithstanding the charters had been solemnly granted and registered before, still the same ceremonies of claims and registry were exacted.³ The palpable object of this practice was to extort money;⁴ for not only did the justices levy a fine upon the registry, but they sought every means of disallowing the claims, and imposing heavy mulcts, by way of redemption for pretended forfeitures.⁵ This was continually remonstrated against as a heavy grievance throughout the kingdom,⁶ and was in all probability the main reason for the opposition so often manifested by the citizens to attend the inquisitions held by the justices in eyre at the Tower.

CITIZENS TO BE TAXED AS THE COMMONALTY, AND NOT AS MEN OF A CITY.—That is, the citizens claimed exemption from tallages, which were arbitrary levies upon *demesnes*, and claimed to be considered in regard to taxation on the same

CHAP. V.

¹ Hargrave's Tracts. Hale concerning Customs, ch. ii.
² The old Reports abound in cases of this claim by the citizens.
³ Vide *supra*, p. 80, note 4, and authorities; and Stat. de quo Warr.

Coke's 2nd Inst. p. 493. Termes de la Leg. 'Claim.'
⁴ Ibid. and the numerous *fines* for liberties. Madox's Hist. Exch. vol. i. ch. xi.
⁵ Ibid.   ⁶ Ibid.

footing as the freemen of counties. Tallages and demesne burthens we have already sufficiently considered.¹

KING'S OFFICERS NOT TO TRADE IN GOODS BELONGING TO THEIR OFFICES.—When we consider that not only the wants of the king's immensely numerous household, but a very great part of the national revenue, was in these times collected by inland tolls and customs on the goods and merchandise of the people, we may form some conjecture of the number and powers of the king's officers spread over the whole kingdom. The purveyors, the king's clerk of the market, the officers of the royal household, the king's butler, were all armed with powers which enabled them to get into their hands merchandise and provision to an almost unlimited extent, professedly for the king's use, at rates and prices much inferior to their real value. It may be easily inferred, therefore what means they would possess of extortion, and what interest in exercising them, if they were allowed to trade in the merchandise in which their offices were concerned. It was to curb these abuses that the present clause of this charter was framed; and for the citizens' more complete security, as well as that of the people at large, it was provided that these officers should trade neither within nor without the City.²

LANDS OF CITIZENS LYING WITHOUT THE CITY TO BE LIABLE TO KEEP THE CITY HARMLESS IN MATTERS CONCERNING THEIR OFFICES, AS WELL AS THOSE WITHIN.—Previous charters had provided that the citizens should be liable to satisfy the ferm and things appertaining to the sheriffwick (though not amerciaments imposed *personally* on the sheriff), in case of the sheriff's default.³ And it had been especially provided by statute, that whole districts should not be fined in common for the particular offence of any individual.⁴ Still, however, when any ministerial officer, other than the

---

¹ Vide *supra*, pp. 30 *et seq.* 51, 88. note 2; and Sullivan's Lectures, Lect. 16.

² For a more detailed proof and explanation of positions in the text, vide Barrington on Statutes, p. 42; Coke's 2nd, 3rd, and 4th Inst. Index 'Officers,' 'Purveyors,' 'Counting-house;' and 4th Inst. Articles against Cardinal Wolsey, p. 89 *et seq*. Vide pp. 108, 122, note 5.

³ Vide *supra*, p. 312, and notes.

⁴ Vide *supra*, p. 110.

sheriff, was amerced and could not pay, or when he or any other civic authority could not discharge his accounts, it was the practice, according to ancient usage, to distrain for such amerciament or debts upon the citizens at large:[1] and as the king looked to the City for these payments by the hands of the City sheriff, whose jurisdiction was bounded by the district, it might have been conceived that there was some irregularity, if not illegality, in resorting to lands or tenements of the citizens situate elsewhere. It was usual, if the citizens did not immediately pay, in a case of default, to seize the whole city into the king's hands, and appoint a custos.[2] The exemption of the citizens from such consequences, while the defaulters had the means of satisfying their debts, will explain the nature and reasons of this clause.

ALL INQUISITIONS BY THE KING'S JUSTICES AND MINISTERS (EXCEPT THOSE AT THE TOWER AND AT THE GAOL-DELIVERY AT NEWGATE) TO BE TAKEN AT ST. MARTIN'S-LE-GRAND.— The City of London possessed by ancient prescription a right, confirmed by charter, of exclusive jurisdiction in pleas of the crown.[3] This, however, did not prevent the king from exercising, by his commissioned judges and others, various judicial functions over the citizens both within and without the walls. Many of these functions were no doubt legal, though others would be hard to reconcile with the chartered privileges of the citizens. The king's coroner, his escheator, and probably some other of his judicial officers, possessed a clear right of jurisdiction within the City,[4] until their functions were transferred to the civic authorities. The king's judges would likewise sit with legal powers at the gaol-delivery at Newgate, associated with the lord mayor; and over the lord mayor and all other citizens at the eyres held at the Tower,

---

[1] Madox's Firma Burgi, ch. ix. & x.; and vide supra, p. 307.

[2] This system of levying the king's debts and amerciaments due by ministerial officers is fully explained and detailed in Madox's Firma Burgi, ch. ix. and x.—Vide also supra, p. 307.

[3] Charter of Henry I., and notes on the passage.

[4] The coroner's jurisdiction was formerly much more extensive than at present. Besides his inquisitions upon violent deaths, which so often led to those forfeitures called deodands, he enquired of waifs, treasure-trove, &c., and abjurations. The king's collectors of customs also held their inquisitions.— Madox's Hist. Exch. vol. i. p. 784; and vide First Charter of Richard II.

for adjudicating upon claims of franchises and the default and misconduct of the civic magistrates. It was not unusual, however, for the king's judges to *hold inquisitions* in criminal matters, and also to *try pleas of the crown* within the City — practice always remonstrated against by the citizens as contrary to law.[1]

By the old common law no inquisitions in criminal matters were held, or pleas of the crown tried, except at the sheriff and the barons' leets, or by the king's sworn judges specially assigned. The *trial* of pleas of the crown was taken away from the leets by Magna Charta; but inquisitions, in the sense of *charges presented* by a grand or rather leet jury, were still taken by the sheriffs and lords of the leet, though more commonly by the grand jury before the king's judges, who likewise tried them. Frequently, however, the king sent judges merely to take criminal inquisitions, which were to be tried by a subsequently constituted tribunal,[2] of which there is a remarkable instance in the second year of this reign; when such a commission of inquisition was issued to the lord mayor, who with his associated justices was afterwards commissioned to try the inquisitions taken.[3]

In the first year of the present reign *justices of the peace* were established. Their original jurisdiction was merely to *keep* or preserve the peace by their individual authority, which was, in fact, to exercise the authority of the sheriff in that particular. But afterwards they were empowered to take inquisitions, and also to *hear and determine* them; and thus the jurisdiction, so well known, of the sessions of the peace came to be founded throughout the realm.[4] This jurisdiction was not specifically conferred on the civic authorities until the reign of Edward IV.

Thus we find a very considerable judicial authority was exercised within the City walls, at this period, both of a civil and criminal kind, calculated to excite jealousy in the minds of the citizens. That the inquisitions here mentioned, when

---

[1] Fabian, pp. 440, 444; and vide *supra*, pp. 86, 112, and notes.
[2] Madox's Hist. Exch. vol. i. p. 140 *et seq.* Maitland's Hist. vol. i. p. 123.
[3] Ibid.
[4] Hale's Pleas of the Crown, vol. ii p. 41.

ken of criminal matters, were more than mere *inquisitions*,
d not *pleas* of the crown, or criminal *trials*, the instance
ove referred to would incline us to disbelieve. That they
terwards gradually became actual sessions of the peace for
ials may be reasonably conjectured: for after the coroner-
ip was granted to the commonalty, and the lord mayor and
dermen came to be justices of the peace in the modern
nse of the word, it was an object to the citizens to have
is court (which we find by the present charter is granted,
a special privilege, to be held *without* the City jurisdiction,
hich St. Martin's-le-Grand was), held *within* it again; and
was so allowed by the charter of Henry VIII., and the lord
ayor and aldermen have held their sessions of the peace ac-
rdingly at Guildhall ever since.

SECOND CHARTER OF EDWARD III.[1]

This charter is directed, 'To all to whom these presents
should come.' It recites a petition of the citizens to the
ing in parliament, complaining that malefactors escaped
nto the village of Southwark, out of the jurisdiction of the
ity, and praying that such village may be granted to them.
The charter, with the consent of parliament, grants the village
t feefarm.[2]

THIRD CHARTER OF EDWARD III.[3]

This charter (which was granted in parliament) recites the
statute of 9th Edward III. c. 1, by which it was enacted, that
all merchants, strangers and English, might trade freely in all

---

[1] Dated March 6, 1st year. To be found in the Inspeximus charters of 7th Richard II. and of Charles II.

[2] The farm-rent was 10*l.* per annum (Strype's *Stow*, vol. ii. p. 2; and First Charter Edward IV.) All that was intended by this grant of Southwark was the shrieval or rather bailiff's jurisdiction over it, which at this time was in most respects merely ministerial. All judicial and seignorial rights, though often contended for by the citizens in this and subsequent reigns under this charter, were not granted to them until the reign of Edward IV.

[3] Dated March 26, 11th year. To be found and directed as the last.

kinds of wares¹ and merchandise in all cities and privileg*
towns, notwithstanding their charters or customs to the co*
trary. It then quotes Magna Charta, by which the liberti*
and customs of London are confirmed, and testifies the kin*
desire that the articles of the Great Charter should be o*
served, and disclaims any intention to infringe them by t*
late statute. It grants that the citizens shall enjoy all th*
liberties and customs notwithstanding the aforesaid statute*

The policy of Edward, in encouraging the introducti*
of foreign merchants and artificers into this kingdom, h*
been before alluded to.² The infringement upon the civ*
right of exclusive trade by the statute of 9th Edward III. c*
was too palpable to be overlooked; and its effects, no doub*
were immediately and severely felt; for we find that it w*
promptly remonstrated against, and remedied. Clear as th*
language of this charter is, yet, as far as regards wholes*
dealing by foreigners with foreigners, its provisions seem t*
have been continually violated, either in open defiance, or b*
a strained construction as to their extent. Petitions and r*
monstrances were continually presented and made to th*
crown, until the civic exclusive rights of trade, both quali*
fied wholesale and retail, were finally established by repeate*
statutes passed from time to time down to the reign o*
Henry VII.³

FOURTH CHARTER OF EDWARD III.⁴

This charter, which was granted June 3, in the 15th yea*
of Edward III.'s reign, is an Inspeximus charter confirmin*

---

¹ *Ponderable* wares they are called in the translations of the City charters; but the term should be *ponderable*, i.e. liable to *poundage*, a duty per pound taken from goods imported. This duty began in Edward I.'s reign, but was established more specifically in the reign of Edward III. by statute Carta Mercatoria, and 47th Edward III. (Hale concerning Customs, part iii. p. 173 *et seq.*) This poundage duty first occasioned the troubles of Charles I.'s reign.

² Vide *supra*. p. 113.

³ As to the nature of these right* and the difference between that b* wholesale and that by retail, vid *supra*, pp. 120, 194 note, 341 note. Vid also Petition 50th Edward III.; Cotton Records, Appendix 11; Rot. Parl. I* Richard II., Nos. 52, 156; Cahboye* l'aigre, p. 1; Stat. 9th Henry IV Coke's Reports, part viii. pp. 254, 256 and 20th Henry VII.

⁴ This charter is to be found in Lit*

ll the preceding charters. It further confirms a privilege
as existing by ancient custom,—that if any customs in 'the
said City, before that time obtained and used, were in any
part hard and defective, or any things in the same City
newly arising, in which no remedy had been ordained,
should need amendment,—the mayor and aldermen, with
the assent of the commonalty, might ordain thereunto a fit
'remedy, as often as it should seem expedient to them; so
'that such ordinance should be profitable to the king and to
'the citizens in general, and all other liege subjects resorting
'to the City, and also consonant to reason and good faith.'
The charter concludes by granting and conferring as 'of more
'abundant favour, that although the citizens may not have
'used some of their liberties, exemptions, articles, or free
'customs in their charters contained, on some occasions, they
'nevertheless may still fully enjoy them for ever.'

FIFTH CHARTER OF EDWARD III.[1]

This charter grants, 'for increase of the honour of the City,'
that the serjeants may, within the civic jurisdiction and without, when in the execution of their office, and on occasions of
ceremony when the civic magistrates go out to meet the king
or any of his family, bear maces of gold or silver, with the
king's arms or others thereon.

The bearing of the City *mace* of gold or silver granted by
this charter is a distinction of some peculiarity. The meaning of the word *mace* seems to be no more than *club* (*massa*);
and the *serjeants at mace*, as they are called, were originally

---

Alb., and is referred to in the Inspeximus charter of 7th Richard II. It is
quoted in Wagoner's case, Coke's Reports, part viii. p. 241; and by Maitland, vol. i. p. 126. As it is not to be
found in Cotton's Abridgment, it may
be presumed that it was not a charter
in parliament. The first clause is a
confirmation of an ancient custom of
the City to make bye-laws.

[1] Dated June 10, 28th year. To be

found in the Inspeximus charters of
Richard II. and Charles II., and also
in the Lib. Alb. There is a record of a
petition to the king in parliament from
Nottingham, in Cotton's Abridgment,
8th Edward III, that no City serjeants
or any but king's serjeants should bear
maces of other metal than of copper,
which is granted with an exception in
favour of London.

O MAKE ORDINANCES.

...ers. It further confirms a privilege
custom,—that if any customs in 'the
...t time obtained and used, were in any
...tive, or any things in the same City
which no remedy had been ordained,
...ment,—the mayor and aldermen, with
...mmonalty, might ordain thereunto a fit
...s it should seem expedient to them; so
...se should be profitable to the king and to
...neral, and all other liege subjects resorting
also consonant to reason and good faith.'
...ludes by granting and conferring as 'of more
...r, that although the citizens may not have
their liberties, exemptions, articles, or free
...ir charters contained on some occasions, they
may still fully enjoy them for ever.'

FIFTH CHARTER OF EDWARD III.

...rter grants, 'for increase of the honour of the City.'
...rjeants may, within the civic jurisdiction and within the execution of their office, and on occasions of
...when the civic magistrates go out to meet the king
...'his family, bear maces of gold or silver, with the
...rms or others thereon.

...earing of the City mace of gold or silver granted by
...arter is a distinction of some peculiarity. The mean-
the word mace seems to be no more than club (massa);
...se serjeants at mace, as they are called, were originally

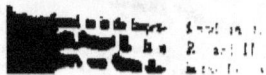

BOOK II.

only the *summoners* or executors of legal process, who were usually termed in Latin *servientes ad clavam*, and who, according to the ancient forms of law amongst all the northern nations of Europe, always performed their office by the exhibition of some wand or club.¹ The more ancient name however of these officers in England was that of beadle (Beodel, Goth.) from Beos, *to bid*.² These officers, though probably of some consideration in ancient times, had long before the date of the present charter sunk to the lowest station amongst the retainers of the law; but the macebearer, who at this period occupied what was perhaps the beadle's original station, seems to have sprung from a different origin, had different functions to fulfil, and enjoyed a higher rank in society. In fact, he seems to have been originally the ancient *esquire*; for, according to ancient records, the persons who ranked next to knights were sometimes termed *servientes ad arma*.³ Accordingly we find the king's macebearer is called his *serjeant at arms*; as are also the macebearers of the two houses of parliament and of the lord chancellor: and the macebearers of the two Universities are still called the *esquire beadles*. The macebearer, as well as the sword-bearer and water-bailiff, in London have always been deemed esquires by virtue of their offices. The grant, therefore, of gold or silver maces, such as preceded the king and the higher dignitaries of state, instead of copper, which were borne by other cities, was a most distinguishing mark of honour conferred on the City, but has no other import.⁴

---

¹ Ed. Rev. vol. xxxiv. p. 185.
² Spelm. Gloss. and Lye's Dict.
³ Seld. Tit. Hon. p. 850.
⁴ It has been a subject of dispute, from the difference in the accounts of the chroniclers, whether the Lord Mayor Walworth did not kill Wat Tyler with a blow from his mace by way of arresting him, or whether he killed him with his dagger. If the first statement is correct, we may reasonably enquire how the mace came into the mayor's own hands (except indeed by the mere impulse of the moment—*furor arma ministrat*), and still more why it came to be used for the purposes of *arrest*. It appears plain from a contemporary record, drawn up in the fourth year of the reign of Richard II., that Walworth slew this rebel chief with his *sword*.—Vide Riley's *Memorials of the City of London*, p. 449.

CHAPTER VI.

FIRST CHARTER OF RICHARD II.—PROTECTION OF PERSONS ENGAGED IN THE KING'S SERVICE NOT TO AVAIL AGAINST SUITS FOR VICTUALS—SECOND CHARTER OF RICHARD II.—FIRST CHARTER OF HENRY IV.—CUSTODY OF CITY GATES—TOLLS OF MARKETS—SECOND CHARTER OF HENRY IV.—FIRST AND SECOND CHARTERS OF HENRY V.—CHARTER OF HENRY VI.—GRANT OF FINES AND FORFEITURES FOR CRIMES—CHATTELS OF FUGITIVE FELONS; ALSO WAIFS, ESTRAYS, ETC.—COMMON LAND WITHIN THE CITY—FORFEITURES AND IMPROVEMENTS—FIRST CHARTER OF EDWARD IV.—CERTIFYING CITY CUSTOMS BY THE RECORDER—SECOND CHARTER OF EDWARD IV.—TRONAGE—THIRD CHARTER OF EDWARD IV.—PURCHASING IN MORTMAIN—FOURTH CHARTER OF EDWARD IV.—SCAVAGE—PACKAGE—PICAGE, ETC.—PORTAGE.

FIRST CHARTER OF RICHARD II.[1]

This is an Inspeximus charter reciting and confirming almost all the preceding charters, with some additional clauses.[2] It was a charter granted in parliament, or, in

---

[1] In the Inspeximus roll of Charles II., another charter, of 4th December (50th Edward III.) is inserted, in which the petition by the citizens mentioned in this charter is recited, and which petition is stated, in the body of the charter quoted in the Inspeximus, to *have been granted*. This, however, is a mistake. The citizens petitioned against the effects of the statute 9th Edward III. as affecting their exclusive rights both in respect of wholesale and retail trade (vide *supra*, p. 151, note); the commons in parliament, in the 51st year of the same king, supported the City petition by a petition of their own, which recited it. The king, thus pressed, granted the petition as far as regarded retail trade (vide Cotton's *Abridgment*, p. 147; and Cotton's *Records*, MS. Brit. Mus. Appendix 2). The citizens were by no means satisfied, and Edward dying immediately after, another petition was presented through parliament to his infant successor, which produced the present charter. This charter is not noticed in the Inspeximus of Charles II., though so much of its contents as is above alluded to is quoted in that Inspeximus as granted by Edward III. The author has seen this charter (bearing date 4th December, 1st Richard II.), with the seal appended, in a most perfect state in the Town Clerk's office. It is also noted in the Liber Albus, and in the Inspeximus of 7th Richard II. The substance of it is also quoted in the Cotton Records of Parliament, Rot. Parl. Rich. I. Nos. 52, 156; and vide Cotton MSS. Brit. Mus. Appendix 2, and his Abridgment, pp. 165, 166. Vide also Calthorpe's *Usages*.

[2] The charters before abstracted, not expressly recited in this Inspeximus

other words, an act of parliament, though passing in form of a charter with the king's seal, which was customary in early times.¹

All the charters recited, and all the liberties, franchises, and customs of the citizens, are there confirmed, with a clause similar to that in the close of the fourth charter of Edward III., declaring that they shall still enjoy them, notwithstanding that they may not sometimes have been used, and even although they may have sometimes been abused.

The charter then proceeds to recite a petition exhibited by the citizens to the king in parliament, setting forth that they used and enjoyed certain free customs in the City until of late years, when the citizens had been unjustly molested—viz. that no foreigner should buy of or sell to another foreigner any merchandise within the liberties of the City, on pain of forfeiting such merchandise, which custom the king confirms, excepting the merchants of Aquitaine.²

The charter next alludes to that part of the citizens' petition which sets forth the nature of the tenure by which the City is held as being immediately of the king himself, and that consequently, the citizens were not bound to obey precepts or process of any inferior authorities or jurisdictions—such as constables, marshals, admirals, or others—but only those of the king's own justices, and those at the king's suit under the great or privy seal, according to their charter. This privilege the king declares shall be enjoyed according to ancient usage.³

---

charter of Richard II., are—1st, the charter of William the Conqueror: 2nd, that of Henry I.: 3rd, that of Henry II.: 4th, the two charters of Richard I.: 5th, the five charters of John: 6th, the second, third, sixth, and eighth charters of Henry III.: 7th, the second charter of Edward II. But the substance of most of these charters is contained in those which are recited by way of Inspeximus in this charter.

¹ Prince's Case, Coke's Rep. Cotton's Abridgment, p. 165. Rot. Parl. Rich. I., No. 52, 156. Cotton MSS. Brit. Mus. Appendix 2.

² These were the French merchants of Guienne and Bourdeaux ; which provinces, descending to the kings of England from Henry II., became the scene of great contests in Edward III.'s wars, who constituted these provinces into the principality of Aquitaine. Their peculiar privileges have been before noticed.—Vide supra, pp. 111. 120, 189 et seq.

³ This clause seems to be merely a confirmation of those exclusive rights of jurisdiction granted by the charter of Henry I., and confirmed by others. These exclusive rights of jurisdiction have been fully commented on under the charter of Henry I.

FIRST CHARTER OF RICHARD III. PROTECTIONS.   369

It is then granted, that inquisitions shall be taken by the citizens themselves, and not by others, for all customs and impositions, and also for all purprestures, and other things of that nature, arising within the City.[1]

The charter further grants to the mayor and chamberlain the custody of all orphans, and the keeping of their lands and goods.[2]

Also that no *protections* granted by the king to persons making voyages upon his service should be valid after the voyage or the service was performed; against pleas of debt brought by citizens for victuals supplied, or against pleas of debt, account, or trespass, wherein a citizen is plaintiff, and the cause of action beyond ten pounds.

That no writs shall issue to bring up a man, confined in Newgate or other City prison for debts or damages adjudged to citizens, before the court of Exchequer to answer debts of the king or others sued in that court; unless the latter debts, upon due examination, shall prove genuine and not feigned,[3] and to have become due before the imprisonment.

It is also granted, if any difficulty or ambiguity should arise upon any article of the charters capable of various senses, that the king, with consent of his council, upon being required, will put such interpretation on it as shall be consistent with good faith and reason.

Lastly, All former charters, and all other rights, liberties, &c. therein expressed, are confirmed; so that, however, the citizens shall not be restrained, by reason of the language of the confirmations here made, in the enjoyment of any of their former liberties and approved customs.

NO PROTECTION OF THE KING TO BE VALID AGAINST PLEAS FOR VICTUALS.—The protections granted by the king against arrest or imprisonment in any suits at law, or for delay in the progress of them, on behalf of particular indivi-

---

[1] The king's judges, but more frequently his coroners and collectors of customs, used to take these inquisitions, commonly called *inquests of office*.—Vide *supra*, p. 361, and the notes. For 'Purprestures,' vide charter of Henry VI.

[2] For an explanation of this clause, vide first charter of James I. 'Office of measurer.'

[3] That is, not feigned for the purpose of giving jurisdiction to the court of Exchequer.

duals supposed to be in the king's service, so contrary to every principle of law and justice, were very common at the period of the present charter. To add to the scandal of the practice, these protections were usually *purchased*; and the records of the king's Exchequer court testify the extent of such abuses.¹ The nature of the system of purveyance by which the king in his progresses and his retinue were supplied with necessaries, has been before commented upon.² The system of purveyance was not the only source of prerogative interference with the legal remedies of the subject: and it is astonishing to contemplate the list of protections granted at this period, and the pretences on which they were founded.³ Whenever the king was disposed to find or feign employment for an individual, the service on which he was engaged was always sufficient to entitle him to the king's protection from all suits during such service. Perhaps the most excusable occasion was that alluded to in the text, when those concerned in victualling vessels by purveyance for expeditions on the royal or public service were protected during the performance of their official duties. From the time of Edward III. to that of Henry IV., scarcely a parliament was held in which the abuses of protections were not remonstrated against.⁴

SECOND CHARTER OF RICHARD II.⁵

This charter is continually spoken of in the older law authorities, and often referred to in records, as the grand charter of confirmation of all the City liberties, franchises, and customs. It is a transcript, *verbatim*, of the last charter, confirming by *inspeximus* that and all the preceding charters recited or referred to in it. The grant was made in parlia-

---

¹ Madox's Hist. Exch.
² Vide *supra*, pp. 108 *et seq.*, 247.
³ Cotton's Abridg. Index, title 'Protections;' and Madox's Hist. Exch.
⁴ Cotton's Abridgment, Index, title 'Protections.' The granting royal protections has long ceased in practice; but the name still survives in the verbiage of Acts of Parliament. Whenever penalties are created, it is still usual to add, that no wager of law essoin or *protection* shall be allowed.
⁵ Dated in the 7th year, directed as the last, and to be found in Liber Albus.

ment, as the last was; and from the date we may conjecture
that it was intended as a ratification of the former charter by
the king, on attaining an age of greater discretion, and in
deference to the services of the citizens and their celebrated
mayor Walworth on the occasion of Tyler's rebellion.[1] It is
a copy of that of the 1st of Richard II.[2]

FIRST CHARTER OF HENRY IV.[3]

This charter grants the custody of Newgate and Ludgate,
as well as all other gates of the City; likewise the gathering
of tolls and customs in Cheap, in Billingsgate, and in Smithfield. It further grants the *tronage*,[4] i.e. the weighing of
goods.

SECOND CHARTER OF HENRY IV.[5]

This charter refers to the statute of 7th Henry IV. cap. 9,
by which merchant strangers were allowed to sell *in gross* (that
is, by *wholesale*) to all the king's subjects as well as to the citizens of London, which was contrary to the franchises of the

---

[1] Vide *supra*, pp. 117, 366, note.

[2] Chamberlain of London's Case, Coke's Reports, part v. Calthorpe's Usages, p. 1. The case of Player and Hutchins, Harg. MSS. Brit. Mus. No. 58, fo. 26, 27. Strype's Stow, vol ii. p. 343, quotes the names of the witnesses, and says, 'One if not two charters were granted by Richard II.' Vide also the quo warranto case; Coke's Reports, part viii. p. 163; and Jones's Reports, p. 283.

[3] To be found in the Inspeximus of Charles II. dated May 26, 1st year. The charter is not stated in full in that Inspeximus, but is said to grant as in the text, 'amongst other things.' For an explanation of the purport of this charter, vide *supra*, pp. 67, 361, and notes.

The custody of the gates seems to be granted for the purpose of collecting the tolls which might grow due there for the transit of merchandise, &c. Madox's Hist. Exch. vol. i. cap. 18, s. 4, and for guarding the City gates, which were also used as prisons. This charter can only be considered as confirmatory of the ancient rights of the City; and in all probability arose out of some peculiar circumstance or claims.

[4] Vide 2nd charter of Edward IV.

[5] This is rather a statute than a charter. It is dated 9th year, and was passed to repeal, as far as regarded London, the stat. 7th Henry IV. cap. 9, by which strangers were allowed to sell by wholesale in London.—Vide Coke's Reports, part viii. p. 254. 4th Inst. p. 249. Cotton's Abridgment. p. 466, and his Records, Brit. Mus.

citizens; and it declares, that no merchant stranger shall traffic by buying of or selling to any other merchant stranger in London for the purpose of selling again, but only for their own use.

FIRST AND SECOND CHARTERS OF HENRY V.[1]

These two charters merely confirm all former charters, customs, and franchises in general terms.

CHARTER OF HENRY VI.—FINES AND FORFEITURES—PURPRESTURES.

This charter grants to the citizens all fines and forfeitures for crimes, chattels of fugitive felons, and also waifs, estrays, common soils, purprestures and improvements, wastes, streets, ways, &c. in the City and suburbs, and in the waters of the Thames, within the limits of the City, and all the profits and rents to be derived therefrom.

PURPRESTURES AND IMPROVEMENTS.—The word *purpresture* is often used in law books as synonymous with nuisance;[2] but, although a purpresture may sometimes be a nuisance, the term seems more strictly applicable to an *encroachment*, which may possibly be an *improvement* and a public benefit. It is not reasonable to suppose that this grant of *purprestures* could be construed to authorise public nuisances; still less to give the City a property in them, especially on the Thames; though such an idea has been apparently entertained.[4] Lite-

---

[1] To be found in Liber Albus. The first is dated July 12, 2nd year; the second, October 6, 7th year.

[2] This charter still exists in the Town Clerk's office, and is copied in Liber Albus. It is only quoted in the Inspeximus of Charles II. as granting 'amongst other things' what is contained in the text, for the purpose of confirming such grant. It is dated 26th October, 23rd year. All grants of lands and tenements made by Henry VI. were declared void by a statute passed in his 28th year; but this grant of Henry VI. was confirmed again by charter in parliament 20th Henry VII.: but doubts still existing, it was regranted again by subsequent charters, and lastly by the general Inspeximus of Charles II. Vide Rex v. Mayor of London, 1 C. M. & R. i. 2; M. & C. 82.

[3] Blacks. Comm. vol. iv. p. 167.

[4] Rex v. Grosvenor and others. Starkie's N. P. Rep. vol. ii. p. 511.

ally, the word signifies *something engrossed or usurped*, and was used to express any invasion of landed property—as by building, or hunting over, or improving common ground, &c.[1]

FIRST CHARTER OF EDWARD IV.[2]

This ample charter begins by reciting that the duties and functions of justices of the peace, both in and out of sessions, had always been, and still were, exercised by the civic authorities, as other justices of the peace were used to exercise them under the statutes of the realm; and to remove all possible doubt as to the legality of such judicial authority, it then proceeds to grant, that the mayor and recorder, and all aldermen who have been mayors, shall be conservators of the peace,[3] to exercise all authority given to justices of the peace by statute, and the same persons (of whom the lord mayor shall always be one) shall sit as justices to hear and determine all felonies and misdemeanors:[4] and the sheriff is directed to give all needful assistance to them in the performance of their duty, saving to the mayor and commonalty all their customs, liberties, and franchises.

The charter then confirms the ancient custom of the City, of recording all City customs, upon certificate of the same made by the mouth of the recorder, before any of the king's justices, without request by jury, even though the citizens themselves be parties in the matter at issue.

It then grants, That the citizens shall fully enjoy all their liberties, 'acquittals, grants, ordinances, articles, and free 'customs,' whether they have been used or not used, and even though they may have been abused, without forfeiture or impeachment.

[1] Spelm. Gloss. Glanville by Beames, bk. 9. Coke's 4th Inst. p. 301.
[2] Dated 9th November, 2nd year: directed to all dignitaries of the realm *nominatim*, and to all the king's subjects generally. To be found in the Inspeximus of Charles II. and in Lib. Alb.
[3] That is, shall act as justices of the peace out of sessions.
[4] That is, shall act as justices of the peace at sessions. As to justices of the peace in London, see 1st charter of Edward III. 'Inquisitions to be taken at St. Martin's le Grand,' &c. pp. 345, 301; *post*, 396.

BOOK II.

It further grants, That all persons, strangers, aliens or denizens, inhabiting and trading within the City, shall contribute according to their faculties to all subsidies, tallages,[1] grants, and other contributions made for the use of the king or his heirs, or for the use of the City, excepting always the merchants of Almain.[2]

The charter further grants, in consideration of the duties of aldermen in the City, and their need of quiet and relaxation in retirement at their possessions in the country, that they shall not be required to serve in any respects as jurymen out of the said City;[3] or as collectors or comptrollers of the king's taxes or subsidies.

Lastly, it grants the borough of Southwark, in language professedly calculated to remove all doubts regarding the civic jurisdiction in that district.[4] It refers to the grant made by the charter of Edward III.; and to 'divers doubts, 'opinions, varieties, ambiguities, controversies, and dissen-'sions' which had arisen with regard to the exercise of the franchises thereby granted; for removing of which for ever it grants in detail, Southwark and its appurtenances, waifs and estrays,[5] treasure-trove, chattels of traitors and felons defamed,[6] escheats and forfeitures, as fully as the king would have had them were the town in his hands; and that the mayor and commonalty may put themselves in possession of all these goods: also that they should have assay and assize of victuals,[7] and exercise the jurisdiction of clerk of the

---

[1] Tallages had by this time become probably a *nomen generale* for taxes of any kind. In their primitive sense they could not be levied in the City. Vide *supra*, pp. 65, 66.

[2] These were the Hanse merchants, or merchants of the Steelyard. For an account of the nature of this establishment, vide *supra*, pp. 159 *et seq*. 167 *et sey*.

[3] Which they were otherwise bound to do by virtue of their residence beyond the City.

[4] Second charter of Edw. III., note 2. Vide *supra*, p. 363.

[5] Waifs were goods stolen and thrown away by the thief upon pursuit, which belonged either to the king or to the lord of the manor by his grant, unless the owner prosecuted promptly. Estrays were stray cattle, which belonged to the king or lord of the manor, unless claimed within a year and a day.

[6] That is, outlawed for felony; and so defamed by matter of record, which produced forfeiture of goods.

[7] The assay was the examination of the quality of provisions sold in the market, deceits in which were punishable by the pillory.—Vide Coke's 3rd Inst. p. 219. The assize was the fixing the price of provisions, a prerogative

market,[1] and have all forfeitures and amercinments: also the
execution of all process, without the interference of the king's
sheriff, or any of the king's officers: also an annual fair on the
7th, 8th, and 9th of September, with a court of *pye powder*:[2]
also a view of frankpledge, and 'all summons, attachments,
'arrests, issues, amerciaments, fines, redemptions, profits, and
'commodities,' pertaining to that jurisdiction: also, that the
mayor and commonalty may arrest all malefactors, and send
them to Newgate,[3] to be delivered according to law; and
generally 'all manner of liberties, privileges, franchises,
'acquittals, customs and rights whatsoever, although not
'expressly mentioned, as the king himself had a right to when
'the town was in his hands; the City paying the ancient
'form of 10l., and saving the rights of the archbishop of Can-
'terbury there:[4] any statute to the contrary notwithstanding.'

CERTIFYING CITY CUSTOMS BY THE RECORDER'S WORD OF
MOUTH.—This custom of certifying the law by word of mouth
is of very high antiquity, and may be traced to the practice
of the ancient and unlettered Scandinavian nations. It was
usual on trials at law amongst the northern nations, who are
considered to have derived their system of jurisprudence from
the same Gothic sources which originally supplied our Saxon
and common law, to have the judgments *recorded*, not in
writing, but by the *oral testimony* of witnesses, whenever the
law, already decided, was inquired about; which witnesses
attended the trials for that express purpose. In the Grand
Custumier of Normandy, it is said 'the king may himself
'*record* decisions made by him, or he may substitute three
'other witnesses'—'but a *record* of the Exchequer shall be

---

[1] exercised time out of mind by the civic authorities, and sanctioned by statute. Interference in market prices was not considered injurious until of late years; assize of bread is now abolished by statute.

[2] Vide supra, p. 105, *mire*; and 1st charter of Edward III.

[3] A court incident to all fairs, held before the steward of the lord of the fair, for adjudicating on all contracts arising at the fair. Vide Coke's 4th Inst. p. 272.

[4] This clause was repealed by statute 8th Edward IV. Vide Cotton's Abridgment, p. 683. It was repealed by the charter of Edward VI.

[5] The Archbishop held the Monastery of Bermondsey in Southwark until the time of Henry VIII., when the monasteries fell into the king's hands; Edward VI. then granted it to the City. Vide his charter, and Strype's Stow, vol. ii. p. 1.

'made by seven witnesses sworn to *record* the truth. Every
'record ought to be made according to what has been said
'and heard.'[1] So again it is said in the Assizes of Jerusalem,[2]
'he who would have judgments in his favour firm, should
'take care to have many friends in court who can well under-
'stand and who have good memories, so that they may know
'how to *record* the plea when it may be required.' This
plainly shows the source of the City law and customs, as well
as the tenacity with which the citizens retained their ancient
forms, in defiance of the Norman improvements and invasions
in jurisprudence.

SECOND CHARTER OF EDWARD IV.[3]—TRONAGE.

This charter grants the tronage of wools brought to London
or to the staple[4] at Westminster, and the housing of such
wools at Leadenhall; with all fees due in respect thereof.

The weighing (*tronage*) of goods brought to the staple
markets, and the warehousing them, was required for the
purpose of ensuring the payment of the king's customs, which
upon wools in particular, were with reference to the times of
large extent.[5] In receiving fees for passing the king's beam,
for measuring, for coquetting, &c. the king's officers were
continually guilty of great abuses.[6] The keeping of the
king's beam for weighing customable goods became therefore,
like most of the petty privileges of the citizens, a valuable
protection from extortion.

To ensure the payment of the king's customs was probably

---

[1] Grand Cust. de Norm. cap. 102, 103, 104, 107. Edinb. Rev. vol. xxxiv. p. 190. Vide also the report of a case tried in a court of Scandinavian extraction (in Ireland) of the date A.D. 931, in which the mode of recording a previous judgment by witnesses on a subsequent trial is detailed.—Edinb. Rev. vol. xxxvi. p. 203.

[2] Grand Cust. de Norm. cap. 45.

[3] Dated 27th August, 3rd year. Directed and to be found as the last, vide supra, pp. 329, 335, 385.

[4] For an explanation of the nature of staples and markets staple, vide *supra*, p. 242.

[5] Coke's Rep. part v. p. 61. Anderson's Hist. Com. vol. i. pp. 216, 231, 254, 315. Madox's Hist. Exch. vol. i. cap. 18; and Hale on Customs, part iii. *passim*, and ch. xxi.

[6] Hale on Customs, part iii. ch. ix. Parliament was petitioned in Edward III.'s reign, that these extortioners should suffer death for their unjust exactions.

the real origin of this office of tronage; for we find that, both in London and in other ports of the kingdom, the officer (usually the chamberlain in London) who collected this duty was, until the reign of Edward II., and perhaps subsequently, appointed by the *Crown*, and accounted to the Crown for the issues of the office, unless exempted specially from rendering any account.¹ The exercise of this office, when in the hands of the Corporation, was extended to the weighing of *all goods* sold above a certain weight by foreigners—that is, those who were not citizens—whether customable or not.² There appears to have been originally two branches of this office; namely, tronage at the king's beam, and tronage at the *common* beam, though the same balance was called by both names. The issues of the latter seem to have been, from the first period of their collection, carried to the account of the commonalty.³

At what time the exercise of this latter branch of the office commenced is difficult to state. It was granted by the 9th charter of Henry III. The charter says, 'That no merchant 'stranger shall sell goods but by weight at the king's beam;' but whether this grant first *created* the office, or whether it granted the exercise of it *to the City*, is doubtful. It certainly was vested in the Corporation before the reign of Edward II., and probably tronage might have been levied by two distinct officers during the latter period, one being appointed by the Crown. As early as the reign of Henry IV. the office of

¹ Madox's Hist. Exch. vol. i. ch. xviii. The appointment of this officer seems by the 3rd charter of Henry VIII. to have been occasionally asserted by the Crown so late as the 13th year of that prince's reign.

² Twelfth article of 1st charter of Edward II. Strype's Stow, vol. ii. pp. 273 et seq. and 421 et seq.; and the acts of Common Council and other authorities there quoted.

³ The 12th article of the 1st charter of Edward II. p. 430, refers to the tronage belonging to the City, the issues of which were accounted for the commonalty as tronage at the common beam. The 3rd charter of Henry VIII. refers to the charter of Edward II. and that of Henry IV. and another by himself, by which *tronage in general terms* is granted, as all alluding to the same office. Tronage of customable goods on behalf of the *king* was a distinct office both in origin and object, which is apparent, not only from the language of this charter, but from its being exercised over merchandise by the king's officers and all other ports, and from the 3rd charter of Henry VIII., and the numerous acts of Common Council referring to and distinguishing the *king's* beam. — Vide authorities quoted in the last note, Madox's *Hist. Exch.* cap. 18. and Hale's *Customs*, part iii. *passim*, and ch. xxi.

tronage was vested in the Corporation by the express words
of a special charter of the Crown. It was no doubt intended
by that grant to convey the entire office to the commonalty;
though it appears that the appointment to the office was
occasionally claimed by the Crown until the reign of
Henry VIII.; it is certain, however, that from the time the
whole office came into the hands of the Corporation only one
duty was levied, the two duties being as it were blended
into the latter branch, as time out of mind exercised by the
citizens.

The real foundation of this toll of tronage, as exercised in
all sales between *merchant and merchant*, was unquestionably
for the purpose of preventing fraud in sales.[1] It was formerly
a source of considerable profit to the City Chamber; but since
the gradual decline of wholesale dealing in open markets
this privilege has with good reason been very considerably
relaxed.[2]

The *warehousing* of merchandise, and more especially of
manufactured cloths, became, in progress of time, the subject
of numerous civic regulations with a view to other objects
besides that of securing the king's customs; chiefly for the
prevention of illegal traffic between stranger and stranger,
and of fraud in the texture, admeasurement, and quality of
the manufactures so deposited. For these purposes *sworn
brokers and factors*, *alnagers* (measurers), and *searchers* were
established, under sanction of ancient customs, acts of Common
Council, or express charters, at Leadenhall and Blackwell
Hall.[3]

---

[1] Vide note 2, p. 377. Vide Riley's Memorials of the City of London, passim.

[2] Strype's Stow, book ii. p. 173; showing that in 1720, the merchants had begun to remonstrate against and to evade this toll.

[3] Player and Hutchins. Sir O. Bridgman's MSS. Hargrave's MSS. Brit. Mus. No. 56. Norton's Exposition, &c. where this subject is discussed at large. Vide supra, p. 160 note. Co. Rep. book v. p. 63. Strype's Stow, vol. ii. p. 276.

THIRD CHARTER OF EDWARD IV.—PURCHASING IN MORTMAIN.

This charter grants, That in consideration of the payment of 1923*l*. 9*s*. 8*d*. the City shall have liberty to purchase in mortmain lands and tenements to the value of 200 marks per annum, without hindrance of the king's justices, escheators, or other officers, and without the necessity of any inquisitions upon the writ of *ad quod damnum*, and notwithstanding the statutes of mortmain.

The writ *ad quod damnum* was a writ of inquisition directed to the king's escheator to inquire into the particulars of the tenancy, the value and the quality of lands, which a person might be desirous of alienating in mortmain. The writ was issued in order to preclude any injustice or deprivation of rights, which the king or mesne lords might suffer, by the tenants so alienating with the king's licence; which it was conceived might be and was continually granted, notwithstanding the statutes of mortmain. For many years after the passing those statutes the licence was not granted until after the return of this inquisition, by which the king was satisfied he did or suffered no wrong. In process of time the rights of the mesne lords grew to be of small importance; and as the king's title was the only consideration, it became about the reign of Edward III. customary to take the king's licence, as in the present charter, with a clause dispensing with the ceremony of executing the writ of *ad quod damnum*.[1]

FOURTH CHARTER OF EDWARD IV.—SCAVAGE—PACKAGE, PICKAGE, PORTAGE, CARTAGE, &c.

This charter, in consideration of the sum of 7000*l*., grants to the citizens the *package* of all merchandise requiring to be 'packed, tunned, piped, barrelled, or in any way inclosed;'

---

[1] Dated 20th June, 18th year. Directed and to be found as the last. For an explanation of this charter, vide supra, 349 *et seq.*

[2] Fitzh. Nat. Br. p. 272. D. Kyd. on Corp. vol. i. p. 90.

[3] Dated and directed as the last. To be found in the Inspeximus of Charles II.

BOOK II.

also the oversight[1] of customable goods at the places where the customs are payable; also the office of picking[2] and poundering customable goods; also that of the portage of goods and merchandise to and from the houses of strangers: also the office of garbling[3] all spices and other goods which should be garbled; also the office of gauger and the carriage of wines; with all the fees and emoluments belonging to such offices,—to be exercised by themselves or their deputies, without rendering any account to the king.

It further grants, That the mayor and commonalty may appoint to the office of coroner within the City of London, and that such office shall no longer be in the appointment of the king's chief butler as claimed by him.

THE OVERSIGHT OF CUSTOMABLE GOODS.—This office, termed in Latin *supervisus*, is translated in another charter by the words *search* and *surveying*,[4] and in the 2nd charter of Charles I. it is termed the *scavage*, which appears to have been its most ancient and common name,[5] and that which is retained at the present day. The origin and nature of this toll of *scavage* seems to have been but little understood. Spelman, who is followed in his explication by other commentators, terms it a toll levied by the owners of markets for the licence given by them to chapmen of *shewing* their merchandise, and derives the expression from the word рсеpan (Sax.), which he translates to *shew* or *inspect*.[6] The latter word, however, seems to be both the more correct and the more applicable translation, and perhaps the French *sçavoir*, to *know*, is the most apt synonym of any. In truth, the explanation given by Spelman in his Glossary, the latter part of which does

---

[1] That is, the *surveying* as it is sometimes termed in other charters, or *scavage*; *searching* also was the same kind of office. It consisted in noting the quality and quantity of goods on which custom was to be levied.—Vide *post*, this charter.

[2] This was the *sorting* or rejecting of improper substances in the merchandise, and was not the same thing as *pickage*, which was a *toll* paid for *picking* up market ground for erecting a stall. For *poundering*, vide 3rd charter of Edward III. p. 364 *note*.

[3] Garbling was the sorting good from bad in quality of the same species of merchandise (vide Coke's 4th Inst. p. 264), and is a term still in use amongst merchants.

[4] Vide 2nd charter of James I.

[5] Madox's Hist. Exch. vol. i. p. 778, where the term and the duty is referred to in the reign of Henry III.

[6] Spelm. Gloss. Termes de Leg.

SCAVAGE. STALLAGE. PICKAGE. PACKAGE, ETC. 381

not seem to have been completed with the same attention and
labour as the former part,¹ is by no means warranted by authority or by law. Tolls in general must be founded *upon
some consideration.*² But the consideration for this toll of
shewage, or for *shewing* merchandise, is in truth no consideration; and it has been long settled that everybody has a right
of access, and of showing his wares, at a fair or market.³
The usual tolls, or duties in the nature of toll recognised as
legal in markets, are for *stallage* or *pickage*; without paying
which, no one can *erect a stall* or *pick up the ground* for such
purpose.⁴

CHAP.
VI.

The real nature of this duty is not a toll for shewing, but
a toll paid for the *oversight of shewing*; and under that name
(*supervisus apertionis*) it was claimed in an action of debt in
the reign of Charles II.⁵ Indeed, the language of the present
charter, and that of others above referred to, plainly indicates
the same exposition. Scavage, like tronage, was an *office* exercised with an express object; and the toll passing by that
name was, like that of tronage, paid in consideration of the
performance of that office.

The object of this office was confined merely to securing
the payment of the king's import customs. The exercise of
it was, therefore, always limited to the *customable* goods of
aliens or sons of aliens.⁶ The duty performed was *seeing* and
knowing the merchandise on which the king's import customs
were paid; in order that no concealment or fraudulent practices by false packing, false admixture, or false ownership by
a citizen, should deprive the king of his just dues.

The office is no doubt as ancient as the customs themselves,
and the duty in all probability contemporaneous with the
office. It was well known under the name of *scavage* in the
reign of Henry III.⁷ and it seems as early as that time to
have been a franchise of the commonalty.⁸ It is secured
in very ample terms by the 2nd charter of Charles I.; and

¹ Spelm. Gloss. preface.
² Vide p. 268, and notes; and authorities there quoted.
³ Sir. p. 1238. Wilson, p. 107.
⁴ Ibid.
⁵ Term. de Pasch.

⁶ 2nd charter of Charles I.
⁷ Madox's Hist. Exch. vol. i. p. 778.
⁸ Ibid. When the money was collected by the king's officers, they collected it as *custodes* of the City.

by that charter certain rates are fixed at which the toll is to be levied.

The king's customs have long since been placed under effectual regulations by statute, and the levying of them is superintended by commissioners and officers appointed under authority of those statutes. The *petty* customs, as the customs paid by aliens were commonly denominated,[1] and in the collection of which only the office of scavage was concerned, have been abolished;[2] but the same statute which abolishes the petty customs, excepts all duties paid to the City of London.

The offices of packing, picking, poundering, garbling, and gauging, were granted to the commonalty originally on the same principle as that of scavage. But these offices, like those of portage and carriage granted by this charter, and that of tronage granted by others, would seem, from the mode of exercising them gradually adopted by the City, to have rested rather on the principle of placing every employment and avocation *of a common or public character* under the regulation and supervision of the local government.

There are some employments which it would be absolutely impossible to leave to general competition in a crowded city, without occasioning disorder, abuse, and disturbances, alike subversive of the public peace and of private accommodation. Amongst these employments may be reckoned those of common carriers, common porters, watermen, fishermen, &c. The rights of the Corporation in controlling and regulating the labour of these classes do not depend upon royal grant, nor, indeed, would such grant, without confirmation in parliament, legally confer such rights; but they rest on ancient usage exercised time out of mind, and naturally springing from the establishment of good government. In ancient times, and down to the Fire of London, almost all the carriage throughout the City was performed by porters: the irregularity and narrowness of the streets, and the clumsy structure of the vehicles, were such as hardly to admit of any other mode. Considering, therefore, the number and quality of the City

[1] Blackstone's Commentaries, vol. i. p. 314; and Hale on Customs.
[2] 24th George III. sess. 2, cap. 16.

porters, the necessity of retaining them under strict rule must be obvious. With regard to carts, whether we refer to the ancient state of the streets or to the modern improvements, both in their arrangement, and in the number and variety of wheeled carriages, we shall be equally convinced of the necessity of placing them also under regulation. In short, the employment of common carriers within crowded districts has always been acknowledged by the legislature to require statutable interference, wherever the municipal authority has been insufficient.

As to those offices which are concerned in the due collection of the king's customs, we can estimate the detriment and the abuses attending the jurisdiction of the king's tax officers in the City in unsettled times, and when no legislative enactments defined and enforced their duties. Besides the security from injustice and oppression afforded to the citizens by the exercise of these duties through their own appointed officers, the profits arising to the Chamber of the City out of them, especially in regard to the fees levied from merchant strangers and foreigners, no doubt greatly enhanced the value of these chartered grants. Many of these offices are still exercised by the City, and are the sources of considerable emolument, and others have been put under statutable regulations.

CHAPTER VII.

CHARTER OF HENRY VII.—WHOLESALE DEALERS—OFFICE OF GAUGER—FIRST CHARTER OF HENRY VIII.—TRONAGE—SECOND CHARTER OF HENRY VIII.—INQUISITIONS AT ST. MARTIN'S-LE-GRAND TRANSFERRED TO GUILDHALL—THIRD CHARTER OF HENRY VIII.—CONFIRMATION OF TRONAGE—CHARTER OF EDWARD VI.—LAND IN SOUTHWARK—FIRST CHARTER OF JAMES I.—CONSERVANCY OF THE THAMES—OFFICE OF MEASURER—METAGE, DUTY ON GOODS ON BEHALF OF FUNDS OF CITY ORPHANS—SECOND CHARTER OF JAMES I.—SEARCH AND SURVEY OF GOODS—THIRD CHARTER OF JAMES I.—WEIGHING—FIRST CHARTER OF CHARLES I.—GENERAL CONFIRMATION OF ALL PRECEDING CHARTERS, NOMINATIM—SECOND CHARTER OF CHARLES I.—SCAVAGE AND WATER BAILLAGE—CHARTER OF CHARLES II.—GENERAL CONFIRMATION OF ALL PREVIOUS CHARTERS, NOMINATIM, AND RECITING AT LARGE THEIR CONTENTS—CHARTER OF WILLIAM AND MARY—CHARTER OF GEORGE II.

CHARTER OF HENRY VII.[1]

BOOK II.

This charter, after referring to the custom as 'time out of mind approved and confirmed by authority of parliament,' that merchant strangers should not buy or sell with other merchant strangers by wholesale within the City, for the purpose of selling again, under pain of forfeiture of the merchandise so sold—proceeds to confirm it, and to authorize the taking all forfeitures in breach of such custom to the use of the mayor, commonalty, and citizens, whether such customs and liberties may have been used, abused, or not used. The charter further grants the office of gauger.[2]

---

[1] Dated 23rd July, 20th year. To be found in the Inspeximus of Charles II.

[2] The office of gauger or of measuring the contents of vessels or barrels was granted by the last charter of Edward IV. almost in the same terms. Some differences it may be presumed had arisen on this subject as well as that of the custom of forfeiture for goods 'foreign bought and foreign sold,' which occasioned this charter of confirmation.

FIRST CHARTER OF HENRY VIII.

This charter is a confirmation of the first charter of Henry IV., by which *tronage* is granted to the City.[1]

SECOND CHARTER OF HENRY VIII.[2]

This charter, referring to that part of the 1st charter of Edward III. by which inquisitions are directed to be taken at St. Martin's le Grand,[3] grants that such inquisitions shall for the future be taken at Guildhall, or other place within the City thought more convenient by the justices before whom such inquisitions shall be taken.

THIRD CHARTER OF HENRY VIII.[4] TRONAGE.

This charter first refers to a grant made in the 13th year of the king's reign, of the tronage or keeping of the great beam and common balance to Sir William Sidney; which grant had been surrendered into the king's hands by him, for the purpose of being made over to the commonalty of the City of London. It then proceeds to recite the charter of Edward II., granted in the 12th year of his reign, by which the weights and beam had been directed to be kept by the citizens of London.[5] It then recites the charter of Henry IV., by which the office of tronage is further secured to the citizens, and also the charter granted in the first year of his reign, confirming the charter of Henry IV.: from which, the charter states, it was evident and clear that the office of tronage did, of ancient right, belong to the citizens of London.

For the end, therefore, of removing all ambiguity, it grants 'the weights and beams for weighing goods and merchandise between merchant and merchant,' and the tronage and office

---

[1] Dated 12th July, in the 1st year of the reign of Henry VIII.
[2] Dated 16th June, 10th year. To be found in the Inspeximus of Charles II.
[3] Vide supra, pp. 361, 376.
[4] Dated 13th April, 22nd year. To be found as the last.
[5] Vide supra, pp. 335, 376.

of keeper of the great beam and common balance, and the power of appointing and removing clerks, and all other officers, deputies, and ministers, and all the profits, fees, and emoluments arising from the exercise of this office, without any account to be rendered thereof to the king.[1]

CHARTER OF EDWARD VI.[2]

By this charter is granted, in the most ample terms, a very extensive property in Southwark, the manor and all manorial rights over it, together with a large jurisdiction over the district, both criminal and civil.

It first describes the lands, tenements, and premises granted to the commonalty for the sum of 647*l*. 2*s*. 1*d*., which are declared to have been purchased by the king's father, Henry VIII., of Charles Duke of Suffolk.[3]

Then it proceeds to grant, for the same consideration, the lordship and manor of Southwark, as late possessed by the Archbishop of Canterbury; and then enumerates a great number of rent-charges belonging to the king, arising out of premises in that manor, which it grants to the commonalty; all which manor, premises, and rent-charges are granted in as full and ample a manner as they were held and enjoyed by Charles Duke of Suffolk, or any other, as Abbot of the dissolved Monastery of Bermondsey, or by the Archbishop of Canterbury.

For the further consideration of 500 marks, the charter proceeds to grant in and through all the town and borough of Southwark, and the parishes of St. Saviour's, St. Olave's, and St. George's, in Southwark; St. Thomas's Hospital, Kentish Street and Blackman Street, and all other places

---

[1] For an explanation of the purport of this charter, vide *supra*, pp. 376 et seq.

[2] Dated 23rd April, 4th year. To be found in the Inspeximus of Charles II.

[3] [This valuable estate has been considered as applicable to the maintenance of London Bridge, and is now charged with the payment of a large sum for rebuilding the new bridge. No trust of this nature is mentioned in the charter, and after payment of the existing charges, the estate ought to revert back to the Corporation.]—EDIT. (of first edition, Mr. Edward Tyrrell, afterwards Remembrancer).

throughout the borough of Southwark;—all waifs, estrays, chattels of felons, and deodands, and all escheats and forfeitures; and that the commonalty may put themselves in possession of all such goods and chattels: also the assay and assize of bread and victuals, &c. and all forfeitures; also the execution of all process: also an annual fair and court of *pye powder* for three days: also the view of frankpledge, and the arrest of felons and malefactors, who may be taken to Newgate.¹ It further grants the franchise of a civil jurisdiction, the same as is exercised in the City courts, to be holden by like actions, bills, plaints, process, arrests, judgments, and executions before the lord mayor, aldermen, and sheriffs, at the Guildhall,² and in like manner and form as all such suits are prosecuted in the City; with power to impanel and enforce the attendance of jurymen from the Borough to try issues arising; and also the cognizance of all pleas personal, to be held in the same courts, and tried by the same jurymen summoned from the Borough.³

Then follows the grant of the coronership over the town and borough and precincts before described, to be executed by two coroners appointed by the commonalty, annually or otherwise; and that the mayor shall be escheator, and clerk of the market of the Borough, and of the king's household in the same district; and that the City shall have all the aforesaid liberties and franchises, and all tolls, stallages, pickages,⁴ and all other jurisdictions, liberties, franchises, and privileges, as fully as the Archbishop of Canterbury, the Duke of Suffolk, the master, brethren, and sisters of the late St. Thomas's Hospital, the Abbot of Bermondsey, or the Prior of

¹ The grants specified in this clause are more detailed particulars of the franchises granted at the close of the charter of Edward IV.

² This jurisdiction is now held in Southwark, and not in Guildhall. Why so valuable a jurisdiction in respect of actions of small debts (which are in effect irremovable) has gone so much into decay, or why foreign attachments are never tried under this jurisdiction, it is not easy to explain.

³ For the nature of 'cognizance of pleas,' vide *supra*, p. 348 *et sq*. This is not the grant of an *exclusive* cognizance of pleas, nor is it an exclusive personal grant to the inhabitants.

⁴ Vide *supra*, pp. 108, 112 note 2, 355, as to king's household, clerk of the market, &c.; 379, as to stallage, &c. The mayor is *by custom* coroner of the City also (Pulling's *London*, 19, 128), and also escheator by statute 1st Edward III. 19.—Vide Pulling. 19.

St. Mary Overy, or any of them had, or as the late King Henry VIII. had.

It further grants, That the inhabitants of Southwark, and of the district before-mentioned, shall be under the jurisdiction and correction of the mayor and City officers, the same as the citizens of London; and that the mayor, recorder, and those aldermen who have passed the chair of the City, shall be justices of the peace throughout those limits.

The charter then grants a market every Monday, Wednesday, Friday, and Saturday, and all things appertaining to a market.

The charter proceeds to except the rights and jurisdictions of the king over his park in Southwark, and the house and garden of the King's Bench, and of the Marshalsea, with their appurtenances, so long as they continue to be used as prisons; and also the jurisdiction of the king's great master steward and marshal of his house over all such parts of the limits aforesaid as are within the verge.[1]

The charter, lastly, grants, That all these lands, tenements, rights and franchises, before granted, shall be held of the king, as of his manor of Greenwich, by fealty only, and in free socage by way of service, and not in chief;[2] and that the mayor and commonalty shall be quit of all manner of account, corrodies,[3] rents, fees, annuities, and sums of money, excepting as before reserved, and except the ancient ferm rent for Southwark of 10l.; and that they may have this charter sealed without any fee to the king in his hanaper[4] or otherwise.

---

[1] This jurisdiction is saved to the king as appurtenant to and in respect of his palace. The master steward and marshal of the king's household had jurisdiction over all conspiracies to kill the king or any of his household in his palace, or within certain limits called *the verge*, and over all misprisions of treason or violence there committed.— Vide Coke's 4th *Inst.* cap. 18, 19, 20, 21.

[2] This was to distinguish it from tenure by knight's service, or in chief simply, according to the feudal principles: the citizens were to be free tenants as to this district of the king's *soc* or manor of Greenwich.—Vide *supra*, p. 44 et seq. p. 289 et seq.

[3] *Corrody* was an allowance of victual which the founder of a monastery, or owner might charge upon such establishment: this acquittance of corrody is granted in respect of the monastery of Bermondsey, which is granted by this charter.—Vide Spelm. *Gloss*. and *Termes de Ley*.

[4] *Hanaper* literally means a *basket* or *hamper*. It was actually used in ancient times as the king's travelling treasury and gave the name to that office in the

Upon the grant of this charter, the court of Aldermen added another to their number, and erected Southwark into a new ward of the liberties of the City, under the name of Bridge Ward Without.¹ The Common Council then passed a bye-law directing the election of an alderman for Bridge Ward Without, to be made by the inhabitants of the Borough; but that ordinance was very soon after repealed by another, passed in the reign of Philip and Mary, placing the election in the court of Aldermen again.²

The Borough of Southwark was not by this charter completely constituted a ward, or component part of the City of London, nor was it detached from the county of Surrey. It continued a distinct borough for the most important of all purposes—that of the election of representatives in parliament; and the justices of the peace, as well as the king's justices on their circuits, still exercise their jurisdiction over this as over every other part of the county. The City possesses jurisdiction over the district by the appointment of leet officers; but in respect of the conservation of the peace it has not an *exclusive* but a *concurrent* jurisdiction. The charter directs, That all felons and malefactors may be taken to Newgate, to be then delivered according to law; but this clause, which had been inserted in the first charter of Edward IV., was repealed by express statute of the 8th Edward IV.;³ the charter was not sufficient to dispense with that statute, and malefactors in Southwark have ceased to be imprisoned or tried in the City. The City has ceased to appoint an alderman for the district;⁴ and the office of alderman, or rather of justice of the peace, is executed by a magistrate of the City of London who has passed the chair. The high steward, appointed by the court of Aldermen, presides in the Borough court of record and at the courts leet, and the high bailiff executes the duties of sheriff. The mayor, recorder, and aldermen who have passed the chair hold the sessions of the peace.

Chancery where money is paid for fixing the king's seal.—Vide Spelm. voce, and 'Fiscus.'

¹ Strype's Stow, vol. ii. p. 2 *et seq.*
² Ibid.
³ Cotton's Abridgment. p. 682.

⁴ There is nominally an alderman for Bridge Ward Without; but his office is a sinecure, and the senior alderman usually holds it, upon translation from his own original ward.

FIRST CHARTER OF JAMES I.

This charter refers to the office of bailiff, and to that of the conservation of the water of the Thames, as having been time out of mind possessed by the mayor and commonalty and exercised by the mayor or his deputy for the time being, from Staines Bridge to Yendall, otherwise Yenland or Yenleet, and in the river Medway, and upon every bank, shore, and wharf, within those limits; together with all wages, rewards, fees, and profits belonging to the office. It also refers to the office of *Measurer* as having been possessed and exercised in the same way, of all coals and grain, also of salt, and of all kinds of fruit and vegetables, and of all other goods and merchandises sold by measure, brought to the port of London, which shall arrive or be laid down within the same limits; together with all wages, rewards, fees, and profits:—in which office of *measuring*, especially in regard to coals, the charter intimates, the citizens had been lately disquieted, though their title was manifest and clear.

The charter, to end all controversies on these subjects, certifies and confirms all the premises, whether the offices have been used or not used.

BAILIFF AND CONSERVATOR OF THE THAMES.—This office has been, time out of mind, possessed by the commonalty, and executed by the lord mayor and his deputies. By virtue of it, both by long usage and by express charters and statutes, the lord mayor has a general authority to remove weare, kiddles, obstructions, and nuisances, and to seize unlawful nets, and fish caught unlawfully or out of season.[1]

For the preservation of the waters of the fishery and of the navigation, various acts of Parliament have from time to time passed, and various ordinances of the Common Council, regulating what nets are to be used and how, and condemning, under penalties and forfeitures, any injurious traffic on the

---

[1] Dated 20th August, 3rd year. To be found in the Inspeximus of Charles II. and in Lib. Alb.

[2] For the nature of the right, and records and authorities collected on the subject, vide Strype's Stow, vol. i. p. 33 et seq.

river;[1] over which offences the lord mayor has jurisdiction, either by action of debt in his mayor's court, or by inquisitions taken in his court of Conservacy. A number of the members of the court of Common Council form an annual committee, called the Navigation Committee, to superintend the general state of the navigation.

The court of Conservacy is a most ancient court of record, held before the lord mayor eight times every year, in the four counties of Middlesex, Kent, Essex, and Surrey, successively, by prescription and by virtue of the king's commission, which is granted by the king on his accession to the lord mayor for the time being. A jury is summoned of residents of those counties; and their jurisdiction may be said to be confined to the inquiry and redress of common nuisances in the river. The commissions which have been from time to time issued from the period of Henry III.'s reign, direct the mayor to *inquire* into, and authorise him to *hear* and *determine* offences in unlawful fishing. In modern times the court has been held with great regularity, and with very beneficial results: the jurisdiction has been chiefly exercised, like the wardmote leet courts, for purposes of inquisition and presentment; and the *redress* of nuisances, when pointed out by such presentment, has been of late years sought by indictments in a superior court.

For the purpose of enforcing his authority as conservator of the Thames, the lord mayor appoints an officer called the water-bailiff, who is called the sub-conservator, and whose office over the river is of the same nature as that of the chief constable appointed by the county sheriff over the hundred. His duties, which are ministerial and partly regulated by statute, are generally to watch over the river, for the detection of and to inform against nuisances—to summon the inquest jury, and to attend them on their view in fulfilment of the charge given them at the Conservacy court—to attend the Corporation on their aquatic processions—to receive the instructions of the Navigation Committee of the Common Council—to license and inspect fishing-nets—to seize forfeitures

---

[1] Strype's Stow, vol. i. p. 35 *et seq.*; Hodges' Bye Laws, and Bohun's Priv. Lond.

for the purpose of condemnation—and to obey the instructions of the civic authorities, in removing obstructions in the navigation of the river.

OFFICE OF MEASURER.—The measuring or *metage*, which is the more common expression, of all articles of consumption sold by measure, brought coastwise into the port of London, and especially of coals and corn, is one of the most lucrative franchises enjoyed by the Corporation. It is founded on the same principle as that of *tronage*,[1] or weighing of goods sold by weight: namely, the collection of the king's customs and the prevention of fraudulent sales. It has long been an object of policy with government, to ascertain the importation and amount of sales of these articles, and more especially that of corn; but the great facility of fraud in measuring them has suggested the necessity of placing all dealings in these articles under public control. In professed imitation of this civic control, exercised time out of mind by the office of metage, the legislature has passed numerous statutes to ensure the just measuring of coals and corn in those districts of the metropolis without the City's jurisdiction and elsewhere;[2] and perhaps it is impossible to point out a subject of civic regulation more productive of reciprocal benefit than this of the office of metage.

Another reason for the public metage of coals and corn is, the collection of the king's customs and other duties. Besides the king's duty upon the importation of coals and the metage duty, the duties known under the name of *the orphans' duty* on coals imported into the port of London, are levied; the origin and purposes of which deserve to be more particularly mentioned.

Formerly the Corporation of London had by ancient custom, confirmed by the first charter in parliament of Richard II., *the custody*, as it was termed, of all orphans,

---

[1] Vide *supra*, pp. 376 *et seq*.
[2] Namely, in regard to coals: 9th & 10th William III. caps. 10 & 13. 9th Anne, cap. 28. 3rd Geo. II. cap. 26. 4th Geo. II. cap. 30. 23rd Geo. II. cap. 26. 32nd Geo. II. cap. 27. 13th Geo. III. cap. 53. 13th Geo. III. cap. 27. 27th Geo. III. cap. 62. 47th Geo. III. cap. 68. 49th Geo. III. caps. 62, 98. 56th Geo. III. cap. 21. 57th Geo. III. caps. 1, 40. —In regard to corn: 1st Anne, st. 4, cap. 26. 2nd Geo. II. cap. 18. 13th Geo. II cap. 22. 31st Geo. III. cap. 30; which last statute refers to many others.

which consisted of the care of their persons and property;[1] and performed this responsible duty through the medium of a court of record, called the Court of Orphans, over which the common-serjeant, *ex officio*, presided. This court, which was part of the jurisdiction of the court of Aldermen, took security from the executors and administrators of deceased citizens for the payment into the City Chamber of all sums due, and accruing due, on behalf of the orphans; and superintended the distribution of such money, according to law and according to the custom of London, in regard to the distribution of personal effects. Since the repeal by statutes of the City custom—under which the citizens were prohibited from disposing by will of more than one-third of their personal estate, and the remaining part was required to be paid into the chamber in trust for their orphans—the functions of this court have entirely ceased: but while this corporate guardianship was fully exercised, large sums were constantly paid into the civic treasury, and the jurisdiction by which the City orphans were protected in their rights was no doubt, in early and unsettled times, both a favourite and valuable privilege amongst the citizens.[2]

In the troublesome times which attended and followed the great rebellion, the *City finances* (which suffered by plunder and extortion in common with the rest of the nation) fell into much confusion and decay; and the distress of the City Chamber was not a little aggravated by the fire of London, in which immense property belonging to the City was consumed, and much more expended in restoring the metropolis in a manner far surpassing in splendour its ancient condition. The arbitrary acts of Charles II. in borrowing great sums of the City, shutting up the Exchequer in which most of the orphans' fund was deposited,[3] and finally seizing on the City charter, completed the ruin of the Chamber; and when the liberties were restored at the Revolution, the City

---

[1] 11th Geo. I. cap. 18; and 5 & 6 William & Mary.
[2] For an account of the Orphans' Court jurisdiction, and the City custom in regard to them and their estates, vide Bohun's *Priv. Lond.*; and the authorities there referred to, Strype's Stow, vol. ii. pp. 323, 324, 372, 373, and Calthorpe's *Rep.* p. 159, Pulling's *Law and Customs of the City of London*, 193 *et seq.*
[3] Vide p. 225.

purse had not only been emptied by the public robbers who usurped the chartered rights of the citizens, but a heavy debt of no less a sum than 750,000l. had accumulated on the responsibility of the Corporation, due to the City orphans and other persons, who were, by the ruin which had thus involved the City, reduced to a state of utter destitution.¹

These circumstances occasioned many petitions to the legislature, and ultimately the passing of the first act for raising what was called an *orphans' fund*; namely, the 5th and 6th of William and Mary. This act provided for the debt thus constituted, by charging the estates of the Corporation with the payment of a perpetual rent of 8,000l., by assigning to the proposed fund certain other small emoluments of the City, and by creating a duty of 2,000l. per annum to be paid by the citizens of London out of their personal property, which was paid till 1795, and then repealed. It also imposed perpetual duties of four shillings per tun on wine, and of fourpence per chaldron on coals and culm imported into the port of London; and a further duty of sixpence per chaldron, which was to last for fifty years, when a charge of 6,000l. per annum was to be fixed upon the Corporation estates, in addition to that of 8,000l. The last-mentioned duties were the only compensation to the citizens of London for taking upon themselves the burthen, partly inflicted by public calamity, but still more by public injustice, and even a large portion of these was contributed by themselves. This arrangement was so unfavourable to the Corporation, that in 1713 the original debt had increased 90,000l. The great addition to the buildings of the metropolis and other circumstances have since rendered these duties very productive, and various acts of parliament have continued the temporary imposition of sixpence; but in the same or in a greater proportion has the fund been burthened. The additional charge of 6,000l. per annum on the Corporation estates has not taken effect; but in 1751, 2,000l. per annum was charged upon them by the 21st George II. cap. 29; and

¹ Reports of the House of Commons on the Orphans' Fund 1812 and 1823; Journals of Proceedings in the Common Council for the years 1818 and 18—, Index titles, 'Orphans' Duty,' 'Co—' (Town Clerk's Office).

n 1767 a further annual sum of 1,500*l.* by the 7th George III. cap. 37. The latter act authorised the application of the whole of the *orphans' fund* to various public purposes, by no means exclusively beneficial to the City of London,¹ and has been followed by several similar acts; so that no less a sum than 840,300*l.* had been devoted to public improvements, and paid for out of this fund, when a committee of the House of Commons made their report on the orphans' fund in 1823. In consequence of these incumbrances, the original debt, which was created by public injustice, has not yet been discharged; and a new debt has been raised and defrayed by the voluntary contribution of the Corporation to the various purposes before mentioned, out of their own private income, besides the share borne by individuals in the payment of the duties; the account of the application of the City revenue forming a part of the fund standing thus:

PAID TOWARDS THE DEBT CREATED BY THE VIOLENCE OF CHARLES II.:

From 1696 to 1751, 8,000*l.* per annum	£440,000
From 1751 to 1782, 10,000*l.* per annum	310,000
	£750,000

VOLUNTARILY CONTRIBUTED TOWARDS PUBLIC IMPROVEMENTS IN LONDON, MIDDLESEX, AND SURREY:

From 1767 to 1782, 1,500*l.* per annum, and from 1782 to 1828, 11,500*l.* per annum	96000
	£1,346,000

The debts so incurred are now in a rapid course of discharge; and the fund still retains the name of the *orphans' fund*, although its object has entirely changed.²

The metage duty both on corn and coals is received for the account of the Corporation. The office is exercised under the control of a committee of the court of Common Council, The coal and corn committee, who appoint a board of

---

¹ Amongst others are included the building of a Sessions House for the county of Middlesex, and another for Westminster; the building of Blackfriars Bridge, paving part of the Borough of Southwark, and improving the avenues in the Strand near Temple Bar. Of late also in aid of the Thames embankment.

² [By 10th Geo. IV. cap. 136, intituled 'An Act for improving the approaches 'to London Bridge,' a further sum of 1,000,000*l.* has been charged upon the coal duties.]—EDIT (Mr. Tyrrell, afterwards Remembrancer.)

principal meters, and also a great number of deputy meters. Both the metage and orphans' duty is collected usually by the same individual, who can of course receive both duties with equal facility at the same time, and which gives ample security for the collection and payment of the duties.

SECOND CHARTER OF JAMES I.[1]

This is a charter chiefly in confirmation of former liberties. It first refers to the many liberties, privileges, franchises, &c. granted from time to time by the kings of England, and then ratifies all such grants, enumerating the various denominations, corporate and otherwise, under which the citizens received their chartered rights; and confirming them whether used or not used, or even abused.[2]

The charter then proceeds to grant and confirm the *search and survey*[3] of 'oil, hops, soap, salt, butter, cheese, and such 'other like things, coming or brought to the port of the City, 'to the intent to be sold by way of merchandise;' and also the *measuring* of corn, coal, and other things measurable, brought for the same purpose.

It proceeds to enlarge the limits of the civic jurisdiction by comprising within it the districts of Duke's Place, Great and Little St. Bartholomew's, Blackfriars and Whitefriars and Cold Harbour; with a proviso, that the inhabitants of Blackfriars and Whitefriars shall be exempt from particular contributions of scot and watch and ward, and from the particular offices of constable and scavenger.

It further grants, That all inhabitants within the City's jurisdiction, who are not freemen, shall nevertheless be liable to all civic contributions in respect of their houses[4] (with the exception before noticed, of the inhabitants of Blackfriars and

---

[1] Dated 20th September, 6th year. To be found in the Inspeximus of Charles II.
Vide similar clauses in the charters 4th Edward III.; 1st Edward IV. and Henry VII.
[2] 4th charter of Edward IV.
[3] Vide sixteenth clause of 1st charter of Edward II. to the same effect.

Whitefriars), with liberty of appeal to the lord chancellor in case of grievance.

The charter then grants, That the mayor, recorder and aldermen who have been mayors, shall be justices of the peace over these new districts: and further, that any four of them (of whom the mayor and recorder shall be two), shall be justices of *oyer and terminer* over the whole civic jurisdiction.

Finally, the charter grants to the Corporation throughout the newly comprised districts, all waifs, estrays, and goods and chattels of felons and fugitives; and that the charter shall be sealed without fine or fee to the hanaper.[2]

THIRD CHARTER OF JAMES I.[3]

This charter commences with some testimonials of the king's regard for the welfare of the City, which induces him to desire not only the confirmation but the enlargement of former grants.

He then refers to some doubts and controversies existing as to the right of the Corporation to the *weighing* as well as the measuring of all coals brought into the port of London, as expressed in his first charter;—to end which, the weighing of all coals weighable and the office of weighing is granted and confirmed to the citizens, in the same language as in the charter confirming the measuring. The fee or duty for weighing is then settled at eightpence per ton weight, and proportionably for a smaller weight. All merchants are enjoined not to land or deliver their coals without measuring or weighing; so that the king may know the quantity of coals imported, and have his duties on them justly paid.

The charter then alludes to the practice of selling coals by retail from lighters and small craft on the Thames, by which means engrossing, regrating, and forestalling was effected,

---

[1] The 1st charter of Edward IV. giving the same jurisdiction to the City authorities, provides only that the mayor (without mentioning the recorder, shall be of the quorum.

[2] Last clause of the charter of Edward VI.

[3] Dated 15th September, 12th year. To be found in the Inspeximus of Charles II., and in Liber Albus.

and more frequent measurings became necessary, to the enhancement of the price; and also the stream of the river was choked by the coals and rubbish falling into it. These practices are accordingly prohibited; and all sales are directed to be transacted either immediately from the ships importing, or in some port, quay, or wharf, near the river.

Lastly, the charter declares, That the king will renew this grant and charter in a more effectual and express way at the desire of the citizens, in case any doubt should arise, or default exist, in regard to the privileges intended to be confirmed to them.

FIRST CHARTER OF CHARLES I.[1]

This is a most ample *inspeximus charter*. It begins by reciting all the charters from William the Conqueror, referred to in the notes of this work as contained in the Inspeximus charter of Charles II. They are all quoted *verbatim*, except the first charter of Edward I., the charter of Henry IV., and the first charter of Henry VII., which are only recited either in substance or in part. The charter of Henry VI. also is but partially mentioned in the subsequent part of this charter.

All these charters are then confirmed; and all grants of lands, tenements, offices, liberties, franchises, &c. to the citizens, under whatever name they may have received them. All free customs, authorities, franchises, &c. are restored,[2] to be enjoyed and used, notwithstanding any hindrances, impediments, or judgments, in times past; and whether they may have been used, not used, or abused; and all the grants made to the citizens by former charters are granted to the citizens as wholly and fully as if they were again severally named and expressed, word for word, to be held by the same rents and services as formerly.

The charters of Henry VI. and the first of Henry VII. are

---

[1] Dated 18th October, 14th year. To be found in the Inspeximus charter of Charles II.

[2] See the numerous violations of the citizens' rights and liberties, *supra*, p. 213 *et seq.*

ABSTRACT OF FIRST CHARTER OF CHARLES I.

then mentioned, and the grants cited from those charters confirmed; the other privileges contained in them are also confirmed, with the provisos and exceptions expressed in the present charter.

The charter proceeds to grant, That the mayor, recorder, and aldermen who have passed the chair, and the three senior aldermen who have not passed the chair,[1] shall be keepers of the peace and justices; and that they or any four of them, of whom the mayor or recorder is to be one,[2] shall also be justices to enquire by the oaths of a jury concerning murders, felonies, and most other offences of an inferior description; and concerning the misconduct of sheriffs, constables, gaolers, and other officers, in reference to such crimes; and also to see into indictments taken before them, and award process upon them against those so indicted: also to hear and determine such offences, and punish them according to law; and to do all other things which justices of the peace may do and execute in counties by force of any laws or statutes.

Next it is granted, That the mayor and commonalty shall have all recognizances taken which may be forfeited—such as for appearance at sessions, for the keeping and maintaining bastard children, and saving the parishes of the City harmless; concerning inmates dividing their dwelling-houses into several habitations, and suppressing ale-houses,[3] and for observation of orders made in the premises; all recognizances taken and forfeited at the sessions of gaol delivery.[4] The charter likewise grants all fines, issues, and amerciaments, for offences committed and tried and adjudged within the City—excepting only, fines and issues *royal*, for offences committed by the City magistrates:[5] also all recognizances forfeited, which are taken for good behaviour and keeping

---

[1] The three senior aldermen who have not passed the chair are hereby first created justices of the peace.

[2] Second charter of James, whereby the mayor and recorder are ordained always to be two of the quorum in all sessions.

[3] This clause refers to the king's proclamations on the subject of buildings and mode of inhabiting houses, very frequent during Elizabeth and James's reigns; they were followed up by numerous acts of Common Council. Vide Maitland and Stow, Index, 'Buildings.' The expediency of these proclamations and ordinances can be much easier defended than their legality.

[4] The great sessions of the king's judges at Newgate.

[5] Vide *supra*, p. 353.

the peace, before justices, or in the court of Conservacy f
preservation of the water of the Thames and the fishing; as
all amerciaments, fines, and penalties there adjudged; and a
penalties and forfeitures imposed, assessed, or adjudged b
force of any commission of sewers.

The charter proceeds to grant and confirm to the commonalty all buildings, and erections, and gutters, and water courses, &c. erected or being in any street or waste ground, or ports, banks, and shores of the Thames: also the field called the Inner Moor and Outward Moor, in the parishes of St. Giles, Cripplegate, St. Stephen, Coleman Street, and St. Botolph, Bishopsgate Street: and the field called West Smithfield and the fairs and markets there held, with pickage stallage,[1] and all profits—the king declaring that he will not allow any of these fields to be built upon, but that they shall be used for the same purposes as heretofore (saving to the king all streets, alleys, and other void or waste places within the City), and to be held by the commonalty for ever, in free or common burgage, and not *in capite* or by knight's service.[2] And that the citizens shall not be liable for any arrearages or issues of the lands and tenements granted; nor should it be necessary to issue a writ of *ad quod damnum*;[3] and that the citizens should be released and exonerated from all entries and intrusions upon these lands any time before made. But that nothing in this charter is to be understood to take away from, or diminish the force of, any proclamations concerning the buildings of the City; and that all contempts and offences against them are to be still punishable, and all encroachments on purprestures are to be reformed by the king and his privy council.[4]

Then the charter grants and confirms the office of garbling all merchandise used to be gurbled, although not hitherto used to be imported, and the fees and profits there-

---

[1] Vide *supra*, p. 379.

[2] That is, the tenure was to be *freehold* in the modern acceptation of the word, and not by tenure *in capite* in free burgage. It is doubtful, however, whether all land within the City was not held by the citizens themselves; and, consequently, the streets and waste ground would not belong to the king, except as lord paramount. Vide *supra*, p. 11 *et seq.* and p. 87 *et seq.*

[3] Vide *supra*, 3rd charter of Edward IV.

[4] In the court of Star Chamber.

unto belonging; and that the chancellor, or treasurer, or president of the council, and the two chief justices of the King's Bench and Common Pleas, or any four of them, shall appoint fees to be taken for garbling spices and other like merchandise, for which no fee has hitherto been taken. The garbling of tobacco is, however, excepted out of this charter, as an office in the appointment of the king. It further grants, with the same provisions as to merchandise not hitherto used to be imported, the offices of gauging[1] and of weighing between merchant and merchant, and at the king's beam.[2]

The charter proceeds to create the office of *Outroper* in the City and Southwark, to be exercised by the appointment of the mayor and commonalty in Common Council, for the selling *by open claim* and *outcry* 'all household stuff, apparel, 'leases of houses, jewels, goods, chattels, and other things,' in open places; and that no one else shall execute this office.[3] A table of fees are added to the charter in a schedule.

It is then granted, That the widows of freemen may carry on their husbands' arts and occupations in the City, notwithstanding the statute of apprentices (5th Elizabeth).

That no market shall be henceforth granted to be kept within seven miles in compass of the City.

---

[1] Vide *supra*, 4th charter of Edward IV.

[2] Second charter of Edward IV.

[3] The term *outroper* or *outrowper*, like that of *bankrupt*, seems to be derived from the *breaking up* (ruptum) of stock; though, as applied to the public selling of effects by *crying them out*, the etymology of the word is somewhat more intricate and involved. The word, and probably the office too, is more ancient than this charter, which professes to *create* it; for the officer called the *common cryer* is perhaps as ancient as the City. The classical reader need hardly be reminded of the importance of the *cryer* in the earlier ages of democratic states, as testified in the character of Homer's Stentor, and of Talmides in Xenophon's *Anabasis*. It may be presumed that a similar duty was performed by the *cryer of London*. It was his task to summon the councils, and call for order in their deliberations. It continues so to the present day; and whoever attends the civic assemblies will still find his voice the most audible, if not the most attended to. His duty, as *outroper*, was that of an auctioneer broker, the performance of which in open places detracted in no small degree from his ancient and also his modern dignity. This has, however, long ago ceased to be noticed in the list of his duties, as the change of the times has produced improvements in public sales, and indeed the legality of this exclusive grant by charter of such an office may be reasonably doubted.

That City customs shall be certified by word of mouth [by] the recorder.¹

That the commonalty and citizens shall have all treasure trove, waifs, estrays, and goods and chattels of felons.

And, That the mayor shall nominate to the chancellor [two] aldermen, one of whom shall be a justice of the peace [for] the county of Middlesex, and the other for the county [of] Surrey.

The charter then alludes to the trade carried on from [the] port of London to other ports by persons who have been apprentices to freemen, or who are sons of freemen, and w[ho] are, consequently, capable of becoming free citizens, but w[ho] delay or refuse to become so; and thereby enjoy many of th[e] privileges of freemen without undergoing the incident char[ges] and burthens: the charter, therefore, declares and ordai[ns] That such persons, residing in the City of London or with[in] ten miles of it, 'shall not be permitted, at any time hen[ce-] 'forth, by themselves or by others, directly or indirectly, 'transport any goods, wares, or merchandise, by way of m[er-] 'chandising, in any way from the port of the said City [of] 'London, to ports foreign, or beyond the seas '—enjoi[n-] ing all societies of merchants, by whatever name kno[wn] (and naming most of them), that they permit not, nor licen[se] such persons to trade or traffic, until they are certified [to] the chamberlain to have become free citizens. The chart[er] requires service by apprenticeship in London and within t[en] miles to extend to seven years, and that these apprentic[es] shall be enrolled.

The charter next alludes to the Court of Conscience A[ct] passed in the third year of James I.,² by which all tradesme[n,] victuallers, and labourers are to sue in that court for deb[ts] under the amount of 40s. due from such individuals, and [in] that court only: and it creates the offices of clerk to t[he] court, for the purpose of entering and registering the bus[i-] ness, and of beadle, to execute the mesne process; and a[lso] a schedule of their fees.

It further creates an office for the registry of goods s[old] or pawned by brokers, in order the better to detect lost a[nd]

¹ Vide supra, 1st charter of Edward IV.   ² Vide supra, p. 147, 149, not[e.]

stolen goods; and gives the appointment of the register to the Court of Common Council; and adds a schedule of his fees.[1]

It grants, That the citizens may hang up, in and over the streets, signs and posts of signs affixed to their houses and shops, without any impediment of interruption, the better to distinguish their dwellings, shops, and occupations.[2]

The charter then proceeds to notice the letters patent of 13th January, granted in the 28th year of Henry VIII., by which the Hospital of Bethlehem, and the lands and tenements thereunto belonging, are made over to the mayor and commonalty, who are thereby constituted masters, governors, and keepers of the hospital, and of such lands, to the use of the hospital, and the better to support the expenses of the poor in West Smithfield; and it confirms fully these letters patent.

The charter further grants, That the commonalty may purchase a certain parcel of land, to the extent of five acres, in the parish of St. Giles-in-the-Fields, although the land may be held of the king *in capite*, notwithstanding the statutes of mortmain. And that such land shall not be reckoned in the valuation of land, to the yearly value of which the commonalty have been allowed by charter to purchase.[3]

And, lastly, the charter declares, That, upon enrolment, it shall be fully valid and sufficient and effectual to all intents and purposes, without any further confirmations or licences, and without any writ of *ad quod damnum*;[4] and notwithstanding the misnaming of any lands, liberties, or privileges, &c., granted, and although no office or inquisition should have been previously found declaratory of the king's title; and notwithstanding any mis-recital or non-recital of any leases, or terms for life or years, of the premises, or of the parish, hamlet, ward, &c., in which the lands may be, or of the names of all the lands granted, or any other defect of

---

[1] This office no longer exists; the London brokers are now put under statutable regulations.

[2] This nuisance existed until the middle of the last century.

[3] Vide supra, 3rd charter of Edward IV.

[4] Ibid.

form; and notwithstanding the statute of Henry VI.,[1] or any of the statutes of mortmain, or any other statutes whatever; and without paying any fee to the hanaper.

SECOND CHARTER OF CHARLES I.[2] SCAVAGE AND WATER-BAILLAGE.

This charter first recites, that the mayor, commonalty, and citizens of London had exercised and claimed the office of package,[3] describing it in the same language as is used in the fourth charter of Edward IV.; and also the office, as well for the surveying, or *scavage*, of all goods of aliens, or of denizens, whose fathers were aliens, brought from foreign parts into the port of London, by way of merchandise, as for the surveying, delivery, or *baillage*, of all goods of such merchants, to be exported by way of merchandise, which might be in any vessel upon the river, or upon any wharf or shore of it, and be delivered or unladen within the City or its liberties or suburbs. These offices the charter declares the citizens to have enjoyed time out of mind, and also by virtue of charters granted in the 1st and 18th years of Edward IV., and in the 3rd year of Henry VIII.[4] It then alludes to some doubts and differences which had arisen concerning these offices; and some hindrance and molestations occasioned thereby to the citizens in the enjoyment of them—to remove which, and for the purpose of confirming, amplifying, and establishing the privileges of the City, this charter, in consideration of the sum of 4,200*l*., creates and constitutes the office of package of all sorts of merchandise, with the survey of the measure, number, and weight of such merchandise, and the survey of customable goods imported and exported; and also the office of carriage and portage of all such goods from the river to the houses of aliens, and from their houses to the river, with

---

[1] For resuming lands, &c., granted. Vide charter of Henry VI.
[2] Directed and to be found as the last. Dated 5th Sept., 16th year.
[3] Vide 4th charter of Edward IV.
[4] The charter of 1st Edward IV., and of 3rd Henry VIII., the author has never been able to meet with; nor does he know of any reference to them except in the present charter. The 4th charter of 18th Edward IV. is abstracted, *supra*, p. 379 *et seq.*

all fees for the execution of such respective offices of package and of portage, as expressed in two schedules annexed to the charter: and it grants these offices, and the appointment of officers for the execution of them, to the citizens, without forfeiture, by reason of not packing goods upon notice of their being ready: and it provides that no porters, not appointed by the citizens, shall intrude into these employments; and that the City porters shall receive fees for their labour according to the schedule annexed.

The charter then grants to the citizens the offices of scavage and baillage, according to the terms recited as to the nature of those tolls; and directs, that the fees for the execution of these offices shall be taken, as expressed in a schedule annexed, according to the statute of 22nd Henry VIII.:[1] to hold these offices 'with the appurtenances, and the 'disputings, orderings, supervisings, and corrections of the 'same,' and all the fees belonging to them for ever; and without forfeiture of them by reason of the not surveying, or delivering, the goods and merchandise to be surveyed or delivered, when ready and upon request. All alien merchants are enjoined to deliver to the collectors of scavage true bills of entry of their merchandise. An annual rent-charge of 3*l*. 6*s*. 8*d*. is then reserved upon these offices, to be paid by the citizens into the Exchequer.

The charter proceeds to notice the practice of some aliens in landing their merchandise at various wharfs between London Bridge and Blackwall, with a view to defraud the citizens of the fees and emoluments of the above offices, and under the notion of those places being without the *port of London, and the liberties, franchises, and suburbs thereof*; namely, at St. Katherine's Wharf, Tower Wharf, Southwark, Dickshore, Wapping, Redriff, Deptford, Greenwich, Blackwall, and other places: and it ordains and declares that aliens so landing merchandise shall pay the fees as in the schedules annexed.

---

[1] Cap. 28; which statute provides, that all tolls and duties taken by the Corporation shall be inserted in a table signed by certain of the king's privy council and judges, and hung up in certain conspicuous places.

Lastly, the charter alludes to the colouring of aliens' goods by other persons not aliens; whereby the king is defrauded of his customs, and the citizens of their duties, payable in respect of the above offices: it authorises the mayor or his deputy to administer oaths to persons suspected of such frauds, colourings, or concealment; and to compel, by all lawful ways and means, such suspected persons to take the oaths so to be administered.

SCAVAGE AND WATERBAILLAGE.—Of the toll called *scavage* we have already spoken.[1] That of *waterbaillage* is somewhat more uncertain, both in origin and extent. Literally, the word signifies a toll for *delivery* by water; and in that sense it seems to be considered by the language of the present charter. The duty is limited precisely to the same kind of merchandise as that of scavage; namely, the merchandise of aliens paying port customs. It appears to be the same toll for merchandise *exported*, as the other is for merchandise *imported*: for as the latter is paid in respect of the *survey* or oversight of customable goods to be shown for sale in England, so the other appears to be a payment for the *delivery by water* of similar articles, for exportation and showing in foreign parts.

There is no doubt that many tolls were formerly paid for the transit of merchandise by the river Thames, which had, previous to the granting of the present charter, become utterly forgotten and unintelligible. Lord Hale enumerates a long list of them of the age of Edward III., but he speaks of them as too obscure to be understood.[2] These water customs, he seems to think, were of the kind usually, in his time, let to farm to the water-bailiff; and probably, therefore, they formerly passed by the name of waterbaillage. However, when in the reign of Charles II. that officer sued for a water toll upon wines, the non-usage of any demand time out of mind overthrew the merit of the evidence of records to show such a duty to be payable, and the waterbailiff was nonsuited.[3]

[1] Vide 4th charter of Edward IV. [2] Hale on Customs, ch. iv. [3] Ibid.

CHARTER OF CHARLES II.[1]

This is a grand Inspeximus charter, usually appealed to as the text of the City charters; although it does not contain the whole of them. It is generally termed, by pre-eminence, *the Inspeximus* charter, and begins by reciting the first charter of Charles I. by way of Inspeximus, and copies the whole of that charter, with all the charters quoted and recited in it, *verbatim.* It proceeds to recite, by way of Inspeximus, the last charter of Charles I., and then concludes with an ample and detailed confirmation of all these charters, and all their contents; and all lands, offices, jurisdictions, privileges, liberties, franchises, customs, &c., by whatever name had, exercised, or enjoyed by the citizens—whether by letters patent or prescription, or by any other lawful means—as fully as if the same were separately, singly, or nominally expressed.

CHARTERS OF WILLIAM AND MARY, AND OF GEORGE II.[2]

These charters were granted solely to constitute *all* the aldermen of London justices of the peace within the City.

The charter of William and Mary, after reciting the first charter of Charles I., appoints the *six* senior aldermen who had not passed the Chair, in addition and next to the *three* senior aldermen who had not passed the Chair, who were created justices by Charles's charter, to be justices of the peace; provided they have served the office of sheriff.

The charter of George II., after reciting the charter of Charles and also that of William and Mary, constitutes *all* the aldermen for the time being justices of the peace, and makes the mayor, recorder, *and all those aldermen who have passed the chair,* of the *quorum.*[3]

The charter of George II. is the last which has been granted to the City of London.

---

[1] Dated 24th June, 15th year.
[2] The first dated 28th July, 4th year; the second dated 25th August, 15th year.
[3] The charter of Charles and William required either the mayor or recorder to be of the quorum.

INDEX.

A

ABUSES. Of franchises not to forfeit chartered rights, 368, 373
Aldermen. Originally synonymous with earl; title of Governor of London, 18, 19, *note* 2; originally presided over gilds, afterwards termed wards, 62; their dignity and authority, 117, 260, 330; impressed as a soldier, another imprisoned for refusing a loan to Henry VIII., 145; how elected, 249, 251; made justices of peace and of sessions, 373, 397, 399
Alfred. His reign; his laws for the City of London, 10; recovers London from the Danes, *ibid*.; encourages ship-building, 157
Allectus. Assumes the sovereignty of Britain, 11
Amerciaments. What. Illegally imposed on cities, and oppressive, 80, 351; granted to the City, 199
Apprentices. Origin of, 138; usual course to freemanship, *ibid*.; statute of Henry IV. restricting, 121; repealed by statute of Henry VI., 160; riots of apprentices' clubs, 205; required by charter of Charles I. to serve seven years, 402
Asclepiodotus. Defeats Allectus A.D. 298, 11
Assise of Victuals. Granted, what, 374
Aula Regis. Jurisdiction of, 272
Aulus Plautius. In command of Britain, 5, 8

B

Bailiage. Confirmed by charter, 404
Barons. Of London, 72; origin and explanation of the term, 260, 261
Bede. His description of London, *circiter* 600 A.D., 15
Benevolences. What, 133, and *note* 2; levied by Henry VII., *ibid*.; and by Henry VIII., 144
Bethel. Elected sheriff in opposition to the Court, 228
Bethlehem. Hospital granted to the City by charter of Charles I., 403
Billingsgate. Tolls and customs granted in, 371
Black Prince. His letter to the Corporation on his victory of Poictiers, 110, *note* 6
Boadicea. Sacks London, 7
Boroughs. Meaning of the term, 29; their quality, 29 *et seq.*
Bridge. London Bridge first built *temp.* Henry II., 63
Bridge Ward. Extended over Southwark, 389; election of aldermen for, *ibid.*; civic jurisdiction over, *ibid.*

Bristoll. What ; Freedom from granted, 301, 303
Brokers. None but freemen to be brokers, and to be sworn before the Mayor, 235
Burgage. Lands held in burgage tenure, what, 50 ; lands in the City held by, 42, 110. *Vide* 'Soc,' 'Socage'
Burghers. *Vide* Barbwaru, Burgage
Burbwaru. Citizens so termed in William L's Charter, 260
By-laws. Right to make, confirmed by charter of Edward III., 361

C

Cade. His rebellion, 122 ; arraigned before the Mayor, defeated by the citizens, *ibid.*
Carausius. Sovereign of Britain, A.D. 288, 11
Carriage. Of goods, confirmed by charter, 403, 405
Certifying City customs, 373, 375, 402
Chamberlain. Partly an officer of the king, 313, 318, 377 ; collected the king's customs, *ibid.* ; originally elected by the Common Council, 335, 343 ; afterwards by the liverymen in Common Hall, 343
Charles I. His personal characteristics, 205 *et seq.* ; review of his reign and measures, 278 ; his illegal and tyrannical measures towards the City, 213 ; citizens side with the Long Parliament, 214 ; personally popular in the City, 215 ; grants ample charters, *ibid.*, 320 ; the five members take refuge in the City, 216 ; appeals personally to the Common Council, *ibid.* ; religious fanaticism in the City, *ibid.* ; political influence of the City during the civil war, 218 ; City turns against Cromwell, *ibid.*
Charles II. General review of his reign and measures, 220, *et seq.* ; religious parties in England, 222 ; and in the City, 227 ; shuts up the Exchequer, 223 ; Popish plot, belief of, in the City, 227 ; disgraceful judicial administration, 228 ; interference of the Court in the appointing and electing sheriffs, 229 ; illegal seizure of the City's charters by writ of quo warranto, 232 ; fire of London, and its re-building, 235
Charters. Meaning and nature of, 255 *et seq.* ; Charter of William the Conqueror, 287 *et seq.* ; Charter of Henry II., 301 *et seq.* ; First Charter of Richard I., 305 ; Second Charter of Richard I., 305 ; First Charter of John, 306 ; Second Charter of John, 308 *et seq.* ; Third Charter of John, 313 ; Fourth Charter of John, 313, 314 ; Fifth Charter of John, 315 *et seq.* ; First Charter of Henry III., 318 ; Second Charter of Henry III., 319 ; Third Charter of Henry III., 319 ; Fourth Charter of Henry III., 320 ; Fifth Charter of Henry III., 320 ; Sixth Charter of Henry III., 321 ; Seventh Charter of Henry III., 323 ; Eighth Charter of Henry III., 324 ; Ninth Charter of Henry III., 324 *et seq.* ; First Charter of Edward I., 332 ; Second Charter of Edward I., 333 ; First Charter of Edward II., 333 *et seq.* ; Second Charter of Edward II., 344 ; First Charter of Edward III., 345 *et seq.* ; Second Charter of Edward III., 363 ; Third Charter of Edward III., 363 ; Fourth Charter of Edward III., 364 ; Fifth Charter of Edward III., 365 ; First Charter of Richard II., 367 *et seq.* ; Second Charter of Richard II., 370 ; First Charter of Henry IV., 371 ; Second Charter of Henry IV., 364 ; First and Second Charters of Henry V., 372 ; Charter of Henry VI., 372 ; First Charter of Edward IV., 374 *et seq.* ; Second Charter of Edward IV., 379 ; Third Charter of Edward IV., 379 ; Fourth Charter of Edward IV., 379 *et seq.* ; Charter of Henry VII., 381 ; First Charter of Henry VIII., 383 ; Second Charter of Henry VIII., 384 ; Third Charter of Henry VIII., 385 ; Charter of Edward VI.

385 *et seq.*; First Charter of James I., 380 *et seq.*; Second Charter of James I., 395; Third Charter of James I., 397; First Charter of Charles I., 398 *et seq.*; Second Charter of Charles I., 404 *et seq.*; Great *Inspeximus* Charter of Charles II., 407; Charter of William and Mary, 407; Charter of George II., 407; Charters not to be forfeited for offences of individuals, 347; all charters to be liberally interpreted, 308

Cheap. Tolls and customs granted in, 371
Chief Justiciar. *Vide* 'Justiciar'
Childwite explained. Exemption from, 201, 202
Citizens. At first associated in territorial guilds, 24, 103; original qualifications of, *ibid.*; not originally members of mercantile guilds, *ibid.*; by redemption, what, 105; claims as gentlemen, 204, *note*; their lands beyond the City liable for City dues, 317, 360. *Vide* 'Elections,' 'Liverymen'
City officers. All process to be served by them only, 347; except that from the king's own justices, *ibid.*
Claudius Cæsar. His invasion of Britain, 6; London not then existing, *ibid.*
Clerks. Of the sheriffs' courts, 333, 337
Clerk of the market. His office, 108, 112, note 2; the king's not to have jurisdiction in the City, 346, 355, 375; office of, granted to the City, 374; also in Southwark, 387
Cnut. His battles around and in London, 22
Coiners. Eight for London, six for Canterbury in Athelstan's reign, 21
Colouring goods. What, 334, 340
Common Council. Court of, first established, 111, 244; irregularities in appointing members, 114; authority to make by-laws, 364; how elected, 211, 219, 251. *Vide* 'Elections'
Common clerk. Now called town clerk, 312; elected by Common Council, 335, 343
Common seal. Having it, a constituent principle of incorporation, 27, 71, *note*; when first obtained, 27; its use explained, 334, 342
Common serjeant. Elected by Common Council, 335, 343
Compurgators. Meaning of the term, 16; trial by, 36, 265, 286; the origin of trial by common jury, *ibid.*
Companies. Origin of trading companies, 25, *note* 2, 103 *et seq.*; corporate freeman required to be member of a City company, 91, 102; none but selected members of companies to be electors, 115; liverymen only of companies to come to elections in Common Hall of mayor, sheriffs, &c., 126; Discussion on the elective franchises of liverymen, 211
Conscience. Court of, established by charter of Charles I., 402
Conservancy. Of the Thames, granted by charter of James I., 390; nature of the right Court of Conservancy, 301
Constable of the Tower. Not to take primage of victuals, 316, 367
Constantine. The Roman general defeats Allectus, A.D. 296, 11
Cookery. Public cookeries *temp.* Henry II., 63
Cornish. Elected sheriff in opposition to the Court, 218; his judicial murder, 237
Coronership. Over Southwark granted, 387; and of London, *ibid.*, *note* 4
Corporation. None existing in Saxon times, 22; origin of, and of that of London, 23, 54, 65, 102, 315; first acquisition of land in a corporate capacity, 71 *note*
Coroneb. Trial by, 36, 265
Councils. Public deliberative and legislative, a general meeting of all the citizens till Edward I., 61; representative Common Council first established, 108. *Vide* 'Common Council'

Courts. London Judicial Courts in Saxon times, 19, 25, 31 et seq., 42, 58, 61 et seq.; abuses in Judicial Courts redressed by Edward I., 78 et seq.; Court Conservancy, 390; Court of Orphans, 321. *Vide* 'Conscience Court'
Cromwell. Citizens side with Parliament against, 218
Cupbearer. Mayor to be, 128
Customs. To be certified by mouth of the Recorder, 173, 375, 402. *Vide* 'Manners'

D

Danegeld. What. Exemptions of citizens from, 283
Danes. In London, 17, 21
Debts. Enrolling debts due to citizens, explained, 325, 329
Debtors. In prison not to be sued in the Court of Exchequer upon feigned suits, 349
Demesnes. What, 29 et seq., 32 et seq.; London not in demesne, 29, 33, 111; not held by feudal tenure, 44, 69. *Vide* 'London,' 'Soc,' 'Socage'
Dress. Proclamation of Elizabeth against sumptuous dress, 156; order of Common Council against it, *ibid*.

E

Edmund Ironside. Battles with Cnut in and near London, 22
Edward I. Parliament first regularly summoned by, 77; his measures to redress judicial abuses and feudal grievances, *ibid*., et seq.; appoints a custos over the City, who held it twelve years, 80; grants two charters, 332, 333
Edward II. Government under, 88
Edward III. Inquisitions by grand jury before trial usual in his time, 111, and note 3; his commercial laws injudicious; encourages manufactures, 111; grants five charters, 332 et seq.
Edward IV. Supported in London on death of his father the Duke of York, 121; his popularity in London, 128; his four charters, 374 et seq.
Edward VI. His Charter, 380 et seq.
Elections. City elected its magistrates in Saxon times, 19, 34, and note 2; elections of the governor and magistrates of the City by the whole body of the citizens till Edward I.'s reign, 60, 74; citizens specially summoned to, by the Mayor, 85, 114; elections to deliberative councils for the government of the City first regulated temp. Richard II., 114; of gild or ward magistrates in the separate wards, 85, 242, 251; elections of mayor, sheriffs, and other officers and members of Parliament in Common Hall transferred to liverymen temp. Edward IV., 128, 244; this course of election confirmed by statute 11. George I., 197, 242 et seq.; summary review of the existing elective franchises, 242 et seq.
Elizabeth. Her reign, 150 et seq.; her proclamations and monopolous grants, 151; attachment of the citizens, 158; demands on the City for soldiers on the Spanish invasion, *ibid*.; her attempt to appoint the Recorder, *ibid*.; her descent from a mayor, 138, note
Escheator. Mayor appointed for Southwark, 377; and in the City, *ibid*., note
Exclusive trade. *Vide* 'Trade'
Eyre. Justices in, their power and oppressions, 79, 80, 112, 361; citizens exempt from their jurisdiction, 348

F

Fair. Annual, in Southwark, granted by charter of Edward IV., 375
Farm. What, in cities and boroughs, 32, 51; Middlesex granted in fee-farm, 207, 268
Fee-farm. *Vide* 'Farm'
Felons. Goods of, granted by charter of Charles I., 402
Feudal system. Explained; in contrast with the City's rights and customs, 40 *et seq.*
Fines. *Vide* 'Amerciaments'
Fire of London, 235
Fitzstephen. His cotemporary account of London *temp.* Henry II., 57 *et seq.*
Folkmote. Original term for wardmotes, 58; also for general assemblies of citizens, 58, 61, 71
Foreign attachment. Nature of this legal custom, 299
Foreigners. Those not citizens so called; jealousies against them, 75, 146; not allowed to reside more than forty days, 75, 87, 120; restriction removed, 120; complaints against merchant strangers, 114, 146, 154; their dealings contrary to City charters, *ibid.*; not allowed to deal by wholesale except with citizens, 120, 363, 364, 368, 371, 384. *Vide* Second Charter of Edward III., and Second Charter of Henry IV., and 'Trade,' 'London'
Foreign merchants. Their residence encouraged by Edward III. and Henry IV., 120; companies of, settled in London with trading privileges, 160 *et seq.*; their privileges abolished, 168 *et seq.*; required to sell within forty days, 316. *Vide* 'Trade'
Foreign pleas. What, 278
Foreign tenures. Pleas of, to oust City jurisdiction explained. 279
Forestalling. Forbidden by charter of Henry III., 325
Forfeitures. Of City charters in early times illegally claimed by royal arbitrary authority, 113. *Vide* 'Charles II.,' 'Abuses'
Foresters. Oppressions by king's foresters, 320
Fortifications. *Vide* 'Streets and Buildings,' 'London'
Frank-pledge. In *gilds* and *leets* in Saxon times, 91, 95, 97 *et seq.*; views of frank-pledge held in the City wards; formerly termed '*leets*' and '*gilds*,' *ibid.*
Free burgage. *Vide* 'Burgage'
Freemen. Of the City, *vide* 'Citizens;' penalty on those entitled to be freemen refusing to become so, 402; this penalty under First Charter of Charles I. repealed by act of Common Council, 104, *note*

G

Garbling. Office of garbler granted, 370, 382, 400
Ganging. Office of granted, *ibid*, 321
Gentlemen. Claims of the citizens as such to the title. *Vide*
Gilds. Independent territorial associations, 21; original ta... cantile gilds different from civic 25, and *note* 3, 32, 8... the latter, 103; gilds of trading companies regu... abolished, 313. *Vide* 'Companies,' 'Mercantile Gil...
Graves of the dead. Swearing on, meaning of, 325, ... *ibid.*
Guildhall. First built *temp.* Henry IV., 121

H

Hanseatic Merchants. *Vide* 'Foreign merchants'
Heirship. A Saxon right preserved to citizens, 18, 41, 265; granted by William the Conqueror's Charter, 265
Henry I. His charter the first step towards incorporation, 41; abstracted and explained, 267 *et seq.*; grants sheriffwick of Middlesex, 60, and note 2
Henry II. Cotemporary account of London in his time 57 *et seq.*; wards then known by that term, 58; his oppressions of the City, 70 *et seq.*
Henry III. Nine charters granted by; almost duplicate—mode of extorting money 72; London supports the barons' war, 72; Parliament first called, *ibid*.
Henry IV. Supported by the citizens throughout his reign, 119; condition of London in his reign, 121
Henry VI. Unpopular in London; citizens side with Richard Duke of York, 121 Cade's rebellion defeated by the citizens, 122
Henry VII. Character of his reign, 131; oppressions on the City, 133; his charter 381
Henry VIII. Civic pageantry, 135; Henry attends the night watch procession 136; state of London and its suburbs; manner of living, 140 *et seq.*; evil May day riots, 146; three charters granted by him, 385; impresses an alderman as a soldier, and imprisons another for refusing a loan, 145
Heregeat. What: same as Jereogita, citizens exempted from, 303
Heriot. *Vide* 'Heregeat'
Housholder. *Vide* 'Citizens,' 'Elections'
Hubert de Burgh. Chief minister of Henry III., 70; his oppressions on the citizens; appoints a custos, 70 *et seq.*
Hunting. Citizens addicted to, *temp.* Henry II., 63; right to, of the citizens, 12
Hustings. Court of, general assemblies of the citizens so called, 38, 61; also called 'Folkmote,' 74, and *note* 297, 417

I

Impressments. In the City both for land and sea service, *temp.* Elizabeth, 153; illegal, *ibid., note* 4
Infangtheft. What: granted by charter, 345; nature of the jurisdiction, 347
Inquisitions. Arbitrary and irregular, 80 and *notes*; usually presentments by a grand jury of offences, 84, 111; from time of Edward III., generally a trial afterwards, *ibid.*, 80, 84; complaints of the citizens against those taken in the City, 112; and of their being summoned to attend them out of the City, *ibid.*; regulated by statute, 113; to be taken only at St. Martin's-le-Grand, the Tower, and at Newgate, 347, 348; those held at St. Martin's-le-Grand transferred by charter of Henry VIII. to Guildhall, 385; on customs leviable, and on encroachments and nuisances to be taken by citizens only, 360
Inspeximus. Charter of Charles II. reciting by inspeximus all previous charters 407
Irish Society. Grants of lands in Ulster to, by charter of James I., 203

INDEX. 415

J

James I. His endeavours at government by prerogative and proclamations, 200; grants three charters, 203. *Vide* 'Irish Society'
James II. Survey of the measures of his reign, 237 *et seq.*; his treatment of Alderman Cornish, 207
Jews. Their trading regulated, 328
Jerragite. *Vide* 'Heregeat,' 'Heriot'
John. Disorders in London during his regency, 64; his restoration of the shrievalty-wick after previous usurpations, 63; first grant of mayoralty by that term, *ibid.*; Magna Charta framed in London, 53, 62; grants five charters, 62
Julius Agricola. Completed the conquest of Britain, A.D. 70, 10
Julius Caesar. In Britain, 5
Justiciar. Reves and the portreve of London so termed in early Norman times, 60, note 2; his functions explained. Appointment granted by charter of Henry I., 267, 278; Chief Justiciar of England; his office and authority, 41; not to have jurisdiction in London, 45; his office abolished, 64
Justice of Peace. Mayor, recorder, and alderman appointed, 373; and to hold sessions, 373, 397, 399

K

King's household. Citizens exempted from lodging, 287; marshal of, to have no jurisdiction in London, 316, 353
King's officers. Trading by, forbidden, 345, 347; to be sued only in the king's special courts, 302
Knight-service. Citizens exempt from; illegally demanded, 110

L

Law-worthy. Citizens to be, by charter of William the Conqueror, 41; meaning of the term, 31, 257, 261
Leets. In London, originally *gilds*, afterwards called *wards*, 25, 62; same as leets in counties, 27; views of frank-pledge held in, *vide* ' Frank-pledge,' ' Wards '
Liverymen. First become electors at Common Hall elections, *temp.* Edward IV., 126; discussion on the elective rights of liverymen, 241, 314. *Vide* ' Companies '
Lodgings. Foreign merchants required to reside in lodgings provided for them, 87, 99 *et seq.*, 120, 282. *Vide* ' King's household '
Lombard merchants. *Vide* ' Foreign merchantmen '
London. Not existing in reigns of Julius or Claudius Caesar, 5, 7; referred to by Tacitus; his narrative of transactions in Britain, 7; founded as a city by the Romans, 10; named Augusta by the Romans, 11; walled and fortified by them, 13; declined on invasion by the Saxons, 14; at first inferior to Canterbury, 14; Bede's description of it, A.D. 600, 15; became the metropolis of Britain under Egbert, A.D. 827, 15; sacked by the Danes, 15–16; recovered from the Danes by Alfred, and repaired by him, 16; its franchises part of the Saxon common law, and date from Alfred's reign, 16–17 *et seq.*; superior to Canterbury, A.D. 847, 18, 21; its first charter from William, 17, 51, 257 *et seq.*; its condition *circiter* 1000, 21, 22; not a corporation in Saxon times, 24 *et seq.*; first became a corporation in the reign of Richard I., 27, 58, 64, 74, note 6, 102, 215; never held in *demesne* under any king or lord, 33, 92; its condition and civil and criminal jurisdiction at the time

of the Norman Conquest, 29 et seq., 34 et seq., 62; Tower of London built by the Conqueror, 40; exemption of the City from Norman changes of the law, 42; elects its own magistrates, ibid.; its lands held on burgage tenure, 62. *Vide* 'Burgage.' its condition and influence *temp.* Stephen and Henry II., 57 et seq.; its supposed military strength in their reigns, ibid.; its assemblies and courts, its wall, and its bridge at that time, 61, 63; outside walls of houses ordered to be built of wood or stone to height of sixteen feet, 64; but houses chiefly of wood till James L, ibid., note; its progressive influence and condition *temp.* Richard L 66, 67; Custos appointed by Hubert de Burgh *temp.* Henry III., 70; lectures on Magna Charta read in London *temp.* Henry III., 71; City supports the barons in their war with Henry III., 73; its opulence at this period, ibid., 74; held no land in its corporate capacity till reign of Edward III., 74, note d; jealousies against foreigners, 76, 146, 151. *Vide* 'Foreigners,' 'Trade,' 'Gilds;' Custos appointed by Edward L, 85; its course of government in his reign, ibid.; doubtful claims of exemption from answering the judges at the Tower, 86; Wat Tyler's insurrection and Walworth's exploit, 117; exactions by Richard II.; invites Bolingbroke to the City, 118; its ordinary military strength *temp.* Henry IV., 119; its condition *temp.* Henry IV. and Henry V., 121; Guildhall built, ibid.; wall in good repair, ibid.; Moorgate built *temp.* Henry V. ibid.; wall impregnable to the Lancastrians *temp.* Henry VI., 126; political influence *temp.* Richard III. 128; Shaw, the mayor, his instrument, and the Duke of Buckingham at a common hall, ibid.; benevolence demanded from the City by Henry VII., 132. *Vide* 'Benevolences;' City oppressed by Henry VII., ibid.; its pageantry, 135 et seq., 146. *Vide* 'Manners and Customs;' condition and manner of living is *temp.* Henry VIII. and Elizabeth, ibid., 140, 145; its condition *temp.* Elizabeth, its riots, 142. *Vide* 'Streets and Buildings;' its political influence *temp.* Edward VI., 142; opposes the Protector Somerset, ibid.; furnished 15,000 soldiers and thirty-eight ships on invasion of the Spanish Armada, 153; political proceedings in the City; conduct and sentiments of the citizens in the reign of Charles L, *vide* 'Charles L;' ditto in the reign of Charles II., *vide* 'Charles II.;' history of the seizure of the City charters by writ of *quo warranto* by Charles II., 231; fire of London; rebuilding of the City, 238; restoration of the charters by James II., 239; citizens summoned to the Convention on flight of James II., 240; franchises of the City confirmed by statute of William and Mary, ibid.; efforts of the Corporation to reform the civic constitution, 241; regulating statute of 11th George L; comments on that Act, 242

Lot. *Vide* 'Scot'
Louis, son of the French king. Invited to oppose John; supported by the citizens, 69
Lucius Septimus Severus, the Roman Emperor. In Britain, A.D. 210, 10
Ludgate. Custody of, granted by Henry IV., 121
Lupicinus, the Roman General. In London, A.D. 358; defeats the Picts and Scots. 11

M

Maces. Granted to be carried; nature of the privilege, 355
Magna Charta. Framed in London, and sworn to at St. Paul's, 63, 68; liberties of the City expressly confirmed by, 69
Manners and Customs. Modes of meeting for civic government and elections *temp.* Henry II., 58, 61; houses, cookeries, schools, sports, huntings, 63; oyer-leser, folkmotes, *temp.* Henry III., 72, 74, 292; pageantry and processions, 135

INDEX.   417

136; manner of living *temp.* Henry VIII. and Elizabeth, 181 *et seq.*, 193, *note*; riots; apprentices and their 'clubs,' *ibid.*, 205; proclamations and ordinances against sumptuous dress, 208; flying to sanctuaries by criminals, 316, 354. *Vide* 'Citizens,' 'Gilds,' 'Apprentices,' 'Folkmotes,' 'Lodgings,' 'Companies,' 'Riots,' 'Gentlemen,' 'Streets'

Market. None to be granted within seven miles of the City, 101; market in Southwark granted, 388

Marshal of the King's Household, 287

Mayor. Of London not existing by that name till Richard I., 36, *note* 1, 88, *note* 1; title of the governor of the City before that 'Reve,' or 'Portreve,' *ibid.*, 55, 61, and *notes*; selects from the citizens his own councils for elections and ordinances, *temp.* Edward I. and Edward II., 85, 88; claims exemption from attending the Judges at the Tower, 86; elected *temp.* Edward I. and Edward II., by twelve selected from the wards by aldermen, 87, 88; made a judge of oyer and terminer by charter of Edward III., 112, 373, 397; assessed as an earl *temp.* Richard II., 117, 260; his right to be cup-bearer at coronations formally recorded *temp.* Richard III., 129; only to serve one year, 333, 337; to be presented to the king's justice, 315, 317; made justice of gaol-delivery at Newgate, 315; made escheator, 316, 357; made justice of peace, and of oyer and terminer, 373, 397. *Vide* 'Elections.'

Mayoralty. First granted by charter of John, 68

May-day. Celebration of, in the City; riots on evil May-day, 148

Measurage. Of coals and other goods, right to, confirmed by charter of James I., 390, 392

Mellitus. First Bishop of London, A.D. 600, 15

Mercantile system. What; its prejudicial effects on trade, 177

Mercantile gilds. *Vide* 'Gilds,' 'Foreigners,' 'Foreign merchants,' 'Companies.' Exclusive privileges and charters of incorporation of foreign companies dissolved *temp.* Edward VI., 168

Merchants. Not to forestall, 325

Merchant adventurers. English company of, established in London, 163, 171

Merchant Courts. Held in the City, 321; presided over by aldermen, 320

Merchant strangers. *Vide* 'Mercantile Gilds'

Merchants of the Staple, 181

Merchants of the Steel-yard, 152

Metage. *Vide* 'Measurage'

Middlesex. Granted to the City in farm, 207, 268

Military service. Citizens exempt from beyond the wall, 34 l, 316

Miskenning. What; forbidden in the City Courts, 294

Monopolies. Granted by Elizabeth, 151; abolished by statute, 200

Moorgate. *Vide* 'Streets and Buildings'

Moore, Mayor. His illegal conduct in the election of sheriffs, 23

Mortmain. Citizens may bequeath in, 316; explanation, 342; liberty to hold in, 403

Murage, 403

Murder. Exemption from, 332; meaning of the term, exemption from, 283, 325

N

Newgate. Mayor to be a justice of gaol-delivery at, by charter of Edward III., 315; custody of, granted by Henry IV., 371

Non-user. Not to work forfeiture of City rights and privileges, 365, 368

Norman Conquest. Rights and liberties of the citizens at, 33 *et seq.*; changes of

E E

the law introduced by the Normans, 41 *et seq.*; London exempted from the, 42 *et seq.*, 81 *et seq.*, 100
North. Sir Dudley North, his illegal intrigues to be made sheriff, 230

O

Occupiers. The true legal construction of 'householders,' 241
Officers. Process to be served only by City officers, 317
Ordeal. Trial by, 36, 255
Orphans. Custody of, granted, 369, 392, 393; origin of orphans' duty on coals, *ibid.*
Outfangtheft. *Vide* 'Infangtheft'
Outroper. Office of, granted, meaning and nature of it, 401

P

Package. What; granted, 379; explained, 382
Pageantry. *Vide* 'Manners'
Parliament. Its original functions those of the king's council, 204; first called as a representative body in Henry III.'s reign, 72
Philpot. Alderman; his exploit *temp.* Richard II., 117
Pickage. What; granted, 379; explained, 382
Picts and Scots. Military muster of the Romans at London to invade, 11; invade southern provinces of Britain, 14
Pie Powder. Court at fairs in Southwark, granted, 375, 397
Pilkington, Alderman. Unjust party sentence against, 232
Pleadings. Without the walls, exemption from, explained, 277, 340. *Vide* 'Miskenning'
Pleas of the Crown. What, 272, 273; abuses arising out of, 75 *et seq.*
Popish Plot. Believed by the citizens, 227
Pontage. Exemption from, 332
Portage. Granted, 404, 405
Port-reve. *Vide* 'Mayor'
Portsoken Ward. Anciently Knighten-gild; history of, 23, 36, *notes* 4-6, 392
Presentment. Of mayor to the king's justice, 315
Presentment. Of the sheriffs at the exchequer, to answer for duties, 307, 312
Presentments. By a jury; in early times operated as convictions, 36, 352
Prisage. Citizens not to be exempt from prisage of wines, 328; to be exempt from prisage of victuals, &c., 346, 357; and also from that of wines, 317
Proves. *Vide* 'City officers'
Protections. Of debtors not to be granted by the king; abuses of, and explanation, 362
Purprestures. What; granted by charter, 372, 400
Purveyances. What; their grievance prohibited by charter of Edward III., 108 122, 287, 347, 355

Q

Queenhithe. Granted, 321

R

Recognizances. Of debt allowed to be enrolled in courts; advantages of, 329; forfeitures of, granted to the City, 322

Recorder. Interference of Elizabeth in the appointment of, resisted, 156; to certify customs by word of mouth, 373, 375; made justice of the peace, 373

Redemption. Citizens how becoming so by purchase or redemption, 106, 247

Reve. One of the names of the original governors of London, 18, 19, 259

Richard I. Progress and influence of London, 64, 66; City first incorporated in his reign, 65

Richard II. Rebellion of Wat Tyler, 117; last king who seised the charters for individual offence, 118; contrary to charter of Edward III., *ibid*.

Richard III. His proclamation to the citizens on the execution of Hastings, 129; political influence of the City, *ibid*.

Romans. Occupation by the, 2 *et seq*.; leave Britain, 1

S

Sanctuaries. Flying to, explained, 344; City charged with the custody of those flying to, *ibid*.

Saxons. East Saxons, London made capital of, A.D. 520, 15

Saxon. Saxon common law the foundation of the City franchises, 15 *et seq*.

Scavage. What: granted, 279 *et seq*., 396, 404

Scot. Scot and lot, what, 100; paying scot and bearing lot, the criterion of the full citizen, 101, 107, 243, 281; citizens exempted by charter from general scot, 281

Scotale. What: exemption from, 301, 304, 324

Seal. Corporate or common seal, the indication of a corporate capacity, 27; its use explained, 334, 312

Serfs. Their quality and condition, 39, 49, 92

Serjeants. Process officers of the City; their abuses, 233, 327

Shaw. Dr. Shaw, brother of the mayor, his abortive sermon at St. Paul's on behalf of Richard III., 128

Sheriff. Reve and portreve the original name of the governor of London, 18, 37, 55, 91; appointment of by the citizens in early Saxon times, 55; appointment of granted, 207; and of amoval, 208; presentment of to answer for dues, 307, 312; how to be amerced for escapes, 351. *Vide* 'Charles II.'

Sheriffwick. Appointment of sheriffs granted by charter of Henry I., 51, 55, 60, 91, 268, 307 *et seq*.; usurped afterwards occasionally by the Crown, 67; sheriffwick granted in express terms by John, 306, 307

Ships. Merchants making three long sea voyages to rank as thanes, by a law of Athelstan, 21; ship-building first began in Alfred's reign, 157; lent them to foreign merchants, 158; supposed enormous navy in Edgar's reign, A.D. 974; ship-building and trading in English bottoms encouraged by Richard II., Henry IV. and Henry V., 166; no English ships then trading in the Mediterranean, *ibid*.; foreign trade in Edward VI.'s reign chiefly in foreign ships, 163; thirty-eight ships required from London on the Spanish invasion, 153; effect of first Navigation Act in encouraging shipping, 172, 186

Smithfield. A market in, used for field sports *temp*. Henry II., 63, 271; fair granted, 400

Soc. Meaning of the term, 34, *note*, 35, *note*, 59, 92, 289; etymology of the *wre* 19, 24, and *notes* 3 and 4; tenure in *socage*, what, 19, 21 *et seq.*; citizens London held their lands by this tenure; *vide* ' Burgage.'

Socage. *Vide* ' Soc'

Socmen. *Vide* ' Soc'

Somerset. The Protector, opposition of the citizens to, 142

Stallage, 321; granted in Southwark, 367; and in London, 404

St. Paul's. First built A.D. 600, 13; liberty of vested in the deanery, 323; sheriff not to account for the issues in, *ibid.*

Steel-yard, 150

Stephen. First saluted king in London, 55; political influence of the City, 56; condition of London in his reign, 57 *et seq.*

Streets and Buildings. *Vide* ' London,' condition and population in time of Nero, 18 *et seq.*; wall built by the Romans and fortifications, 13; St. Paul's founded A.D. 600, 16; decayed after the Romans, 14; Bede's description of London, 15; houses of wood in Edgar's reign A.D. 974, 21; Fitzstephen's cotemporary description *temp.* Henry II., 63; London Bridge first begun to be built *temp.* Henry II. *ibid.*; general assemblies of the citizens held at St. Paul's Cross, and convened by bell till time of Edward III., 74; Guildhall first built *temp.* Henry IV., 121; walls and fortifications then in complete condition, *ibid.*, pageantry in the streets, *vide* ' Manners;' its wall impregnable to the Lancastrians *temp.* Henry VI., 126; state of the streets and houses, and of the area of the City and suburbs *temp.* Henry VIII., 140 *et seq.*; brick houses few, if any, in the City till reign of James I., 143; proclamation of James I. against increase of buildings, *ibid.*; fire of London, and rebuilding of the City in Charles II.'s reign, 216; purprestures (entrenchments) and waste grounds granted to the City, 371, 402. *Vide* ' Purprestures;' allowance to hang up street signs by charter of Charles I., 403

Suetonius in command of Britain. Abandons London to sack by Boadicea, 7

Southwark. Jurisdiction granted over in fee-farm, 362, 374; lands, manor, and jurisdiction granted in, 386

T

Tacitus. His account of London in Nero's time, 7

Tallages. What: levied on lands held in *demesne*, 66; London illegally tallaged though not in demesne, *ibid.*, note 5, 72; forbidden by statute of Edward I., 83; illegally levied by Edward II., 88; sometimes levied by Edward II., 88; sometimes levied by the sole authority of the mayor and sheriffs, 89; citizens expressly exempted from by charter of Edward III., 108, 347, 359

Taxes. Citizens to be taxed on the same footing as the rest of the commonalty, 359

Testaments. The making of, an ancient Saxon right in London, 30, 31

Theodosius, the Emperor. His victory near London, A.D. 368, 11

Toll. What: citizens exempted from, 287, 324, 339; remedy for taking illegal tolls by cities and boroughs from citizens, 298

Tower of London. Built by William the Conqueror, 40

Town Clerk. *Vide* ' Common Clerk'

Trade. Wholesale dealing restricted to open markets till the reign of Charles II., 121, 161; quality of trade in England in early times, 157; progress of trade in England and the City, 157 *et seq.*; establishment in London of foreign companies

159 et seq.; first statute of highways by Edward I., 102; woollen manufactures encouraged by him and by Edward III., ibid.; increase of by the reign of Henry VI., 165; impediments to trade through arbitrary taxation, 161 et seq., 171; abolition of foreign monopolies companies temp. Edward VI., 187; Navigation Act, 172; its immediate effects in the encouragement of commerce and ship-building, 172; discussion on the exclusive trading privileges of the City, 174 et seq., 331, 341. Vide 'Foreigners,' 'Foreign merchants,' 'Ships,' 'Mercantile system.'

Treasure-trove. With waifs and estrays and goods of felons, granted by charter of Charles I., 102

Trials. Modes of trial in Saxon times, 20, 38, 43, 264

Tronage. What; granted to the City, 325, 329, 335, 376, 385

V

Villeins. Vide 'Serfs'
Vice-comes. Latin term for sheriff, 259

W

Wager of battle, 20, 43; citizens exempted from, 20, 267, 284; explained, 283
Waifs and strays, 102. Vide 'Treasure-trove'
Wager of law. Vide 'Trials'
Wall. Vide 'Streets'
Ward. Unjust judgment against Sir Patience Ward temp. Charles II., 232
Wards. Derivation of the term, applied to City districts as early as Henry II., 58; previously called gilds, 24, 25; leet jurisdiction similar to that over hundreds of counties and socs, 58, 97, 269; known by district names first in Edward I.'s reign, 59, 85; before that by name of the alderman or owner, ibid.; elect councilmen to assist aldermen temp. Edward I., 85, 289, 291. Vide 'Gilds,' 'Leets'
Warren of Staines. Disafforested by charter of Henry III., 320
Waste grounds. Vide 'Purprestures'
Watch. Annual processions in setting the night watch, 136. Vide 'Manners'
Wat Tyler. His rebellion, 117
Wears. By charter of Richard I. to be removed from the Thames, 305
Weavers' Gild. Vide 'Gilds'
Weighing. Granted by charter of James I., 397
Weres. Citizens not to be mulcted beyond their weres, 267, 282; meaning of the term, ibid., 281
Widows. Of citizens authorised to trade in the City, 401
Will. Vide 'Testament'
William the Conqueror. His charter, text and translation, 17, 257
Wittenagemote. This national council ordered by Alfred to be held in London, 20
Wholesale dealing. Vide 'Trade'
Woollen manufactures. Vide 'Trade'

6137

STANFORD UNIVERSITY LIBRARIES
CECIL H. GREEN LIBRARY
STANFORD, CALIFORNIA 94305-6004
(415) 723-1493

All books may be recalled after 7 days

DATE DUE

JUN 1 9 1997

www.ingramcontent.com/pod-product-compliance
Lightning Source LLC
Chambersburg PA
CBHW022140300426
44115CB00006B/271